Adoption, Impact, and Challenges of International Financial Reporting Standards

Azzouz Elhamma
Ibn Tofaîl University, Morocco

IGI Global
Scientific Publishing
Publishing Tomorrow's Research Today

Vice President of Editorial	Melissa Wagner
Director of Acquisitions	Mikaela Felty
Director of Book Development	Jocelynn Hessler
Production Manager	Mike Brehm
Cover Design	Jose Rosado

Published in the United States of America by
IGI Global Scientific Publishing
701 East Chocolate Avenue
Hershey, PA, 17033, USA
Tel: 717-533-8845
Fax: 717-533-7115
Website: https://www.igi-global.com E-mail: cust@igi-global.com

Library of Congress Cataloging-in-Publication Data

Names: Elhamma, Azzouz, 1979- editor
Title: Adoption, impact, and challenges of International Financial Reporting Standards / [edited by] Azzouz Elhamma.
Description: Hershey, PA : IGI Global Scientific Publishing, [2026] | Includes bibliographical references and index. | Summary: "This book aims to highlight 50 years of IFRS adoption"-- Provided by publisher.
Identifiers: LCCN 2025019841 (print) | LCCN 2025019842 (ebook) | ISBN 9798337319025 hardcover | ISBN 9798337319032 paperback | ISBN 9798337319049 ebook
Subjects: LCSH: Accounting--Standards
Classification: LCC HF5681.B2 .A36 2025 (print) | LCC HF5681.B2 (ebook) | DDC 657.3--dc23/eng/20250718
LC record available at https://lccn.loc.gov/2025019841
LC ebook record available at https://lccn.loc.gov/2025019842

British Cataloguing in Publication Data
A Cataloguing in Publication record for this book is available from the British Library.

Editorial Advisory Board

Table of Contents

Detailed Table of Contents

This article aims to investigate the mediating role of economic growth in the relationship between mandatory International Financial Reporting Standards (IFRS) adoption and unemployment in the Middle East and North Africa (MENA) region. The study was conducted based on panel data from 11 MENA countries during the period 2000–2020. The study results show three main findings. First, mandatory IFRS adoption affects positively and significantly economic growth. Second, economic growth has a significant negative impact on unemployment. Third, mandatory IFRS adoption influences negatively and significantly unemployment through economic growth (full mediation). This implies that IFRS adoption increases economic growth, which in turn decreases unemployment. To the author's knowledge, this is the first research study to investigate the impact of mandatory IFRS adoption on unemployment and the mediating effect of economic growth on this relationship. Results of the present research have important implications for both academics and policymakers.

The adoption of International Financial Reporting Standards (IFRS) by various countries has consistently sparked debate regarding its impact on the quality of financial reporting. This study aims to evaluate the perceptions of Moroccan financial professionals concerning the effect of IFRS adoption on the quality of financial statements. To achieve this objective, a questionnaire was distributed to a sample of 134 professionals active in the Moroccan financial market. The data collected were analyzed using the Partial Least Squares (PLS) method, which is particularly well-suited to studies with relatively small sample sizes. The findings reveal a notable improvement in the quality of financial communication following the adoption of IFRS. Moreover, respondents believe that IFRS implementation has positively influenced the financial performance of adopting companies, while also offering substantial benefit to those listed on the Casablanca Stock Exchange.

This study aims to analyze the trend of 96 articles published on the subject of IFRS adoption and financial reporting quality in the Web of Science (WoS) database between 2010-2025 in terms of authors, citations, author's keywords, co-ocurrence, specific terms frequency, corresponding author's countries. The method of the study is scientometric (bibliometric) analysis used to reveal the publication trends of the articles. Findings have demonstrated that the researches related to IFRS adoption and financial reporting quality have increased since the last decade. Moreover, this study has indicated that the top three most frequently used keywords by authors are financial reporting quality, IFRS, IFRS adoption, and the top keywords plus are earnings management, IFRS adoption, impact, mandatory IFRS adoption and corporate governance, respectively. In addition, the study has concluded that IFRS adoption and financial reporting quality studies are mostly published in the Accounting Review, Journal of Applied Accounting Research and Journal of International Accounting Auditing and Taxation.

The main purpose of this study is to identify the determinants of the International Financial Reporting Standard for small and medium-sized entities (IFRS for SMEs) adoption in African countries. This study used the diffusion of innovation theory to explain why countries choose to adopt IFRS for SMEs. Based on logistic regression analysis, our results show that quality of governance, trading networks, and normative isomorphism have a strong and positive effects on a country's adoption of IFRS for SMEs. However, mimetic isomorphism has a negative impact on IFRS for SMEs adoption in African countries. Furthermore, tax system and coercive isomorphism system have no effect on the adoption of IFRS for SMEs standards. Our study contributes to facilitate the implantation of IFRS for SMEs in African countries and to better understanding the factors influencing the implementation of IFRS for

The Kingdom's General Treasury's accession to the IPSAS board in 2012 represents a significant advancement in public sector accounting reform in Morocco. This initiative aligns with the principles of the Moroccan Constitution of 2011 regarding transparency and accountability, as well as with the requirements of Organic Law No. 130-13 on finance, which mandates the State to maintain comprehensive accounts alongside budgetary accounts. This move aims to enhance good governance and improve the management of public finances. Our research is based on a quantitative study involving a sample of 84 respondents, aimed at assessing the level of IPSAS adoption among Moroccan public sector practitioners and analyzing its impact on the comparability, reliability, relevance, and intelligibility of financial information. The results indicate that, despite increasing awareness, the level of IPSAS adoption remains low in Morocco. Nevertheless, respondents unanimously acknowledge that these standards significantly enhance the quality of financial information.

This chapter examines the early adoption of IFRS S1 and S2 within a non-mandatory regulatory environment, using a qualitative case study of Air Canada. Guided by neo-institutional theory, it investigates how institutional dynamics influence the voluntary implementation of sustainability disclosure standards. The chapter draws on insights from a semi-structured interview with Air Canada's Director of Corporate Sustainability Reporting, offering a detailed view of the internal motivations, operational challenges, and strategic considerations that underpin early engagement with the ISSB framework. The findings show that IFRS S2 is more readily integrated due to its alignment with existing climate disclosure practices, whereas IFRS S1 presents interpretive and practical difficulties. In the absence of regulatory obligation, the decision to adopt is shaped by investor expectations, peer influence, and professional norms. This study contributes to the literature by offering grounded evidence on how organizations internalize and operationalize ESG standards in a voluntary setting.

Preface

Accounting has long been regarded as the language of business par excellence. However, with the rise of economic and financial globalization, this role has increasingly been challenged, particularly regarding the comparability of financial statements. The existence of country-specific accounting rules and standards has made it difficult—and sometimes impossible—to compare the financial reports of companies operating under different regulatory frameworks. To address this issue, nine countries—Canada, the United Kingdom, the United States, Australia, France, Germany, Japan, the Netherlands, and Mexico—decided in 1973 to establish an independent organization responsible for developing and issuing international accounting standards. This organization, initially known as the International Accounting Standards Committee (IASC), was replaced by the International Accounting Standards Board (IASB) in 2001. The standards, originally called International Accounting Standards (IAS), were subsequently rebranded as International Financial Reporting Standards (IFRS). In our view, IFRS can be defined as follows: "IFRS are international accounting standards developed and issued by the International Accounting Standards Board (IASB). They provide guidance for the preparation of accounting and financial information that is both high in quality (through the application of advanced actuarial and statistical techniques) and comprehensible (easily understood by non-experts). These standards address a wide range of topics, including tangible and intangible assets, inventories, financial instruments, leases, employee benefits, and more. The primary objective of these standards is to enhance the comparability, transparency, and reliability of financial information across countries and companies". This book commemorates the 50th anniversary of IFRS by examining their evolution over the past five decades.

This book is highly relevant to current discussions, especially in the aftermath of recent global financial crises that have raised concerns about the quality of financial information. Its primary objective is to provide an in-depth examination of key topics such as the adoption of IFRS and IFRS for SMEs, sustainability, foreign direct investment, employment, and governance. The book offers valuable insights that enhance our understanding of the contemporary challenges facing international accounting standards.

TARGET AUDIENCE

This book, comprising high-quality scientific articles on the adoption, impacts, and regulatory framework of IFRS, targets a broad audience of accounting researchers and practitioners. It is primarily intended for researchers, PhD students, lecturers, and students in management sciences, particularly in accounting, finance, and economics. It also targets accounting and auditing professionals, standard-setters, public policymakers, and international organizations with a shared interest in international accounting standards—especially IFRS and IPSAS—such as the International Accounting Standards Board (IASB), the International Public Sector Accounting Standards Board (IPSASB), the International Federation of Accountants (IFAC), and the International Organization of Securities Commissions (IOSCO), among others.

The particularity of this book lies in the diversity of its chapters, which expands its target audience to include both academics and practitioners. The themes covered, such as the adoption of IFRS in emerging and African countries, the quality of financial information, foreign direct investment, sustainability, governance, employment, and IFRS for SMEs, closely align with the current concerns of investors, accounting standard-setters, and international institutions. This renders the book especially relevant to an international and interdisciplinary audience.

COVERAGE AND CONTENT OF THE BOOK

To cover all areas related to IFRS, we structured our book, *Adoption, Impact, and Challenges of International Financial Reporting Standards,* around four main thematic groups. The first group explores IFRS adoption and its determinants, focusing on the factors that influence the uptake of IFRS standards in various contexts, including developing countries **(Chapter 8)** and Small and Medium-Sized Enterprises (SMEs) in Africa **(Chapter 4)**, as well as the voluntary adoption of IFRS in emerging and developed economies **(Chapters 5, 10, and 12)**. The second group examines the impact of IFRS adoption on the quality of financial reporting, assessing how the implementation of these standards affects the reliability, comparability, and overall quality of financial information in both the private **(Chapters 2 and 3)** and public **(Chapter 9)** sectors. The third group investigates the economic and macroeconomic effects of mandatory IFRS adoption, particularly its relationship with unemployment **(Chapter 1)** and foreign direct investment **(Chapter 7)** in regions like the MENA countries. The fourth group addresses regulatory frameworks, harmonization, and standardization, discussing the challenges and progress in aligning international standards with regional regulations and sustainability reporting requirements **(Chapters 6 and 11).**

Together, these themes reflect the diverse dimensions of IFRS research, covering adoption practices, reporting quality, economic outcomes, and regulatory convergence.

This book comprises 12 scientific chapters that employ various methodologies and is organized as follows:

Chapter 1, titled *"The Impact of Mandatory IFRS Adoption on Unemployment: The Mediating Role of Economic Growth in the MENA Region,"* examines the indirect impact of the mandatory adoption of International Financial Reporting Standards (IFRS) on unemployment through economic growth. In other words, it investigates the mediating effect of economic growth on the relationship between the mandatory adoption of IFRS and unemployment in the Middle East and North Africa (MENA) region. The study utilizes panel data from 11 MENA countries over the period 2000–2020.

Chapter 2, titled *"Assessing the Impact of IFRS Adoption on Financial Information Quality: A Structural Equation Modeling Approach,"* aims to evaluate financial professionals' perceptions of the impact of International Financial Reporting Standards (IFRS) adoption on the quality of financial statements. To this end, a questionnaire was administered to a sample of 134 professionals active in the financial market. The collected data were analyzed using the Partial Least Squares (PLS) method.

Chapter 3, titled *"The Impact of IFRS Adoption on Financial Reporting Quality: A Comprehensive Scientometric Analysis,"* employs scientometric (bibliometric) methods to analyze a broad range of articles published between 2010 and 2025 in the Web of Science (WoS) database on the topic of International Financial Reporting Standards (IFRS) adoption and financial reporting quality. The analysis focuses on authorship, citation patterns, author keywords, term co-occurrence, term frequency, and the countries of corresponding authors.

Chapter 4, titled *"Determinants of IFRS for SMEs Adoption in African Countries,"* applies the diffusion of innovation theory and logistic regression analysis to examine the key factors influencing the adoption of the International Financial Reporting Standard for Small and Medium-sized Entities (IFRS for SMEs) across African countries.

Chapter 5, titled *"The Impact of Firm Characteristics on Voluntary IFRS Adoption: An Empirical Analysis in an Emerging Country,"* aims to identify the key factors influencing the voluntary adoption of International Financial Reporting Standards (IFRS) by Moroccan companies. To this end, the study is based on a survey of 82 companies operating across various economic sectors and regions within the Kingdom of Morocco, and the collected data were analyzed using logistic regression analysis.

Chapter 6, titled *"Sustainability and Integration of ESG Reporting: Regulatory Frameworks, Standardization, and the Role of the ISSB,"* examines the current landscape of sustainability and ESG reporting through a review of key regulatory frameworks and standards, with particular emphasis on the International Sustainability Standards Board (ISSB) and its IFRS Sustainability Disclosure Standards S1 and S2. The chapter also highlights the challenges arising from the coexistence of global standards with regional regulations and voluntary frameworks, and explores the resulting implications for companies, investors, and regulators.

Chapter 7, titled *"The Impact of Mandatory IFRS Adoption on Foreign Direct Investment: Evidence from Jordan, Morocco, and the United Arab Emirates,"* examines the effect of the mandatory adoption of International Financial Reporting Standards (IFRS) on foreign direct investment (FDI) in three selected countries from the Middle East and North Africa (MENA) region—Jordan, Morocco, and the United Arab Emirates—over the period 1980 to 2019. The study employs descriptive statistics and fixed-effects panel regression analysis.

Chapter 8, titled *"Macroeconomic and Institutional Determinants of IFRS Adoption: Evidence from Developing Countries,"* investigates the macroeconomic and institutional factors influencing the adoption of International Financial Reporting Standards (IFRS) in developing countries. Using panel data from seven countries—Morocco, South Africa, Egypt, Tunisia, Algeria, Qatar, and Jordan—spanning the period from 2010 to 2022, the study aims to identify which economic and institutional variables, such as GDP per capita, foreign direct investment, trade openness, rule of law, and regulatory quality, significantly affect IFRS adoption..

Chapter 9, titled *"The Impact of IPSAS on the Quality of Financial Reporting in Public Sector Organizations: An Empirical Study,"* is based on a quantitative study involving a sample of 84 accounting professionals. The study aims to assess the level of IPSAS (International Public Sector Accounting Standards) adoption among Moroccan public sector practitioners and to analyze its impact on the comparability, reliability, relevance, and intelligibility of financial information.

Chapter 10, titled *"IFRS S1 and S2 Adoption in a Non-Mandatory Environment: Institutional Drivers and Insights from Air Canada,"* examines the institutional factors driving the voluntary adoption of the IFRS Sustainability Disclosure Standards S1 (General Requirements for Disclosure of Sustainability-related Financial Information) and S2 (Climate-related Disclosures) in a non-mandatory context. Using Air Canada as a case study, the chapter explores the internal motivations, strategic considerations, and implementation challenges associated with early adoption, drawing on insights from neo-institutional theory.

Chapter 11, titled *"Accounting Harmonization in French-Speaking African Countries: Dynamics and Prospects,"* employs a historical approach and analyzes diverse documentary sources to investigate the process of accounting harmonization in French-speaking African countries. Framed within the broader context of the international diffusion of IAS/IFRS standards, the chapter explores the dynamics shaping this harmonization and assesses its future prospects.

Chapter 12, titled *"Understanding the Impact of IFRS for SMEs in Morocco: A Qualitative Study Based on Semi-Structured Interviews,"* investigates the impact of IFRS (International Financial Reporting Standards) adoption for SMEs (Small and Medium-sized Enterprises) in Morocco, aiming to understand how this standard affects accounting practices and financial reporting within small and medium-sized enterprises. The study adopts a qualitative methodology, relying on semi-structured interviews with accounting professionals to gather in-depth insights.

In conclusion, this book makes a valuable contribution to the field of international accounting standardization for two main reasons. First, it brings together recent and diverse research on the adoption of IFRS and IFRS for SMEs, as well as the effects of this adoption on the quality of financial information, investment, employment, and sustainability. Second, it addresses multiple regions of the world—including Africa, the Middle East, North America, and Europe—offering a global and comparative perspective on contemporary accounting challenges. Overall, this book serves as a key reference for understanding the dynamics of accounting convergence at the international level.

Azzouz Elhamma
National School of Business and Management-ENCG, Ibn Tofaîl University, Kenitra, Morocco

Acknowledgment

We would like to express our sincere gratitude to all the authors who contributed to this volume. Thanks to the high quality of their research, the project was carried out under the best possible conditions. Their contributions—covering a wide range of timely and significant topics—have given this book both international scope and interdisciplinary relevance.

This volume is the result of a collective effort involving the editor, the authors, and the anonymous reviewers. We extend our sincere thanks to all the anonymous reviewers whose valuable recommendations significantly contributed to enhancing the quality of the chapters.

We hope that this work will be useful to the scientific community, practitioners, and students alike, and that it will contribute to enriching the ongoing debate on international accounting standards.

Chapter 1
The Impact of Mandatory IFRS Adoption on Unemployment:
The Mediating Role of Economic Growth in the MENA Region

Azzouz Elhamma
https://orcid.org/0000-0003-3382-0278
Ibn Tofaîl University, Morocco

ABSTRACT

This article aims to investigate the mediating role of economic growth in the relationship between mandatory International Financial Reporting Standards (IFRS) adoption and unemployment in the Middle East and North Africa (MENA) region. The study was conducted based on panel data from 11 MENA countries during the period 2000–2020. The study results show three main findings. First, mandatory IFRS adoption affects positively and significantly economic growth. Second, economic growth has a significant negative impact on unemployment. Third, mandatory IFRS adoption influences negatively and significantly unemployment through economic growth (full mediation). This implies that IFRS adoption increases economic growth, which in turn decreases unemployment. To the author's knowledge, this is the first research study to investigate the impact of mandatory IFRS adoption on unemployment and the mediating effect of economic growth on this relationship. Results of the present research have important implications for both academics and policymakers.

DOI: 10.4018/979-8-3373-1902-5.ch001

1. INTRODUCTION

Nowadays, unemployment is considered as a key issue facing both developing and developed countries. According to the International Labor Organization (ILO, 2021, p.128), between 2005 and 2020, the global unemployment figure increased significantly, rising from 177 million to 220 million individuals. Certainly, this remarkable increase has negative effects on health, economy, and society, etc. Unemployment has negative effects both economically and socially. Economically, it results in decreased consumer spending and slower economic growth (Mohseni and Jouzaryan, 2016; Hjazeen et al., 2021). Socially, it can lead to many problems, including isolation, psychological stress, mental health issues, family tensions, etc. (Pohlan, 2019). An unemployed person is defined by ILO (2021) as "a person aged 15 or over without a job during a given week; available to start a job within the next two weeks; actively having sought employment at some time during the last four weeks or having already found a job that starts within the next three months". Economists, researchers and policymakers agree that economic growth is regarded as a key factor that plays role in decrease of unemployment. The American economist Arthur Okun was the first to examine the relationship between unemployment and economic growth in the earlier 1960s. Okun (1962) has found a negative correlation between GDP (Gross Domestic Product) and unemployment in the United States between 1948 and 1960. These results are known by okun's law. Afterward, an abundant literature has examined the relationship between unemployment and economic growth in the world. Most of these research studies have concluded that a higher growth rate tends to raise the employment rate or reduce the unemployment rate (Bayrak and Tatli, 2018; Alabed et al., 2022).

For several years, numerous developing and emerging economies have actively pursued economic growth through policies aimed at attracting investment, facilitating trade, and promoting a conducive business environment. Among these policies is the mandatory adoption of credible and well-known accounting standards. According to Zhang (2013), the adoption of credible accounting standards could have positive consequences on the growth of countries. Generally, adopting the International Financial Reporting Standards (IFRS) is seen as a way to enhance legitimacy in the eyes of external users of financial information, including investors, creditors, and customers (Elhamma, 2025a). In this context, Nurunnabi (2021) indicates that there are "significant evidences of adopting a high-quality set of harmonized accounting standards (i.e. IFRS) fosters trade and foreign direct investment (FDI), financial transparency, and comparability and reduces information asymmetries". In the same vein, Owusu et al. (2022, p.75) show that "IFRS improves accounting information quality, enhances allocation of capital and promote FDI inflows to a country, its adoption should promote economic growth".

In recent years, particularly following the reform of the IASB (formerly the IASC) in 2001 and the mandatory adoption of IFRS by the European Union in 2005, the adoption of IFRS has shown a significant upward trend in both developed and developing countries (Elhamma, 2025c). In our view, IFRS can be defined as follows: "IFRS are international accounting standards developed and issued by the International Accounting Standards Board (IASB). They provide guidance for the preparation of accounting and financial information that is both high in quality (through the application of advanced actuarial and statistical techniques) and comprehensible (easily understood by non-experts). These standards address a wide range of topics, including tangible and intangible assets, inventories, financial instruments, leases, employee benefits, and more. The primary objective of these standards is to enhance the comparability, transparency, and reliability of financial information across countries and companies".

The economic consequences of mandatory IFRS adoption have been the subject of some research studies. Samaha and Khlif (2016) identified four main areas of study: the "relationship between IFRS and foreign direct investment" (e.g., Gordon et al., 2012), "IFRS and the cost of equity capital" (Daske, 2006), the "impact of IFRS on value relevance" (Ahmed et al., 2013), and "IFRS and earnings quality". However, empirical research in accounting and economics examining the relationship between IFRS adoption and macroeconomic indicators such as unemployment and economic growth remains scarce (Elhamma, 2023a).

In this context, the current study investigates whether economic growth serves as a mediating factor in the relationship between mandatory IFRS adoption and unemployment in the Middle East and North Africa (MENA) countries. The key question in this research is therefore does economic growth mediate significantly the relationship between mandatory of IFRS adoption and unemployment in the MENA region? In other words, does the mandatory adoption of IFRS indirectly affect unemployment through its impact on economic growth in the MENA region? According to the ILO (2024), the MENA region has unemployment rate very high compared to other regions. This is attributable especially to high rate of unemployment among youth. "the youth unemployment rate in the Middle East and North Africa (MENA) region, at 24.4 per cent in 2023, is almost double the global average" (ILO, 2024, p.1).

This study aims to analyze the dynamics of unemployment in the MENA region by examining the link between the mandatory adoption of IFRS and economic growth. To address this objective, we employ panel data from 11 MENA countries spanning the period from 2000 to 2020, resulting in a total of 231 observations. The findings show three key results. First, the mandatory implementation of IFRS is positively and significantly associated with economic growth. Second, economic growth exerts a significant negative effect on unemployment. Third, the adoption of

IFRS indirectly reduces unemployment through its positive influence on economic growth, indicating a full mediation effect. These results suggest that mandatory IFRS adoption contributes meaningfully to fostering economic growth, which, in turn, plays a crucial role in reducing unemployment across the examined MENA countries. More specifically, the mandatory adoption of IFRS reduces the unemployment rate by 1.39% through its effect on economic growth.

The remainder of this chapter is structured as follows: the next section is devoted to the literature review and formulation of hypotheses (Section 2), followed by a presentation of our methodological choices (Section 3). Section 4 presents the research results, and finally, Section 5 provides the conclusion.

2. LITERATURE REVIEW AND FORMULATION OF HYPOTHESES

This section begins by presenting key demographic and economic statistics for the MENA region (2.1), followed by a discussion of the potential effects of IFRS adoption on economic growth (2.2), and concludes with an investigation of how economic growth affects unemployment (2.3).

2.1. Key Demographic and Economic Indicators of the MENA Region

The Middle East and North Africa (MENA) region includes countries from both the Middle East and North Africa, such as Morocco, Saudi Arabia, Egypt, the United Arab Emirates, Tunisia, Qatar, Iraq, Iran, and Jordan. However, there is no consensus among international organizations on the exact list of countries in the MENA region (Elhamma, 2024a). The MENA region is considered as a strategic link between Europe, Asia, and Africa. It is also known for its large natural resource reserves, especially oil and gas. In fact, MENA "proved oil reserves are estimated at 860 billion barrels (bbl), representing 52% of the global total, and MENA proved natural gas reserves are estimated at 88 trillion cubic meters (Tcm), representing 42% of the global total" (Griffiths, 2017). According to British Petroleum's Statistical Review of World Energy (2021), the statistics on proven oil and gas reserves in the MENA region at the end of 2020 are presented in Table 1.

Table 1. MENA region's share of proven Oil and Gas reserves in the world at the End of 2020

	Oil	**Natural gas**
Middle East	48.3%	40.3%
Algeria	0.7%	1.2%
Egypt	0.2%	1.1%
Libya	2.8%	0.8%
Tunisia	(Not available)	-
Total MENA	52%	43.4%

Source: BP Statistical Review of World Energy (2021, p.16 & 34)

Figure 1. The MENA region's share of proven oil reserves in the world at the end of 2020

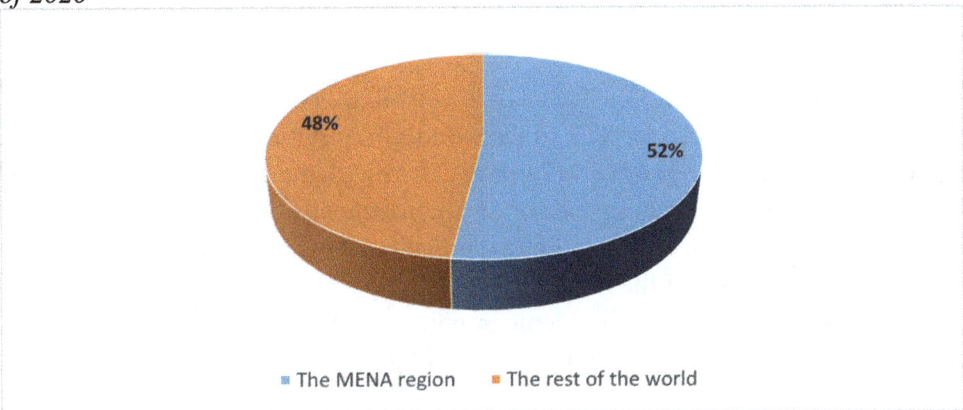

Source: Authors, based on BP Statistical Review of World Energy (2021)

Figure 2. The MENA region's share of proven natural gas reserves in the world at the end of 2020

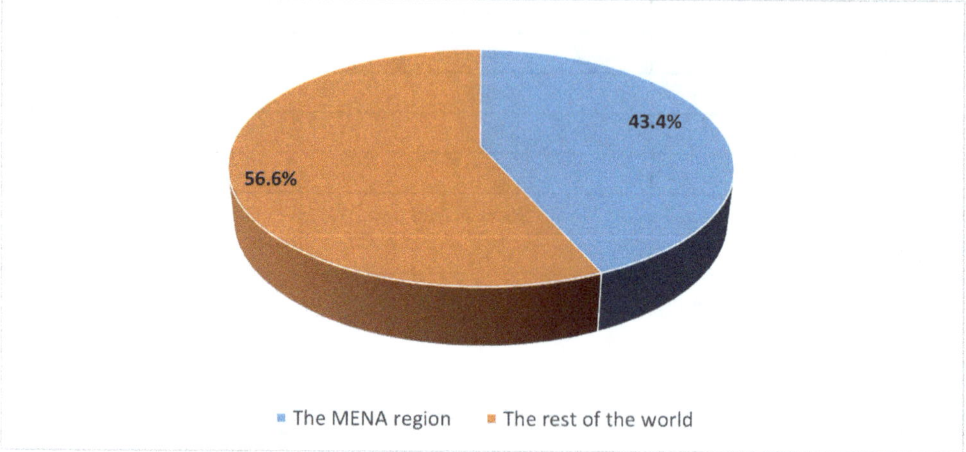

Source: Authors, based on BP Statistical Review of World Energy (2021)

According to these statistics, the total proven oil reserves in the MENA region at the end of 2020 accounted for 52% of the world's oil reserves (Figure 1) and 43.4% of the world's natural gas reserves (Figure 2). This highlights the region's significant importance in the global energy sector and, consequently, in the global economy. This significant importance prompts an examination of various demographic, social, and economic statistics of the region.

Table 2 summarizes the main demographic, social and economic statistics for the MENA region in comparison to the rest of the world.

Table 2. Comparative Demographic, Economic, and Social Indicators: MENA Region vs. World

		1980	1990	2000	2010	2020
Total population (in Billion)	MENA region	0.183	0.255	0.319	0.397	0.482
	The World	4.44	5.3	6.16	7	7.86
	% in the world	4.12%	4.81%	5.17%	5.67%	6.13%
GDP (current US dollars; in Trillion)	MENA region	0.595	0.794	0.995	2.82	3.21
	The World	11.45	22.99	33.86	66.61	85.76
	% in the world	5.19%	3.45%	2.93%	4.23%	3.74%

continued on following page

Table 2. Continued

		1980	1990	2000	2010	2020
Unemployment rate.	MENA region		11.4% (1991)	12.1%	9.8%	10.6%
	The world	-	5.1% (1991)	6.1%	6.3%	6.6%

Source: Authors, based on WDI

Figure 3. Total Population of the MENA Region Compared to the Global Population

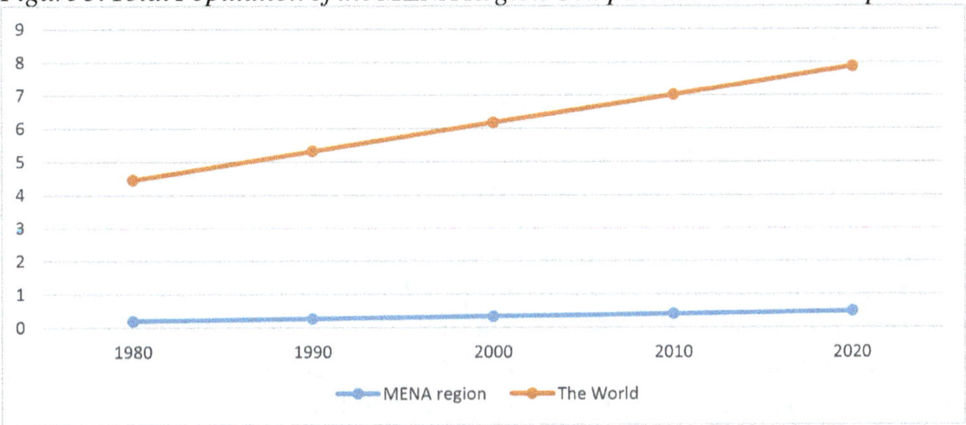

Source: Authors, based on WDI

Figure 4. GDP of the MENA Region Compared to Global GDP

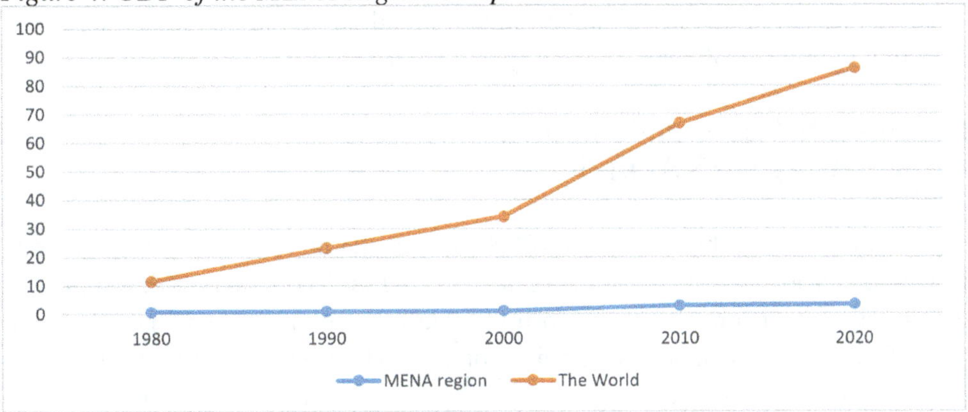

Source: Authors, based on WDI

Figure 5. Unemployment Rates of the MENA Region Compared to Global Unemployment Rates

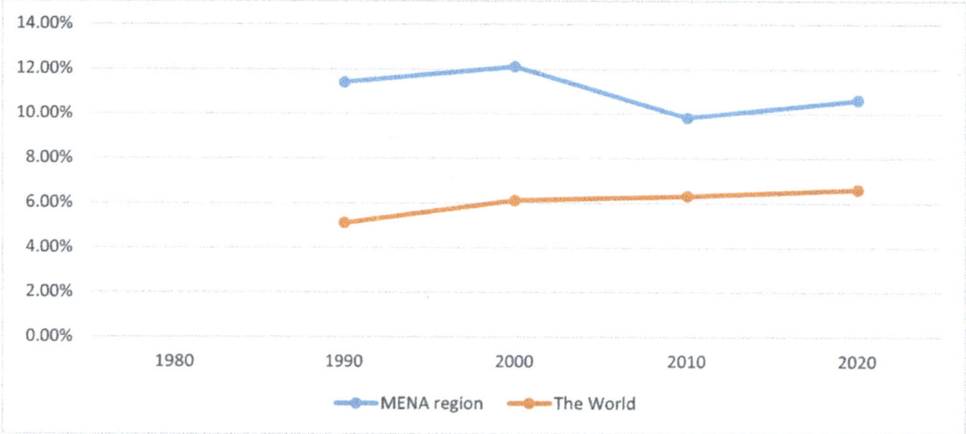

Source: Authors, based on WDI

Between 1980 and 2020, the MENA region experienced steady population growth, increasing from 183 million to 482 million people (Figure 3). Its share of the global population rose from 4.12% to 6.13%, indicating that population growth in MENA was faster than the world average. During the same period, the region's GDP in current US dollars grew from USD 0.595 trillion to USD 3.21 trillion (Figure 4). However, its share of global GDP declined from 5.19% to 3.74%, suggesting that economic growth in the region did not keep pace with global trends. In terms of unemployment, the MENA region consistently showed higher rates than the world average. In 2000, for example, the unemployment rate in MENA was 12.1%, compared to 6.1% globally. Although it decreased to 9.8% in 2010, it increased again to 10.6% in 2020, while the global average reached 6.6% (Figure 5). These figures highlight ongoing challenges in the region's labor markets.

2.2. Potential Economic Growth Effects of Mandatory IFRS Adoption

For several years, the adoption of IFRS has been the subject of numerous theoretical and empirical research projects aimed at better understanding its development, determinants, and consequences. However, studies examining the potential effects of IFRS adoption on macroeconomic indicators (FDI, economic growth, unemployment, etc.) remain relatively scarce (Elhamma, 2023a, 2023b). Most empirical investigations conducted across both developed and developing nations suggest that the mandatory implementation of IFRS significantly contributes to enhancing the quality of financial reporting (Bartov et al., 2005; Liu & Liu, 2007; Armstrong et al., 2010; Iatridis, 2010 Elhamma, 2025b). For instance, Chai et al. (2010) evaluated the accounting practices of publicly listed firms across 15 European Union (EU) countries, comparing pre- and post-IFRS adoption periods. Their results indicated notable improvements in key indicators of accounting quality following the 2005 IFRS adoption. Similarly, Yrisandi and Puspitasari (2015) examined the link between IFRS adoption and financial reporting quality among companies listed on the Indonesian Stock Exchange. Their findings revealed that the qualitative attributes of financial reports, such as relevance, understandability, and comparability, experienced measurable enhancement after IFRS implementation.

Furthermore, according to a substantial body of research, adoption of IFRS has been positively correlated with an increase in FDI inflows (Elhamma, 2025a). For example, Márquez-Ramos (2008), in an analysis covering 27 European Union member states between 1999 and 2007, found evidence supporting a favorable association between IFRS implementation and FDI levels. These findings have been reinforced by subsequent studies, including those by Gordon et al. (2012), Akisik (2014), Lungu et al. (2017), Owusu et al. (2017), Yousefinejad et al. (2018), Golubeva (2020), and Musah et al. (2020), etc. More broadly, numerous empirical studies have demonstrated a positive link between FDI inflows and economic growth. Rehman (2016), for instance, identified FDI as a key contributor to Pakistan's economic development. Similarly, using data from 104 countries over the period 1996 to 2015, Hayat (2018) concluded that FDI inflows exert a statistically significant and positive impact on economic growth.

Despite growing interest in the role of international accounting standards, empirical research directly assessing the potential influence of full or partial IFRS adoption on GDP growth remains limited in both advanced and emerging economies. Akisik (2013) explored this relationship by analyzing data from 51 countries (1997–2009). The study examined how accounting regulation—measured through the use of high-quality international standards—affects financial development and, in turn, economic growth. The findings indicate that international accounting standards have a meaningful positive effect on economic growth across both groups of countries. Similarly, Özcan (2016) investigated the connection between IFRS adoption and economic performance by comparing 41 countries that adopted IFRS with 29 non-adopting countries during the 2005–2015 period. The results demonstrated a significant improvement in economic growth among the countries that had implemented IFRS. Further evidence comes from Oppong and Aga (2019), who focused on 28 EU countries from 2005 to 2014. Their study found that IFRS adoption contributes positively to economic growth, with a more pronounced effect observed in developing nations. Based on these insights, the authors advocated for broader IFRS implementation, particularly in less developed economies.

Akisik et al. (2020) examined "the relationships of IFRS, FDI, human development and economic growth in Anglophone and Francophone African countries between 1997 and 2017". Their analysis produced two main insights. First, they found that "there is a negative and insignificant relationship between IFRS and GROWTH". Second, "the interaction term, FDI x IFRS has a significant and positive effect on GROWTH", implying that while IFRS adoption alone may not drive growth, it strengthens the beneficial influence of FDI on economic performance. In a related study, Owusu et al. (2022) explored "whether the adoption of International Financial Reporting Standards (IFRS) affects economic growth in developing economies", with a particular focus on the moderating role of institutional quality. Utilizing panel data from 78 developing economies spanning 1996 to 2013, their findings indicate that countries implementing IFRS generally experience higher levels of economic growth than those that do not. Moreover, the analysis shows that robust institutional frameworks amplify the positive effect of IFRS adoption on economic outcomes. More recently, Elhamma (2023a) investigated the link between mandatory IFRS adoption, economic growth, and the economic impact of the COVID-19 pandemic across a sample of 30 developing countries—15 from the MENA region and 15 from Sub-Saharan Africa—over the period 2017 to 2020. The results demonstrate that the compulsory adoption of IFRS contributes positively to economic growth across the sample, even in the context of crisis-related disruptions.

Nevertheless, the conclusions drawn from existing studies should be approached with caution, as some research has yielded contrasting results. For example, Zaidi and Huerta (2014) analyzed the impact of IFRS adoption on economic growth in 102 countries (51 IFRS adopters and 51 non-adopters). They found "a negative and significant relationship between IFRS adoption and economic growth rate".

Based on the literature presented above, the following hypothesis can be formulated:

> **Hypothesis H1:** *"Mandatory IFRS adoption has a positive impact on economic growth".*

2.3. The Effect of Economic Growth on Unemployment

In the field of economics, the relationship between unemployment and economic growth generally reflects a negative correlation, with higher economic growth associated with lower unemployment rates. In the early 1960s, Okun (1962) demonstrated that a 1% decrease in unemployment was typically accompanied by a 3% increase in Real Gross Domestic Product (RGDP). The findings of several recent studies examining the link between economic growth and unemployment are summarized in Table 3.

Table 3. Recent literature summary on the relationship between unemployment and economic growth

Authors	Sample	Main findings
Mosikari (2013)	South Africa with annual data covering the period 1980–2011.	"The relationship between unemployment rate and economic growth is no significant".
Abdul-Khaliq et al. (2014)	9 Arab countries with annual data covering the period 1994–2010.	"the economic growth had a negative and significant effect on the unemployment rate".
Alhdiy et al. (2015)	Egypt the quarterly data between 2006Q1 and 2013Q2.	"The study results show a Granger causality between unemployment rate and economic growth in the short term, but no causality relationship was obtained in the long term".
Sadiku et al. (2015)	FYR of Macedonia. quarterly data covering the period 2000-2012	"The empirical results do not confirm the inverse relationship between unemployment rate and economic growth, as the Okun's Law suggests".
Misini and Badivuku-Pantina (2017)	Kosovo from 2004 to 2014.	"The study results show that if the nominal GDP increases by 1% unemployment is negatively affected and decreases by an average of 0.43%".
Bayrak and Tatli (2018)	31 OECD countries from 2000- 2015.	"Empirical results reveal the adverse effects of economic growth on youth unemployment".
Xesibe and Nyasha (2020)	South Africa from 1994 to 2017.	"The results reveal that there is a negative correlation between the unemployment rate and economic growth rate".
Hjazeen et al. (2021)	Jordan over the period 1991–2019.	"The empirical findings show a negative linkage between economic growth and unemployment".
Alabed et al. (2022)	Panel of 20 MENA countries for the period (1996-2017)	"The study showed that 1% rise in GDP growth rate contributes to decreasing unemployment by 0.104%".

Source: Author construction

Thus we can formulate these two hypotheses:

Hypothesis H2: *"Economic growth has a negative impact on unemployment"*
Hypothesis H3: *"Economic growth mediates the relationship between mandatory IFRS adoption and unemployment. Specifically, mandatory IFRS adoption has an indirect and negative impact on unemployment through its effect on economic growth".*

3. METHODOLOGY

This section outlines the methodological approach employed in this research. We begin by describing the study sample (3.1), followed by the operationalization of the variables and their respective sources (3.2), and conclude with a presentation of the econometric model utilized in the analysis (3.3).

3.1. Study Sample and Data

In the field of management sciences, researchers typically choose between quantitative or qualitative methodologies (Elhamma, 2024b). In this study, a quantitative approach is adopted. The empirical analysis encompasses 11 countries from the MENA region over the period 2000 to 2020. The sample consists of seven Middle Eastern countries (Jordan, Lebanon, Oman, Qatar, Saudi Arabia, the United Arab Emirates, and Iran) and four North African countries (Algeria, Egypt, Morocco, and Tunisia). Data for this study is sourced from the "World Development Indicators (WDI)", the "World Governance Indicators (WGI)", the websites of Deloitte and the IFRS Foundation.

3.2. Variable Measurement and Data Sources

This study utilizes seven variables:

- Unemployment (the dependent variable);
- Mandatory IFRS Adoption (the independent variable);
- Economic Growth (the mediating variable);
- Foreign Direct Investment, Inflation, Political Stability, and Regulatory Quality (control variables).

The measurement of these variables and their corresponding data sources are outlined in Table 4.

Table 4. Variable Measurement and Data Sources

Variable		Acronym	Measurement	Source of data
Dependent variable	Unemployment	UneRat	The annual Unemployment rate.	The WDI: https://datatopics .worldbank.org/
Independent variable	Mandatory IFRS adoption	IFRS	Mandatory IFRS adoption is measured by using a dummy variable coded as • "1" for "years after mandatory IFRS adoption" • and "0" "for before adoption". Mandatory adoption of IFRS means in this study "requirement" for some or all companies.	• The official website of Deloitte: www.iasplus.com • The official website of IFRS Foundation: www.ifrs.org
Mediator variable	Economic growth	lnGdp	Natural logarithm of annual GDP constant (2015 USD).	The WDI: https://datatopics .worldbank.org/
Control variables	Inflation	Inflat	Annual inflation rate.	The WDI: https://datatopics .worldbank.org/
	Foreign direct investment	lnFdi	Natural logarithm of annual Net FDI inflows	The WDI: https://datatopics .worldbank.org/
	Political Stability	PolSta	"Political Stability and Absence of Violence/ Terrorism"	The World Governance Indicators (WGI).
	Regulatory Quality	RegQua	"Regulatory Quality"	The World Governance Indicators (WGI).

Source: Authors

3.3. Specification of the Econometric Model

To examine empirically whether economic growth mediates the relationship between mandatory IFRS adoption and unemployment, we have chosen to use Baron and Kenny's (1986) model modified by Zhao et al. (2010). According to Baron and Kenny (1986), "a variable may be called a mediator to the extent that it accounts for the relation between the predictor and the criterion" (p.1176). To test the mediation hypothesis, Baron and Kenny (1986) proposed a three-step approach: "first, regressing the mediator on the independent variable; second, regressing the dependent variable on the independent variable; and third, regressing the dependent variable on both the independent variable and on the mediator" (Baron and Kenny, 1986, p. 1177). The mediation hypothesis will be validated if: "first, the independent variable must affect the mediator in the first equation; second, the independent variable must be shown to affect the dependent variable in the second equation; and third, the mediator must affect the dependent variable in the third equation" (Baron and Kenny, 1986, p. 1177).

This model was partially criticized by Zhao et al. (2010). According to these researchers, the significant relationship between independent variable and dependent variable in the second regression is not necessary. They indicated that "all that matters is that the indirect effect is significant" (Zhao et al., 2010). In this regard, three equations need to be tested.

Equation (1):

$$lnGdp = f(IFRS, lnFdi, Inflat, PolSta, RegQua)$$

$$\ln Gdp_{it} = \beta_0 + \beta_1 IFRS_{it} + \beta_2 \ln Fdi_{it} + \beta_3 Inflat_{it} + \beta_4 PolSta_{it} + \beta_5 \mathrm{Reg}Qua_{it}$$

Equation (2):

$$UneRat = f(IFRS, lnFdi, Inflat, PolSta, RegQua)$$

$$UneRat_{it} = \beta_0 + \beta_1 IFRS_{it} + \beta_2 \ln Fdi_{it} + \beta_3 Inflat_{it} + \beta_4 PolSta_{it} + \beta_5 \mathrm{Reg}Qua_{it}$$

Equation (3):

$$UneRat = f(IFRS, lnGdp, lnFdi, Inflat, PolSta, RegQua)$$

$$UneRat_{it} = \beta_0 + \beta_1 IFRS_{it} + \beta_2 \ln Gdp_{it} + \beta_3 \ln Fdi_{it} + \beta_4 Inflat_{it} + \beta_5 PolSta_{it} + \beta_6 \mathrm{Reg}Qua_{it}$$

Where: UneRat represents "Unemployment Rate". lnGdp represents "Natural Logarithm of Annual GDP Constant (2015 USD)". IFRS is "Mandatory of IFRS Adoption". lnFdi is "Natural Logarithm of Net Foreign Direct Investment Inflows". Inflat is "Inflation". PolSta represents "Political Stability". RegQua represents "Regulatory Quality". "i" denotes "the country subscript". "t" is the "time period". "βi" is "the coefficient related to different types of variables" and "ε_{it}" is "the error term".

To test the indirect effect of mandatory IFRS adoption on unemployment trough economic growth, we will use the Sobel (1982) test:

Equation 4:

$$z - value = (\beta_1 * \beta_2) / \sqrt{(\beta_2{}^2 * s_{\beta 1}{}^2 + \beta_1{}^2 * s_{\beta 2}{}^2)}$$

Where: β_1 is the coefficient of IFRS in equation 1. β2 is the coefficient of lnGdp in equation 3. $s_{\beta 1}$ and $s_{\beta 2}$ are Standard errors of β_1 and β2.

4. RESULTS AND DISCUSSION

This section presents the results of our analysis. We begin by discussing the descriptive statistics, correlations, and stationarity of the variables (4.1), followed by the presentation of the regression results (4.2).

4.1. Descriptive Statistics, Correlations and Stationarity Tests

Table 5 presents the descriptive statistics of the main data.

Table 5. Summary of Descriptive Statistics

Variables	Mean	St. Dv.	Min.	Max.	Obs.
UneRat	0.0885	0.0534	0.001	0.298	231
lnGdp	4.7673	0.9963	2.9112	6.5766	231
IFRS	0.5064	0.5010	0	1	231
lnFdi	2.6526	0.2643	2.1246	3.9247	231
Inflat	0.0527	0.0835	-0.049	0.849	231
PolSta	-0.3117	0.8745	-2.12	1.22	231
RegQua	-0.1409	0.6546	-1.7201	1.1205	231

Notes. "UneRat represents Unemployment Rate". "lnGdp represents Natural Logarithm of Annual GDP Constant (2015 USD)". "IFRS represents Mandatory of IFRS Adoption". "lnFdi represents Natural Logarithm of Net Foreign Direct Investment Inflows". "Inflat represents Inflation". "PolSta represents Political Stability". "RegQua represents Regulatory Quality".

The average unemployment rate (UneRat) in the sample is 8.85%, with values ranging from 0.1% to almost 30%, indicating strong variation across countries and years. The average of the logarithm of GDP (lnGdp) is 4.77, with moderate dispersion, suggesting notable economic differences among countries. Approximately 50% of the observations correspond to countries that have adopted IFRS. The logarithm of FDI (lnFdi) is relatively stable, with low variation around a mean of 2.65. Inflation averages 5.27%, but some observations show negative values, indicating instances of deflation. Lastly, institutional indicators such as political stability (PolSta) and regulatory quality (RegQua) show wide variation, reflecting diverse institutional environments within MENA countries.

Table 6 presents the results of the Pearson pairwise correlation analysis.

Table 6. Correlation Matrix

	UneRat	lnGdp	IFRS	lnFdi	Inflat	PolSta	RegQua
UneRat	1						
lnGdp	-0.251*	1					
IFRS	-0.433*	-0.383*	1				
lnFdi	-0.235*	0.477*	-0.037	1			
Inflat	0.157**	0.213*	-0.237*	0.100	1		
PolSta	-0.667*	-0.099	0.413*	-0.012	-0.34*	1	
RegQua	-0.562*	-0.242*	0.628*	0.136**	-0.451*	0.757*	1

Notes. "UneRat represents Unemployment Rate". "lnGdp represents Natural Logarithm of Annual GDP Constant (2015 USD)". "IFRS represents Mandatory of IFRS Adoption". "lnFdi represents Natural Logarithm of Net Foreign Direct Investment Inflows". "Inflat represents Inflation". "PolSta represents Political Stability". "RegQua represents Regulatory Quality". Stars indicate statistical significance:*p<1%; **p<5%; ***p<10.

The unemployment rate (UneRat) is negatively correlated with GDP (lnGdp) (Correlation coefficient=-0.25; p<1%), IFRS adoption (Correlation coefficient =-0.43; p<1%), FDI (Correlation coefficient=-0.23; p<1%), political stability (Correlation coefficient=-0.67; p<1%), and regulatory quality (Correlation coefficient=-0.56; p<1%). This suggests that stronger economic performance and better institutional frameworks are associated with lower unemployment levels. IFRS adoption shows positive correlations with political stability (Correlation coefficient=0.41; p<1%) and regulatory quality (Correlation coefficient=0.62; p<1%), indicating that countries with more stable and effective institutions are more likely to adopt IFRS. GDP is positively related to FDI (Correlation coefficient=0.47; p<1%) and inflation (Correlation coefficient=0.21; p<1%), while its correlation with political stability is relatively weak. The correlation coefficients indicate the absence of multicollinearity among the study variables. This finding is further supported by the Variance Inflation Factor (VIF) test (see Table 8).

To test the stationarity of the variables, the Levin–Lin–Chu (LLC) test was used. The results of this test are summarized in the table below (Table 7).

Table 7. Levin–Lin–Chu (LLC) Unit Root Test Results

Variables	Unadjusted t	Adjusted t*	p-value
UneRat	-5.8284	-1.5365	0.0622***
lnGdp	-5.8014	-4.7567	0.0000*
lnFdi	-7.0685	-2.4451	0.0072*
Inflat	-6.8084	-1.5663	0.0586***
PolSta	-6.4054	-3.5233	0.0002
RegQua	-5.5178	-1.8838	0.0298

Significant at:*p<1%; **p<5%; ***p<10.

The LLC test results indicate that all variables are stationary at level, with p-values below the 10% significance threshold. This allows us to reject the null hypothesis of a unit root. GDP (lnGdp), FDI (lnFdi), and political stability (PolSta) are stationary at the 1% level, suggesting strong stability in their time-series structure. The unemployment rate (UneRat) and inflation (Inflat) are stationary at the 10% level, which is still considered acceptable. These findings support the use of these variables in econometric analyses without concerns about non-stationarity bias.

4.4. Regression Analysis

The fixed effects regression results are reported in the table below (Table 8).

Table 8. Regression results

Dependent variable	lnGdp	VIF	UneRat	VIF	UneRat	VIF
IFRS	0.4295* (0.0652)	1.754	-0.0097 (0.0062)	1.754	0.0041 (0.0064)	1.858
lnGdp					-0.0324* (0.0061)	1.692
lnFdi	0.1271*** (0.0746)	1.136	-0.0151** (0.0071)	1.136	-0.0110 (0.0067)	1.588
Inflat	-0.2942 (0.2297)	1.316	0.0148 (0.0219)	1.316	0.0053 (0.0207)	1.318

continued on following page

Table 8. Continued

Dependent variable	lnGdp	VIF	UneRat	VIF	UneRat	VIF
PolSta	-0.3731* (0.0476)	2.482	-0.0202* (0.0045)	2.482	-0.0323* (0.0048)	2.635
RegQua	0.1209 (0.0792)	4.022	0.0215* (0.0075)	4.022	0.0254* (0.0071)	4.250
Constant	4.1286* (0.1976)	All VIF<5	0.1297* (0.0188)	All VIF<5	0.2638* (0.0309)	All VIF<5
R-squared	0.38		0.35		0.21	

Notes. "UneRat represents Unemployment Rate". "lnGdp represents Natural Logarithm of Annual GDP Constant (2015 USD)". "IFRS represents Mandatory of IFRS Adoption". "lnFdi represents Natural Logarithm of Net Foreign Direct Investment Inflows". "Inflat represents Inflation". "PolSta represents Political Stability". "RegQua represents Regulatory Quality". Standard errors in parentheses. Stars indicate statistical significance:*p<1%; **p<5%; ***p<10.

According to the results presented in Table 8, the mandatory adoption of IFRS significantly enhances economic growth in the countries studied ($\beta = 0.42$; $p < 0.01$). These findings provide strong support for the first hypothesis (H1), which posits that IFRS adoption has a significant positive impact on economic growth in MENA countries. It suggests that nations implementing IFRS tend to experience stronger economic growth compared to those that do not. These findings are consistent with several previous studies conducted in different regions and employing various methodologies. Akisik (2013) examined the links between "accounting regulation, financial development, and economic growth" across 51 countries between 1997 and 2009. The findings revealed that "accounting regulation has a strong effect on economic growth even after controlling for a number of macroeconomic and socioeconomic variables" (Akisik, 2013, p.33). Özcan A. (2016), using data from 70 countries (41 IFRS adopters and 29 non-adopters) between 2005 and 2015, demonstrated that "IFRS adoption has significantly increased countries' economic growth" (Özcan, 2016, p.78). Following a similar line of reasoning, Oppong and Aga (2019), using data from 2005 to 2014 across 28 European countries, found that "IFRS adoption improves the economic growth and that IFRS adoption matters for developing economies than developed ones" (Oppong and Aga, 2019, p.792). In the same vein, Owusu et al. (2022), examining 78 developing countries from 1996 to 2013, demonstrated that "countries that adopt IFRS experience better economic growth than non-adopting countries" (Owusu et al., 2022, p.73). More recently, Elhamma (2023a) investigated the relationship between "mandatory IFRS adoption, economic growth and Covid-19 crisis" in 30 developing countries. The results of the study showed that the "mandatory IFRS adoption has a positive and significant impact on economic growth" (Elhamma, 2023a, p.565).

According to our findings, lnGdp has a significant negative effect on the unemployment rate (UneRat) (β = -0.03; $p < 0.01$). Thus, the results support the second research hypothesis (H2), which posits that economic growth significantly and negatively affects unemployment. These findings are consistent with previous research demonstrating that economic growth has a substantial negative impact on unemployment. Abdul-Khaliq et al. (2014) examined the relationship between GDP growth and unemployment in nine Arab countries over the period 1994–2010. Their findings indicate that the unemployment rate is negatively and statistically significantly affected by economic growth. Specifically, a 1% increase in GDP growth is associated with a 0.16% decrease in the unemployment rate. Similarly, Bayrak and Tatli (2018) investigated the relationship between economic growth and the youth unemployment rate using data from 31 OECD countries. Their findings indicate that economic growth negatively affects youth unemployment. In the same vein, in Jordan, Hjazeen et al. (2021) investigated the effects of unemployment on the economic growth from 1991 to 2019. The findings show that unemployment and economic growth are negatively correlated. Along the same lines, Alabed et al. (2022) used panel data from 20 countries between 1996 and 2017 to investigate the primary factors influencing unemployment rates in the MENA region. Their findings demonstrated that economic variables, including GDP growth, significantly affect unemployment in this region.

The results of our analyses show, as already presented above, that the mandatory IFRS adoption, as an independent variable, has a positive significant impact on economic growth, as a mediator variable ($\beta 1$=0.4295; p-value < 0.01). When both mandatory IFRS adoption and economic growth are included in the regression model, two notable results emerge. First, mandatory IFRS adoption has no significant direct effect on unemployment (β = 0.0041; not significant). Second, economic growth has a significant negative effect on unemployment (β = -0.0324; $p < 0.01$). Thus, the indirect effect ($\beta 1 * \beta 2$) is -0.0139 (0.4295*-0.0324). According to Sobel–Goodman test results, the indirect effect of mandatory IFRS adoption on unemployment through economic growth is statistically significant (z-value=-4.41; p-value=0.00001). According to Zhao et al. (2010), these results indicate full mediation, because the indirect effect is significant, but the direct effect (β=0.0041; ns) is not significant. Therefore, the third research hypothesis (H3) is validated by our analysis according to which the mandatory IFRS adoption impacts significantly the unemployment through the economic growth. Specifically, the analysis suggests that mandatory IFRS adoption may contribute to a reduction in the unemployment rate by approximately 1.39% in the countries examined. These empirical results offer novel insights into the relationship between the adoption of credible accounting standards, such as IFRS, and labor market outcomes. The evidence supports the notion that enhanced financial reporting standards can foster economic growth, which subsequently leads to lower unemployment.

Based on the results obtained in this research, two key recommendations can be made. The mandatory adoption of IFRS should be encouraged in other MENA countries. the results of this study indicate that the mandatory adoption of IFRS positively impacts economic growth, which in turn helps reduce the unemployment rate. Specifically, IFRS adoption could decrease the unemployment rate by 1.39% through its effect on economic growth. Therefore, governments in MENA countries that have not yet adopted this standard should consider making IFRS mandatory, especially to stimulate economic growth and create a more favorable environment for job creation. Second, training and support for IFRS implementation should be strengthened to ensure effective application and compliance. While the adoption of IFRS has shown positive effects, it is crucial to ensure that companies and professionals possess the necessary skills to apply these standards effectively. It is recommended to invest in training, awareness, and certification programs for accountants, auditors, and managers to facilitate smooth implementation and maximize its impact on economic growth and employment.

5. SUMMARY AND CONCLUSION

The objective of this research is to examine in depth the indirect impact of mandatory IFRS adoption on unemployment rates through economic growth. In other words, it aims to investigate the mediating role of economic growth in the relationship between mandatory IFRS adoption and unemployment. A panel data of 11 MENA countries from 2000 to 2020 was analyzed. Our study found a significant full mediation effect of economic growth between mandatory IFRS adoption and unemployment in the MENA region. This suggests that the indirect effect of IFRS adoption on unemployment through economic growth is both negative and significant. Specifically, mandatory IFRS adoption enhances economic growth, which subsequently leads to a reduction in unemployment. More precisely, the mandatory adoption of IFRS could lower the unemployment rate by 1.39% in the countries studied, driven by its impact on economic growth.

The findings of this research carry significant implications for both scholars and policymakers. From an academic perspective, the study enhances the understanding of the intricate relationship between mandatory IFRS adoption and two key macroeconomic variables: economic growth and unemployment. To the best of the author's knowledge, this is the first empirical investigation to assess the indirect effect of IFRS adoption on unemployment via its influence on economic growth.

For policymakers, the results suggest that implementing mandatory IFRS may yield both beneficial and adverse outcomes for economic growth and employment.

Like any research, this research has certain limitations. First, it is confined to a single geographical area, the MENA region. Future studies should focus on other regions, such as Asia or Latin America, to obtain a more thorough understanding of the relationship between economic growth, unemployment, and the mandatory adoption of IFRS. Additionally, this study focuses exclusively on countries that have adopted IFRS as issued by the IASB. Future research could examine countries that have modified their national accounting standards to align with IFRS.

REFERENCES

Abdul-Khaliq, S., Soufan, T., & Shihab, R. A. (2014). The relationship between unemployment and economic growth rate in Arab countries. *Journal of Economics and Sustainable Development, 5*(9), 56–59.

Ahmed, A. S., Neel, M., & Wang, D. (2013). Does mandatory adoption of IFRS improve accounting quality? Preliminary evidence. *Contemporary Accounting Research, 30*(4), 1344–1372. DOI: 10.1111/j.1911-3846.2012.01193.x

Akisik, O. (2013). Accounting regulation, financial development, and economic growth. *Emerging Markets Finance & Trade, 49*(1), 33–67. DOI: 10.2753/REE1540-496X490103

Akisik, O. (2014). Financial reporting and foreign direct investments in Latin America. In *Accounting in Latin America* (pp. 41–47). Emerald Group Publishing., DOI: 10.1108/S1479-356320140000014000

Akisik, O., Gal, G., & Mangaliso, M. P. (2020). IFRS, FDI, economic growth, and human development: The experience of Anglophone and Francophone African countries. *Emerging Markets Review, 45*, 100725. DOI: 10.1016/j.ememar.2020.100725

Alabed, Q., Said, F. F., Karim, Z. A., Zaidi, M. A. S., & Mansour, M. (2022). Determinants of unemployment in the MENA region: New evidence using dynamic heterogeneous panel analysis. In A. E. Hassanien, R. Y. Rizk, V. Snášel, & R. F. Abdel-Kader (Eds.), *The 8th International Conference on Advanced Machine Learning and Technologies and Applications (AMLTA 2022)*. https://doi.org/DOI: 10.1007/978-3-031-03918-8_34

Alhdiy, F. M., Johari, F., Daud, S. N. M., & Rahman, A. A. (2015). Short and long term relationship between economic growth and unemployment in Egypt: An empirical analysis. *Mediterranean Journal of Social Sciences, 6*(4), S3, 454–462. https://doi.org/DOI: 10.5901/mjss.2015.v6n4s3p454

Armstrong, S. C., Barth, M. E., Jagolinzer, A. D., & Riedl, E. J. (2010). Market reaction to the adoption of IFRS in Europe. *The Accounting Review, 85*(1), 31–61. DOI: 10.2308/accr.2010.85.1.31

Baron, R. M., & Kenny, D. A. (1986). The moderator–mediator variable distinction in social psychological research: Conceptual, strategic, and statistical considerations. *Journal of Personality and Social Psychology, 51*(6), 1173–1182. DOI: 10.1037/0022-3514.51.6.1173 PMID: 3806354

Bartov, E., Goldberg, S. R., & Kim, M. (2005). Comparative value relevance among German, US, and international accounting standards: A German stock market perspective. *Journal of Accounting, Auditing & Finance, 20*(2), 95–119. DOI: 10.1177/0148558X0502000201

Bayrak, R., & Tatli, H. (2018). The determinants of youth unemployment: A panel data analysis of OECD countries. *The European Journal of Comparative Economics, 15*(2), 231–248. DOI: 10.25428/1824-2979/201802-231-248

British Petroleum. (2021). *Statistical review of world energy* (70th ed.). https://www.bp.com/content/dam/bp/business-sites/en/global/corporate/pdfs/energy-economics/statistical-review/bp-stats-review-2021-full-report.pdf

Chai, H., Tang, Q., Jiang, Y., & Lin, Z. (2010). The role of international financial reporting standards in accounting quality: Evidence from the European Union. *Journal of International Financial Management & Accounting, 21*(3), 220–278. DOI: 10.1111/j.1467-646X.2010.01041.x

Daske, H. (2006). Economic benefits of adopting IFRS or US-GAAP – Have the expected cost of equity capital really decreased? *Journal of Business Finance & Accounting, 33*(3–4), 329–373. DOI: 10.1111/j.1468-5957.2006.00611.x

Elhamma, A. (2023a). Impact of mandatory IFRS adoption on economic growth: The moderating role of COVID-19 crisis in developing countries. *Journal of Accounting and Management Information Systems, 22*(3), 554–568. DOI: 10.24818/jamis.2023.03007

Elhamma, A. (2023b). *Cinquante ans des normes comptables internationales IAS/IFRS: Adoption, conséquences et où en est-on au Maroc?* In R. M'Rabet & M. A. Issami (Eds.), *50 ans de management: Regards croisés d'un demi-siècle du management* (pp. 121–136). Éditions EDISCA.

Elhamma, A. (2024a). Determinants of national IFRS adoption: Evidence from the Middle East and North Africa region. *International Journal of Accounting. Auditing and Performance Evaluation, 20*(1–2), 69–90. DOI: 10.1504/IJAAPE.2024.135535

Elhamma, A. (2024b). Participant observation as a qualitative research method in management sciences: Interests, conditions, and limitations. In Bentalha, B., & Alla, L. (Eds.), *Applying qualitative research methods to management science* (pp. 75–91). IGI Global., DOI: 10.4018/979-8-3693-5543-5.ch004

Elhamma, A. (2025a). Impact of mandatory IFRS adoption on foreign direct investment: The moderating role of conflict of interest regulation. *Journal of Financial Reporting and Accounting, 23*(3), 936–958. DOI: 10.1108/JFRA-04-2022-0145

Elhamma, A. (2025b). Perceived benefits of IFRS adoption in Morocco and French-speaking Sub-Saharan African countries. In F. Albuquerque & P. G. Dos Santos (Eds.), *Contemporary innovations in reporting and analysis* (pp. 183–210). IGI Global. https://doi.org/DOI: 10.4018/979-8-3693-5923-5.ch007

Elhamma, A. (2025c). A half-century of international accounting standards (IAS/I-FRS): Assessing the mandatory adoption, impact, and Morocco's position in the convergence process. In Vardari, L., & Qabrati, I. (Eds.), *Aligning financial reporting standards with global trade needs* (pp. 185–204). IGI Global., DOI: 10.4018/979-8-3373-0887-6.ch007

Golubeva, O. (2020). Maximising international returns: Impact of IFRS on foreign direct investments. *Journal of Contemporary Accounting & Economics*, *16*(2), 100200. DOI: 10.1016/j.jcae.2020.100200

Gordon, L. A., Loeb, M. P., & Zhu, W. (2012). The impact of IFRS adoption on foreign direct investment. *Journal of Accounting and Public Policy*, *31*(4), 374–398. DOI: 10.1016/j.jaccpubpol.2012.06.001

Griffiths, S. (2017). A review and assessment of energy policy in the Middle East and North Africa region. *Energy Policy*, *102*, 249–269. DOI: 10.1016/j.enpol.2016.12.023

Griffiths, S. (2017). A review and assessment of energy policy in the Middle East and North Africa region. *Energy Policy*, *102*, 249–269. DOI: 10.1016/j.enpol.2016.12.023

Hayat, A. (2018). FDI and economic growth: The role of natural resources? *Journal of Economic Studies (Glasgow, Scotland)*, *45*(2), 283–295. DOI: 10.1108/JES-05-2015-0082

Hjazeen, H., Seraj, M., & Ozdeser, H. (2021). The nexus between economic growth and unemployment in Jordan. *Future Business Journal*, *7*(1), 42. DOI: 10.1186/s43093-021-00088-3

Iatridis, G. (2010). International financial reporting standards and the quality of financial statement information. *International Review of Financial Analysis*, *19*(3), 193–204. DOI: 10.1016/j.irfa.2010.02.004

IFRS Foundation. (2018). *Use of IFRS standards around the world*. https://www.ifrs.org/content/dam/ifrs/around-the-world/adoption/use-of-ifrs-around-the-world-overview-sept-2018.pdf

International Labour Organization. (2024). *Employment trends for youth in the Middle East and North Africa*. https://doi.org/DOI: 10.54394/GFEA7064

International Labour Organization (ILO). (2021). *World employment and social outlook trends 2021*. International Labour Office.

Liu, J., & Liu, C. (2007). Value relevance of accounting information in different stock market segments: The case of Chinese A-, B-, and H-shares. *Journal of International Accounting Research, 6*(2), 55–81. DOI: 10.2308/jiar.2007.6.2.55

Lungu, C. I., Caraiani, C., & Dascălu, C. (2017). The impact of IFRS adoption on foreign direct investments: Insights for emerging countries. *Accounting in Europe, 14*(3), 331–357. DOI: 10.1080/17449480.2017.1374546

Marquez-Ramos, L. (2008). The effect of IFRS adoption on trade and foreign direct investments. *International Trade and Finance Association Conference Papers, bepress*(19).

Misini, S., & Badivuku-Pantina, M. (2017). The effect of economic growth in relation to unemployment. *Journal of Economics and Economic Education Research, 18*(2), 1–9.

Mohseni, M., & Jouzaryan, F. (2016). Examining the effects of inflation and unemployment on economic growth in Iran (1996–2012). *Procedia Economics and Finance, 36*, 381–389. DOI: 10.1016/S2212-5671(16)30050-8

Musah, A., Adjei, E., & Ahmed, I. A. (2020). The effect of IFRS adoption on foreign direct investment in Africa. *Journal of Applied Accounting and Taxation, 5*(2), 117–126. DOI: 10.30871/jaat.v5i2.1481

Nurunnabi, M. (2021). Implementation of international financial reporting standards (IFRS) in developing countries. In *International financial reporting standards implementation: A global experience (Contributions to International Accounting)* (pp. 11–76). Emerald Publishing. https://doi.org/DOI: 10.1108/978-1-80117-440-420211002

Okun, A. (1962). Potential GNP: Its measurement and significance. In *The 1962 proceedings of business and economic statistics section*. American Statistical Association.

Oppong, C., & Aga, M. (2019). Economic growth in the European Union: Does IFRS mandatory adoption matter? *International Journal of Emerging Markets, 14*(5), 792–808. DOI: 10.1108/IJOEM-01-2018-0010

Owusu, G. M., Saat, N. A. M., Suppiah, S. D. K., & Siong, H. L. (2017). IFRS adoption, institutional quality, and foreign direct investment inflows: A dynamic panel analysis. *Asian Journal of Business and Accounting, 10*(2), 43–75.

Owusu, G. M. Y., Suppiah, S. D. K., Saat, N. A. M., & Law, S. H. (2022). IFRS adoption and economic growth in developing economies. *International Journal of Economics and Accounting*, *11*(1), 73–98. DOI: 10.1504/IJEA.2022.119613

Özcan, A. (2016). Assessing the effects of IFRS adoption on economic growth: A cross-country study. *ACU International Journal of Social Sciences*, *2*(2), 65–80. DOI: 10.22466/acusbd.v2i2.5000202321

Pohlan, L. (2019). Unemployment and social exclusion. *Journal of Economic Behavior & Organization*, *164*, 273–299. DOI: 10.1016/j.jebo.2019.06.006

Rehman, N. U. (2016). FDI and economic growth: Empirical evidence from Pakistan. *Journal of Economic and Administrative Sciences*, *32*(1), 63–76. DOI: 10.1108/JEAS-12-2014-0035

Sadiku, M., Ibraimi, A., & Sadikucal, L. (2015). Econometric estimation of the relationship between unemployment rate and economic growth of FYR of Macedonia. *Procedia Economics and Finance*, *19*, 69–81. DOI: 10.1016/S2212-5671(15)00009-X

Samaha, K., & Khlif, H. (2016). Adoption of and compliance with IFRS in developing countries: A synthesis of theories and directions for future research. *Journal of Accounting in Emerging Economies*, *6*(1), 33–49. DOI: 10.1108/JAEE-02-2013-0011

Xesibe, Z., & Nyasha, S. (2020). Unemployment and economic growth in South Africa: A re-examination. *International Journal of Sustainable Economy*, *12*(2), 101–116. DOI: 10.1504/IJSE.2020.110261

Yousefinejad, M., Ahmad, A., Salleh, F. M., & Rahim, R. A. (2018). Causal relationship between international financial reporting standard (IFRS) and foreign direct investment (FDI): A panel data analysis of ASEAN countries. *Asian Journal of Accounting and Governance*, *10*, 61–72. DOI: 10.17576/AJAG-2018-10-06

Zaidi, S., & Huerta, E. (2014). IFRS adoption and enforcement as antecedents of economic growth. *International Journal of Accounting and Financial Reporting*, *4*(1), 1. Advance online publication. DOI: 10.5296/ijafr.v4i1.5410

Zhang, G. (2013). Accounting standards, cost of capital, resource allocation, and welfare in a large economy. *The Accounting Review*, *88*(4), 1459–1488. DOI: 10.2308/accr-50375

Zhao, X., Lynch, J.Jr, & Chen, Q. (2010). Reconsidering Baron and Kenny: Myths and truths about mediation analysis. *The Journal of Consumer Research*, *37*(2), 197–206. DOI: 10.1086/651257

KEY TERMS AND DEFINITIONS

Economic growth: Economic growth refers to the sustained increase in the production of goods and services in an economy over a specific period. It is typically measured by the change in real Gross Domestic Product (GDP).

IFRS (International of Financial Reporting Standards): IFRS are international accounting standards developed and published by the IASB, aiming to ensure the comparability, transparency, and reliability of financial information.

Mandatory IFRS adoption: Mandatory adoption of IFRS occurs when a country requires some or all companies to apply IFRS in their financial reporting.

Mediation effects: A mediation relationship occurs when an intermediate variable (called a mediator) explains all or part of the effect of an independent variable on a dependent variable. Mediation can be classified as either total or partial, depending on the extent of the mediator's influence.

MENA region: The MENA region comprises countries in North Africa (such as Morocco and Egypt) and the Middle East (such as Jordan and Lebanon). However, the exact list of countries included in this region varies among international organizations.

Unemployment: Unemployment refers to the situation in which individuals of working age, typically over 15, are without a job and are actively seeking employment during a specified period.

Chapter 2
Assessing the Impact of IFRS Adoption on Financial Information Quality:
A Structural Equation Modeling Approach

Adil Laouane
https://orcid.org/0009-0005-5065-2474
Faculty of Law, Economic and Social Sciences, Ain Sebâa Hassan II University, Casablanca, Morocco

ABSTRACT

The adoption of International Financial Reporting Standards (IFRS) by various countries has consistently sparked debate regarding its impact on the quality of financial reporting. This study aims to evaluate the perceptions of Moroccan financial professionals concerning the effect of IFRS adoption on the quality of financial statements. To achieve this objective, a questionnaire was distributed to a sample of 134 professionals active in the Moroccan financial market. The data collected were analyzed using the Partial Least Squares (PLS) method, which is particularly well-suited to studies with relatively small sample sizes. The findings reveal a notable improvement in the quality of financial communication following the adoption of IFRS. Moreover, respondents believe that IFRS implementation has positively influenced the financial performance of adopting companies, while also offering substantial benefit to those listed on the Casablanca Stock Exchange.

DOI: 10.4018/979-8-3373-1902-5.ch002

1. INTRODUCTION

The growth of economic and financial markets in a globalized context presents development opportunities and constraints. This prompts companies to collaborate to address these new challenges. Similarly, the internationalization of companies has created the need for a reliable financial information tool common to all market participants.

In this sense, the International Financial Reporting Standards (IFRS) are fully aligned with this approach. They represent a shift from a tax- and legal-inspired accounting approach to a financial reporting logic that focuses on investors and seeks to preserve their confidence in the financial markets.

The stated objective of international standard setters in adopting IFRS is to help designers of financial information to produce high quality financial statements that serve as a basis for optimal investment decisions (Laouane, 2023). In this regard, the concept of the usefulness of accounting and financial information is at the heart of the concerns of international standards. The latter stipulate that the purpose of accounting is not limited to its predictive role, but also includes presenting a faithful reflection of the financial and economic situation, the results and the assets of the company. In addition, financial information is a fundamental management tool on which all companies rely in order to maintain relations with their stakeholders, and it is therefore necessary to provide them with transparent accounting information that best reflects the economic reality of transactions.

The specificity of the international framework is demonstrated by the introduction of qualitative characteristics, in particular: reliability, relevance, comparability, comparability and understandability (Elhamma, 2025). The Financial Accounting Standards Board (FASB) considers the first two characteristics to be the primary or fundamental criteria. The European Community has chosen the path of harmonizing accounting practices and rules at the level of Member States, with the aim of providing users with relevant, accessible financial Compliance with these qualities will yield financial statements that accurately represent the true and fair view of the entity and will ensure the communication of financial information that is of high value to users information that is legally recognized by the various stakeholders within the Union. As a result, the application of these standards became mandatory for certain categories of companies from 1 January 2005.

The Moroccan authorities have recognized the importance of adopting international standards for companies operating in the country. In this sense, integrating IFRS has become a necessity in order to keep pace with international developments and adopt the same accounting language. The first application in Morocco is scheduled for January 1, 2008, for certain categories of companies.

Adopting international accounting standards undoubtedly represents an opportunity for companies operating in several financial markets. Indeed, there have been a number of moves in this direction in various contexts. However, such implementation is often accompanied by difficulties due to the divergent approaches on which the two accounting systems are based.

This transition to the new accounting standards unavoidably prompts inquiries on the effect of this shift on the quality of the financial information generated. In this framework, we will endeavor to address the subsequent inquiry: **To what degree does the implementation of IFRS enhance the quality of financial reporting as regarded by its primary users within the Moroccan context?**

To understand the opinions of the main designers and users of accounting and financial information regarding the relevance of IFRS. We distributed a 69-question survey to achieve this goal. Starting from a positivist paradigm, within hypothetico-deductive reasoning, the transition from the theoretical base to the empirical side of the study through an investigation based on structural equation modeling using the Partial Least Squares (PLS) approach.

Verification of the structural model empirically revealed a significant link between IFRS adoption and the quality of annual financial statements. The results of our survey show that users of financial information have similar perceptions regarding financial communication, financial performance, and the benefits of adopting IFRS in a Moroccan context. Conversely, they have different opinions regarding changes in working methods and the main themes addressed by the new accounting standards.

In Morocco, we observe a gradual integration of the new framework by a limited number of companies. To our knowledge, no studies has analyzed how Moroccan financial actors perceive the impact of IFRS on financial reporting quality in Morocco.

To address this question, we will first provide a literature review to construct the theoretical context of our research. We then present the research hypotheses to be tested empirically. Finally, the perspectives and possible tracks of research will be proposed, after presenting its main limitations.

2. LITERATURE REVIEW AND RESEARCH HYPOTHESES

A preliminary examination of extant research findings reveals a state of discordance, with equivocal outcomes that fail to establish definitive conclusions. In this regard, the initial body of research substantiates the notion that the implementation of IFRS enhances the quality of financial reporting. Elhamma (2023), Hassan (2019), Barth et al. (2017), and Laouane & Torra (2024) have demonstrated that the significance of financial communication is subject to alteration subsequent to the implementation of International Financial Reporting Standards (IFRS). In a similar vein, Outa et al. (2017) discovered a robust and substantial association between the adoption of IFRS and the enhancement of firm value. This correlation is primarily attributable to the impact of the application of the fair value principle. Nevertheless, the predominance of International Financial Reporting Standards (IFRS) over domestic accounting standards is called into question by the supposition that the significance of accounting data is contingent not solely on the accounting framework employed, but also on institutional factors in the nations where financial information is generated and interpreted (Garanina & Kormiltseva, 2013).

As part of our research, we sought to understand the perceptions of Moroccan financial actors regarding the impact of International Financial Reporting Standards (IFRS) on the quality of financial information. To this end, we examined five aspects: financial communication, working methods, financial performance, the advantages of implementing IFRS, and the main issues addressed by IFRS. In summary, the set of hypotheses can be outlined as such:

Figure 1. Presentation of research hypotheses

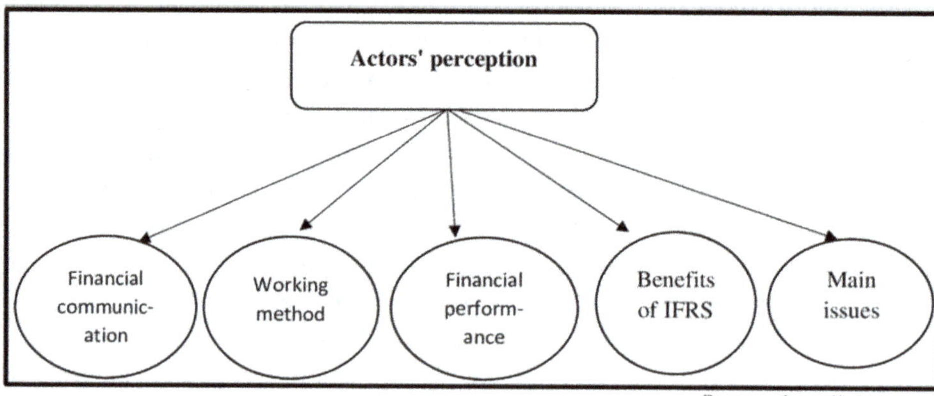

Source: Compiled by us

Source: *Compiled by us*

2.1. The Effect of IFRS Adoption on Financial Reporting

To restore investor confidence, the International Accounting Standards Board (IASB) required the use of International Financial Reporting Standards (IFRS) for publicly listed firms preparing consolidated financial statements effective January 1, 2005. The principal aim of the IASB is to provide an international regulatory framework for the dissemination of high-quality financial information (Barth et al., 2017). Consequently, Cormier et al. (2007) contend that investors and creditors are recognized as the primary users of accounting and financial information. Moreover, the IASB asserts that the fundamental purpose of financial statements is to furnish information that is beneficial to investors in making investment decisions.

In the same vein, Almaqtari and al., (2021) considers that accounting is recognized as a useful information system for stakeholders. Similarly, the updated conceptual framework of IFRS states that the primary recipients of financial information are, in particular, capital providers (investors and creditors).

Conversely, Lenormand et al. (2012) assert that IFRS will lead enterprises to generate and provide more comprehensive information to satisfy users' requirements. Consequently, the initial hypothesis is articulated as follows:

> **Hypothesis 1:** Users of financial information contend that the introduction of IFRS improvers financial communication;

2.2. The Effect of IFRS Implementation on Working Practices

Research regarding the effects of IFRS implementation on working practices is plentiful and inconsistent. Amaefule and al., (2018) argue that international accounting standards require preparers of financial statements, as well as auditors and financial analysts, to understand the accounting problem in its economic and legal context. Furthermore, Daske and al., (2013) have analyzed the effect of various accounting methods on the financial analysis of financial statements.

As a result, the adoption of IFRS has forced preparers of financial information to change their working methods. Numerous adjustments must be implemented to assess specific accounting and financial indicators and ratios. Moreover, the implementation of certain standards has forced a change in vision and approach to the design of financial information. Hence our second hypothesis:

> **Hypothesis 2:** Financial information users believe that the implementation of IFRS influences the working practices of financial information preparers.

2.3. The Effect of IFRS Adoption on Financial Performance

According to the financial and accounting literature, there is a significant association between adopting IFRS and improving the quality of financial performance indicators (Elhamma,(2023; Laouane &Torra (2024) ; Alnodel, 2018; Ahmadi and Bouri, 2018).

The adoption of IFRS can be justified by the relevance of the financial information produced compared to local accounting standards. In this regard, Do Hoon et al. (2019), believe that IFRS improve The quality of the informational content of accounting performance indicators enhances the elucidation of the company's market value. The authors identify a positive correlation between stock market performance and accounting performance indicators.

Furthermore, Garza Sánchez et al. (2017) state that accounting measures of performance and financial measures can be complementary in that they separately show statistically significant and differentiated explanatory power.

For their part, Watts and Zimmerman (1986) consider that the use of recognized accounting standards can be viewed as an effective method for optimizing the firm's value for capital providers. Similarly, and referring to the work of the following authors, Turki et al. (2020) Hassan(2019), Ahmadi et Bouri (2018), the implementation of international standards should improve the informational quality of accounting figures by optimizing the explanatory power of financial performance indicators, which are the main elements used by investors to assess the value of the firm. In this context, our third hypothesis is as follows:

> **Hypothesis 3:** Users of financial information assert that the implementation of IFRS enhances the financial performance of adopting firms.

2.4. The Principal Topics Covered by IFRS

As our objective is not to go into detail about the issues addressed by these standards, we have limited ourselves to nine topics in this section. First, we have compiled a list of the main topics in IFRS that have attracted the interest of researchers. As a result, some agreement was reached on the importance of fair value measurement as a topic that has left its mark on the existing literature. We then suggested certain standards whose application could cause certain difficulties. The consensus was that IAS 39 'Financial Instruments: Recognition and Measurement' would be unduly burdensome to apply, and that IAS 17 'Leases' and IAS 16 'Intangible Assets' would not cause major difficulties. The changes to the rules on how to calculate revenue, provisions, contingent liabilities and contingent assets made the adoption of IFRS difficult and limited the benefits expected from the change.

Furthermore, Lenormand et al. (2012) examine the notion of fair value and scrutinize the effective improvement of financial information published under IFRS. They conclude that the choice given to managers to choose the accounting treatment that best reflects economic reality provides opportunities to manipulate accounting figures, especially in the selection of valuation model. In addition, Bernheim et al (1999) analyze the advantages and disadvantages of fair value and its limitations, concluding that its reliability, objectivity and neutrality are not assured characteristics that can be attributed to it, but are nevertheless recognized as indispensable in accounting. Finally, our fourth hypothesis is as follows:

Hypothesis 4: Users of financial information have the same perception of the main issues in IFRS.

2.5. The Benefits of Using IFRS inside the Moroccan Context

Barth et al., (2017) believe that there is a growing interest in joining the international accounting standard-setting process. In fact, the adoption of IFRS brings several advantages to companies and plays a key role in enhancing the relevance of the main accounting and financial indicators reported.

In the same vein, Cormier, Magnan and Zeghal (2000) find that the relevance of accounting figures is highly dependent on the orientation of the accounting standards. In addition, Lenormand et al (2012) argue that the most expected benefits from the adoption of IFRS are to be found in the emphasis placed on fair value measurement and its role in providing a vision more rooted in economic reality, as well as in the production of financial information with greater predictive value. Similarly, Soderstrom and Sun (2007) confirm that the implementation of IFRS facilitates comparisons between companies over time and space. However, despite the importance of these standards in producing accounting figures that best reflect economic reality, several limitations have been identified that have constrained the anticipated advantages of this accounting change. As a result, our fifth hypothesis can be formulated as follows:

Hypothesis 5: Users of financial information consider IFRS to be of great interest to listed companies.

3. METHODOLOGY

Our study focuses on the Moroccan context. Morocco is one of the countries in Africa and the MENA region that has chosen to apply IFRS selectively, making it mandatory for some companies (banks and financial institutions) and optional for others (listed companies) (Elhamma, 2024, 2025).

In order to draw valid conclusions, it is essential to select the right respondent profiles for our questionnaire. Accordingly, our target will be the main actors of financial and accounting information in Morocco, namely: statutory auditors, chartered accountants, financial analysts, accountants and financial managers. For various reasons: cost optimization, time constraints and accessibility of respondents, we were not able to interview the entire population. In fact, we restricted our investigation to a sample of 134 actors from the primary users of financial information community.

3.1. Sampling Method

In this study, we have used the non-probability sampling technique, and more specifically convenience sampling, which remains the most appropriate for our study as it allows us to interview people who are accessible and want to participate in our survey. In addition, this technique is preferred when the time frame for the study is very short, the identification of the target remains a difficult task and the budget allocated to the study is very low.

3.1.1. Sample Size

From a methodological point of view, it is essential to collect at least 30 responses in order to carry out the analysis using the PLS method (Marien and Beaud, 2003). Furthermore, our respondents are users of financial information. They were selected on the basis of prior consent, position and proximity. As a result, our final sample consists of 134 major players in the financial market. The limited number of companies adopting IFRS in Morocco explains the limited size of the sample.

3.1.2. Choice of Scale

The questionnaire consists of 69 questions, divided into 5 themes or blocks, and the survey essentially seeks the opinions of the main users of financial information. In addition, our questionnaire includes questions relating to the profile of the respondents. In the end, our questionnaire would be structured as follows:

Table 1. Topics covered in the questionnaire

Topics or blocks	Number of questions
1- Respondent profile	02 questions
2- General perception of IFRS	13 questions
3- Financial communication under IFRS	07 questions
4- Financial performance under IFRS	13 questions
5- IFRS and working methods	04 questions
6- Key IFRS topics	14 questions
7- Benefits of IFRS	16 questions

Source: Compiled by us

In the light of the literature study of diverse theoretical and empirical works related to our research question in one way or another, we were able to define a conceptualization of our questionnaire. To do this, we first operationalized the variables to be measured. We then scaled the expected responses on the five-point Likert scale.

4. RESULTS

We wanted to find out what the primary designers and users of accounting and financial information thought about the relevance of this new set of standards. We developed and distributed a 69-question questionnaire.

First, we will present the results of our descriptive study. Then, as mentioned above, our structural model estimation is made up of two elements: (1) the measurement model, representing the relationships between latent and manifest variables, and (2) the structural model, relating latent variables. Our study will conclude with a discussion of the results.

4.1. Descriptive Analysis

The structure of our questionnaire allows us to identify a section dedicated to the characteristics of the respondents, as well as their experience in their current position. Therefore, it would be very interesting to discuss the descriptive analysis of our study.

4.1.1. Breakdown of the Sample by Profile

The choice of our target group remains essential if we are to arrive at convincing conclusions. Consequently, we distributed our questionnaire to a sample of 134 prominent participants in the Moroccan financial market. Between statutory auditors, accountants, financial analysts and other financial professionals.

Figure 2. Profile of respondents

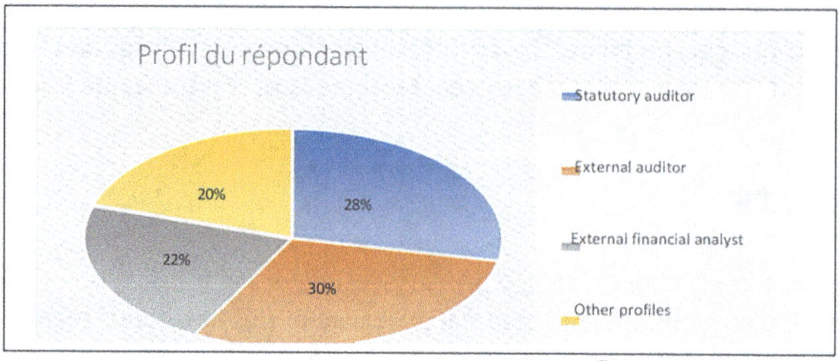

Source: Compiled by us

Source: Compiled by us

Table 2. Profile of respondents

		Number	Percentage	Valid Percentage	Cumulative Percentage
Valid	Statutory auditor	38	28,35	28.35	28.35
	External auditor	40	29.85	29.85	58,20
	External financial analyst	29	21,64	21.64	79,84
	Other	27	20,14	20.14	100,0
	Total	134	100,0	100,0	

Source: Author's calculations in SPSS V22

The findings of our descriptive study, derived from the respondents' profiles, result in the subsequent conclusions:

- The profile with the highest response rate to our questionnaire is that of external auditors, representing (29.85%) of the population surveyed, followed by the category of statutory auditors with a rate of (28.35%). The remaining respondents were financial analysts (21.64%) and others (20.14%).
- The "other" category includes the following functions: administrative and financial manager, internal auditor, administrative and financial director, accounting director.

4.1.2. Description of the Experience of the Target Population

The figure below shows the level of experience of the target population for our empirical study:

Figure 3. Breakdown of experience

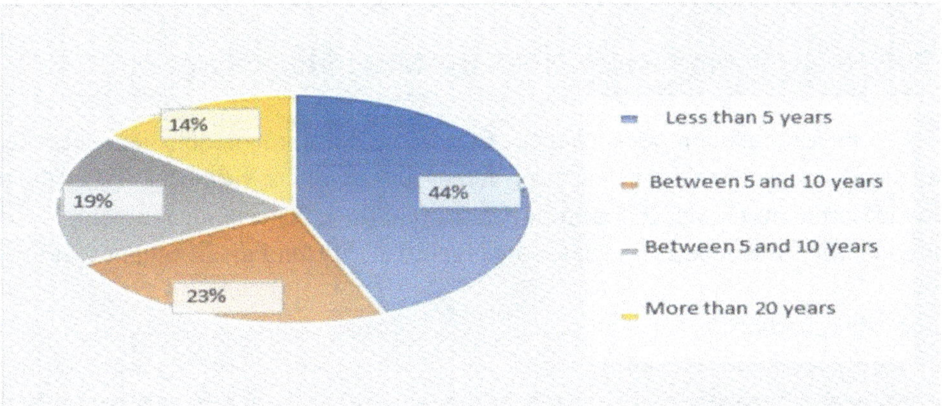

Source: Compiled by us

Source: Compiled by us

Table 3. Breakdown of experience

		Number	Percentage	valid percentage	Cumulative percentage
Valid	Less than 5 years	58	43,28	43,28	43,28
	Between 5 & 10 années	32	23,88	23,88	67,16
	Between 10 & 20 years	25	18,65	18,65	85,81
	More than 20 years	19	14,17	14,17	100,0
	Total	134	100,0	100,0	

Source: Author's calculations in SPSS V22

In terms of experience, our descriptive study shows that the majority of respondents to our survey on the Moroccan financial market have less than 20 years of professional experience. Thus, 43.28% have less than 5 years of experience, 23.88% of respondents have less than 10 years of experience, 18,65% of the population surveyed have between 10 and 20 years of experience and only 14.17% of the sample have more than 20 years of experience.

4.2. Results of the Test of the Measurement Model

According to Benitez et al. (2020), assessing the internal structural model is presumed absurd and irrelevant if the external measurement model does not meet minimum reliability and validity requirements. In other words, a consistent measurement model is necessary before engaging in a quality assessment of the internal structural model or relying on the statistical magnitude of its estimated parameters.

4.2.1. Results of the Validation of the Measurement Scales

The measurement model, also known as the external model, delineates the presumed linear correlations between latent and manifest variables. To evaluate the measurement model, literature indicates that three criteria must be employed: the reliability of measuring scales, convergent validity, and discriminant validity.

a. Scale reliability

In our case, the results calculated using SmartPLS are more reliable, with all constructs showing composite reliability above 0.7. The reliability of items and measurement scales is confirmed when they meet the validation standards described in the table below.

Table 4. The reliability of the measurement scales

	Number of items before PCA	Number of items after PCA	Cronbach's alpha	KMO index	Bartlett's sphericity test		
					Approximate chi-square	ddl	Significance Barteltt
Perception	14	6	0,916	0,514	258,542	10	0,000
Financial communication	8	6	0,922	0,657	345,536	10	0,000
Financial performance	15	5	0,938	0,799	302,214	6	0,000
Work method	6	4	0.785	0.707	77.178	6	0.000
Major themes	15	5	0,908	0,786	195,197	10	0,000
Interest of IFRS	14	5	0.906	0.814	191.251	10	0.000

Source: Output from SPSS V23

After reviewing the table, we conducted a principal component analysis (PCA), as previously mentioned. The table below summarizes the results. The KMO index shows a value greater than 0.5, which is considered satisfactory. This indicates that the correlations between the items and their constructs are of good quality. Additionally, the evaluation shows that all selected items have factor contributions above 0.5. Internal reliability is representative, as indicated by a Cronbach's alpha above 0.7. Therefore, we can conclude that the reliability and unidimensionality of the measurement scales meet the criteria set forth in the literature review of model estimation processes using the PLS approach.

b. Convergent validity

Given the utilization of multiple indicators within the context of an "individual" construct, researchers must prioritize the reliability of individual measurement items while also assessing the extent to which these items can demonstrate convergent validity (Hulland J. 1999).

Convergent validity involves computing the average variance shared by a construct and its items. Researchers have employed one or two metrics of convergent validity: Cronbach's alpha and internal consistency as established by Fornell and Larcker (1982). Since the interpretation of the obtained values is similar, the guideline offered by Nunnally (1978) can be adopted. The author considered a threshold of 0.7 to be exceptional for "modest" composite reliability applied in earlier stages of research. The table below shows the results:

Table 5. Significance and composite reliability (ρ)

Constructs	Composite Reliability
Financial communication	0,960476
Financial performance	0,902158
Interest of IFRS	0,945862
Work Method	0,878522
Actors' perception	0,915200
Major themes	0,895212

Source: Smart PLS software output

c. Discriminant validity

The conventional methodological complement to convergent validity is discriminant validity. It is a quantitative metric that quantifies the discrepancy between the measurement indicators attributed to the latent variables and the measurements of other constructs in the model.

Discriminant validity is demonstrated by the greater variance shared between a construct and its measures (AVE) compared to the variance shared between two constructs (r^2ij). Fornell and Larcker (1982) suggest using "average variance extracted" to apply discriminant validity. This is the average variance shared between the construct and its measurement indicators. This measure must exceed the variance shared between the construct and the other constructs in the model, which is represented by the square correlation between two constructs.

This can be demonstrated in the correlation matrix, which shows the correlations between constructs as the values along the lower left diagonal and the square root of the AVE values for each construct positioned along the diagonal. The table below shows the results of the discriminant validity of the scales.

Table 6. The discriminant validity of the scales

	AVE	Fin_Com	Fin_Per	Inter_IFRS	Work_Meth	Percep	Maj_Them
Fin_Com	0,830732	0,911445007					
Fin_Per	0,760569	0,814086	0,872106072				
Inter_IFRS	0,816976	0,858498	0,836652	0,903867247			
Work_Meth	0,656829	0,276751	0,219188	0,245763	0,810449875		
Percep	0,764612	0,859052	0,858892	0,782207	0,253166	0,874420951	
Maj_Them	0,732157	0,229273	0,294822	0,220666	0,132986	0,241384	0,855661732

Source: Smart PLS software output

A perusal of the table reveals that the correlation matrix contains the correlations between the constructs in the items located on the bottom left of the diagonal of the matrix and the values of the square root of the AVE calculated for each construct along the diagonal. This provides discriminant validity.

d. Overall model quality: the goodness-of-fit test (GoF)

The quality of the measurement model can generally be evaluated based on its explanatory power. This is evaluated by the coefficient of determination (*R*2) of the endogenous variables. The value of the GoF index must be greater than (0.30), as this is the recommended threshold.

Table 7. The goodness-of-fit test (GoF)

Constructs	R^2 (variance explained)	Redundancy	Communality
Financial Comm		0,830732	0,830732
Financial Perfo		0,760569	0,760569
IFRS Interests		0,816976	0,816976
Work Method		0,656827	0,656827
Perception	**0,985421**	**0,486422**	0,764612
Major themes		0,712452	0,712452
Total	**0,985421**		

continued on following page

Table 7. Continued

Constructs	R^2 (variance explained)	Redundancy	Communality
Average	0,984521		0,75421224
Gof	0,854842121		

Source: Smart PLS software output

According to the results in the table above, the GoF index is very satisfactory: GoF = 0.87 (the recommended threshold is 0.30). As a result, our measurement model, after adjustment, can be presented as follows:

Figure 4. Measurement model after adjustment

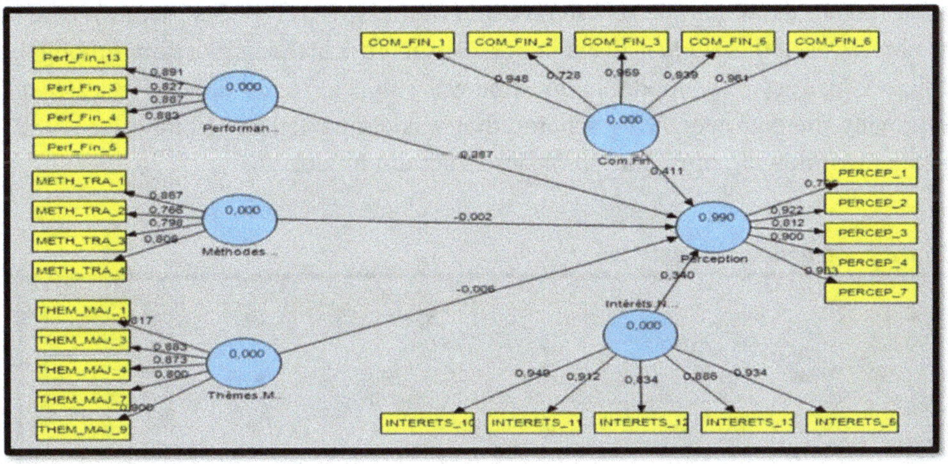

Source: Smart-PLS output

When reading the measurement model, we can say that the selected items contribute effectively to the explanation of each selected latent variable. As a result, all the items have a value that exceeds the recommended threshold of 0.5. On the basis of the various tests carried out, we may ascertain that the measuring model's quality is very satisfactory. Consequently, it is essential to advance the development of the structural model.

4.3. Results of the Structural Model Test

Upon validating the dependability of the items inside the measurement module, the subsequent phase involves a multi-group assessment of the structural model outcomes.

The structural model is central to structural equation theory. It comprises a set of regression equations that illustrate the assumed associations between theoretical concepts (Hair et al., 2016).

4.3.1. The Synthesis Model

The model obtained comprises of six latent variables (five exogenous and one endogenous), including the schema (output of the SMART PLS software). One of the objectives of this study is to evaluate a causal order in the interactions among the various constructs. The model in question was subjected to an internal assessment, employing the path weighting scheme that was delineated by (Lohmöller, 1989). Hence the following presentation of our structural model:

Figure 5 .Structural model

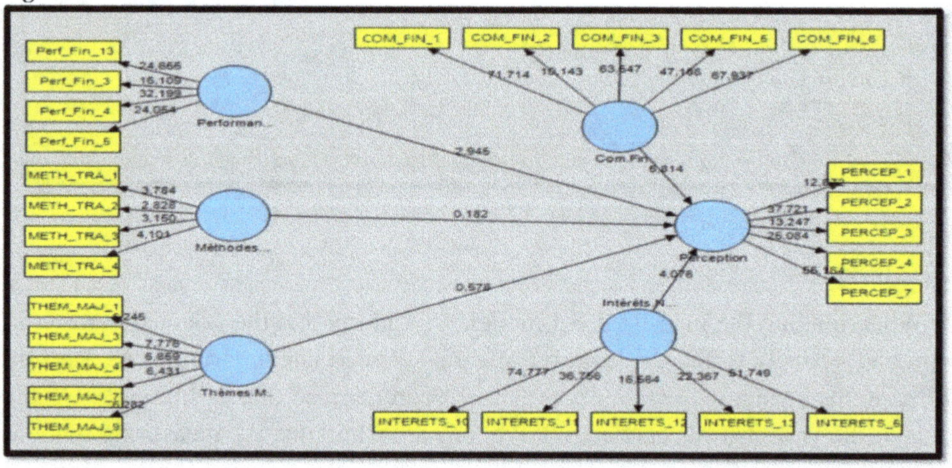

Source: Smart-PLS output

Source: Smart-PLS output

Reading the structural model, we can propose the existence of a substantial correlation between our explanatory variable. i.e. the perception of financial actors, and the following explanatory variables: financial communication, financial performance and the benefits of adopting IFRS.

4.3.2. Hypothesis Testing

The first step in hypothesis testing is to check the relevance level of the estimation parameters (path coefficients) of the correlations between the latent variables. A bootstrap simulation is used for this purpose. Following the recommendations of Chin (1998), we employed the bootstrapping technique (utilizing a sample size of 500) to evaluate the statistical significance of each coefficient.

The table below shows the postulated hypotheses, the coefficients (β) and the results of the Student's T-test.

Table 8. Estimation of the parameters of the causal model using the bootstrap method

Hypothesis	β (Correlation coef)	T-Student (Bootstrap) (>1,96)	Significance
Financial _ Comm-> Perception	0,396	4,120452	**Validated**
Financial_ Perf-> Perception	0,288	2,995212	**Validated**
Interest_IFRS -> Perception	0,312	3,241521	**Validated**
Work_Method -> Perception	-0,003	0,214525	**Non Validated**
Major_Themes -> Perception	-0,004	0,525412	**Non Validated**

Source: Smart-PLS output

Based on the table above, the correlation coefficient B must be positive and the Student's T test must exceed the threshold of 1.96. The subsequent conclusions may be inferred:

- There are substantial correlations between the dependent variable and the three explanatory variables: financial communication, financial performance and the benefits of adopting IFRS.
- Non-significant correlations between the perceptions of Moroccan financial actors and the other dependent variables, in this case working methods and the main topics covered by IFRS.

4.4. Discussion

With regard to the first independent variable related to financial communication under IFRS, The findings obtained allow for the conclusion that the conversion of Moroccan companies to international accounting standards has substantially influenced their financial communication of the adopting enterprises. Indeed, the implementation of these standards significantly changes the perception of users of financial information with regard to the expected effects of this accounting conversion. Consequently, users of financial information assert that the implementation of IFRS will improve the quality of financial accounts.

On the other hand, financial statements prepared in compliance with IFRS fully meet the the prerequisites of investors, financial analysts and managers and increase the level of detail, which will facilitate audit assignments and/or financial analysis for the majority of our respondents. This conclusion matches the findings of (Cormier et al., 2007), who believe that the application of IFRS would contribute to the production of useful financial statements that would serve as a basis for facilitating decision-making by key financial stakeholders, in particular investors and creditors. Furthermore, the estimates obtained show that the relationship between the explanatory variable and the variable to be explained has a coefficient B, the value of which can be considered very satisfactory ($\beta = 0.410$). Furthermore, the analysis of the T-Student value reveals it to be 6.053 (>1.96), indicating a substantial correlation between the aforementioned variables. As a result, it can be said that the first hypothesis is accepted.

With regard to the second hypothesis, the study indicated that the majority of the selected financial actors (all profiles taken together) do not agree that the introduction of IFRS influences working methods. In fact, the results show that there is no consensus on the direct impact of the introduction of IFRS on the working methods of our respondents. The estimates obtained show a negative correlation between the perception of Moroccan financial actors and the impact of the application of IFRS on working methods. The B coefficient indicates a negative correlation ($\beta = -0.002$). Furthermore, an examination of the t-value shows that it is equal to 0.181 (<1.96), which implies a non-significant correlation between the two variables mentioned above. In conclusion, the second hypothesis is therefore not supported.

With regard to the variable "financial performance", the findings of this study demonstrate that the adoption of International Financial Reporting Standards generates a number of advantages and is behind the relevance of the main indicators measuring the financial performance of Moroccan companies which are listed on the Casablanca Stock Exchange. In addition, our respondents believe that the introduction of the international benchmark has made it possible to produce financial information with a high predictive value, which serves as a basis for stakeholders' decisions regarding the allocation of their resources. The findings align with the research of Barth et al. (2017), Hassan (2019), and Laouane and Torra (2024), which established that the measures employed to evaluate financial performance altered following the implementation of IFRS.

Taiwo and Adejare (2014) identified a robust and significant correlation between the implementation of IFRS and the enhancement of financial performance.

Furthermore, the estimates obtained indicate a positive association between these two variables (β =0.267). Examination of the t-value shows that it is equal to 3.025 (>1.96), this indicates a substantial correlation between the two variables. This hypothesis is therefore accepted.

With regard to the fourth hypothesis, users of financial information assert that the implementation of IFRS would be advantageous for the adopting companies. Survey respondents assert that the advantages of implementation of IFRS are evident in the enhanced relevance of fixed asset valuation and in the facilitation of sectoral and regional comparisons.

However, despite the importance of these standards in producing accounting figures that better reflect economic reality, certain factors were identified that have limited the benefits of moving to this process of international accounting standardization. In fact, according to our contributors, the application of International Financial Reporting Standards would be an opportunity to accentuate the increase in the volatility of net income and the increase in the manipulation of accounting income through the leeway given to company directors to draw up "tailor-made" accounts.

The estimates obtained show a positive correlation (β = 0.340). Examination of the t-value shows that it is equal to 4.170 (>1.96), this finding indicates the presence of a substantial correlation between the two variables. This hypothesis is therefore accepted.

Finally, we find that respondents have different perceptions of the main issues addressed by IFRS. The estimates obtained show a negative correlation between the perception variable and the major themes variable (β =-0.006). Furthermore, an analysis of the t-value reveals that it is equivalent to 0.665 (less than 1.96), thereby indicating a non-significant correlation between the two aforementioned variables. In conclusion, our last hypothesis is not confirmed.

5. CONCLUSION

The acceleration of this harmonization process was mainly motivated by the decompartmentalization of markets and the multiplication of international exchanges.

The main criticism of the directives adopted in Europe was the slowness of the procedure, requiring a strong political consensus among EU member states to adopt a text or law relating to accounting legislation. This prompted the European Union to officially support the harmonization of accounting practices through the creation of the IASC (International Accounting Standards Council).

Morocco is no exception to the process of internationalization. The Moroccan authorities recognize that IFRS standards present an excellent opportunity to align with global requirements for producing reliable information acceptable to all users.

In the case of Morocco, we have observed a gradual integration of the new standard by a limited number of companies. Consequently, the transition to IAS/IFRS has been described as a true accounting revolution. These standards are based on theoretical principles and have characteristics that distinguish them from other standards.

The effects of IFRS adoption on the enhancement of financial statement quality have garnered significant interest from researchers and have been examined in various studies across different financial markets. As a result, the analysis of the information quality of the international framework compared to other local frameworks is one of the topics that has attracted the interest of several academics and professionals.

The aim of this study is to validate many hypotheses regarding users' perceptions of accounting and financial information concerning the effect of IFRS adoption on the quality of financial statements. In order to respond to our problem and to confirm or refute our research hypotheses, we relied on structural equations, as we have already mentioned. In this sense, the PLS approach is widely used to analyze the complexity of certain real-life situations. The PLS method is suitable for research where the unit of analysis is the firm, even if the sample is small.

The primary focus of our study is the examination of IFRS's role in enhancing the quality of financial statement information, which are an essential element for assessing the effectiveness of the strategic choices made by Moroccan companies listed on the Casablanca Stock Exchange.

The findings of our empirical investigation indicate that users of financial information hold similar perceptions regarding specific issues, namely financial communication, financial performance, and the advantages of adopting International Financial Reporting Standards in the Moroccan context. On the other hand, they have different opinions on the working methods and the main issues addressed by this new corpus of standards.

The results of our analysis may be pertinent not just to investors but also to other stakeholders and organizations directly or indirectly impacted by these new standards. The findings indicate that the adoption of International Financial Reporting Standards provides substantial advantages to implementing organizations. Nevertheless, future research efforts can be invested in taking into account the economic environment. In this sense, the improvement in published accounting and financial information is in some cases due to the economic environment and not to the quality of the standards.

Regarding our questionnaire-based study, the limitations of the results obtained mainly concern the composition of our sample and the small number of respondents to the survey. We aimed to expand our research by engaging with various categories of financial information users in Morocco. However, our efforts to diversify our stakeholders were hindered by the low response rate from certain respondents, which resulted in the dispersion of our efforts. To compensate for the low number of participants, we adopted the PLS method, which is well suited to company-level research with a small sample size.

Furthermore, the number of questions and topics covered was insufficient. Therefore, a more detailed and targeted investigation would add value to the work.

Based on this, our research aims to contextualize knowledge according to the specific situation in which it is used, providing benchmarks designed to enlighten financial players and stimulate their reflection and questioning.

REFERENCES

Ahmadi, A., & Bouri, A. (2018). The accounting value relevance of earnings and book value: Tunisian banks and financial institutions. *International Journal of Law and Management, 60*(2), 342–354. DOI: 10.1108/IJLMA-11-2016-0131

Almaqtari, F., Hashed, A., & Shamim, M. (2021). Impact of corporate governance mechanism on IFRS adoption: A comparative study of Saudi Arabia, Oman, and the United Arab Emirates. *Heliyon, 7*(2), e05848. DOI: 10.1016/j.heliyon.2020.e05848 PMID: 33490662

Alnodel, A. A. (2018). The impact of IFRS adoption on the value relevance of accounting information: Evidence from the insurance sector. *International Journal of Business and Management, 13*(4), 138–148. DOI: 10.5539/ijbm.v13n4p138

Amaefule, L., Onyekpere, U., & Kalu, E. (2018). International Financial Reporting Standards and manufacturing firms' financial performance in Nigeria: A study of selected quoted firms. *International Journal of Accounting and Taxation, 6*(1), 102–114. DOI: 10.15640/ijat.v6n1a9

Barth, M. E., Li, K., & McClure, C. G. (2017). Evolution in value relevance of accounting information. *Stanford University Graduate School of Business Research Paper No. 17-24*, 78. https://doi.org/DOI: 10.2139/ssrn.2933197

Benitez, J., Henseler, J., Castillo, A., & Schuberth, F. (2020). How to perform and report an impactful analysis using partial least squares: Guidelines for confirmatory and explanatory IS research. *Information & Management, 57*(2), 103168. Advance online publication. DOI: 10.1016/j.im.2019.05.003

Bernheim, Y., Escaffre de Mazars, L., & Guerard. (1999). Point de vue. Évaluation à la juste valeur. Un nouveau modèle comptable ? *Comptabilité - Contrôle – Audit, 5*(2), 25–45.

Chin, W. W. (1998). The partial least squares approach to structural equation modeling. *Modern Methods for Business Research*, 295–336.

Cormier, D., Demaria, S., & Lapointe-Antunes, P. (2007). Le référentiel IFRS: Nous dirigeons nous vers une comptabilité au delà du réel ? *Comptabilité – Contrôle – Audit*, Numéro thématique, décembre, 43–56.

Cormier, D., Magnan, M., & Zéghal, D. (2000). Le contenu informationnel et la capacité prédictive des mesures de performance financière: Une comparaison France, États-Unis et Suisse. *Comptabilité – Contrôle – Audit, 6*(1), 77–105.

Daske, H., Hail, L., Leuz, C., & Verdi, R. (2013). Adopting a label: Heterogeneity in the economic consequences around IAS/IFRS adoptions. *Journal of Accounting Research, 51*(3), 495–547. DOI: 10.1111/1475-679X.12005

Do Hoon, K., Leem, W. B., & Yuk, J. H. (2019). The effect of IFRS adoption on the value relevance of accounting information: Evidence from South Korea. *Investment Management and Financial Innovations, 16*(2), 78–88. DOI: 10.21511/imfi.16(2).2019.07

Elhamma, A. (2023). Cinquante ans des normes comptables internationales IAS/IFRS: Adoption, conséquences et où en est-on au Maroc? In R. M'Rabet & M. A. Issami (Eds.), *50 ans de management: Regards croisés d'un demi-siècle du management* (pp. 121–136).

Elhamma, A. (2024). Determinants of national IFRS adoption: Evidence from the Middle East and North Africa region. *International Journal of Accounting. Auditing and Performance Evaluation, 20*(1–2), 69–90. DOI: 10.1504/IJAAPE.2024.135535

Elhamma, A. (2025a). Impact of mandatory IFRS adoption on foreign direct investment: The moderating role of conflict of interest regulation. *Journal of Financial Reporting and Accounting, 23*(3), 936–958. DOI: 10.1108/JFRA-04-2022-0145

Elhamma, A. (2025b). Perceived benefits of IFRS adoption in Morocco and French-speaking Sub-Saharan African countries. In F. Albuquerque & P. G. Dos Santos (Eds.), *Contemporary innovations in reporting and analysis* (pp. 183–210). IGI Global. https://doi.org/DOI: 10.4018/979-8-3693-5923-5.ch007

Fornell, C., & Bookstein, F. L. (1982). Two structural equation models: LISREL and PLS applied to consumer exit-voice theory. *JMR, Journal of Marketing Research, 19*(4), 440–452. DOI: 10.1177/002224378201900406

Garanina, T. A., & Kormiltseva, P. S. (2013). The effect of International Financial Reporting Standards (IFRS) adoption on the value relevance of financial reporting: A case of Russia. *Research in Accounting in Emerging Economies, 13*, 27–60. DOI: 10.1108/S1479-3563(2013)0000013007

Garza Sánchez, H. H., Cortez Alejandro, K. A., Méndez Sáenz, A. B., & Rodríguez García, M. D. P. (2017). Efecto en la calidad de la información ante cambios en la normatividad contable: Caso aplicada al sector real mexicano. *Contaduría y Administración, 62*(3), 761–774. DOI: 10.1016/j.cya.2015.11.012

Hassan, M. (2019). Analysis of effects of IFRS adoption on the comparability of financial reporting: Evidence from Saudi listed companies. *Journal of Emerging Issues in Economics. Finance and Banking, 8*(1), 2698–2714.

Hulland, J. (1999). Utilisation des moindres carrés partiels (PLS) dans la recherche en gestion stratégique: Une revue de quatre études récentes. *Journal de gestion stratégique, 20*, 195–204.

Laouane, A. (2023). Informations financières issues du référentiel international et performance financière: Analyse de l'impact des IFRS sur la valeur des indicateurs comptables et boursiers. *Alternatives Managériales Economiques, 5*(3), 200–218. https://doi.org/DOI: 10.48374/IMIST.PRSM/ame-v5i3.41917

Laouane, A., & El Hijazi, M. (2024). Le passage aux IFRS par les entreprises marocaines: Contexte d'avènement, voies de recherche et principales divergences par rapport au CGNC. *Revue de Gestion et d'Économie, 1*(1), 91–108. DOI: 10.34874/PRSM.jbe.48062

Lenormand, G., Bessieux-Ollier, C., & Piot, C. (2012). Les IAS/IFRS: Bilan et perspectives. *Revue Française de Gestion, 38*(222), 55–66. DOI: 10.3166/rfg.222.55-66

Lohmöller, J. B. (1989). *Latent variable path modeling with partial least squares*. Springer., DOI: 10.1007/978-3-642-52512-4

Marien, B., & Beaud, J.-P. (2003). *Guide pratique pour l'utilisation de la statistique en recherche: Le cas des petits échantillons*. Réseau sociolinguistique et dynamique des langues, Agence Universitaire de la Francophonie.

Nunnally, J. C. (1978). *Psychometric theory* (2nd ed.). McGraw-Hill.

Outa, E., Ozili, P. K., & Eisenberg, P. (2017). IFRS convergence and revisions: Value relevance of accounting information quality from East Africa. *Journal of Accounting in Emerging Economies, 7*(3), 352–368. DOI: 10.1108/JAEE-11-2014-0062

Soderstrom, N. S., & Sun, K. J. (2007). IFRS adoption and accounting quality: A review. *European Accounting Review, 16*(4), 675–702. DOI: 10.1080/09638180701706732

Turki, H., Wali, S., Ali, Z., & Mohammed, M. (2020). IFRS and financial performance: Study in the French context. *International Journal of Financial Research, 11*(2), 424–434. DOI: 10.5430/ijfr.v11n2p424

Watts, R. L., & Zimmerman, J. L. (1986). *Positive accounting theory*. Prentice Hall.

KEY TERMS AND DEFINITIONS

Financial actors: Financial actors in Morocco play a crucial role in producing and analyzing accounting and financial information. This includes statutory auditors, accountants, financial analysts and other financial professionals.

Financial communication: is a fundamental pillar of a company's overall strategy. It encompasses all activities related to transmitting financial information from a company to its stakeholders.

Financial performance: is a measure of a company's efficiency in managing its financial resources. It allows us to evaluate a company's profitability and its capacity to generate profits and create value for its shareholders.

IFRS: International Financial Reporting Standards are international accounting standards issued by the International Accounting Standards Board (IASB) to help companies produce transparent, consistent and internationally comparable financial statements.

Perception: refers to the term used to describe the mechanisms and procedures that allow us to recognize phenomena based on information processed by our senses.

Quality of information: Information is considered high quality if it meets five criteria: reliability, relevance, timeliness, originality, and accessibility. Obtaining this information usually comes at a cost, which must be reasonable in relation to the objective to be achieved.

The structural equations: Structural equation modeling represents causal relationships between latent and observed variables. Observed variables are those that can be measured directly. Latent concepts, on the other hand, are inferred and cannot be measured directly.

Chapter 3
The Impact of IFRS Adoption on Financial Reporting Quality:
A Comprehensive Scientometric Analysis

Hamide Ozyurek
https://orcid.org/0000-0002-2574-954X
OSTIM Technical University, Turkey

Buket Atalay Aycan
Ufuk University, Turkey

ABSTRACT

This study aims to analyze the trend of 96 articles published on the subject of IFRS adoption and financial reporting quality in the Web of Science (WoS) database between 2010-2025 in terms of authors, citations, author's keywords, co-ocurrence, specific terms frequency, corresponding author's countries. The method of the study is scientometric (bibliometric) analysis used to reveal the publication trends of the articles. Findings have demonstrated that the researches related to IFRS adoption and financial reporting quality have increased since the last decade. Moreover, this study has indicated that the top three most frequently used keywords by authors are financial reporting quality, IFRS, IFRS adoption, and the top keywords plus are earnings management, IFRS adoption, impact, mandatory IFRS adoption and corporate governance, respectively. In addition, the study has concluded that IFRS adoption and financial reporting quality studies are mostly published in the Accounting Review, Journal of Applied Accounting Research and Journal of International Accounting Auditing and Taxation.

DOI: 10.4018/979-8-3373-1902-5.ch003

1. INTRODUCTION

In 2002, the European Union (EU) made a decision that International Financial Reporting Standards (IFRS), issued by the International Accounting Standards Board (IASB), has been adopted for the listed EU companies since 2005 (Elhamma, 2023, 2024, 2025).

According to IASB (2010), financial reporting mainly aims to enable financial information users to get useful information about the financial reporting of economic entities for making economic decisions. According to the conceptual framework for Financial Reporting, qualitative characteristics provide useful information to those who need it (Mensah, 2021). With IFRS adoption, it is aimed to increase financial reporting quality (FRQ) through providing useful information to shareholders, managers, investors and creditors. This useful financial information enables them to make accurate investment or financing decisions. According to Psaros and Trotman (2004), FRQ has enhanced with the adoption of a uniform accounting standard.

Moreover, mandatory adoption of IFRS brings regulatory compliance, uniformity and transparency to financial reports. Therefore, it improves accounting quality and makes financial statements easily comparable. FRQ makes financial reports of companies more relevant, accurate, understandable, comparable and ready for its users. In this sense, it is important to make decisions for investors, stakeholders and other financial information users.

In the literature, there are lots of articles which demonstrate that IFRS adoption has enhanced FRQ. In contrast, there are also some articles which indicate that FRQ has decreased or has not been affected with IFRS adoption.

In these studies, the topic of IFRS adoption and FRQ is examined with respect to earnings management, cost of equity, internal control system, cost of debt, audit fees, corporate governance, value relevance, investment efficiency and so on.

With IFRS adoption, studies on IFRS adoption and FRQ have increased since 2005. Although there are lots of articles on IFRS adoption and FRQ, there are not any publication on research trends of articles in this subject. Bibliometric analysis is a kind of statistical method applied to explain the trends of publication (Rashmi and Kataria, 2021). In the literature, there is only one publication (Kumari & Naresh, 2023) on research productivity of IFRS using this method. In this research, publication trend of articles indexed in the Scopus database was examined. In this sense, there is no publication which reveals the research trends of articles published on the subject of IFRS adoption and FRQ and indexed in the Web of Science (WoS) database.

In this sense, this study significantly contributes to the accounting literature. This chapter aims to review literature regarding the effect of IFRS adoption on FRQ. It also gives an analysis of articles published in the WoS database and related to the subject of IFRS adoption and FRQ.

This study applies bibliometric (scientometric) analysis in order to investigate the research trend of articles which are indexed in the WoS database and are concerning the subject of IFRS adoption and FRQ. With the use of this method in the study, it aims to understand the evolution and development of studies and identify the gaps and future research opportunities in this field.

In this study, bibliometric analysis depends on the articles published between the years of 2010 and 2025. Moreover, this analysis reveals the research trend of these articles in terms of the authors, citations, author's keywords, co-ocurrence, specific terms frequency, corresponding author's countries. In this sense, this study differs from previous studies in terms of its coverage of long period of time and comprehensive analysis which enables the identification of gaps in the literature and helps highlight future research trends.

By uncovering hidden structures in the literature and offering a roadmap for future inquiry, this study makes a novel and timely contribution to both bibliometric research and the ongoing global discourse on financial reporting standards.

The rest of the chapter is structured as follows: Section 2 covers the regulatory framework which explains the framework of IFRS adoption and FRQ. Section 3 discusses the related literature concerning how FRQ is affected by IFRS adoption. Section 4 presents the selection of data and methodology of the chapter. Section 5 highligths the results of findings. Finally, section 6 covers conclusion and future research trends.

2. REGULATORY FRAMEWORK

2.1. Adoption of IFRS

Various research have been carried out with the IFRS adoption since the EU became a member in 2002 (De George et al., 2016). Although these studies have examined the impact of IFRS adoption on several kinds of subjects such as audit and regulatory enforcement (Chen & Zhang, 2010), internal audit (Alzeban, 2018) and direct foreign investment (Gordon et al., 2012), the effect of IFRS adoption on FRQ (Bonetti et al., 2016; Klish et al., 2022) has mostly investigated in the literature.

In this context, IFRS adoption is regarded as a notable trend during the past twenty years (Elhamma, 2023, 2024, 2025).

IFRS consists of standards required for all firms listed on European security markets by the EU since 2005. The International Accounting Standards Committee (IASC) underwenting a reorganization in order to become the IASB released the first set of International Accounting Standards (IAS) in 1971 (De George et al., 2016). IASB developed IFRS to be globally used to provide harmonization in financial statements and guidance for companies while preparing their financial reports (Mbir et al., 2020).

IASB has fundamentally transformed financial reporting framework, as seen by the extensive IFRS adoption by numerous countries. In the EU, the majority of listed companies on stock exchanges have been mandated to prepare their financial reports in compliance with IFRS since the beginning of the year 2005. In this sense, the financial statements of listed companies are significantly affected by IFRS adoption. When IFRS adoption becomes mandatory for more than 140 countries, this subject has become popular in accounting research (El Guindy & Trabelsi, 2020). Since 2018, 158 countries around the world have accepted IFRS (Mbir et al., 2020). Since then the topic of FRQ and IFRS adoption has emerged as a key focus of accounting study.

IFRS adoption is an important issue among countries all over the world thanks to the search for reliability, standardization, comparability and uniformity of financial statements of their organizations (Okpala, 2012). There are some important differences between Generally Accepted Accounting Principles (GAAP) and IFRS. The first difference is that fair value measurement is used in IFRS. Moreover, IFRS gives importance on the core of transactions. IFRS and GAAP also differ with respect to the requisites for disclosure and presentation of financial statements (El Guindy & Trabelsi, 2020).

IFRS adoption is one of the most crucial transformation for the accounting profession with the adoption of new conceptual framework for financial reporting (Mensah, 2021). IFRS adoption has a great impact on companies' financial reports, even in countries where there is no significant differences in terms of GAAP and IFRS. However, there is a chance to investigate how such a significant regulation change affects FRQ.

The IFRS advocators assert that IFRS is a set which consist of high-quality standards (De George et al., 2016). They also advocate that adoption of IFRS improves the FRQ (Klish et al., 2022). Many studies have stated that the quality of IFRS is higher than that of GAAP and with its adoption comparability and transparency of financial reports have increased (Levitt, 1998). As FRQ increases, information asymmetry reduces and managers' investment decisions are positively affected

(Biddle and Hilary, 2006). However, Barth et al. (2007) have indicated that FRQ decreases due to the decrease in the reliability of financial information.

2.2. Financial Reporting Quality

IFRS Adoption, the conversion from GAAP to IFRS, increases not also transparency but also comparability. As a result of this, FRQ has enhanced.

According to Robinson & Henry (2009), FRQ indicates that how accurately a firm's financial report demonstrates its financial performance and how useful it is in predicting cash flows for future.

IASB issued Conceptual Framework for Financial Reporting in 2010. In 2018, IASB revised the conceptual framework. In the Conceptual Framework, it is stated that the aim of general objective financial reporting is providing useful information on the reporting company to its investors, creditors or lenders, which enables them to make decisions (IFRS Foundation, 2018, p.7).

Main qualitative characteristics consist of faithful representation and relevance. Information can be useful when it is relevant and faithfully represented (IFRS Foundation, 2018, p.13). Financial information is regarded as relevant if it makes a difference or in other words, if it is useful for its users. Faithful representation must contain three dimensions: completeness, neutrality and freedom from error (IFRS Foundation, 2018, p.14). Understandability, comparability, timeliness and verifiability are defined as enhancing qualitative qualities in the Conceptual Framework, which making information more useful (IFRS Foundation, 2018, p.16).

The usefulness of the information relies on the high-quality of that information (Önce & Çavuş, 2019, p. 387). In this sense, high-quality financial reports are useful for its users. Value relevance research (Bath et al., 2001) depends on whether the financial information is beneficial for its investors. Value relevance models (Francis et al., 2004; Bath et al., 2008) were developed in order to identify the impact of IFRS on financial information quality.

3. RELATED LITERATURE

In the literature, there are lots of publications concerning the effects of IFRS adoption on FRQ. Some of the aims and/or results of these studies are given below.

Kim et al. (2012) investigates that the impact of mandatory IFRS adoption in 2005 on FRQ in terms of audit fees for European Union countries. The results demonstrate that when IFRS adoption becomes mandatory for EU countries, there is an increase in audit fees and audit fee premium because of the rise in complexity of audit, on the other hand there is a decrease in them with the increase in the FRQ.

The article by Palea (2013) discusses how IFRS adoption influences FRQ in terms of value-relevance. Likewise, the article by Bonetti et al. (2016) investigates how mandotary IFRS adoption affects FRQ in European companies in terms of governance at firm and country level. They find that there is a rise in FRQ of companies who have strong corporate governance at board level.

In the article by De George and Shivakumar (2016), the impacts of IFRS adoption is examined. They find that IFRS adoption has increased international investments, the number of foreign analysts followers, transparency and comparability of financial reports. However, it has decreased cost of capitals.

The study by Bassemir and Novotny Farkas (2018) has discussed how voluntary IFRS adoption for private German GAAP and IFRS reporting firms is affected by earnings quality and disclosure practices. They concludes that the guality of earnings and information disclosure in the financial reports has increased for firms which report in accordance with IFRS.

In the article by Habib et al. (2019), it is investigated how IFRS adoption influences cost of equity and FRQ for Australian listed companies. They conclude that FRQ has decreased. Although, cost of equity has enhanced with IFRS adoption. Moreover, the study demonstrates that the older Australian listed firms have more advantages than younger ones with IFRS adoption.

The research by Cameran and Campa (2020) has discussed the impact of voluntary IFRS adoption cost of debt on the FRQ for the European companies. They find that IFRS adoption enhances FRQ, but it decreases cost of debt.

The research by Klish et al. (2022) demonstrates that after IFRS is adopted in the region of MENA, earnings management has reduced for IFRS adopters when compared to adopters of local standards.

In the study by Mensah (2021) indicates that there is a negative effect on earnings management in the period of post-IFRS adoption, on the other hand there is an rise in the financial reports quality for the manufacturing companies listed on the Ghana Stock Exchange.

The study by Ajibade et al. (2022) demonstrates that IFRS adoption and corporate governance have influenced the quality of financial reporting for Nigeria's development banks thanks to providing faithful representation.

Similarly, Elhamma (2025) conducts a perception-based study involving 75 accounting professionals and researchers from Morocco and 11 French-speaking Sub-Saharan African countries. The study show that the majority of respondents believed IFRS adoption significantly improved the reliability (52%), relevance (57.4%), and comparability (54.7%) of financial reporting. However, Moroccan respondents have expressed greater concern than their Sub-Saharan counterparts regarding improvements in relevance and understandability. These findings have emphasized the importance of regional context and subjective perceptions in assessing the effect of IFRS implementation.

In the research by Houcine et al. (2022), it is investigated whether investment efficiency has an effect on FRQ, IFRS and corporate governance for French listed companies. They conclude that the relation between FRQ and investment efficiency increases together with the rise in corporate governance and the IFRS adoption.

The research by Carjaval and Campa (2024) investigates whether bilateral trade made among IFRS countries affects the relation between FRQ and adoption of IFRS. They find that there is a negative relationship between IFRS adoption and accruals-based earnings management in terms of bilateral trade. In that sense, they concludes that the increase in bilateral trade among IFRS countries enhances FRQ due to the decrease in earnings management which is based accruals.

In the research by Kateb (2024), it is examined that how IFRS adoption affects the quality of financial reporting in Saudi Arabia in terms of mediating effect of audit committees and earnings management practices. The result indicates that IFRS adoption has an adverse impact on earnings management practices.

The research by Johri (2024) investigates the relation between IFRS adoption and FRQ focusing the moderating effect of the internal control system for Indian multinational corporations. It is concluded that IFRS adoption improves FRQ, which makes financial reports of these companies more relevant, accurate, understandable, comparable and ready for its users.

These examples of studies show that the subject of IFRS adoption and quality of financial reporting is examined with regard to earnings management, cost of equity, internal control system, cost of debt, audit fees, corporate governance, value relevance, investment efficiency and so on.

Moreover, these studies demonstrate that IFRS has increased, decreased or has been no effect on FRQ. These studies are summarized in the table below in terms of the impact of IFRS adoption on FRQ.

Table 1. Impact of IFRS adoption on FRQ

Author	Presence of Impact	Direction of Impact	Reason of Impact
Levitt (1998)	Yes	+	-Increase in financial transparency and comparability.
Psaros and Trotman (2004)	Yes	+	-The adoption of a uniform accounting standard.
Biddle and Hilary (2006)	Yes	+	-Decrease in information asymmetry and increase in managers' investment decisions.

continued on following page

Table 1. Continued

Author	Presence of Impact	Direction of Impact	Reason of Impact
Barth et al. (2007)	Yes	-	-Decrease in the reliability of financial information.
Jeanjean and Stolowy (2008)	Yes	-	-Rise in earnings management.
Lin et al. (2012)	Yes	-	-Rise in earnings management and fall in value relevance.
Agyei-Mensah (2013)	Yes	+	-Increase in accounting disclosure quality.
Ahmed et al. (2013)	Yes	-	-Changes in the discretion of management or use of judgment.
Kao (2014)	No	0	-No important impact on faithful representation.
Christensen et al. (2015)	No	0	-No significant impact on accounting quality.
Amidu et al. (2016)	Yes	+	-Increase in earnings quality.
Bonetti et al. (2016)	Yes	+	-Strong board-level corporate governance.
De George and Shivakumar (2016)	Yes	+	-Decrease in costs of capital, -Increase in international investments, the number of foreign analysts followers, transparency and comparability of financial reports.
Bassemir and Novotny Farkas (2018)	Yes	+	-Increase in earnings quality and information disclosure in financial reports for IFRS reporting firms.
Habib et al. (2019)	Yes	-	-Increase in cost of equity.
Mensah (2021)	Yes	+	-Fall in earnings management in the post-IFRS adoption period
Ajibade et al. (2022)	Yes	+	-The faithful representation.
Houcine et al. (2022)	Yes	+	-Increase in investment efficiency.
Klish, et al. (2022)	Yes	+	-Decrease in earnings management in terms of IFRS adopters.
Carjaval and Campa (2024)	Yes	+	-Increase in bilateral trade among IFRS countries -Decrease in accruals-based earnings management.
Kateb (2024)	Yes	+	-Decrease in earnings management.
Johri (2024)	Yes	+	-Providing more relevant, accurate, understandable, comparable financial reports for its users.

Table 1 indicates that the number of studies demonstrating an increase in FRQ with IFRS adoption is higher than that of showing the contrary.

Although there has been a rise in research exploring the relationship between IFRS adoption and FRQ, there are not any publication on research trends of articles in this subject. In other words, there is a significant lack of study that comprehensively examine the evolution of this research area through bibliometric methods. To our knowledge, only one prior study (Kumari & Naresh, 2023) applied bibliometric analysis to this topic, but it was limited to the Scopus database. In this study, the Web of Science (WoS) database is used.

4. DATA AND METHODOLOGY

Three techniques are used in science mapping studies: scientometric analysis, informatics and bibliometric analysis (Hosseini et al., 2018). When compared with the bibliometric analysis, the content of scientometric analysis is broader than bibliometric analysis. Scientometric analysis contains not only bibliometric methods but also its tools and data in order to evaluate the literature (Hosseini et al., 2018).

Bibliometric analysis is a widely used method in order to reveal and analyze large amount of data (Donthu et al., 2021). In other words, bibliometric analysis is a kind of research trend in order to see the global research trends in a specific subject through the output of academic publications in Scopus or WoS databases (Alsharif et al., 2020).

We used advanced bibliometric techniques such as keyword co-occurrence analysis, co-citation analysis, co-word analysis, trending topics, thematic evolution, conceptual structure map, content analysis and scientometric mapping.

The articles reached by scanning WoS database with the keywords "IFRS Adoption" and "Financial Reporting Quality" were recorded for analysis. The recorded 96 documents indexed in WoS database between the years 2010 and 2025 were scanned and analyzed using VOSviewer, R and MAXQDA programs. In this research, Biblioshiny and Bibliometrix's R-based graphical interface were used due to their text mining capabilities that reveal the intellectual and conceptual structure of the literature. MAXQDA was used in content analysis and VOSviewer was applied to visualize the findings.

The foundation of systematic literature reviews is protocol preparation, which guarantees careful planning, reliable execution, and openness for possible replication. To direct the tasks of assembling, organizing, and evaluating, we use the Scientific Procedures and Rationales for Systematic Literature Reviews (SPAR-4-SLR) protocol, which was created by Paul et al. (2021) and has been widely used by other authors (Raman et al., 2022) (Figure 1).

Figure 1. SPAR-4-SLR protocol-based research design.

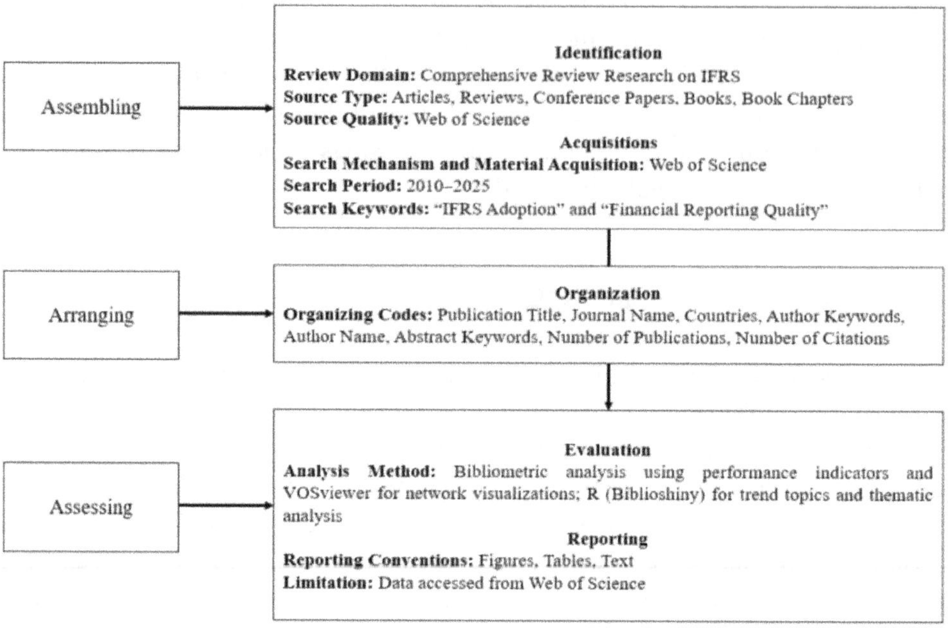

Table 2. Descriptive summary of bibliometric data (2010–2025)

Description	Results
Timespan	2010:2025
Sources	67
Documents	96
Annual Growth Rate %	7,6
Document Average Age	5,21
Average citations per doc	22,05
References	4817
Single-authored docs	21
Co-Authors per Doc	2,66
International co-authorships %	42,71
Article	82
Article; book chapter	2
Article; early access	3
Proceedings paper	8

continued on following page

Table 2. Continued

Description	Results
Review	1
Keywords Plus (ID)	309
Author's Keywords (DE)	343
Authors	237
Authors of single-authored docs	20

In this study, the literature published between 2010 and 2025 was reviewed, resulting in the identification of 96 documents. These documents were disseminated across 67 different sources which have an annual growth rate of 7.6%. The average age of the documents was 5.21 years. The average number of citations per document was 22.05. A total of 4,817 references were cited across all documents. Regarding document types, the majority consisted of articles (n=82), followed by proceedings papers (n=8), early access articles (n=3), book chapters (n=2), and only one review article. In terms of keywords, 343 were provided by the authors, while 309 were assigned through Keywords Plus. Analysis of authorship patterns revealed that 21 documents were single-authored, which have an average of 2.66 co-authors per document. The rate of international collaboration was notably high at 42.71%. In total, 237 authors contributed to the documents, among whom 20 were responsible for single-authored papers. These findings indicate that the number of publications in the field has increased steadily, that collaborative authorship is prevalent, and that there is a significant degree of international academic cooperation (Table 2).

5. RESULTS OF FINDINGS

Figure 2. Yearly trends in the articles (2010–2025)

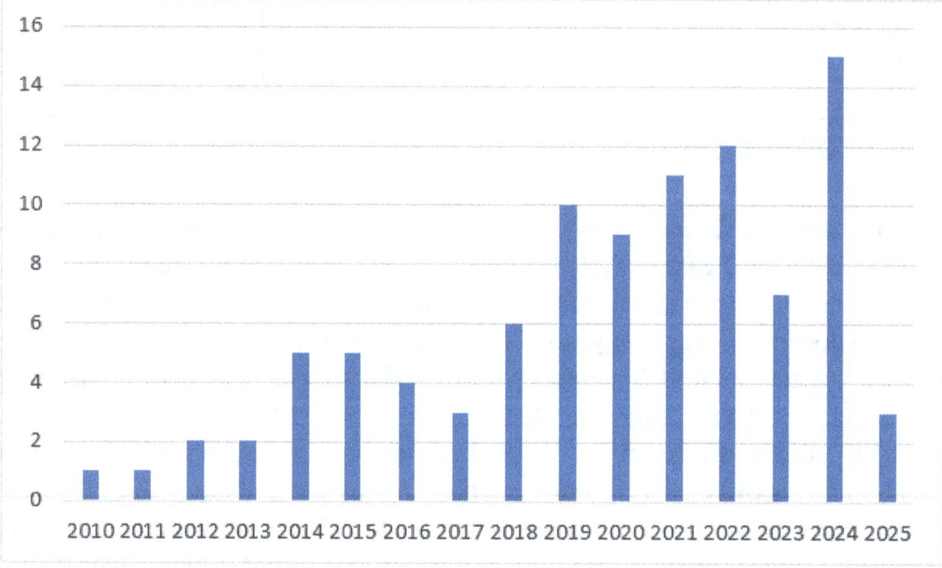

The articles published between 2010 and 2025 shows an overall upward trend, with a marked increase after 2018. While publication numbers remained low and stable until 2013, a significant rise is observed especially between 2019 and 2024, peaking at 15 articles in 2024. The slight decrease in 2025 may be due to the year not yet being completed (Figure 2).

Figure 3. Annual trends in mean citation rates (2010–2025)

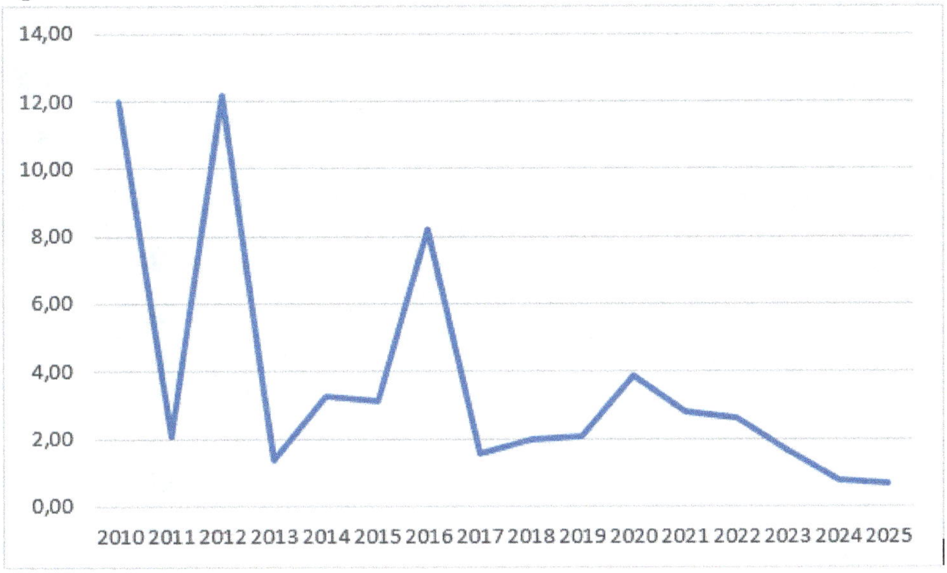

The mean number of citations per year indicates notable fluctuations between 2010 and 2025. High citation averages were observed in 2010 (12.00) and 2012 (12.18), while in the following years, the citation impact generally declined, with a slight resurgence in 2016 (8.18). After 2020, a gradual decrease is evident, likely reflecting the shorter time available for newer publications to accumulate citations (Figure 3).

Figure 4. Top 10 journals

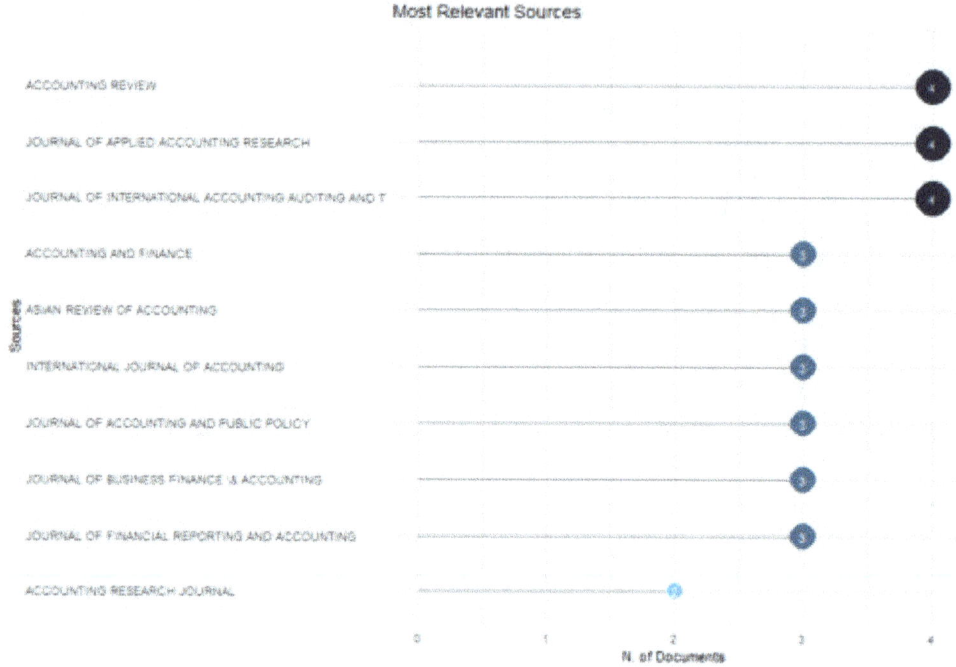

Figure 4 shows that the distribution of articles across various academic journals, highlighting the sources most frequently referenced in the bibliometric analysis. It shows that *Accounting Review*, *Journal of International Accounting Auditing and Taxation* and *Journal of Applied Accounting Research*, are the leading journals, each contributing four articles to the dataset.

Table 3. Overview of academic journals in accounting

Source	Documents	Citations	Total link strength
AR	4	310	13
JAAR	4	23	7
JIAAT	4	10	6
AF	3	57	3
ARA	3	42	2
JAPP	3	188	8
JBFA	3	78	8
JFRA	3	2	2

continued on following page

Table 3. Continued

Source	Documents	Citations	Total link strength
IJA	3	190	14
ARJ	2	29	3
CJAR	2	57	8

AR: Accounting Review; JAAR: Journal of Applied Accounting Research; JIAAT: Journal of International Accounting Auditing and Taxation; AF: Accounting and Finance; ARA: Asian Review of Accounting; JBFA: Journal of Business Finance & Accounting; JFRA: Journal of Financial Reporting and Accounting; IJA: International Journal of Accounting; JAAP: Journal of Accounting and Public Policy; ARJ: Accounting Research Journal; CJAR: China Journal of Accounting Research

Table 3 provides an overview of various accounting journals, highlighting their respective citations, number of documents and total link strength. *Accounting Review* and *International Journal of Accounting* exhibit high citation counts and link strengths, indicating their significant impact and widespread influence within the academic accounting community. In contrast, journals with fewer citations and link strengths, such as *Journal of Financial Reporting and Accounting*, reflect more specialized or emerging contributions to the literature.

Figure 5. The top ten authors

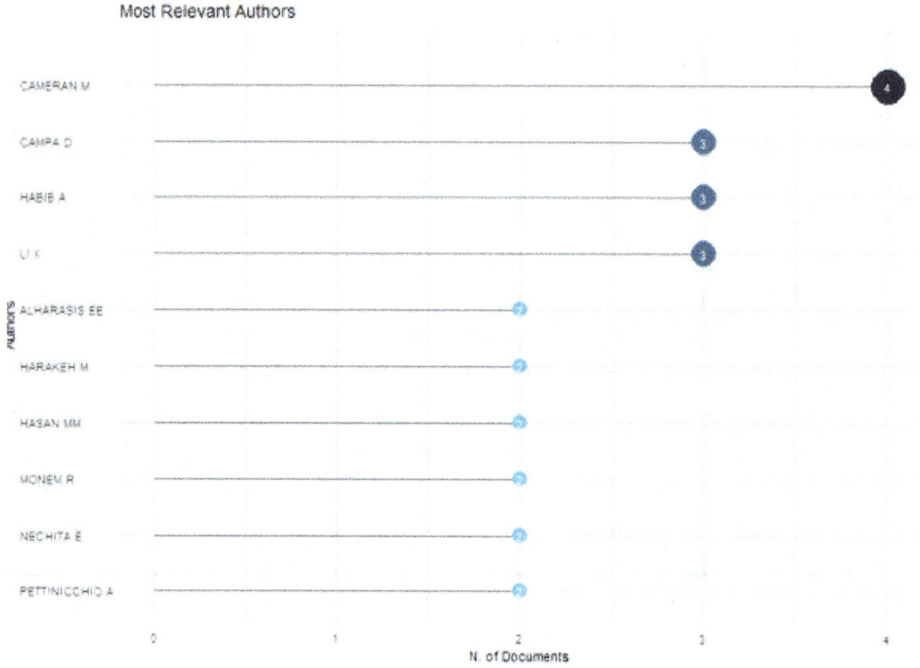

Figure 5 shows that most active researchers in the field depends on the number of articles included in the bibliometric analysis. Cameran M leads with four publications, followed by Campa D, Habib A, and Li X, each contributing three articles.

Table 4. Top ten countries

Countries	Documents	SCP	MCP	Freq.	MCP_Ratio
China	12	7	5	0,125	0,417
Italy	7	4	3	0,073	0,429
United kingdom	7	1	6	0,073	0,857
USA	6	5	1	0,063	0,167
Australia	5	4	1	0,052	0,2
New zealand	4	1	3	0,042	0,75
Romania	4	4	0	0,042	0
Saudi arabia	4	1	3	0,042	0,75
France	3	1	2	0,031	0,667
Greece	3	3	0	0,031	0

Table 4 illustrates the corresponding author's country-wise distribution of articles, highlighting China as the leading contributor with 12 articles, followed by Italy and the United Kingdom with seven each. Notably, the United Kingdom shows a high level of international collaboration, with a Multi-Country Publication (MCP) ratio of 0.857, compared to China's 0.417.

Table 5. Countries distribution of article frequency

Countries	Freq.
China	43
Australia	26
USA	25
UK	24
Italy	19
Jordan	15
Saudi arabia	13
New zealand	11
France	10
Malaysia	10

Table 5 presents the regional distribution of article frequency, with China leading at 43 occurrences, followed by Australia (26) and the USA (25). Other notable contributors include the United Kingdom, Italy, and Jordan - each demonstrating significant research activity within the analyzed dataset.

Figure 6. Keywords Analysis

Table 6. Keywords Analysis

Keywords	**F**
Earnings management	39
IFRS adoption	24
Impact	24
Mandatory ifrs adoption	24
Corporate governance	19
Accounting standards	17
Incentives	17
Information	15
Disclosure	14
International accounting standards	14
Standards	14
Investor protection	13
Quality	13
Management	12
Ownership	11
Financial-reporting quality	10
Accruals	9

continued on following page

Table 6. Continued

Keywords	F
Determinants	9
Economic consequences	9
Accounting quality	8

Frequency

Table 6 and Figure 6 present the frequency of keywords in the literature, focusing on key concepts related to earnings management (Almaqtari et al., 2021; Alruwaili et al., 2023; Can, 2021; Carvajal & Cahan, 2024; Elemes & Filip, 2022; Florou et al., 2020; Gardi et al., 2023; Gomes & Costa, 2025; Habib et al., 2019; Kosmidou et al., 2020; Lopez et al., 2022; Ma et al., 2021; Mensah, 2021; Palea, 2013; Riccardi, 2019; Ulah et al., 2024; Vishnani et al., 2021), IFRS adoption (Ajibade et al., 2022; Bajra & Čadcž, 2018; Dcfond ct al., 2019; Florou et al., 2020; Himanshu et al., 2020; Palea, 2013; Saji, 2022; Tawiah & Borgi, 2022), corporate governance (Ajibade et al., 2022; Alruwaili et al., 2023; Bajra & Čadež, 2018; Bonetti et al., 2016; Golmohammadi Shuraki et al., 2021; Hsu & Yang, 2022; Saji, 2022; Mahmood et al., 2021), accounting standards (Acar, 2023; Barghathi, 2019; Cameran & Campa, 2020; Carvajal & Cahan, 2024; Riccardi, 2019) and financial reporting. Among the most frequently discussed terms, "Earnings management" (39) stands out as the dominant topic, indicating significant attention to the manipulation of earnings and its effect on financial reporting. The terms "IFRS adoption", "Impact" and "Mandatory IFRS adoption" (all with a frequency of 24) suggest a strong focus on the adoption of IFRS, particularly the implications and mandatory nature of such adoption.

"Corporate governance" (19) appears as another key term, reflecting its critical role in forming financial reporting practices and the broader governance framework within organizations. The term "Accounting standards" (17), "International accounting standards" (14) and "standards" (14) also emerge frequently, pointing to the importance of formalized rules and guidelines that govern financial reporting.

"Incentives" (17), "Information" (15) "Disclosure" (14) "Investor protection" (13) and "Quality" (13), "Financial-reporting quality" (10), "Accounting quality" (8) are among the most frequently used keywords in the research examined. "Incentives" emphasizes the role of financial managers' behaviour in decision-making processes in accounting information systems. "Information" identifies the importance of accurate, comparable and timely information in all decision making processes. "Disclosure" highlights the importance of sharing information produced by the accounting information system with all internal and external stakeholders in a timely manner. "Investor protection" (13) and "Quality" (13) indicate their role in protecting investors' interests and ensuring the quality of financial reporting.

The other most frequently used keywords are "Management" (12), which emphasizes the role of management in financial reporting decisions and "Ownership" (11), which shows the impact of ownership structures on financial transparency and reporting practices. In these studies keywords frequently used to define the factors impacting FRQ include "Accruals" (9), "Determinants" (9), and "Economic consequences" (9).

These findings show a strong focus on the effects of IFRS adoption, quality corporate governance, earnings management and other factors affecting the quality of financial reporting.

Figure 7. Author's keywords

Table 7. Author's keywords

Terms	Frequency
Financial reporting quality	32
IFRS	20
IFRS adoption	13
Financial reporting	11
Corporate governance	8
Earnings management	8
Quality	8
Audit fees	6
Earnings quality	6
International financial reporting standards	5
Accounting quality	4
Corruption	4
Faithful representation	4
Financial	4
International	4
Investment efficiency	4
Reporting quality	4
Value relevance	4
Accruals	3
Comparability	3

Table 7 and Figure 7 show the results of author keywords analysis. These author keywords include IFRS, financial reporting quality, corporate governance, and financial reporting processes. The most frequently keywords are "Financial reporting quality"(32) (Alomair et al., 2022; Gietzmann & Isidro, 2013; Manawadu et al., 2019), "IFRS" (20), (Al-Enzy et al., 2023; Gietzmann & Isidro, 2013; Li & Saffar, 2021; Lopez et al, 2022; Manawadu et al, 2019) and "IFRS adoption" (13) focus the attention given to the implementation and adoption of IFRS, accents its importance in the field.

The keyword "Financial reporting" (11) shows that there are general research on financial reporting processes (Isidro et al, 2020). "Corporate governance" (8) and "Earnings management" (8) keywords focus on the impact of corporate governance and earnings manipulation on financial reporting. "Audit fees" (6) (Cameran & Perotti, 2014) and "Earnings quality" (6) (Al-Enzy et al., 2023) show that studies that explore the relationship between audit processes and the quality of financial information. "Accounting quality" (4) (Lopez et al., 2022) and "Accruals" (3) show that studies focus on technical aspects related to the accuracy and reliability of financial reporting. Keyword "Corruption" (4) focus on external factors, particularly corruption, that may influence financial reporting processes. "Faithful representation" (4) show up the principle that financial reports should be presented properly, accurately and on time. "Comparability" (3) define the importance of comparability in financial data of companies. "Investment efficiency" and "Value relevance" focus on the effectiveness and value of financial information for investors. These findings show that research are focused on key topics such as financial reporting quality, corporate governance, and IFRS.

Figure 8. Co-occurence (Author's keywords)

Table 8. Co-occurence (Author's keywords)

Keywords	Cluster	Betweenness	Closeness	PageRank
Financial reporting	1	49,9072063	0,01852	0,05649
Corporate governance	1	18,7941323	0,01724	0,03710
Quality	1	46	0,01370	0,04458
Financial	2	0	0,01010	0,01658
Reporting quality	2	24	0,01333	0,02610
Discretionary accruals	3	24	0,01053	0,02738
Earnings	3	0	0,00840	0,01699
Financial reporting quality	4	209,22375	0,02381	0,17097
IFRS	4	27,0826923	0,01613	0,04464

continued on following page

Table 8. Continued

Keywords	Cluster	Betweenness	Closeness	PageRank
Audit fees	4	0	0,01515	0,01228
Accounting quality	4	12,8220074	0,01639	0,03539
Comparability	4	0	0,01515	0,01228
Financial statement comparability	4	0	0,01515	0,01228
Audit quality	4	0	0,01515	0,01228
Corruption	5	46	0,01282	0,04031
Earnings management	6	25,2954545	0,01724	0,05175
International	6	4,54134615	0,01639	0,03819
Accruals	6	0	0,01220	0,01269
Companies	6	0	0,01613	0,02682
IFRS adoption	7	53,3058473	0,01887	0,06951

Table 8 and Figure 8 present the results of Co-occurence (Author's keywords) analysis. This analysis explains keywords in the field of financial reporting and related areas based on their cluster affiliations, centrality measures, betweenness, closeness, and PageRank. The analysis shows that the concept of financial reporting quality holds a central position within the research. Betweenness (209.22) and PageRank (0.17097) are the highest values for this keyword (see, Table 8 and Figure 8).

Figure 9. Keywords Plus

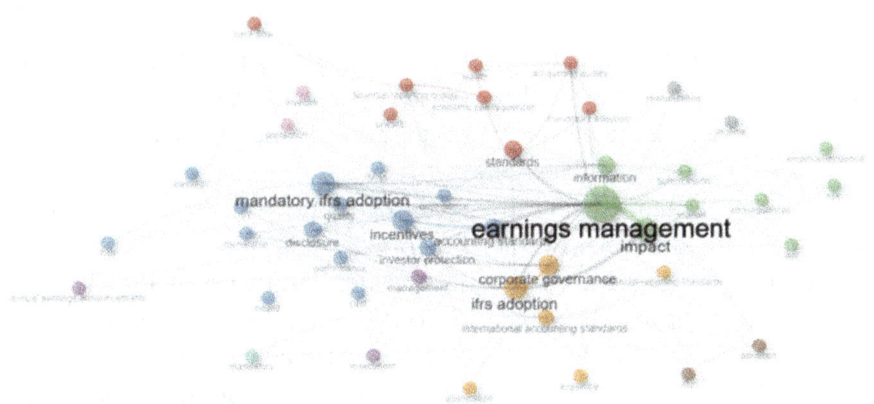

Table 9. Keywords Plus

Keywords	Cluster	Betweenness	Closeness	PageRank
Standards	1	20,1482102	0,01299	0,03389
Financial-reporting quality	1	10,7874255	0,01250	0,02368
Economic consequences	1	12,9431068	0,01205	0,02420
Accounting quality	1	4,65448567	0,01190	0,02171
Mandatory adoption	1	0,10810811	0,01087	0,01350
Private	1	1,97262538	0,01176	0,01621
Equity	1	0,05882353	0,01075	0,01107
Cash flow	1	0,11111111	0,00952	0,00783
Mandatory IFRS adoption	2	113,264174	0,01493	0,05533
Accounting standards	2	23,4115328	0,01333	0,03450
Incentives	2	30,1897319	0,01389	0,04303
Disclosure	2	8,26912342	0,01299	0,02939
Investor protection	2	40,391079	0,01351	0,03508
Quality	2	34,8443504	0,01316	0,02777
Ownership	2	2,70051391	0,01235	0,02064
Accruals	2	2,9639608	0,01220	0,01775
Firms	2	2,0361245	0,01220	0,01951
Governance	2	0,55603284	0,01163	0,01602
Earnings	2	3,73975151	0,01124	0,01308
Performance	2	0,65345872	0,01176	0,01653

Table 9 and Figure 9 present the results of Co-occurence, Author's keywords and Keywords plus analysis. This analysis explains keywords in the field of financial reporting and related areas based on their cluster affiliations and centrality measures, betweenness, closeness, and PageRank.

When Table 9 is examined, it shows that there are two clusters. The first cluster consists of the words Standards, Financial-reporting quality, Economic consequences, Accounting quality, Mandatory adoption, Private, Equity, Cash flow. The second cluster consists of the words Mandatory IFRS adoption, Accounting standards, Incentives, Disclosure, Investor protection, Quality, Ownership, Accruals, Firms, Governance, Earnings, Performance. The most effective word in the first cluster is "Standards" (Betweenness: 20.14).

Although "Financial-reporting quality" and "Economic consequences" are also important concepts, it is understood that their areas of influence are lower. The second cluster focuses on the mandatory implementation of IFRS and their consequences. The central keyword is seen to be Mandatory IFRS adoption (Betweenness: 113.26).

Other effective words were found to be "Investor protection" (40.39), "Quality" (34.84) and "Incentives" (30.18).

The clustering in both tables suggests that while Table 8 reflects a micro-level technical focus, Table 9 incorporates macro-level regulatory implications. Although *financial reporting quality* dominates in Table 8 with the highest PageRank (0.17097), its PageRank in Table 9 drops to 0.02368, where *mandatory IFRS adoption* becomes the most influential (0.05533). This shift indicates that when author keywords are used (Table 8), technical aspects are prioritized; however, when Keywords Plus are used (Table 9), the literature focuses more on policy-level impacts. Keywords such as *accounting quality*, *earnings*, and *accruals* appear in both tables, but their positioning and metrics vary. For instance, *accounting quality* has higher PageRank and closeness in Table 8, indicating its technical alignment with reporting quality.

The clustering of keywords illustrates their relationships within the research field. For example, the keywords "mandatory adoption" and "IFRS adoption" which are found in Cluster 2, show a strong relationship with "regulatory" and "standard-setting" discussions. Additionally, these keywords serve as a bridge between "accounting standards" and "investor protection". The keyword "financial-reporting quality" functions as a central node, connecting multiple related topics. These topics include "disclosure", "incentives," and "accounting standards".

In conclusion, the Co-occurence keywords analysis reveals detailed relationships among various keywords in the financial reporting field. "Earnings management", "IFRS adoption" and "Financial reporting quality" are the best main keywords, which have high centrality measures for this field.

Figure 10. Trends topic

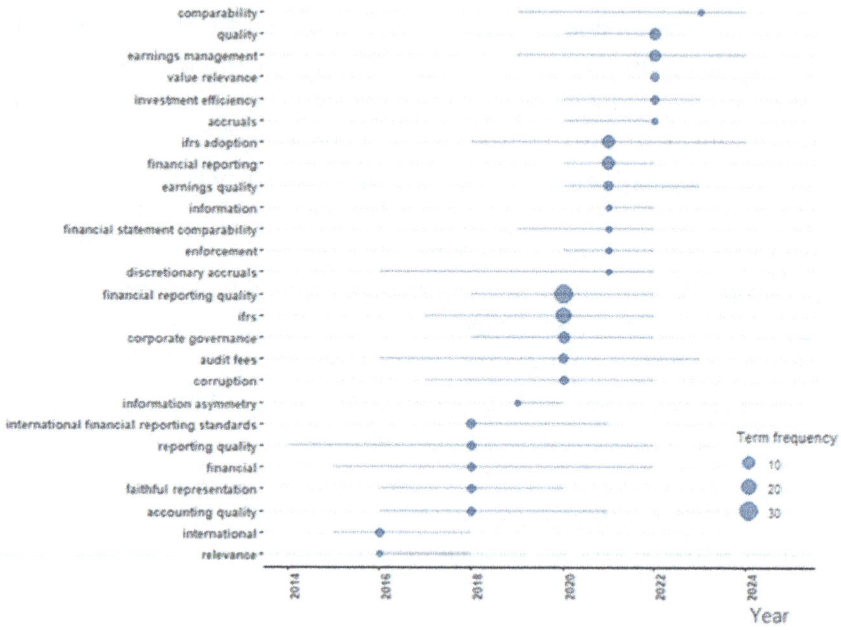

Figure 10 shows that trending topics in the literature, keywords and their frequency of occurrence over time. The table also includes these keywords were cited, historical insights into their temporal evolution and relevance in academic research. Topics such as "international", "Relevance", "IFRS", "faithful representation", "accounting quality", "Audit fees", "corruption", "earnings quality" and "Earnings management" have seen a gradual rise in interest in 2015 through 2024.

The keyword "international" emerge with an increasing trend from 2015 to 2018. This trend indicates growing interest in global perspectives in financial reporting. "Relevance" gains importance starting in 2016 and continuing through to 2018. This trend appears to reflect the growing focus on the relevance of financial information for decisions.

The interest in "IFRS" seems to have gained importance since 2018. This increasing interest continues throughout 2021. This trend explains the increasing importance of IFRS and its applications in global financial reporting standards.

The analysis shows that other keywords "accounting quality" and "faithful representation" emerged around 2016, a peak in 2018 and keep up through 2021. This trend explains the ongoing interest in enhancing the quality of financial statements in research. At the same time, "Financial reporting quality" increased in 2018 and continued to increase through 2022. This trend indicates that the accuracy, reliability, and transparency of financial reporting have been of significant concern in recent years.

The trend analysis shows that focus of research in the field of financial reporting, with “Financial reporting quality”, “Earnings management” and “IFRS adoption” trending in recent years. These trends reflect academic interest in improving the transparency and also quality of financial reporting, the role of international standards, and the management of financial reports in the context of evolving global markets.

Figure 11. Thematic map

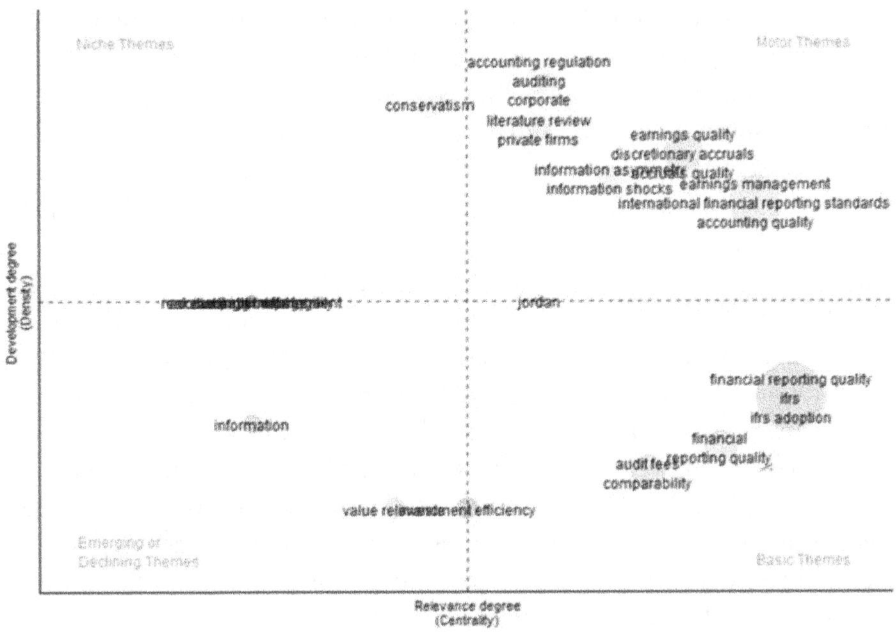

The findings from the thematic map analysis show that landscape of research in financial reporting and accounting (Figure 11). Niche themes consist of conservatism, accounting quality, earnings quality, accounting regulation, earnings management, and IFRS adoption. These themes have been central to the research and also include the transparency, reliability, and comparability of financial reporting. Basic themes including reporting quality, IFRS adoption, and financial reporting quality underscore the importance of global standards in enhancing financial transparency and comparability. Emerging themes consist of information, value relevance, and efficiency.

Financial Reporting Quality; The reports produced by the accounting information system are used by internal and external stakeholders in the decision-making. The timely comparison and relevance of these reports ensures that the right decisions are made. It is observed that the quality of financial reports has increased with IFRS applications. It is show that the "comparability","relevance", "timeliness" and "understandability" features of financial reports have improved after the IFRS application. In this way, investors can access more reliable information in their decision-making processes (Yurisandi & Puspitasari, 2015; Ciocan & Georgescu, 2019). These developments ensure that financial reports are transparent and at the same time support investor confidence by ensuring transparency in capital markets (Johri, 2024).

Earnings Management; Studies on the reducing effect of IFRS on earnings management use accrual-based and real activity-based earnings management measurements. IFRS application allows for more accurate reports to be prepared and presented by limiting the manipulation of data (Mensah, 2021). However, there are studies that explain that this effect is limited (Doukakis, 2014; Kateb, 2024).

Corporate Governance and Audit; Corporate governance practices include the independence, expertise and effectiveness of audit committees, gender distribution, shareholder rights, relations with stakeholders, transparency, accountability, public disclosure activities and responsibility. IFRS practices are seen to have positive effects on corporate governance and auditing (Silva et al., 2025; Gardi et al., 2023). It has been determined that FRQ is higher in companies working with Big 4 auditing firms that conduct audits taking into account IFRS practices (Riccardi, 2019).

Investor Behavior and Cost of Capital; Investment decision-making is important not only for managers but also for investors to plan the future correctly. Accurate and timely financial reports contribute to accurate and timely decision-making. The adoption and implementation of IFRS allows investors to provide more reliable information in the decision-making process. In this context, it increases investor confidence. Investors reduce their risk perception thanks to more transparent and comparable financial statements (Habib et al., 2019; Beneish et al., 2015).

Legal Infrastructure; The success of IFRS implementation varies from country to country. The legal system, investor protection level, institutional capacity and audit infrastructure of the countries are effective in this. It is stated that IFRS implementation is more successful in countries where there are regulations to protect investors (Houqe et al., 2012). It is emphasized that the implementation of legal regulations makes IFRS implementation more effective (Alruwaili et al., 2023; Chakroun & Ben Amar, 2025).

Voluntary / Mandatory adoption of IFRS; IFRS is implemented in two ways all over the world: mandatory and voluntary. The most important motivations of companies that voluntarily switch to IFRS include public offering, attracting investors or internationalization. It is determined that the reporting quality of companies that act with this motivation increases when they voluntarily switch to IFRS (Bassemir & Novotny-Farkas, 2018). Mandatory compliance is enforced through legal regulations and they switch to IFRS in order to comply with the legislation. It is explained that the results are shaped positively, especially in terms of information asymmetry, audit fees and earnings management, as there are stronger corporate intentions and strategic planning behind the voluntary transition (Cameran & Campa, 2020).

Internal Control Systems; The success and effective implementation of IFRS does not depend solely on its acceptance. It varies according to the structural characteristics of the company, its size, age (Ciocan & Georgescu, 2019), internal control system, audit committee expertise (Kateb, 2024), and the characteristics of audit committees. It is observed that the success of IFRS implementation increases in large-scale and publicly traded companies with developed internal audit systems (Johri, 2024).

Tax Avoidance and Ethics; IFRS increases financial transparency. As a result, the financial structures of companies are revealed more clearly. Manipulations decrease. Since IFRS application increases transparency, it can deter companies from engaging in tax avoidance. Research indicates that tax avoidance behavior is more pronounced, especially in family companies and structures with low levels of control. It is emphasized that it contributes to the institutionalization of a transparent reporting culture (Chakroun & Ben Amar, 2025).

Audit Fees and Workload; IFRS increases the workload of auditors, especially in the first implementation period, which leads to an increase in audit fees. However, these costs can be balanced with increasing experience and systems over time (Kim et al., 2012). Some studies indicate that IFRS increases audit costs, especially for small businesses, because it creates more complex reporting structures (Cameran & Perotti, 2014).

6. CONCLUSION AND FUTURE RESEARCH TRENDS

IFRS adoption, as a transition from GAAP to IFRS, enhances not only transparency but also comparability in financial statements. This shift has consequently led to improvements in the quality of financial reporting, which makes reports more relevant, accurate, understandable, and accessible to their users. According to the Conceptual Framework (IFRS Foundation, 2018), the two fundamental qualitative characteristics that define high quality financial information are faithful representation and relevance. Faithful representation comprises neutrality, completeness and freedom from error, while enhancing characteristics include comparability, understandability, verifiability, timeliness all of which contribute to the usefulness of financial information for investors and stakeholders (IFRS Foundation, 2018, pp. 13–16).

Value relevance research further supports this perspective by emphasizing the degree to which financial information is useful to investors. As such, high-quality financial reporting serves as a cornerstone of sound investment and credit decisions. IASB developed IFRS to serve as a globally recognized framework to standardize and guide financial reporting across diverse jurisdictions (Mbir et al., 2020). Since becoming mandatory in the EU in 2005, IFRS has been widely adopted and recognized as a transformative force in global accounting (Mensah, 2021).

The empirical literature largely supports the positive impact of IFRS on FRQ (Levitt, 1998; Psaros and Trotman, 2004; Biddle and Hilary, 2006; Bonetti et al., 2016; Klish et al., 2022). However, there are contrasting findings indicating negative or insignificant effects (Barth et al., 2007; Christensen et al., 2015). This diversity of findings underscores the complexity of IFRS adoption effects and the need for further empirical validation across contexts.

Despite the growing volume of research, the analysis reveals several key gaps and priorities for future investigation. First, while earnings management has been widely studied, research on concrete mechanisms to mitigate it -particularly in post-IFRS contexts- remains underdeveloped. Moreover, there is limited comparative research on IFRS adoption experiences between developed and emerging economies, especially with regard to regulatory enforcement, capacity-building, and contextual adaptation.

First, while earnings management has been widely studied, research on concrete mechanisms to mitigate it -particularly in post-IFRS contexts- remains underdeveloped. Moreover, there is limited comparative research on IFRS adoption experiences between developed and emerging economies, especially concerning regulatory enforcement, capacity-building, and contextual adaptation.

Additionally, corporate governance has been predominantly studied in large or listed firms, leaving a gap in understanding how governance affects financial reporting in small and medium-sized enterprises (SMEs). Similarly, although audit fees and audit quality are recognized as influencing reporting reliability, their long-term relationship with trust in financial statements warrants deeper analysis. The bibliometric results also suggest that themes such as corruption, technology (e.g., AI and blockchain), and investor access to information are emerging but still insufficiently explored.

- In light of these findings, future research should focus on:
- The role of governance mechanisms in enhancing FRQ in SMEs;
- The effect of technological innovations on comparability and transparency in financial reporting;

- The country-level comparative studies on IFRS implementation challenges and adaptations;
- The relationship between audit quality, audit fees and stakeholder trust;
- The mechanisms to curb corruption in financial reporting, especially in developing economies;
- The tools and platforms that improve individual investor access to accurate financial information.

This chapter also acknowledges several limitations. First, the bibliometric analysis is restricted to the WoS database and may not capture relevant research indexed elsewhere, such as Scopus or Google Scholar. Second, while bibliometric methods allow for the identification of patterns and trends, they do not offer direct insights into the theoretical depth or methodological rigor of the included studies. Lastly, the time window (2010–2025) captures current trends but may exclude newer developments not yet reflected in citation networks.

In conclusion, this research contributes to the accounting literature by systematically mapping the intellectual landscape of IFRS adoption and FRQ. It identifies central themes, highlights emerging research areas and proposes a roadmap for future inquiry. Addressing the identified gaps will not only enrich academic knowledge but also enhance the practical effectiveness of financial reporting systems for global investor confidence.

REFERENCES

Acar, M. (2023). Who affects whom? Impact of the national culture of international audit firms and their affiliates on the financial reporting quality of audit clients. *Borsa Istanbul Review*, *23*(1), 113–135. DOI: 10.1016/j.bir.2022.09.011

Agyei-Mensah, B. K. (2013). Adoption of international financial reporting standards (IFRS) in Ghana and the quality of financial statement disclosures. Macrothink Institute, *International Journal of Accounting and Financial Reporting*, ISSN, 2162-3082. https://doi.org/DOI: 10.5296/ijafr.v3i2.4489

Ahmed, A. S., Neel, M., & Wang, D. (2013). Does mandatory adoption of IFRS improve accounting quality? Preliminary evidence. *Contemporary Accounting Research*, *30*(4), 1344–1372. DOI: 10.1111/j.1911-3846.2012.01193.x

Ajibade, A. T., Okutu, N., Akande, F., Kwarbai, J. D., Olayinka, I. M., & Olotu, A. (2022). IFRS adoption, corporate governance and faithful representation of financial reporting quality in Nigeria's development banks. *Cogent Business & Management*, *9*(1), 2139213. DOI: 10.1080/23311975.2022.2139213

Al-Enzy, N. S. K., Monem, R., & Nahar, S. (2023). IFRS experience and earnings quality in the GCC region. *International Journal of Managerial Finance*, *19*(3), 670–690. DOI: 10.1108/IJMF-09-2021-0410

Almaqtari, F. A., Hashed, A. A., & Shamim, M. (2021). Impact of corporate governance mechanism on IFRS adoption: A comparative study of Saudi Arabia, Oman, and the United Arab Emirates. *Heliyon*, *7*(1), e05848. Advance online publication. DOI: 10.1016/j.heliyon.2020.e05848 PMID: 33490662

Alomair, A., Farley, A., & Yang, H. H. (2022). The impact of IFRS adoption on the value relevance of accounting information in Saudi Arabia. *Accounting and Finance*, *62*(2), 2839–2878. DOI: 10.1111/acfi.12902

Alruwaili, W. S., Ahmed, A. D., & Joshi, M. (2023). IFRS adoption, firms' investment efficiency and financial reporting quality: A new empirical assessment of moderating effects from Saudi listed firms. *International Journal of Accounting & Information Management*, *31*(2), 376–411. DOI: 10.1108/IJAIM-10-2022-0226

Alsharif, A. H., Salleh, N. O. R. Z. M. D., & Baharun, R. O. H. A. I. Z. A. T. (2020). Bibliometric analysis. *Journal of Theoretical and Applied Information Technology*, 98(15), 2948-2962, E-ISSN: 1817-3195.

Alzeban, A. (2018). The association between internal audit department characteristics and IFRS compliance. *Asian Review of Accounting*, *26*(3), 336–358. DOI: 10.1108/ARA-03-2017-0054

Amidu, M., Yorke, S. M., & Harvey, S. (2016). The Effects of Financial Reporting Standards on Tax Avoidance and Earnings Quality: A Case of an Emerging Economy. *Journal of Accounting & Finance* (2158-3625), 16(2).

Bajra, U., & Čadež, S. (2018). Audit committees and financial reporting quality: The 8th EU Company Law Directive perspective. *Economic Systems*, *42*(1), 151–163. DOI: 10.1016/j.ecosys.2017.03.002

Barghathi, Y. (2019). Financial reporting quality and earnings management in Libyan banks: Stakeholders' perceptions. *African Journal of Accounting. Auditing and Finance*, *6*(3), 177–200. DOI: 10.1504/AJAAF.2019.10020488

Barth, M. E., Landsman, W. R., Lang, M., & Williams, C. (2007). Accounting quality: International accounting standards and US GAAP. Manuscript, Stanford University. https://citeseerx.ist.psu.edu/document?repid=rep1&type=pdf&doi=092af2d5624226dba00e8cd39e5fa302d635e0ae

Bassemir, M., & Novotny-Farkas, Z. (2018). IFRS adoption, reporting incentives and financial reporting quality in private firms. *Journal of Business Finance & Accounting*, *45*(7-8), 759–796. DOI: 10.1111/jbfa.12315

Beneish, M. D., Miller, B. P., & Yohn, T. L. (2015). Macroeconomic evidence on the impact of mandatory IFRS adoption on equity and debt markets. *Journal of Accounting and Public Policy*, *34*(1), 1–27. DOI: 10.1016/j.jaccpubpol.2014.10.002

Biddle, G. C., & Hilary, G. (2006). Accounting quality and firm-level capital investment. *The Accounting Review*, *81*(5), 963–982. https://www.jstor.org/stable/4093094. DOI: 10.2308/accr.2006.81.5.963

Bonetti, P., Magnan, M. L., & Parbonetti, A. (2016). The influence of country-and firm-level governance on financial reporting quality: Revisiting the evidence. *Journal of Business Finance & Accounting*, *43*(9-10), 1059–1094. DOI: 10.1111/jbfa.12220

Cameran, M., & Campa, D. (2020). Voluntary IFRS adoption by unlisted European firms: Impact on earnings quality and cost of debt. *The International Journal of Accounting*, *55*(03), 2050013. DOI: 10.1142/S1094406020500134

Cameran, M., & Perotti, P. (2014). Audit fees and IAS/IFRS adoption: Evidence from the banking industry. *International Journal of Auditing*, *18*(2), 155–169. DOI: 10.1111/ijau.12019

Can, G. (2021). Does Sharia compliance affect financial reporting quality? An evidence from Muslim majority countries. *International Journal of Islamic and Middle Eastern Finance and Management*, *14*(1), 16–33. DOI: 10.1108/IMEFM-04-2019-0149

Carvajal, M., & Cahan, S. (2024). International trade, mandatory IFRS adoption and financial reporting quality. *Pacific Accounting Review*, *36*(2), 185–210. DOI: 10.1108/PAR-01-2023-0014

Chakroun, S., & Ben Amar, A. (2025). The IFRS adoption, corporate tax avoidance and the moderating effect of family ownership. *International Journal of Law and Management*, *67*(1), 16–36. DOI: 10.1108/IJLMA-06-2023-0135

Chen, J. J., & Zhang, H. (2010). The impact of regulatory enforcement and audit upon IFRS compliance–Evidence from China. *European Accounting Review*, *19*(4), 665–692. Advance online publication. DOI: 10.1080/09638180903384684

Christensen, H. B., Lee, E., Walker, M., & Zeng, C. (2015). Incentives or standards: What determines accounting quality changes around IFRS adoption? *European Accounting Review*, *24*(1), 31–61. DOI: 10.1080/09638180.2015.1009144

Ciocan, C. C., & Georgescu, I. (2019). Quality of financial reporting in Romania: Measuring qualitative characteristics pre and post IFRS adoption. *European Union Financial Regulation and Administrative Area EUFIRE*, *2019*, 405–428.

De George, E. T., Li, X., & Shivakumar, L. (2016). A Review of the IFRS Adoption Literature. *Review of Accounting Studies*, *21*(3), 898–1004. DOI: 10.1007/s11142-016-9363-1

DeFond, M., Gao, X., Li, O. Z., & Xia, L. (2019). IFRS adoption in China and foreign institutional investments. *China Journal of Accounting Research*, *12*(1), 1–32. DOI: 10.1016/j.cjar.2018.07.006

Donthu, N., Kumar, S., Mukherjee, D., Pandey, N., & Lim, W. M. (2021). How to conduct a bibliometric analysis: An overview and guidelines. *Journal of Business Research*, *133*, 285–296. DOI: 10.1016/j.jbusres.2021.04.070

Doukakis, L. C. (2014). The effect of mandatory IFRS adoption on real and accrual-based earnings management activities. *Journal of Accounting and Public Policy*, *33*(6), 551–572. DOI: 10.1016/j.jaccpubpol.2014.08.006

El Guindy, M. N., & Trabelsi, N. S. (2020). IFRS adoption/reporting and auditor fees: The conditional effect of audit firm size and tenure. *International Journal of Accounting & Information Management*, *28*(4), 639–666. DOI: 10.1108/IJAIM-09-2019-0107

Elemes, A., & Filip, A. (2022). Financial reporting quality and private firms' access to trade credit capital. *The International Journal of Accounting*, *57*(02), 2250010. DOI: 10.1142/S109440602250010X

Elhamma, A. (2023). Impact of mandatory IFRS adoption on economic growth: The moderating role of Covid-19 crisis in developing countries. *Journal of Accounting and Management Information Systems*, *23*(3), 554–568. DOI: 10.24818/jamis.2023.03007

Elhamma, A. (2024). Determinants of national IFRS adoption: Evidence from the Middle East and North Africa region. *International Journal of Accounting. Auditing and Performance Evaluation*, *20*(1-2), 69–90. DOI: 10.1504/IJAAPE.2024.135535

Elhamma, A. (2025), *Perceived benefits of IFRS adoption in Morocco and French-speaking Sub-Saharan African countries.* In F. Albuquerque & P. G. Dos Santos (Eds.), *Contemporary innovations in reporting and analysis* (pp. 183–210). IGI Global. DOI: 10.4018/979-8-3693-5923-5.ch007

Elhamma, A. (2025). Impact of mandatory IFRS adoption on foreign direct investment: The moderating role of conflict of interest regulation. *Journal of Financial Reporting and Accounting*, *23*(3), 936–958. DOI: 10.1108/JFRA-04-2022-0145

Florou, A., Morricone, S., & Pope, P. F. (2020). Proactive financial reporting enforcement: Audit fees and financial reporting quality effects. *The Accounting Review*, *95*(2), 167–197. DOI: 10.2308/accr-52497

Francis, J., LaFond, R., Olsson, P. M., & Schipper, K. (2004). Costs of equity and earnings attributes. *The Accounting Review*, *79*(4), 967–1010. https://www.jstor.org/stable/4093083. DOI: 10.2308/accr.2004.79.4.967

Gardi, B., Aga, M., & Abdullah, N. N. (2023). Corporate governance and financial reporting quality: The Mediation Role of IFRS. *Sustainability (Basel)*, *15*(13), 9869. DOI: 10.3390/su15139869

Gietzmann, M. B., & Isidro, H. (2013). Institutional investors' reaction to SEC concerns about IFRS and US GAAP reporting. *Journal of Business Finance & Accounting*, *40*(7-8), 796–841. DOI: 10.1111/jbfa.12027

Golmohammadi Shuraki, M., Pourheidari, O., & Azizkhani, M. (2021). Accounting comparability, financial reporting quality and audit opinions: Evidence from Iran. *Asian Review of Accounting*, *29*(1), 42–60. DOI: 10.1108/ARA-06-2020-0087

Gomes, L. R., & Costa, J. C. (2025). Financial reporting quality dynamics in India: The role of IFRS convergence and corporate governance. *Corporate Governance (Bradford)*, *25*(3), 441–454. DOI: 10.1108/CG-10-2023-0439

Gordon, L. A., Loeb, M. P., & Zhu, W. (2012). The impact of IFRS adoption on foreign direct investment. *Journal of Accounting and Public Policy, 31*(4), 374–398. DOI: 10.1016/j.jaccpubpol.2012.06.001

Habib, A., Bhuiyan, M. B. U., & Hasan, M. M. (2019). IFRS adoption, financial reporting quality and cost of capital: A life cycle perspective. *Pacific Accounting Review, 31*(3), 497–522. DOI: 10.1108/PAR-08-2016-0073

Himanshu, S., Singh, J. P., & Kumar, A. (2020). Prioritizing and establishing cause and effect relationships among financial reporting quality metrics. *Vision (Basel), 24*(3), 330–344. DOI: 10.1177/0972262920925600

Hosseini, M. R., Martek, I., Zavadskas, E. K., Aibinu, A. A., Arashpour, M., & Chileshe, N. (2018). Critical evaluation of off-site construction research: A Scientometric analysis. *Automation in Construction, 87*, 235–247. DOI: 10.1016/j.autcon.2017.12.002

Houcine, A., Zitouni, M., & Srairi, S. (2022). The impact of corporate governance and IFRS on the relationship between financial reporting quality and investment efficiency in a continental accounting system. *EuroMed Journal of Business, 17*(2), 246–269. DOI: 10.1108/EMJB-06-2020-0063

Houqe, M. N., van Zijl, T., Dunstan, K., & Karim, A. W. (2012). The effect of IFRS adoption and investor protection on earnings quality around the world. *The International Journal of Accounting, 47*(3), 333–355. DOI: 10.1016/j.intacc.2012.07.003

Hsu, Y. L., & Yang, Y. C. (2022). Corporate governance and financial reporting quality during the COVID-19 pandemic. *Finance Research Letters, 47*, 102778. DOI: 10.1016/j.frl.2022.102778 PMID: 35250396

IFRS Foundation. (2018), Conceptual framework for financial reporting, Retrieved from https://www.ifrs.org/content/dam/ifrs/publications/pdf-standards/english/2021/issued/part-a/conceptual-framework-for-financial-reporting.pdf Isidro, H., Nanda, D., & Wysocki, P. D. (2020). On the relation between financial reporting quality and country attributes: Research challenges and opportunities. The Accounting Review, 95(3), 279-314. https://doi.org/DOI: 10.2308/accr-52607

Jeanjean, T., & Stolowy, H. (2008). Do accounting standards matter? An exploratory analysis of earnings management before and after IFRS adoption. *Journal of Accounting and Public Policy, 27*(6), 480–494. DOI: 10.1016/j.jaccpubpol.2008.09.008

Johri, A. (2024). Examining the Impact of International Financial Reporting Standards Adoption on Financial Reporting Quality of Multinational Companies. *International Journal of Financial Studies, 12*(4), 96. DOI: 10.3390/ijfs12040096

Kao, T. H. W. H. S. (2014). The effect of IFRS, information asymmetry and corporate governance on the quality of accounting information. *Asian Economic and Financial Review*, *4*(2), 226.

Kateb, I. (2024). The bridge to quality financial reporting: Audit committees' mediating role in IFRS implementation for emerging markets. *Journal of Corporate Accounting & Finance*, *35*(1), 250–268. DOI: 10.1002/jcaf.22664

Kim, J. B., Liu, X., & Zheng, L. (2012). The impact of mandatory IFRS adoption on audit fees: Theory and evidence. *The Accounting Review*, *87*(6), 2061–2094. DOI: 10.2308/accr-50223

Klish, A. A., Shubita, M. F. S., & Wu, J. (2022). IFRS adoption and financial reporting quality in the MENA region. *Journal of Applied Accounting Research*, *23*(3), 570–603. DOI: 10.1108/JAAR-08-2020-0155

Kosmidou, K., Kousenidis, D., Ladas, A., & Negkakis, C. (2020). Regulation of capital flows: Effects on liquidity and the role of financial reporting quality. *Journal ofEconomic Behavior & Organization*, *175*, 86–97. DOI: 10.1016/j.jebo.2020.04.005

Kumari, R., & Naresh, G. (2023). Adoption of International Financial Reporting Standards and its effect on quality of financial reporting-a bibliometric study. *International Journal of Managerial and Financial Accounting*, *15*(3), 255–281. DOI: 10.1504/IJMFA.2023.131760

Levitt, A. (1998). The importance of high quality accounting standards. *Accounting Horizons*, *12*(2), 79–82. https://www.proquest.com/openview/113ef6fb20852f7024ae491923c7e84c/1?cbl=3330&pq-origsite=gscholar

Lin, S., Riccardi, W., & Wang, C. (2012). Does accounting quality change following a switch from US GAAP to IFRS? Evidence from Germany. *Journal of Accounting and Public Policy*, *31*(6), 641–657. DOI: 10.1016/j.jaccpubpol.2012.10.006

Lopez, D. M., Schuldt, M. A., & Vega, J. G. (2022). Do industry specialist auditors enhance accounting quality in the EU? Evidence from the pre-IFRS and mandatory post-IFRS periods. *Asian Review of Accounting*, *30*(4), 398–431. DOI: 10.1108/ARA-04-2022-0077

Ma, L., Ma, T., & Friedman, H. L. (2021). Financial reporting quality and noise in stock returns: Evidence from Chinese AB Twin shares. *Journal of Financial Reporting*, *6*(1), 137–162. DOI: 10.2308/JFR-2019-0019

Mahmood, K., Barghathi, Y., & Lasyoud, A. A. (2021). Exploring the potentials of clawbacks to check earnings management practices and enhance financial reporting quality: Perceptions from the UAE. *Qualitative Research in Financial Markets, 13*(3), 359–382. DOI: 10.1108/QRFM-05-2020-0081

Manawadu, I., Che Azmi, A., & Mohamed, A. (2019). Moderating effect of IFRS adoption on FDI and conditional accounting conservatism in South Asia. *Journal of Accounting in Emerging Economies, 9*(1), 51–74. DOI: 10.1108/JAEE-03-2017-0035

Mbir, D. E. G., Agyemang, O. S., Tackie, G., & Abeka, M. J. (2020). IFRS compliance, corporate governance and financial reporting quality of GSE-listed non-financial firms. *Cogent Business & Management, 7*(1), 1759856. DOI: 10.1080/23311975.2020.1759856

Mensah, E. (2021). The effect of IFRS adoption on financial reporting quality: Evidence from listed manufacturing firms in Ghana. *Economic research-. Ekonomska Istrazivanja, 34*(1), 2890–2905. DOI: 10.1080/1331677X.2020.1860109

Okpala, K. E. (2012). Adoption of IFRS and financial statements effects: The perceived implications on FDI and Nigeria economy. *Australian Journal of Business and Management Research, 2*(5), 76–83. DOI: 10.52283/NSWRCA.AJBMR.20120205A10

Önce, S., & Çavuş, G. (2019). Evaluation of the Effects of Corporate Governance on Financial Reporting Quality. *Journal of Modern Accounting and Auditing, 15*(8), 385–395.

Palea, V. (2013). IAS/IFRS and financial reporting quality: Lessons from the European experience. *China Journal of Accounting Research, 6*(4), 247–263. DOI: 10.1016/j.cjar.2013.08.003

Paul, J., Lim, W. M., O'Cass, A., Hao, A. W., & Bresciani, S. (2021). Scientific procedures and rationales for systematic literature reviews (SPAR-4-SLR). *International Journal of Consumer Studies, 45*(4), O1–O16. DOI: 10.1111/ijcs.12695

Psaros, J., & Trotman, K. (2004). The impact of the type of accounting standards on preparers judgments. *Abacus International Journal of Accounting. Finance and Business Studies, 40*(1), 76–93.

Raman, R., Subramaniam, N., Nair, V. K., Shivdas, A., Achuthan, K., & Nedungadi, P. (2022). Women entrepreneurship and sustainable development: Bibliometric analysis and emerging research trends. *Sustainability (Basel), 14*(15), 9160. DOI: 10.3390/su14159160

Rashmi, K., & Kataria, A. (2021). Work–life Balance: A Systematic Literature Review and Bibliometric Analysis. *The International Journal of Sociology and Social Policy*, *42*(11/12), 1028–1065. DOI: 10.1108/IJSSP-06-2021-0145

Riccardi, W. N. (2019). Do audit firm tenure and size moderate changes in financial reporting quality due to mandatory IFRS adoption? *Auditing*, *38*(4), 201–224. DOI: 10.2308/ajpt-52406

Robinson, T. R., & Henry, E. (2009). International financial statement analysis. CFA Institute Investment Series. Retrieved from https://books.mec.biz/tmp/books/G2L68QLOCEX7RSFY1UU1.pdf

Saji, T. G. (2022). Asymmetric financial reporting quality and firm size: Conditional evidence from an emerging market. *Journal of Applied Accounting Research*, *23*(5), 977–1004. DOI: 10.1108/JAAR-10-2021-0264

Silva, A., Jorge, S., Rodrigues, L. L., & Proença, C. (2025). The role of internal and external enforcers in enhancing financial reporting quality. *Journal of Accounting & Organizational Change*.DOI: 10.1108/JAOC-01-2024-0027

Tawiah, V., & Borgi, H. (2022). Impact of XBRL adoption on financial reporting quality: A global evidence. *Accounting Research Journal*, *35*(6), 815–833. DOI: 10.1108/ARJ-01-2022-0002

Vishnani, S., Gupta, S., & Gupta, H. (2021). Convergence of Indian accounting standards to IFRS: Impact on quality of financial reporting of Indian industries. *International Journal of Managerial and Financial Accounting*, *13*(1), 1–24. DOI: 10.1504/IJMFA.2021.116205

Yurisandi, T., & Puspitasari, E. (2015). Financial reporting quality-before and after IFRS adoption using NiCE qualitative characteristics measurement. *Procedia: Social and Behavioral Sciences*, *211*, 644–652. DOI: 10.1016/j.sbspro.2015.11.091

KEY TERMS AND DEFINITIONS

Bibliometric Analysis: A kind of analysis used to reveal the trends and evolution of scientific research on a specific issue.

Financial Reporting Quality: The extent to which a company's financial report is useful for its investors, stakeholders, and other financial information users to make decisions.

Financial Reporting: The process of preparing and presenting financial documents in order to consistently disclose the financial position, performance and cash flow of a company.

IFRS: Abbreviation of International Financial Reporting Standards

International Financial Reporting Standards: A set of standards established by the International Accounting Standards Board (IASB) that standardizes the financial statement preparation of companies around the world.

Scientometric Analysis: A kind of analysis that reveals the quality of scientific research and its development trends.

Web of Science: One of the worlds' biggest bibliometric database used to follow and evaluate scientific research.

WoS: Abbreviation of Web of Science

Chapter 4
Determinants of IFRS for SME Adoption in African Countries

Nesrine Sassi
https://orcid.org/0000-0003-2090-7235
IHEC Carthage, Tunisia

Salma Damak-Ayadi
IHEC Carthage, Tunisia

ABSTRACT

The main purpose of this study is to identify the determinants of the International Financial Reporting Standard for small and medium-sized entities (IFRS for SMEs) adoption in African countries. This study used the diffusion of innovation theory to explain why countries choose to adopt IFRS for SMEs. Based on logistic regression analysis, our results show that quality of governance, trading networks, and normative isomorphism have a strong and positive effects on a country's adoption of IFRS for SMEs. However, mimetic isomorphism has a negative impact on IFRS for SMEs adoption in African countries. Furthermore, tax system and coercive isomorphism system have no effect on the adoption of IFRS for SMEs standards. Our study contributes to facilitate the implantation of IFRS for SMEs in African countries and to better understanding the factors influencing the implementation of IFRS for SMEs in African countries and could be used to predict a country's decision to adopt this standard.

DOI: 10.4018/979-8-3373-1902-5.ch004

1. INTRODUCTION

In today's globalized economy, the rise of interconnected financial systems and international trade has intensified the demand for harmonized accounting standards. In response to this need, the International Accounting Standards Board (IASB) introduced the International Financial Reporting Standard for Small and Medium-sized Entities (IFRS for SMEs) in 2009. This standard was specifically developed to support SMEs—particularly in emerging economies—in aligning with international accounting practices and improving the quality of financial reporting.

The IFRS for SMEs promotes harmonization by enabling the preparation of transparent, comparable, and high-quality financial statements. These statements are designed to meet the needs of users and support informed decision-making, while balancing implementation benefits with associated costs.

In Africa, SMEs represent over 90% of all businesses and contribute approximately 80% of total employment on the continent (African Business, 2022). This sector plays a pivotal role in driving economic development and job creation. However, despite their importance, African SMEs face numerous structural challenges. According to Center for Strategic and International Studies (2021), a major issue is the lack of reliable financial information, which limits SMEs' access to external financing. Additionally, high borrowing costs and limited investor confidence further constrain their growth potential.

The adoption of IFRS for SMEs can help address these barriers. By improving the quality, credibility, and transparency of financial statements, SMEs can enhance their access to credit and attract both local and foreign investment (Chamisa, 2000). Understanding the factors that influence the adoption of this standard is therefore crucial for improving the financial ecosystem in Africa.

Although several studies—such as those by Kaya and Koch (2015), Bonito and Pais (2018), Sellami and Gafsi (2018), Zahid and Simga-Mugan (2019), and Mhedhbi and Essid (2022) have examined IFRS for SMEs adoption globally, there remains a significant gap in the literature regarding African countries specifically.

This research aims to address that gap by identifying the key determinants influencing IFRS for SMEs adoption across African nations. In particular, the study evaluates the roles of corporate governance quality, trade networks, tax systems, and institutional isomorphism. The analysis covers a sample of 42 African countries over a seven-year period, including all countries that have adopted the IFRS for SMEs during that time. To our knowledge, this is one of the few empirical studies focusing exclusively on the African context.

The results indicate that governance quality, trade relationships, and normative institutional pressures positively influence IFRS for SMEs adoption. In contrast, mimetic isomorphism appears to negatively affect adoption, while neither the tax system nor coercive pressures show a significant impact.

The structure of this paper is as follows: Section 1 provides background on IFRS for SMEs in the African context. Section 2 introduces the theoretical foundations of standard adoption. Section 3 presents a literature review on governance, economic networks, taxation, and institutional pressures. Section 4 outlines the research design, followed by Section 5, which discusses the empirical results.

2. IFRS FOR SMES AND AFRICAN COUNTRIES

2.1. IFRS for SMEs

In 2002, the IASB registered several sollicitation requesting a version of international standards dedicated to SMEs. Thus, the IASB Council decided to launch the project of developing standards specific to SMEs. Indeed, the Trustees of the IFRS Foundation noted that "the Trustees (administrators) also support the efforts made by the IASB (2009) to examine issues specific to emerging economies and small and medium-sized entities. In July 2005, the Trustees of the IFRS Foundation confirmed the objectives of the IASB by adding another which indicates that IFRS must take into account the specific needs of SMEs in emerging countries.

The draft IFRS standard for SMEs went through several stages to, in the end, bring out this standard: firstly the discussion paper, secondly the questionnaire on possible modifications and thirdly the exposition draft. The IFRS for SMEs standard was inspired by Full IFRS. It is developed by a "top down" approach. Indeed, this standard is based on the modification and simplification of the rules and measures related to IFRS standards and the elimination of standards deemed inappropriate and inadequate for SMEs (Ernst & Young, 2016). As a result, the information provided is more appropriate and better meets the needs of SMEs. Despite the intensive use of full IFRS standards, the IFRS for SMEs standard remains independent.

Generally, SMEs are not obliged to provide complex and expensive accounting information. Therefore, in order to meet the needs of SMEs in financial information, the IASB worked on the simplification of the accounting and valuation methods designated by Full IFRS. In what follows, we will present the subjects not dealt with at the level of the IFRS for SMEs standard, the simplification of the methods of recognition and measurement, the elimination of certain accounting options retained by the Full IFRS as well as the simplification of the methods of presentation financial statements and relieving disclosures.

The adoption of international standards is a political decision. For this, the decision to implement international standards is taken according to the specificities of each country. Albu and Albu (2014) indicated that Factors such as culture, accounting traditions, and the economic and political environment influence how IFRS is applied in practice. Indeed, political decision-makers often recognize the importance of harmonizing national accounting practices with international standards. (Callao et al., 2007, p.149). In addition, the application of international standards could be mandatory or voluntary.

2.2. Objectif of the IFRS for SMEs

The main objective of the IFRS for SMEs (Small and Medium-sized Enterprises) standard is to enable small and medium-sized enterprises worldwide to prepare high-quality, transparent, and comparable financial statements. These financial statements must meet the needs of users to help them make economic decisions while balancing benefits and costs. The IASB (International Accounting Standards Board) and the IASC (International Accounting Standards Committee) aim, through the publication of the IFRS for SMEs standard, to address the specificities of SMEs and emerging economies (IASB, 2009)

Financial information prepared in accordance with an international accounting framework should be understandable, relevant, and reliable. In addition, the provided information must be comprehensible, appropriate, and meaningful for decision-making, and it should reflect a true and fair view of the reality, financial situation, and financial performance of SMEs. Such information helps internal and external users and aids them in making appropriate decisions. Furthermore, funders need high-quality accounting information that allows them to assess the financial situation of SMEs. Therefore, financial statements prepared in accordance with IFRS for SMEs offer quality information and a clear vision of the financial performance of SMEs, which helps investors make informed decisions.

Furthermore, Financial statements are considered the primary source of financial information. Therefore, internal users such as owners, managers, and directors, as well as external users such as investors and funders, need transparent information that reflects the financial position of the

SME and assists in decision-making. As such, the transparency of financial information helps reduce information asymmetry btween various stakeholders (Masoud, 2017).

However, small and medium-sized enterprises (SMEs) are defined using quantitative criteria, such as the number of employees, annual turnover, or total assets. The International Accounting Standards Board (IASB) has adopted a different approach by offering a qualitative definition of SMEs. This definition is based on the primary users of the financial statements and the nature of the entity's operations, in order to ensure that the financial information provided meets the specific needs of these users.

Unlike many national regulations, the IASB has not established a fixed quantitative threshold to classify an entity as an SME. Although the standard was developed with an indicative threshold of approximately 50 employees in mind, each country retains the discretion to set its own quantitative criteria for defining SMEs (Obert, 2009).

According to the IASB, an SME is an entity that:

- Does not have public accountability, and
- Publishes general-purpose financial statements intended for external users, including owners who are not involved in managing the business.

An entity is deemed to have public accountability if it has issued debt or equity instruments in a public market, is in the process of issuing such instruments, or holds assets in a fiduciary capacity for a broad group of external parties—typical examples include banks, insurance companies, securities brokers, and mutual funds.

Additionally, some stakeholders have suggested that an entity may also be considered publicly accountable if it is economically significant within its national context, based on indicators such as total assets, net income, number of employees, market dominance, or the scale of its external borrowings.

2.3. Opportunities Offered by the IFRS for SMEs Standard

The adoption of the IFRS for SMEs standard offers numerous benefits for small and medium-sized enterprises. By implementing this standard, SMEs can pursue international growth, improve their accounting practices, and enhance governance structures (Ouvrard, 2010). Adopting IFRS for SMEs enables businesses to produce high-quality financial information, which increases transparency and visibility, thereby attracting foreign investors. Vilardell (2013) argued that companies presenting financial statements in accordance with international standards are more likely to encourage foreign investment.

Chamisa (2000) emphasized the critical role international accounting standards play in developing countries by attracting foreign investors who are essential for financing economic and industrial activities. According to Chamisa (2000), countries can secure foreign capital through three main channels: government aid, loans from international institutions such as the World Bank and IMF, and private foreign investments, primarily by multinational corporations.

Nobes and Parker (2006) further stressed that applying international standards is a strategic approach for developing countries, allowing them to establish robust accounting systems at a reasonable cost. Moreover, adopting IFRS for SMEs helps reduce transaction costs associated with international business expansion. These costs arise from the need to gather information that mitigates uncertainty and reduces risks linked to opportunistic behavior and limited rationality during transactions (Chourou, 2005). Transparent, reliable, and accurate financial information alleviates these transaction costs by lowering uncertainties.

Accounting information prepared under international standards functions as a network of exchanges between SMEs across global markets. Degenne and Forsé (1994) describe exchange networks as concrete, informal, and personalized links among groups of actors. Managers benefit from developing social networks that facilitate information sharing within this system (Filion, 1991).

Indeed, preparing financial statements according to national standards may hinder SMEs' internationalization and pose challenges for foreign investors. Zeghal and Mhedhbi (2010) highlighted that internationally understandable and comparable accounting information enables investors to better assess company performance globally and make informed investment decisions. Chtourou (2006) noted that such information is crucial for international development. Supporting this, Elhamma (2025) found that IFRS adoption in Sub-Saharan African countries significantly enhances the reliability, relevance, and comparability of financial reporting.

From an SME development perspective, the IFRS for SMEs standard promotes improved business management by encouraging a new approach focused on optimizing the performance of various operational processes within the enterprise (Hedfi & Sethom, 2010). As a result, SMEs are evaluated based on resource allocation efficiency.

Additionally, the IFRS for SMEs provides effective accounting rules that enable SMEs to produce high-quality financial statements, thereby improving their access to international capital markets. Adopting an accounting regulatory framework helps ensure greater recognition of the accounting function internally and facilitates communication externally, supporting business growth. The IFRS for SMEs standard allows SMEs to assess their performance using comparable and universal indicators, which enhances their ability to benchmark against other businesses.

2.4. IFRS for SME in Africa

In 2019, 17 African countries adopted the IFRS for SMEs standard. South Africa is the first country who adopt the IFRS standard for SMEs and it was on 14 August 2009. Ghana adopted this standard in 2010. In addition, other countries have voluntarily adopted the standard. Moreover, the scope of the standard is defined by the authorities of each country (figure 1). Thus, some countries have authorized the application of the standard by all SMEs.

Figure 1. Percentage of countries by adoption

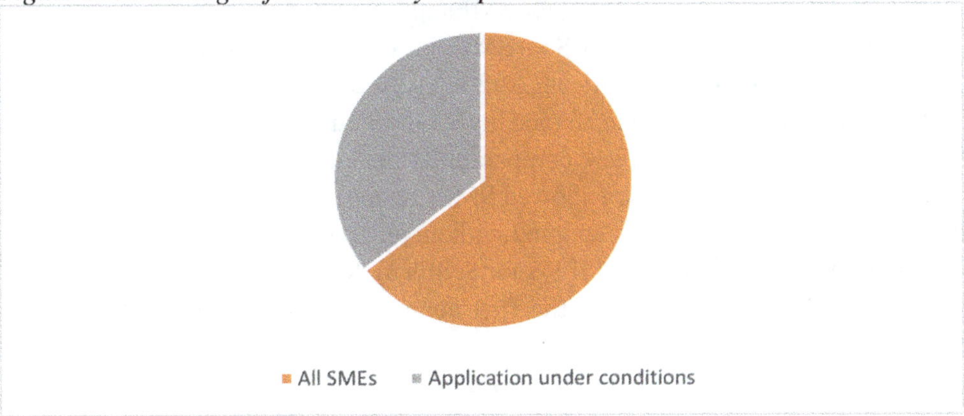

Source: IASB

While other countries have specified the characteristics entities that are authorized to apply the IFRS for SMEs standard.

It should be noted that the authorities that have authorized the application of IFRS for SMEs standard have left SMEs the choice between the IFRS for SMEs, full-IFRS and local standards. Several African countries have adopted the International Financial Reporting Standard for Small and Medium-sized Entities (IFRS for SMEs). Here's an overview:

Botswana: IFRS for SMEs is used by non-public interest entities. The implementation of this standard was supported by Botswana Institute of Chartered Accountants (BICA).

Ethiopia: The implentation of IFRS for SMEs in Ethiopian strating from 2018 for public interest entities and to SMEs from 2020. The procedure has conducted by expert in accounting.

Gambia: The Gambia considers IFRS for SMEs as the accounting standards to be used by to non-listed companies. The Gambia Institute of Chartered Accountants has managed this adoption.

Ghana: In 2010 Ghana has required the application of IFRS for SMEs to improve transparency and governance for SMEs.

Kenya: Kenya officially adopted IFRS for SMEs in 2010 ;

Lesotho: Lesotho adopted IFRS for SMEs in 2009 ;

Madagascar: Madagascar adopted IFRS for SMEs in 2010. All SMEs are authorized to apply this standard.

Malawi: Malawi adopted IFRS for SMESs in 2013

Mauritius: Mauritius adopted IFRS for SMEs in 2010 for small and medium-sized enterprises that are not publicly accountable ;

Namibia: Namibia adopted IFRS for SMEs in 2010 ;

Nigeria: Nigeria adopted IFRS for SMEs in 2014 ;

Rwanda: Rwanda adopted IFRS for SMEs in 2012 in phases starting with smaller company that do not have significant external stakeholders.

Sierra Leone: Sierra Leone aligned his local statement for SMEs with IFRS for SMEs to improve the quality and comparability of financial statements.

South Africa: South Africa allowed SMEs to apply IFRS for SMEs, starting in the 2000s. this statements was adopted without any modifications.

Tanzania: Tanzania adopted IFRS for SMEs in 2013.

Uganda: Uganda was one of the first countries in Africa to adopt IFRS for SMEs, starting in 2009.

Zambia: Zambia adopted IFRS for SMEs in 2011.

Zimbabwe: this country **adopted** IFRS for SMEs in 2010.

The following figure summarizes adoption frequency by year:

Figure 2. Number of countries by year of adoption.

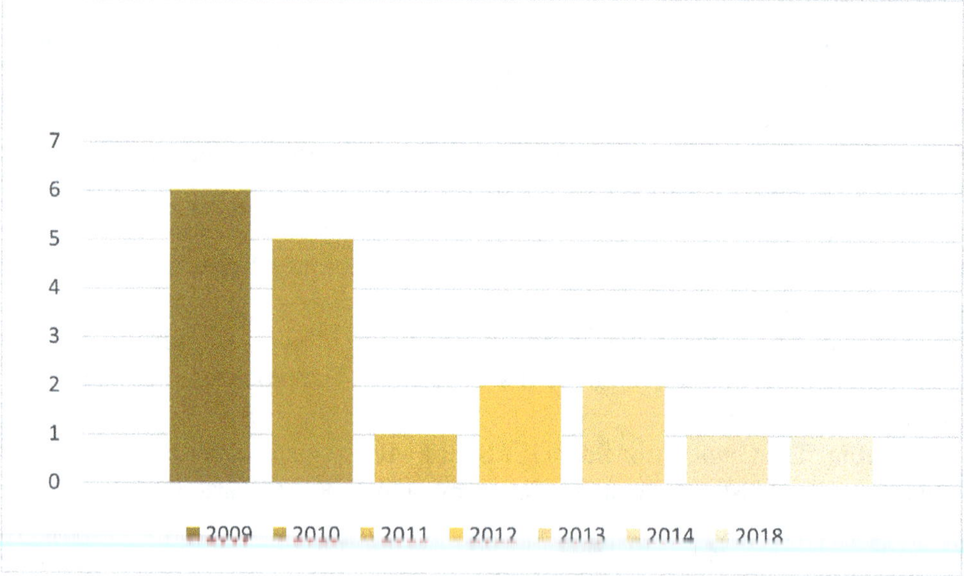

To identify the characteristics of countries adopting IFRS for SMEs, Deaconu et al. (2012) and Bohušova and Blaškova (2011) distinguished between emerging and developed countries. Emerging markets tend to be less open than developed markets, which are more accessible to foreign investors. Additionally, frontier markets often face economic and regulatory challenges that hinder their development. According to global country classifications, all countries that have mandated IFRS for SMEs adoption are emerging economies.

The primary motivation behind the IFRS for SMEs standard is to address the specific needs of SMEs in transitional and developing economies (OECD, 2004). The IASB (2009) has also highlighted the importance of considering the unique characteristics of emerging economies when developing international standards, noting that the existing accounting system can either impede or facilitate the adoption of new regulations.

3. THEORETICAL FRAMEWORK, LITERATURE REVIEW, AND FORMULATION OF HYPOTHESES

This section introduces the Diffusion of Innovation (Rogers, 1962) as the primary theoretical framework to explain the factors that drive the adoption of the International Financial Reporting Standard for Small and Medium-sized Entities (IFRS for SMEs). The diffusion of innovation theory provides a structured lens through which to analyze how, why, and at what rate new ideas and technologies—such as IFRS for SMEs—spread across organizations, sectors, or countries. The theory identifies key elements that influence adoption, including the perceived attributes of the innovation (e.g., relative advantage, compatibility, complexity, trialability, and observability), the type of innovation-decision, communication channels, the nature of the social system, and the extent of change agents' promotion efforts. In addition to this theoretical perspective, a comprehensive literature review is conducted to explore the effect's of quality of corporate governance, trading networks, tax system and institutional isomorphism on implementation of IFRS for SMEs.

3.1. Framework Theory: Diffusion Of Innovation

The IFRS for SMEs was published in 2009 and over time the number of countries has been mandatorily adopted or increased. Therefore, this standard can be considered as a new innovative product. Moreover, Rogers (1962) argues that innovation is a new idea that is available but it requires long periods to be diffused. Therefore, it needs time to be communicated between the members of a social system (Rogers, 1962).

That said, the speed and extent of the adoption of this new practice may be different from one individual/country to another (El-Helaly et al., 2020 & Rogers, 1962). Indeed, some African countries have adopted the standard as soon as it was published in 2009, such as Botswana, Kenya and Rwanda, while other countries have adopted it as desired, such as Ghana and Guatemala. In addition, some countries have adopted the IFRS for SMEs in a mandatory way (this is the case of Ghana while others have done so.

Robey (1986) distinguishes between administrative innovations and technical innovations. Administrative innovations relate to administrative and company policy changes. While, technical innovations that affect technological changes. Therefore, the implementation of a new accounting system is considered as an administrative innovation that allows to upset the accounting procedures as well as the tax policy of companies.

Therefore, it is important to study the diffusion of the adoption of IFRS in order to understand which variables can influence the decision of a country to adopt or not this specific type of accounting innovation.

3.2. Literature Review

3.2.1. Quality of Corporate Governance

Corporate governance is widely recognized as a key factor influencing the adoption of international financial reporting standards. Chen et al. (2013) argue that strong governance structures promote adherence to global standards by ensuring transparency and the reliability of financial information. Similarly, Chen and Razaee (2012), based on a study of Chinese firms, found that companies with effective governance mechanisms are more inclined to adopt full IFRS.

In line with this, Veriest (2011) highlighted that robust corporate governance practices enhance the consistent implementation of international standards. Furthermore, Ibrahim and Jaafar & El-Shawa (2009) confirmed the influence of internal and external governance systems on voluntary IFRS compliance. Their findings suggest that internal governance mechanisms play a pivotal role in driving alignment with global standards.

Goodwin et al. (2009), analyzing the Australian context, observed that companies with sound governance experience fewer forecast errors when transitioning to IFRS. Kothari (2001) further emphasized that the quality of financial disclosures is shaped not only by governance frameworks but also by the legal system and regulatory enforcement. Kabir and Hartini (2013) support this view, suggesting that governance quality reinforces financial reporting credibility and institutional trust.

> H1: Higher corporate governance quality positively influences the adoption of IFRS for SMEs in African countries.

3.2.2. Trading Networks

Network theory suggests that the decision to adopt an innovation is influenced by the interdependence between economic actors and the perceived value of standardization (Katz & Shapiro, 1985). Applying this framework to IFRS adoption, Ramanna and Sletten (2009) distinguished between the direct value of using IASB standards and the synchronization value derived from aligning with global peers.

Phuong and Nguyen (2012) illustrated how external commercial relationships can shape domestic accounting policies, noting that Vietnam adapted its standards in response to pressure from key trade partners. Similarly, Kossentini and Ben Othman (2014) demonstrated that developing economies with stronger trade ties to IFRS adopters are more likely to adopt the standards themselves. This was further supported by Shima and Yang (2012) and Ben Salem et al. (2017), who found positive correlations between international trade integration and IFRS alignment.

Other scholars, such as Zahid and Simga-Mugan (2019) and Sellami and Gafsi (2018), found that economic openness and liberalization are positively associated with IFRS for SMEs adoption. However, Zehri and Chouabi (2013) offered a more cautious view, indicating that openness alone does not guarantee standard adoption. Still, it remains clear that countries integrated into IFRS-compliant trade networks have a stronger rationale to harmonize their accounting practices for consistency and investor confidence.

> H2: The strength of a country's economic trade network positively impacts its adoption of IFRS for SMEs.

3.2.3. Tax System

In many jurisdictions, tax and accounting systems are closely interconnected (Alford et al., 1993; Ali & Hwang, 2000; Bushman & Piotroski, 2006). This overlap can create resistance to accounting reforms, particularly when they disrupt existing fiscal structures. Hail et al. (2010) note that transitioning to IFRS often incurs compliance costs due to necessary changes in tax-related accounting calculations.

Empirical evidence from emerging economies shows that this tax-accounting alignment may hinder IFRS adoption. Studies by Rodrigues et al. (2012), Phuong and Nguyen (2012), and Albu et al. (2011) revealed that where taxation heavily relies on accounting outputs, governments are less inclined to shift to IFRS. In Tunisia, for instance, Trabelsi (2010) found the tax system to be a barrier to IFRS implementation due to its rigid dependence on traditional accounting rules.

Kossentini and Ben Othman (2014) supported this by showing that tax-driven economies are less open to new accounting standards. Shima and Yang (2012), as well as Ramanna and Sletten (2009), further concluded that regulatory environments anchored in tax systems often discourage IFRS transitions. Kaya and Koch (2015) added that higher tax revenues—indicative of a stable fiscal base—reduce the perceived need for reform. Sellami and Gafsi (2018) also stressed that tax-related administrative burdens and political costs can impede IFRS for SMEs adoption.

Nonetheless, Bonito and Pais (2018) reported no significant correlation between tax-accounting linkage and IFRS for SMEs uptake. Despite this, the general trend suggests that countries with tightly integrated tax and accounting regimes may be less receptive to global accounting reforms.

> H3: A country's tax system has a negative influence on its likelihood of adopting IFRS for SMEs.

3.2.4. Institutional Isomorphism

Institutional isomorphism, a core concept in sociological institutionalism, refers to the tendency of organizations to become similar when exposed to similar environmental pressures (DiMaggio & Powell, 1983). It helps explain how and why organizations conform to shared norms, practices, or regulations over time. According to Trabelsi (2013), isomorphic pressures influence the standardization of organizational behavior within a given field.

DiMaggio and Powell (1983) differentiate between **competitive isomorphism**, driven by market dynamics, and **institutional isomorphism**, shaped by non-market pressures. Their framework identifies three types of institutional pressures:

- **Coercive isomorphism**, resulting from political or regulatory mandates ;
- **Mimetic isomorphism**, stemming from the tendency to imitate successful peers;
- **Normative isomorphism**, influenced by professional standards and educational systems.

In the context of IFRS for SMEs, external institutional actors such as international financial institutions, trade partners, and global standard-setters can exert coercive or normative influence. Elhamma (2023) highlighted factors such as external financial aid conditions, the openness of an economy, and the competence of accounting professionals as key drivers of compliance.

These institutional pressures lead countries to adopt similar standards not just for efficiency, but to gain legitimacy within the global financial system.

H4: Coercive isomorphism positively affects the adoption of IFRS for SMEs in African countries.
H5: Mimetic isomorphism has a positive effect on IFRS for SMEs adoption in African countries.
H6: Normative isomorphism positively influences the adoption of IFRS for SMEs in African countries.

4. METHODOLOGY

In this section, we begin by describing the research sample. Next, we provide a detailed explanation of the measurement and operationalization of key variables, including governance quality, the tax system, economic exchanges, and institutional isomorphism. Then, we introduce the panel logistic regression model employed to analyze the determinants of IFRS for SMEs adoption. Finally, we present and interpret the results of the empirical analysis.

4.1 Sample

This research draws upon a final sample of 42 African countries. Of these, 17 have either allowed or mandated the use of the IFRS for SMEs framework, while the remaining 25 have not adopted the standard (see Table I). Notably, Ghana stands out as the only country in the sample to have made IFRS for SMEs adoption compulsory. The analysis spans a seven-year period, from 2009 to 2015, with data on country-level variables sourced from the World Bank's publicly available datasets.

Table 1. African countries of our sample

Countries		
Adoption	**Non Adoption**	
BOTSWANA	**ALGERIA**	**MOZAMBIQUE**
GAMBIA. THE	BENIN	SENEGAL
GHANA	BURKINA FASO	SEYCHELLES
KENYA	CENTRAL AFRICAN REPUBLIC	SOMALIA
LESOTHO	CHAD	SOUTH SUDAN
MADAGASCAR	CONGO. DEM. REP.	SUDAN
MALAWI	CONGO. REP.	TOGO
MAURITIUS	CÔTE D'IVOIRE	TUNISIA

continued on following page

Table 1. Continued

Countries		
Adoption	**Non Adoption**	
BOTSWANA	**ALGERIA**	**MOZAMBIQUE**
NAMIBIA	ERITREA DJIBOUTI	
NIGERIA	ERITREA	
RWANDA	GABON	
SIERRA LEONE	LIBERIA	
SOUTH AFRICA	LIBYA	
TANZANIA	ETHIOPIA	
UGANDA	MALI	
ZAMBIA	MAURITANIA	
ZIMBABWE	MOROCCO	

Source: World Bank website World Bank Open Data I Data

4.2 Measurement of Variables And Data Collection

4.2.1 Dependent Variables

To construct the dependent variable, countries that implemented the IFRS for SMEs standard between 2010 and 2015 were assigned a value of 1, indicating adoption. Conversely, countries that did not adopt the standard during this period were coded as 0. Information regarding adoption status was obtained from authoritative sources, including the IFRS Foundation website (www.ifrs.org) and the IAS Plus portal maintained by Deloitte (IASB, 2016; Deloitte & Touche, 2016).

4.2.2 Independent Variables

To investigate the factors influencing IFRS for SMEs adoption, several explanatory variables were constructed:

- **Governance Quality (GOV):** Governance performance was assessed using the composite average of six key indicators introduced by Kaufmann et al. (2007) and previously utilized by Kaya and Koch (2015). These include regulatory quality, rule of law, control of corruption, government effectiveness, political stability, and voice and accountability. Data were retrieved from the World Bank's Worldwide Governance Indicators (WGI) database (World Bank, 2016).

- **Trading Networks (NETWORK):** This variable measures the extent of a country's trade with other nations that have already adopted IFRS for SMEs. It captures the influence of economic integration and international trade partnerships on standard adoption, based on the framework proposed by Ramanna and Sletten (2009, 2010). Data were sourced from the CIA World Factbook (www.cia.gov).
- **Tax System (TAXATION):** To approximate the relationship between tax dependence and accounting standards, the study uses tax revenue as a percentage of GDP. This proxy reflects the degree of fiscal reliance on existing accounting structures, in line with Kaya and Koch (2015).
- **Coercive Isomorphism (COERCIVE):** Coercive pressures are proxied by the volume of foreign aid received by a country, as international financial institutions may condition support on the implementation of global standards (Judge et al., 2010; Ritsumeikan, 2011).
- **Mimetic Isomorphism (MIMETIC):** This construct captures the influence of economic openness by measuring the share of direct imports of goods and services as a percentage of GDP. Higher levels imply stronger exposure to international norms and practices.
- **Normative Isomorphism (NORMATIVE):** Educational attainment and professional norms contribute to normative pressures. Literacy rate serves as a proxy, reflecting the capacity of a country's institutional environment to absorb international standards (Hassan, 2008; Bonito & Pais, 2018; Shima & Yang, 2012).
- **Country Size (SIZE):** Rather than geographical size, the variable refers to the number of SMEs within a country, reflecting the potential scope of IFRS for SMEs application. Data were drawn from the World Bank's World Development Indicators (2016b).

4.3 The Econometric Model Of Logistic Regression

Some African countries have chosen to apply IFRS for SMEs while others they didn't. To Study determinates of IFRS for SMEs adoption of African countries, we use a Panel logistic regression model:

$$ADOPTION_{it} = \beta_1 QUGOV_{it} + \beta_2 NETWORK_{it} + \beta_3 TAXATION_{it} + \beta_4 COERCIVEit + \beta_5 MIMETIC_{it} + \beta_6 NORMATIVE_{it} + \beta_7 SIZE_{it} + \varepsilon_{it}$$

ADOPTIONit = Adoption of IFRS for SMEs by country;

QUGOVit = Governance quality;

NETWORKit= Trading networks;

TAXATIONit = Tax revenue as a percentage of GDP;

COERCIVEit = Coercive isomorphism;

MIMETICit = Mimetic isomorphism;

NORMATIVEit = Normative isomorphism;

SIZEit = Country size;

α = Constant;

β = Coefficient vector;

ε: Error term.

5. RESULTS AND DISCUSSION

This section begins with a presentation of the descriptive statistics, offering an overview of the key characteristics of the dataset used in the analysis. These statistics provide insights into the distribution, central tendencies, and variability of the variables considered, including governance quality, trade intensity, tax revenue, institutional isomorphism dimensions, and SME size. Understanding these baseline features is essential for interpreting the subsequent econometric findings.

Following the descriptive analysis, we report the results of the binary logistic regression model, which serves to empirically assess the determinants of IFRS for SMEs adoption across African countries. The dependent variable is dichotomous, capturing whether or not a country adopted the IFRS for SMEs standard during the period under study. The regression analysis allows us to examine the individual and combined effects of governance quality, trading networks, taxation, coercive pressures, mimetic tendencies, normative influences, and country size on the likelihood of adoption.

5.1 Descriptive Statistics

Tables II and III present the descriptive statistics of our study. These tables show that, on average, 33.67% of the countries in our sample were coded 1 (indicating adoption of IFRS for SMEs) over the seven-year period. The average governance quality index is -0.652, reflecting generally low governance quality in African countries. This index ranges from a minimum of -2.41 to a maximum of 0.852. The trade network variable (NETWORK) averages 23.2%, representing the percentage of trade with IFRS-adopting partners. The average total tax rate is 52.078%, with the lowest recorded at 13.6% and the highest in Congo at 339.1%.

Table 2. Descriptive statistics results of our study

	Mean	SD	MIN	MAX
GOV	-0,652	0,644	-2,41	0,852
NETWORK	0,232	0,211	0	80%
TAXATION	52,62	52,078	13,6	339,1
CORECIVE	9,801	9,126	0,085	55,252
MIMETIC	46,948	23,686	12,074	147,146
NORMATIVE	67,301	18,21	31,099	97,812
SIZE	88755	230344	726	1376000

Table 3. Descriptive statistics results continued.

ADOPTION	Frequency	%
0	195	66,33
1	99	33,67
Total	294	100

Source: Statistical Results

5.2 Correlation Test

Table IV of Pearson correlation matrix reveals that there is no problem of significant correlation between variables. Therefore, we conclude the inexistence of multi-collinearity between the independent variables (Groebner et al.,2011).

Table 4. Pearson correlation matrix

	ADOPTION	GOV	NETWORK	TAXATION	CORECIVE	MIMETIC	NORMATIVE	SIZE
ADOPTION	1	0.3946	-0.0115	-0.0846	-0.0645	0.0064	0.3269	-0.0846
GOV	0.3946	1	-0.0872	-0.2277	-0.1805	0.1811	0.3761	0.0877
NETWORK	0.1831	-0.0872	1	-0.1933	0.1528	-0.1817	-0.0129	-0,0115
TAXATION	-0.0846	-0.2277	-0.1933	1	0.0653	-0.1338	-0 .1551	0 .0221
CORECIVE	-0.0645	-0.1805	0.1528	0.0653	1	-0.2960	-0.2025	0.2239
MIMETIC	0.0064	0.1811	-0.1817	-0.1338	-0.2960	1	0.1338	-0.2847
NORMATIVE	0.3269	0.3761	-0.0129	-0.1551	-0.2025	0.1338	1	0.0866
SIZE	-0.0824	-0.1901	-0.0115	0.0221	0.2239	-0.2847	0.0866	1

Source: Statistical Results

5.3 Panel analysis: the results of randomized logistic regression

Table V summarizes the outcomes of the logistic regression analysis, revealing that governance quality (GOV) has a statistically significant and positive association with IFRS for SMEs adoption. This supports earlier findings, such as those of Kothari (2001), who argued that robust governance frameworks promote adherence to international accounting standards. Furthermore, the introduction of IFRS for SMEs may serve as a catalyst for strengthening internal governance within small and medium-sized enterprises. According to Hoarau and Teller (2007), IFRS adoption can function as a governance instrument, while Raffournier (2009) described a reinforcing relationship wherein IFRS implementation enhances managerial oversight by limiting financial manipulation and increasing the reliability of financial data. This dynamic ultimately contributes to greater investor protection and improved governance through mechanisms such as performance-based accountability.

The results also demonstrate that trading networks (NETWORK) play a significant role in shaping adoption behavior. Countries with stronger trade ties to IFRS-adopting partners are more likely to implement the standard themselves. This finding echoes previous studies by Chua et al (2006) and Kossentini and Ben Othman (2014), who noted that harmonized accounting systems facilitate international trade and investment. As highlighted by Ramangalahy (2001), the use of standardized reporting frameworks improves transparency and reduces transaction costs, making cross-border investments more accessible and attractive.

In contrast, the variables representing tax system (TAXATION) and coercive isomorphism (COERCIVE) were not found to have a statistically significant impact on the likelihood of adoption. This suggests that, in the African context, neither fiscal dependence on taxation nor conditionalities imposed by external donors appear to exert meaningful influence on IFRS for SMEs adoption decisions.

Table 5. Result of our logistic regression

Variables	**Coefficient (z-statistics)**	**Sig.**
NETWORK	6.837	**0.014****
TAX	1.001	0.723
QUGOV	5.659	0.000***
COERC	-0.981	0.221
MIMET	-0.982	**0.019****
NORM	1.013	**0.017****
SME	-0.999	0.617
Log-likelihood	**-152.450**	
Wal Chi-2	**81.65**	
	(0,0000)***	
OBS	**294**	

Source: Statistical Results

The regression results presented in Table V indicate that mimetic isomorphism (MIMETIC) exerts a statistically significant negative effect on the adoption of IFRS for SMEs. This finding implies that higher levels of economic openness—typically associated with imitation of international practices—do not necessarily translate into greater uptake of IFRS for SMEs (Ritsumeikan, 2011). While previous research, such as Dumontier and Raffournier (1998), suggested that export-oriented economies are more inclined to adopt IFRS due to their need for financial statement comparability and transparency, this may not hold true for the SME sector. In many African countries, SMEs are minimally engaged in export activities, often contributing less than 10% of total national exports. Consequently, their exposure to international financial reporting demands remains limited. Elhamma (2024) also found that although IFRS adoption is more prevalent in highly open MENA economies, this openness does not always extend to the SME segment.

In contrast, normative isomorphism (NORM) shows a positive and significant relationship with IFRS for SMEs adoption. This suggests that professional and educational influences—such as those exerted by universities, accounting bodies, and training institutions—encourage the adoption of international standards. As observed by Sellami and Gafsi (2018), academic and institutional actors often advocate for globally recognized reporting frameworks, contributing to their diffusion across developing economies.

The role of external auditors is also highlighted in this context. As Dumontier and Raffournier (1998) and Hodgdon et al. (2009) emphasized, audit professionals help promote convergence with international norms by influencing accounting practices. While audits are typically not mandatory for SMEs, studies by Murphy (1999), Guerrerio et al. (2008), and Kilic et al. (2016) show that firms that voluntarily engage audit services are more likely to adopt IFRS for SMEs, due to increased exposure to professional guidance and compliance expectations.

6. CONCLUSION

This study explored the institutional and economic determinants influencing the adoption of the International Financial Reporting Standard for Small and Medium-sized Entities (IFRS for SMEs) across a sample of 42 African countries over the 2009–2015 period. Specifically, it examined how governance quality, trade integration, tax policy, and institutional isomorphism (coercive, mimetic, and normative pressures) affect national decisions to adopt this international standard.

The empirical findings reveal that governance quality, economic trading networks, and normative isomorphism have a positive and statistically significant impact on the adoption of IFRS for SMEs. These results suggest that countries with well-functioning governance structures, strong trade ties to IFRS-compliant nations, and influential educational and professional accounting structures are more inclined to embrace international standards. These environments foster conditions of transparency, institutional learning, and professional alignment that are conducive to reform.

In contrast, mimetic isomorphism—often associated with economic openness and imitation of global trends—was found to have a negative effect on adoption. This counterintuitive result implies that openness to global trade does not automatically lead to regulatory convergence in the SME sector. In fact, countries with higher levels of economic openness may prioritize more flexible or customized frameworks rather than fully aligning with global templates like IFRS for SMEs. Moreover, tax systems and coercive pressures, including foreign aid conditionality, were not found to exert a significant influence, indicating that fiscal constraints and external institutional demands are not primary drivers of adoption in this context.

These insights contribute meaningful implications for policymakers, regulatory authorities, and stakeholders involved in SME financial management. By identifying the key institutional levers that support IFRS for SMEs implementation, this research offers practical guidance for improving financial transparency, expanding access to capital, and fostering investor confidence in the African SME sector. Strengthening governance systems, developing professional accounting education, and reinforcing trade-related regulatory cooperation may be critical pathways toward broader adoption.

Despite its contributions, this study acknowledges several limitations. First, it does not include all African countries due to the lack of comprehensive or reliable data for some nations. Second, the range of explanatory variables, though grounded in theory, may not capture the full complexity of factors influencing standard adoption—such as cultural norms, political economy considerations, or legal infrastructure. Future studies could broaden the analytical scope by incorporating additional dimensions, including firm-level characteristics, sectoral dynamics, or qualitative institutional assessments.

Furthermore, future research would benefit from differentiating between non-adopters, voluntary adopters, and mandatory adopters of IFRS for SMEs. This typology could provide deeper insight into the nature and intensity of institutional commitment to international standards, offering a more nuanced understanding of adoption patterns and policy impacts across the African continent.

REFERENCES

African Business. (2022, April 5). *Unlocking SME potential through the power of emerging technology*. African Business. https://african.business/2022/04/technology-information/unlocking-sme-potential-through-the-power-of-emerging-technology

Albu, N., & Albu, C. N. (2014). Strategies for and implications of the IFRS for SMEs implementation in emerging economies. *Comptabilités et innovations*, Grenoble, France.

Alford, A., Jones, J., Leftwich, R., & Zmijewski, M. (1993). The relative informativeness of accounting disclosures in different countries. *Journal of Accounting Research, 31*, 183-223.Ben Salem, R., Damak-Ayadi, S., & Saïhi, M. (2017). Determinants of full IFRS adoption. *International Journal of Managerial and Financial Accounting*, *9*(2), 105–123.

Ali, A., & Hwang, L.-S. (2000). Country-specific factors related to financial reporting and the value relevance of accounting data. *Journal of Accounting Research, 38*(1), 1–21. DOI: 10.2307/2672920

Bonito, A., & Pais, C. (2018). The macroeconomic determinants of the adoption of IFRS for SMEs. *Revista de Contabilidad, 21*(2), 116–127. DOI: 10.1016/j.rcsar.2018.03.001

Bushman, R. M., & Piotroski, J. D. (2006). Financial reporting incentives for conservative accounting: The influence of legal and political institutions. *Journal of Accounting and Economics, 42*(1–2), 107–148. DOI: 10.1016/j.jacceco.2005.10.005

Callao, S., Jarne, J. I., & Laínez, J. A. (2007). Adoption of IFRS in Spain: Effect on the comparability and relevance of financial reporting. *Journal of International Accounting, Auditing & Taxation, 16*(2), 148–178. DOI: 10.1016/j.intaccaudtax.2007.06.002

Center for strategic and international studies. (2021). Supporting Small and Medium Enterprises in Sub-Saharan Africa through Blended Finance. Daniel F. Runde, Conor M. Savoy, and Janina Staguhn.

Chamisa, E. E. (2000). The relevance and observance of the IASC standards in developing countries and the particular case of Zimbabwe. *The International Journal of Accounting, 35*(2), 267–286. DOI: 10.1016/S0020-7063(00)00049-2

Chen, C., Young, D., & Zhuang, Z. (2013). Externalities of mandatory IFRS adoption: Evidence from cross-border spillover effects of financial information on investment efficiency. *The Accounting Review, 88*(3), 881–914. DOI: 10.2308/accr-50384

Chen, Y., & Rezaee, Z. (2012). The role of corporate governance in convergence with IFRS: Evidence from China. *International Journal of Accounting & Information Management.*

Chourou, B. (2005). *Promoting human security: Ethical, normative and educational frameworks in the Arab states.* UNESCO.

Chtourou, W. (2006). Le développement international des PME. *Gestion, 31*(1), 88–97. DOI: 10.3917/riges.311.0088

Chua, J. H., Steier, L. P., & Chrisman, J. J. (2006). How family firms solve intra-family agency problems using interlocking directorates: An extension. *Entrepreneurship Theory and Practice, 30*(6), 777–783. DOI: 10.1111/j.1540-6520.2006.00150.x

Deaconu, A., Buiga, A., & Strouhal, J. (2012). SMEs financial reporting: Attitudes towards IFRS for SMEs. *Studia Universitatis Babe -Bolyai, Oeconomica, 57*(1).

Degenne, A., & Forsé, M. (1994). *Social networks: A structural analysis in sociology* (U series, Sociology). Paris: Armand Colin.

DiMaggio, P. J., & Powell, W. W. (1983). The iron cage revisited: Institutional isomorphism and collective rationality in organizational fields. *American Sociological Review, 48*(2), 147–160. DOI: 10.2307/2095101

Dumontier, P., & Raffournier, B. (1998). Why firms comply voluntarily with IAS: An empirical analysis with Swiss data. *Journal of International Financial Management & Accounting, 9*(3), 216–245. DOI: 10.1111/1467-646X.00038

El-Helaly, M., Ntim, C., & Al-Gazzar, M. (2020). Diffusion theory, national corruption and IFRS adoption around the world. *Journal of International Accounting, Auditing and Taxation, 38*, 100305. Harvard Business School, available at: *SSRN*: https://ssrn.com/abstract=1590245. https://doi.org/DOI: 10.2139/ssrn.1590245

Elhamma, A. (2023). Cinquante ans des normes comptables internationales IAS/IFRS: Adoption, conséquences et où en est-on au Maroc? In R. M'Rabet & M. A. Issami (Eds.), *50 ans de management: Regards croisés d'un demi-siècle du management* (pp. 121–136). Éditions EDISCA.

Elhamma, A. (2024). Determinants of national IFRS adoption: Evidence from the Middle East and North Africa region. *International Journal of Accounting. Auditing and Performance Evaluation, 20*(1-2), 69–90. DOI: 10.1504/IJAAPE.2024.135535

Elhamma, A. (2025). Perceived benefits of IFRS adoption in Morocco and French-speaking Sub-Saharan African countries. In F. Albuquerque & P. G. Dos Santos (Eds.), *Contemporary innovations in reporting and analysis* (pp. 183–210). IGI Global. https://doi.org/DOI: 10.4018/979-8-3693-5923-5.ch007

Ernst & Young. (2016). Accounting System of Enterprises and IFRS Standards for SMEs – Comparative Study, EY Tunisia Financial Reporting Group, 2016 Edition.

Filion, L. J. (1991). Vision and relations: Elements for an entrepreneurial metamodel. *International Small Business Journal*, *9*(2), 26–42. DOI: 10.1177/026624269100900202

Goodwin, J., Ahmed, K., & Heaney, R. (2009). The effects of IFRS adoption and the influence of agency costs on earnings management: Evidence from Australia. *Journal of Contemporary Accounting & Economics*, *5*(2), 1–17. DOI: 10.1016/j.jcae.2009.08.001

Groebner, D. F., Shannon, P. W., Fry, P. C., & Smith, K. D. (2011). *Business Statistics: A Decision-Making Approach*. Prentice Hall/Pearson.

Hail, L., Leuz, C., & Wysocki, P. D. (2010). Global accounting convergence and the potential adoption of IFRS by the U.S. (Part I): Conceptual underpinnings and economic analysis. *Accounting Horizons*, *24*(3), 355–394. DOI: 10.2308/acch.2010.24.3.355

Hassan, M. K. (2008). The development of accounting regulations in Egypt: Legitimating the International Accounting Standards. *Managerial Auditing Journal*, *23*(5), 467–484. DOI: 10.1108/02686900810875299

Hedfi, M. R., & Sethom, K. (2010). *Norme IFRS pour PME: Présentation et étude d'opportunité pour la Tunisie*.

Hoarau, C., & Teller, R. (2007). IFRS: Les normes comptables du nouvel ordre économique global? *Comptabilité-Contrôle-Audit*, *13*(3), 3–20. DOI: 10.3917/cca.133.0003

Hodgdon, C., Tondkar, R. H., Adhikari, A., & Harless, D. W. (2009). Compliance with International Financial Reporting Standards and auditor choice: New evidence on the importance of the statutory audit. *The International Journal of Accounting*, *44*(1), 33–55. DOI: 10.1016/j.intacc.2008.12.003

International Accounting Standards Board. (2009). Basis of des conclusions. Available at: https://www.ifrs.org/use-around-the-world/use-of-ifrs-standards-by-jurisdiction (Accessed in 2022).

International Accounting Standards Board. (2022). International financial reporting standards for SMEs jurisdiction. Available at: https://www.ifrs.org/use-around-the-world/use-of-ifrs-standards-by-jurisdiction (Accessed in 2022).

Jaafar, A., & El-Shawa, M. (2009). Ownership concentration, board characteristics and performance: Evidence from Jordan. In Tsamenyi, M., & Uddin, S. (Eds.), *Accounting in Emerging Economies* (Vol. 9, pp. 73–95). Emerald Group Publishing Limited., DOI: 10.1108/S1479-3563(2009)0000009005

Judge, W., Li, S., & Pinsker, R. (2010). National adoption of international accounting standards: An institutional perspective. Corporate Gouvernance. *International Review (Steubenville, Ohio)*, *18*(3), 161–174.

Kabir, I., & Hartini, J. (2013). Corporate governance and disclosure on segment reporting: Evidence from Nigeria. In *Global Business and Finance Research Conference, 5*(2), 98-113.

Katz, M. L., & Shapiro, C. (1985). Network externalities, competition, and compatibility. *The American Economic Review*, *75*, 424–440.

Kaufmann, D., Kraay, A., & Mastruzzi, M. (2007). *Worldwide Governance Indicators 2006*. World Bank.

Kaya, M., & Koch, D. (2015). Countries' adoption of the International Financial Reporting Standard for Small and Medium-sized Entities (IFRS for SMEs) – Early empirical evidence. *Accounting and Business Research*, *45*(1), 93–120. DOI: 10.1080/00014788.2014.969188

Kiliç, M., Uyar, A., & Ataman, B. (2016). Preparedness of the entities for the IFRS for SMEs: An emerging country case. *Journal of Accounting in Emerging Economies*, *6*(2), 156–1. DOI: 10.1108/JAEE-01-2014-0003

Kossentini, A., & Ben Othman, H. (2014). A study of the institutional and economic determinants of IFRS adoption in emerging economies. *Business Illinois*. Available at: https://business.illinois.edu

Kothari, C. R. (2001). *Research methodology: Methods and techniques* (2nd rev. ed.). New Age International Publishers.

Masoud, N. (2017). The effects of mandatory IFRS adoption on financial analysts' forecast: Evidence from Jordan. *Cogent Business & Management*, *4*(1), 1–18. DOI: 10.1080/23311975.2017.1290331

Mhedhbi, Z., & Essid, A. (2022). National cultural dimensions and adoption of the International Financial Reporting Standard (IFRS) for Small and Medium-sized Entities (SMEs). *The International Journal of Accounting*, *57*(1), 2250004. DOI: 10.1142/S1094406022500044

Murphy, K. J. (1999). Executive compensation. Handbook of labor economics, 3, 2485-2563.

Nobes, C., & Parker, R. (2006). *Comparative international accounting* (9th ed.). Prentice Hall.

Obert, R. (2009). Des IFRS pour les PME. Revue Française de Comptabilité, 424.

Ouvrard, S. (2010). *IFRS for SMEs*. 17th IAE–Chartered Accountants Conference, Toulouse.

Phuong, N. C., & Nguyen, T. D. (2012). International harmonization and national particularities of accounting: Recent accounting development in Vietnam. *Journal of Accounting and Organizational Change*, *8*(3), 431–451. DOI: 10.1108/18325911211258371

Raffournier, B. (2009). IFRS et gouvernance d'entreprise: un cercle vertueux ? ». DerSchweizerTreuhänder = L'expert-comptable suisse, 11, 802-809.

Ramangalahy, C. (2001). Capacité d'absorption de l'information, compétitivité et performance des PME exportatrices: Une étude empirique (Absorptive capacity of information, competitiveness, and exporting SMEs' performance: Empirical study). Doctoral dissertation, University of Montréal, Montréal.

Ramanna, K., & Sletten, E. (2010). Network effects in countries' adoption of IFRS. *Working paper, Harvard Business School*. Available at: *SSRN*: https://ssrn.com/abstract=1590245. DOI: 10.2139/ssrn.1590245

Ritsumeikan, L. (2011). An institutional perspective on international financial reportingstandards adoption in developing countries. *Academy of Accounting and Financial Studies Journal*, *15*(2), 61–71.

Robey, D. (1986). Evaluating the organizational impact of computer-based information systems. *Accounting Management and Information Technologies*, *1*(1), 3–15. DOI: 10.1016/0959-8022(86)90005-6

Rodrigues, L. L., Schmidt, P., & dos Santos, J. L. (2012). The origins of modern accounting in Brazil: Influences leading to the adoption of IFRS. *Research in Accounting Regulation*, *24*(1), 15–24. DOI: 10.1016/j.racreg.2011.12.003

Rogers, E. M. (1962). *Diffusion of Innovations*. Free Press.

Sellami, Y. M., & Gafsi, Y. (2018). What drives developing and transitional countries to adopt the IFRS for SMEs? An institutional perspective. *Journal of Corporate Accounting & Finance*, *29*(2), 34–56. DOI: 10.1002/jcaf.22331

Shima, K. M., & Yang, D. C. (2012). Factors affecting the adoption of IFRS. *International Journal of Business*, *17*(3), 276–298.

Trabelsi, R. (2013). Vers un dispositif d'appréciation de la pertinence des IFRS dans un contexte pré-implémentation. *International Journal of Innovation and Applied Studies*, *3*(3), 626–650.

Veriest, A. (2011). *IFRS for SMEs: Evolution and challenges.*

Vilardell, I. (2013). *The Spanish accounting plan for SMEs and the IFRS for SMEs.* DRM/CREFIGE, University of Paris-Dauphine.

World Bank. (2016). *Governance index.* Retrieved June 23, 2016, from http://info.worldbank.org/governance/wgi/index.asp

Zahid, R. M. A., & Simga-Mugan, C. (2019). An analysis of IFRS and SME-IFRS adoption determinants: A worldwide study. *Emerging Markets Finance & Trade*, *55*(2), 391–408. DOI: 10.1080/1540496X.2018.1500890

Zehri, F., & Chouabi, J. (2013). Adoption determinants of the international accounting standards IAS/IFRS by developing countries. *Journal of Economics, Finance and Administrative Science*, *18*(35), 56–62. DOI: 10.1016/S2077-1886(13)70030-1

KEY WORDS AND DEFINITIONS

IFRS for SMEs (International Financial Reporting Standards for Small and Medium-sized Entities): A simplified version of accounting standards published by the International Accounting Standards Board (IASB) that is designed to meet the needs and capabilities of small and medium-sized entities that do not have public accountability;

Adoption: The governmental or organizational uptake and implementation of a new system, regulation, or standard by an organization, government, or state;

African countries: States on the African continent;

SMEs (Small and Medium-sized Enterprises): Firms whose numbers of employees, revenues, or assets fall below certain levels established by regulatory bodies; they are usually smaller in scale than large corporations and face distinctive economic, legal, and operational issues;

Determinants: Variables or factors that have a causal influence on some result or phenomenon; in empirical research, determinants are independent variables used to explain variations in a dependent variable;

Institutional Isomorphism: A concept in institutional theory explaining why and how organizations within a specific industry begin to look like each other over time, driven by coercive, mimetic, and normative pressures;

Quality of Corporate Governance: The extent to which corporate policies, structures, and practices ensure accountability, equity, and transparency in a company's interactions with its stakeholders, including shareholders, employees, customers, and regulators;

Trading Networks: Organized systems of exchange among firms or countries in the form of goods, service, capital, and information flow, often analyzed in economic sociology and international trade theory;

Tax System: The legal and administrative framework within which a government levies and collects revenue from individuals and organizations, along with institutions for assessing, collecting, and enforcing taxes;

Panel Logistic Regression Model: A statistical technique used to model binary (yes/no) responses in statistical panel data, which consists of multiple observations over time for the same units (e.g., countries, firms). It accounts for individual-specific effects that may influence the dependent variable.

Chapter 5
The Impact of Firm Characteristics on Voluntary IFRS Adoption:
An Empirical Analysis in an Emerging Country

Soumaya Outellou
https://orcid.org/0000-0002-9323-2921
Higher Institute of Nursing Professions and Health Techniques, Rabat, Morocco

Noureddine Abdelbaki
National School of Commerce and Management, Kenitra, Morocco

Omar Taouab
National School of Commerce and Management, Kenitra, Morocco

ABSTRACT

In light of the transformations resulting from globalization, the Moroccan economy is now characterized by greater international openness. In this regard, Moroccan companies must ensure transparent and comprehensive financial reporting to improve their competitiveness and attract international investors. This chapter aims to identify the key factors influencing the adoption of IFRS by Moroccan companies. This choice is justified by the scarcity of studies analyzing the determinants of this adoption, particularly in the specific context of Morocco. Thus, this study is grounded in a thorough examination of previous research, followed by an empirical study consisting of a survey of 82 companies operating in various economic sectors

DOI: 10.4018/979-8-3373-1902-5.ch005

and different regions of the Kingdom of Morocco. The results reveal that company size is the only significant contingent factor favoring the adoption of IFRS. In other words, larger companies appear more likely to adopt these international standards.

INTRODUCTION

During the 20th century, the world experienced several events in terms of world wars, debt economy and financial scandals, the most widespread of which are the Wall Street crash of 1929 and the two financial scandals of the American companies Enron and WorldCom. Faced with these circumstances, the world found itself obliged to create several international organizations in order to achieve objectives in different areas:

- **Security domain**: Characterized by the creation of the UN in 1945, whose objective is to ensure international peace and economic and social development at the level of different countries;
- **Monetary domain**: After the two world wars, the world suffered from a certain monetary instability and a collapse of international economic relations, hence the obligation to set up a consistent and stable monetary system. Indeed, the Bretton-Woods agreements of 1945 gave birth to two organizations, namely the International Monetary Fund (IMF) and the International Bank for Reconstruction and Development (IBRD) (now known as the World Bank), whose main vocation is to achieve macroeconomic and financial stability, and to preserve solid economies;
- **Commercial domain**: There was the creation of the GATT body (General Agreement on Tariffs and Trade), in order to harmonize and order international trade in goods;
- **Accounting and financial field**: The majority of countries around the world, especially those classified as emerging economies, needed to create a set of international accounting standards that can be used by different companies, while allowing them to open up internationally and be competitive, and thus facilitating economic decision-making by all users of financial information. We are talking about the creation of two accounting standardization bodies, namely the IASC (International Accounting Standards Committee) in Europe, which will be replaced by the IASB (International Accounting Standards Board), and the FASB (Financial Accounting Standards Board) in the United States of America. These two bodies were then able to give birth to the two accounting frameworks US-GAAP (United States Generally

Accepted Accounting Principles) for the United States and IFRS (International Financial Reporting Standards) for Europe.

Indeed, these latest norms were applied in a mandatory manner by the EU in 2005 for all listed companies. Thus, the recognized effectiveness of these standards has encouraged several companies from countries around the world, other than those of the European Union, to adopt this international standard, as is the case in Morocco.

In this way, some Moroccan companies are required to prepare their consolidated financial statements in accordance with IFRS standards, in particular credit institutions. In addition, there are other companies that adopt these standards early, in order to contribute to the enhancement of international competitiveness.

The objective of this chapter is to determine the key factors influencing the adoption of IFRS standards by Moroccan companies. For this purpose, an empirical study was conducted among 100 companies, with a response rate of 82%. Thus, the study relied on the development of a carefully designed questionnaire to collect accurate and relevant data from the companies concerned. This questionnaire was constructed taking into account the research hypotheses formulated from a literature review. Furthermore, the importance of this chapter lies in the fact that it deals with a topic that has been little studied, particularly in the Moroccan context.

In this context, it appears essential to raise several key questions in order to address the issue of IFRS adoption, namely:

- How did these accounting and financial standards appear?
- How can these international accounting standards be defined?
- What are the advantages presented by these standards?
- What are the determinants of the adoption of IFRS standards by Moroccan companies?

The responses of these questions will be organized into four sections: The first section will present the historical background to IFRS standards and define the main concepts associated with them; the second outlines the methodology and explains the importance of the study; the third presents the findings and the final section offers a discussion of the results.

1. LITERATURE REVIEW

The main objective of each company is the achievement of a maximum profit, while improving its competitiveness whether at the level national or international. To achieve this target, the presentation of these companies' accounting and financial statements must be clear, readable, and understandable to investors; a goal that can only be realized through the adoption of IFRS.

This literature review is structured around two subsections. The first focuses on the historical context of IFRS standards, while the second subsection highlights the key concepts of the study, such as the origin of the name of IFRS standards (International Financial Reporting Standards) and the notion of conceptual framework as well as the major contributions of these international accounting standards.

1.1. The Historical Context of IFRS Standards

This axe aims to explain the historical motivations which led accounting bodies, especially standard-setting bodies, to consider the establishment of common accounting and financial standards at the international level.

Indeed, several authors have tried to identify the most significant factors of the diversity of accounting systems at the international level, the most important being the sources of financing of companies, the difference in environment, the culture of the different countries and the legal, economic and financial factors.

1.1.1 Sources of Business Financing

Nobes and Parker (2003) suggests that one of the main reasons for international differences in financial reporting lies is the type of financing used (Involving the choice between debt-based and equity-based financing).

In countries such as Italy, France, Germany and Belgium, for example, the majority of companies turn to banks as their primary source of financing. Consequently, these companies tend to rely more on debt than on raising funds from shareholders (The Rhineland model of capitalism). (Table 1)

Table 1. Comparison of countries according to the dominant financing method

Countries funded by shareholders «Shareholders oriented»	Countries financed by credit «Credit oriented»
The United States	Germany
The United Kingdom	France
The Netherlands	Japan
Sweden	Belgium
Australia	Italy
Canada	Spain

Source: *Alexander et al.* (2007), p. 26-27

On the other hand, in the United States of America and the United Kingdom, the majority of company financing is based mainly on funds provided by shareholders (The Anglo-Saxon model of capitalism). (Table 1)

Internal financing, also known as self-financing or equity financing, is often perceived by investors as a sign of a company's financial health. However, its cost remains relatively high, as shareholders assume a higher level of risk than that incurred by a bank in the case of a loan.

Regarding external financing, particularly debt, its cost is generally fixed and predictable, unlike that of external financing through capital increases, the cost of which can vary over time. However, excessive use of debt can weaken the company's financial structure and compromise its solvency in the medium and long term.

This distinction therefore provides a clearer understanding of the difference between the accounting systems derived from Rhineland and Anglo-Saxon capitalism.

1.1.2 Difference in Environment

On the other hand, Nobes (1983) explained the dichotomy that characterizes accounting systems by the difference of environments. He distinguished two types of accounting systems:

- "Microeconomic accounting systems with commercial influence";
- "Macro-economic accounting systems with government and fiscal influence".

This distinction is presented in figure 1 as follows:

Figure 1. Different Environments, Different Accounting Standards

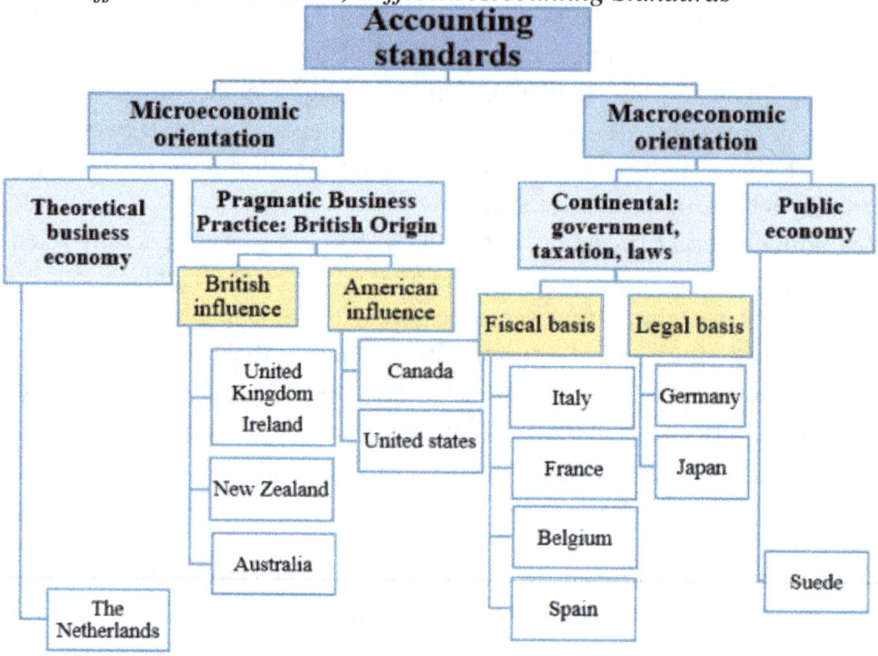

Source: Colasse (2000), p. 373

1.1.3 Culture of Different Countries

Before addressing this key factor in the diversity of accounting systems, it is essential to provide a relevant definition of the concept of "culture". According to Belkaoui (1995), culture is defined using a typology based on the contributions of literature:

- Culture is an instrument in a functionalist vision, meaning it provides a response to every psychological and biological need. Therefore, accounting differs from one country to another, or even from one culture to another;
- Culture is an adaptation and a regulation uniting individual. Accounting is then defined by an interaction with the environment;
- Culture is a system of shared cognition. Accounting is a shared system of rules established by individuals;
- Culture is the expression of shared meanings; hence, accounting is a language that is expressed while relying on symbols (different accounting concepts). (Wilfrid, (2000))

On the other hand, the work of Hofstede (1980) which, based on data collected from IBM (International Business Machines Corporation) employees in more than 50 countries, made it possible to identify four variables which, according to him, can characterize any culture: individualism, power distance, aversion to uncertainty and masculinity (Colasse, 2000):

- **"Individualism or Collectivism" (IDV)**: reveals the degree to which individuals are attached to groups. If one has a high IDV for a country, the culture of that country is more individualistic and therefore the individual is the center of interest;
- Strong or weak **"Power Distance"** (or **Power Distance Index (PDI)**): defines the degree of distance from power. If a country's power distance is weak, it is said that power is distributed democratically;
- High or low **Uncertainty Avoidance Index (UAI):** this index describes how strongly a culture perceives threats from unfamiliar situations or unexpected events. In a society with a high Uncertainty Avoidance Index, people fear change. Conversely, in a culture with low uncertainty control, uncertainty about the future does not scare people.
- The "**Masculinity or Femininity**" dimension **(MAS)**: determines the division of gender roles in a society. A very high index defines a masculine culture and makes a clear distinction between exclusively female roles and exclusively male roles.

This model was developed by Gray (1988), while making the equivalence between its cultural dimensions (**professionalism**, **uniformity**, **conservatism** and **secrecy**) and those of Hofstede (1980).

Table 2. The relationship between the Gray (1988) and Hofstede (1980) models

Gray's accounting values	Hofstede's cultural dimensions			
	PDI	**IDV**	**MAS**	**UAI**
Professionalism	Negative	Positive	No hypothetical relationship	Negative
Uniformity	Positive	Negative	No hypothetical relationship	Positive
Conservatism	No hypothetical relationship	Negative	Negative	Positive
Secrecy	Positive	Negative	Negative	Positive

Source: *Koleśnik (2013*, p. 36)

The table 2 above highlights the links between Hofstede's theoretical framework, accounting concepts and practices and the cultural dimensions defined by Gray. For example, according to Gray (as shown in the first row of the table), the level of individualism in a country is correlated with a greater importance given to professional judgment. In other words, in cultural contexts marked by strong individualism, the decisions of professionals and specialized organizations carry more significant weight. In contrast, individualism tends to be negatively related to the dimensions of secrecy, uniformity and even conservatism.

Furthermore, Gray (1988) related his accounting values to accounting practices, as illustrated in the table 3 below:

Table 3. The relationship between Gray's cultural values and accounting practices

Gray's accounting values	Accounting practices
Professionalism/Legislative Control	Power and execution
Uniformity/Flexibility	
Conservatism/Optimism	Valuation of assets and profits
Secrecy/Transparency	Disclosure of information

Source: *Doupnik, et al. (2006)*, p. 239

Gray (1988) was able to demonstrate through this table the causal link between cultural dimensions or even national accounting values and accounting practices.

For example, the two cultural values of secrecy and conservatism have a profound effect on the content of a company's financial reports. Conservatism affects how assets and profits are valuated, while secrecy determines the level of information disclosure.

1.1.4 Legal, Economic and Financial Factors

The diversity of accounting practices at the international level is explained in particular by the coexistence of multiple legal, economic and financial factors. As Elhamma (2012) highlights in his scholarly book "Understanding International Accounting Standards (IAS/IFRS) in the Context of Morocco", this is illustrated in Table 4:

Table 4. Factors influencing international accounting system practices

Factors	Anglo-Saxon countries	Continental Europe
The legal system	The main characteristics of the legal system: To state general principles and leave a wide margin of appreciation to the judges to decide on each question submitted to their attention. Impact on accounting: Accounting standard setters: professional organizations (FASB in the USA, IASB in the UK).	The main characteristics of the legal system: Detailed legislation, principles and regulations specific to each question, limit the margin of appreciation of judges. Impact on accounting: Accounting rules are included in laws (commercial code in France for example).
The economic and financial system	The main source of financing: the stock markets. Imapct on accounting: A faithful image is the main concern of investors when assessing the state of health of companies.	The main source of financing: financial institutions (banks). Imapct on accounting: Strict application of the principle of prudence in order to protect banks' claims.
The taxation	The tax result is calculated independently of the accounting result. Imapct on accounting: The accounting objective is the search for a faithful image.	Strong link between taxation and accounting. Imapct on accounting: Trying to minimize the taxable base.
Economic and political connections	A great similarity between the accounting systems of the countries allied to the British crown within the framework of the commonwealth and the accounting system in force in the United Kingdom.	A great convergence exists between the countries of French-speaking Africa (Morocco for example) and France.

Source: *Elhamma, (2012)*, p. 10-11

1.2. IFRS Standards

Under this subsection, two aspects will be addressed: the definition of IFRS Standards and their contributions.

1.2.1. Definition of IFRS Standards

International accounting standards aim to improve the competitiveness of companies in the medium and long term, while providing greater visibility and clarity regarding the company's financial situation. The adoption of IFRS (International Financial Reporting Standards) will then allow companies to reflect a positive image in the eyes of their environment (suppliers, investors, etc.) (Elhamma, 2025a, 2025b). To better understand the concept of "International Financial Reporting Standards," we will define the origin of each component, as follows:

- International: IFRS standards are international and, as such, they aim to provide a framework of reference for various listed companies operating in national financial markets and, by their very nature, confronted with diverse and varied market cultures and practices. How can we propose a common language for entities that are so different (1) operationally (for example, can the banking and insurance sectors use the same reporting techniques as the retail sector?); (2) economically (can companies operating in developed economies communicate as well and with equivalent tools as their counterparts operating in developing economies?); and (3) culturally (for example, do management methods and the influence of local culture influence the way they communicate?) (Ramond et al., 2012)
- Financial Reporting: IFRS are, above all, financial reporting standards that rely on financial techniques. They implement valuation methods that were previously only encountered marginally in accounting reporting departments and were more the preserve of the financial world (bankers, insurers, financial analysts, external valuators, etc.). The purpose of these valuation methods is not only the value they result in, but also the means of conveying this value. For example, a fluctuation in the value in financial instruments will affect market participants in different ways (for example, financial analysts) if it is transcribed into equity or income statement, since depending on the accounting allocation, different performance measures will be impacted (for example Economic Asset).
- Standards: IFRS standards convey a philosophy, even an Anglo-Saxon ideology, that differs from those anchored in the regulatory accounting frameworks previously used by continental European countries. This philosophy, which is highly oriented toward financial markets, has the primary characteristic of presenting itself, by nomenclature, as a norm (or standards), and not as a law.

The transition to IAS/IFRS standards by companies represents a real opportunity to review and revalue the accounting function. A good strategic opportunity for a reproduction of traditional financial data, in order to be able to exhibit it internationally (Falikou, 2010)

1.2.2. Conceptual Framework of IFRS Standards

The IASB's conceptual framework is not an international accounting standard, and therefore does not include any normative provisions regarding measurement or disclosures. Nothing in this framework supersedes a specific international accounting standard. The conceptual framework first defines the objectives and recipients of the financial information published in the statements prepared in accordance with the new standards. These financial statements are intended to first and foremost objective of providing investors; in other words, essentially to providers of risk capital, information on the financial situation of the group and its evolution, on the measurement of the company's performance, on its profitability and on the creation of value (financial, as opposed to the creation of economic value traditionally measured by added value) (Moukil, 2011)

Among the concepts defined by the conceptual framework, we cite:

- Scope of application: This is where the conceptual framework addresses these various basic questions: the recipients and purpose of financial statements, the principles to be followed in preparing financial statements, and the qualitative characteristics, etc.
- Users of financial statements: There are several people who will be interested in the use of published financial statements; we are, of course, talking about existing or prospective investors, lenders, suppliers and other creditors, governments and their public bodies, clients, and the public. Each of these users will view the published information according to their own vision and needs.
- The objective of financial statements: The objective of financial statements is to deliver relevant and reliable information regarding a company's financial position, performance, and financial evolution, with the aim of supporting various stakeholders in making informed and effective economic decisions.
- Basic assumptions: Two assumptions on which financial statements must be prepared, namely:
    - Accrual accounting: Every transaction or event must be recorded in the accounting records as of its date of occurrence and presented in the financial statements for the periods to which they relate;
    - Going concern: The preparation of financial statements is based on the going concern assumption, which presumes that the company will continue its operations for the foreseeable future. In other words, it does not anticipate the cessation of its operations or the significant liquidation of its assets.

If it exists such intention or necessity, the company must present its financial statements on a different basis, and, if so, the basis used must be indicated.

1.2.3 Contributions of IFRS Standards

The main objective of the IASB's creation of international accounting standards is to harmonize companies' accounting and financial documents in order to enable them to open up on an international scale. Thus, these standards aim to ensure the presentation of transparent, high-quality and comparable accounting information and financial statements, meeting the needs of all relevant stakeholders, namely: investors, lenders and other creditors.(Păşcan, 2015)

Thus, the table 5 explains the benefits of IFRS for the various stakeholders:

Table 5. Users and their respective needs

Users	Needs	Source documents	Accessible information	Time to obtain information
Direction	Information for planning, deciding strategy and resource allocation and controlling	Financial statements.	Full access from basic documents to financial statements.	Information continually accessible. Accessibility depends only on the organization
Shareholders and Investors	Concern about risk and return on their investments: - Useful information for deciding when to buy, hold, or sell securities. - Data used to assess the company's ability to distribute dividends.	Financial statements.	Financial statements, along with publicly accessible information about the company's performance in its markets and operations.	The date of publication of the financial statements must be before the general meeting. This date is regulated in each country. The trend is towards earlier publication.
Banks and lenders	Information to determine if their loan payments and related interest will be paid when due.	Retrospective and forecast financial statements.	Financial statements.	The company must produce documents when it wants to raise funds from a bank or on the market.
Suppliers and other commercial creditors	Information to determine whether their debts will be repaid to them when due. Trade creditors are interested in the company for a shorter period than lenders, unless they are dependent on the company's continued existence when it is a major customer for them.	Financial statements.	Theoretically, these users have no right to more information than that of the financial statements. By making comparisons and organizing intelligence monitoring, get a more precise idea.	Case by case.
Customers	Information about the company's business continuity, especially if they have a long-term relationship with it or are dependent on it. Customers are particularly interested in the company's sustainability.	Financial statements.	Like suppliers, customers ask for direct information and will cross-reference it to be alerted to possible opportunities or difficulties.	Case by case.
Competitors	To compare relative performance.	Financial statements.	Competitor analysis is based on databases compiling financial statements. This information is cross-referenced with intelligence research and a good understanding of the sector.	On a case-by-case basis depending on the resources allocated to intelligence gathering.
Staff members	Information on the stability and profitability of their employer. Information to estimate the company's ability to pay its employees and pay them retirement benefits and employment opportunities.	Financial statements.	Access to information is regulated in each country.	On a case-by-case basis, taking into account the law of the country concerned.

continued on following page

Table 5. Continued

Users	Needs	Source documents	Accessible information	Time to obtain information
States and public organizations	Are concerned with how resources are allocated and distributed, and therefore the activities of business. Furthermore, they impose information requirements in order to regulate these activities, define tax policies, and provide a reliable basis for the development of national statistics.	Financial statements often restructured into regulatory forms.	Tax forms are routinely required. In the event of a tax audit, access to all basic documents is provided.	Each country has its own rules. For example, in France, tax forms must be submitted to the administration 3 ½ months after the close of the accounting year.
Public	Companies have an impact on individuals and the community. For example, a company can contribute significantly to the country's economy, in particular, by contributing to job creation and soliciting the services of local suppliers. Financial statements can thus provide the general public with relevant information on the evolution of the company's performance, recent trends in its prosperity, as well as the scale of its activities.	Financial statements.	Regulated access.	Case by case.

Source: *Stolowy et al. (2006)*, p. 27-28

1.2.4 Significant Impacts Expected From the Adoption of IFRS or IFRS for SMEs

The adoption of international accounting and financial standards, IFRS or IFRS for SMEs, can have numerous repercussions on the various departments and functions of a company subject to these standards. These impacts are evident at several levels. At the fiscal level, the application of IFRS calls into question the traditional link between taxation and accounting, in particular due to the divergences between international accounting rules and national tax benchmarks. In terms of education, this transition requires a revision of accounting training programs to integrate the conceptual and technical specificities of IFRS standards, which implies an adaptation effort for both teachers and students. Furthermore, from an economic and financial perspective, the adoption of international standards can contribute to greater transparency of financial information, thus facilitating comparisons between companies on an international scale, which strengthens the attractiveness of local financial markets and investor confidence.

1.2.4.1 Impact on the Various Departments of the Company Subject to IFRS Standards

The adoption of IFRS by companies could change the company's entire strategy and therefore have a direct or indirect impact on its various departments, as can be seen below:

- General Management: The implementation of IAS/IFRS will have an impact on financial reporting and therefore on financial communication. This impact occurs on two levels:
    - A direct impact on financial statements and, consequently, on ratios and performance indicators;
    - An impact on the information to be provided, which will be more numerous, more sensitive, et also strategic.

In this case, companies will have to adapt their communications and prepare for this transition with various stakeholders (shareholders, analysts, media, partners, customers, suppliers, employees, etc.). Legal professionals' knowledge of IAS/IFRS principles will make it easier for accountants and operational staff to understand a contract in international language.

- Legal Department: The legal department must analyze both contractual clauses, taking into account penalties in the context of construction contract revenue (IAS 11) and the legal protection of intangible assets (IAS 38).

The legal department will be directly involved in the assessment of provisions, particularly to determine whether the related risk is "more likely than not" to materialize. A provision can only be recognized if this probability is verified. A second condition for recognizing a provision is the company's ability to reliably estimate the resources required to settle an obligation. Legal experts will specify, for each contract, whether the performance of the obligation involves a probable outflow of resources and whether a reliable estimate of this outflow can be established. They should also be consulted to confirm the existence of contingent liabilities. (Zouak, 2012)

- Human Resources: The Human Resources department will be involved at three levels: training, compensation, and litigation:
  - Training: The implementation of IAS/IFRS represents a change in financial language, and various stakeholders must be trained to use this standard.

IFRS training must be both technical (to meet the needs of accounting and finance teams) and general (to train teams in other functions that need to understand the standards), in order to understand the overlaps and be able to respond to requests from general management.

- Compensation: The use of IAS/IFRS will have an impact on the financial indicators used as the basis for variable compensation (profit-sharing, bonuses based on objectives, etc.). The Human Resources department will therefore need to analyze all possible impacts to assess the relevance of the calculation bases for certain compensation. Furthermore, personnel expenses must include all pension expenses (IAS 19) and expenses related to the granting of stock options (IFRS 2).
- Disputes: Finally, the Human Resources department is involved in the management of disputes with staff and must therefore be involved in the monitoring of provisions and contingent liabilities (IAS 37) related to staff.
  - Marketing and Sales: Taking into account the famous "4P" of the marketing mix (Price, Product, Place, and Promotion). The impacts of IAS/IFRS standards on Marketing/Sales departments are:
- Price: The analysis of commercial contracts, which allows the identification of assets, liabilities, income and expenses, as well as the evaluation of certain balance sheet items, is based in part on estimates of future sales and costs (IAS 36 and IAS 37), thus requiring sales representatives to calculate and provide accountants with more information;

- Product: Inventories should be valued at the lower of their cost and their net realizable value, the latter being the estimated selling price in the normal course of business, after deducting the estimated costs of completion and the estimated costs necessary to make the sale (IAS2);
- Place (Distribution): The definition and communication of sectors (IAS 14) are an important point for IAS/IFRS standards; it is necessary to be able to harmonize marketing sector positioning and segmentation with the typology of the selected sectors. In addition, it will be necessary to anticipate and measure the accounting impact of a change in exclusive distribution network following the acquisition of a new distribution network for a company or brand (IAS 38);
- Promotion: Promotional operations at the point of sale must be carried out and not treated as end-of-year discounts, which must be subtracted from revenue and not constitute expenses.
  - The financing and treasury department: This department must analyze all financing operations from the perspective of IAS/IFRS because the economic presentation of some operations may call into question the merits of certain choices. For example, the component accounting of hybrid debt/equity instruments (IAS 32) results in the restatement of financial interest, which is recalculated by applying the effective interest rate method.
  - The Production/R&D Department: This department will be involved in the implementation of all standards. In particular, it will need to provide information for:
- Inventory valuation: definition of normal activity (IAS 2);
- Construction contract accounting (IAS 11): separation/grouping of contracts, determination of the stage of completion, costs at completion, and distinction of costs attributable to each construction contract;
- The breakdown of different assets by sector (IAS 14) and their allocation to cash-generating units (IAS 36);
- The distinction between research and development phases (IAS 38), compliance with the criteria for activating development costs and their segment allocation (IAS 14).

1.2.4.2 Impact on the Tax-Accounting Connection

In some countries that are gradually moving towards the adoption of IAS/IFRS international accounting standards, such as Morocco, there is a strong interdependence between fiscal rules and national accounting rules (Elhamma and Boutafrout, 2025). Indeed, in accordance with the provisions of the General Tax Code (CGI), the taxable income, which constitutes the basis of corporate tax, is determined from individual accounts established according to the rules of the General Code of Moroccan Accounting Standards (CGNC).

The introduction of IFRS in Moroccan companies could therefore have significant repercussions on the structure and content of individual financial statements. This development is likely to have an impact not only on the calculation of taxable income, but also the calculation of other tax obligations, such as VAT, business tax, or the social solidarity contribution. This would result in a need to adapt the mechanisms liking accounting and taxation, or even to rethink certain fundamentals of corporate taxation, in order to ensure the consistency and reliability of the tax system in a changing regulatory environment.

1.2.4.3 Impact on Accounting Education

The introduction of IFRS/IFRS for SMEs in Morocco requires significant efforts by the Moroccan government to ensure a smooth transition to these standards. For the education sector, the scarcity of courses addressing the topic of international accounting standards may pose a real challenge for students wishing to work in various accounting professions in the future. One possible approach is to introduce IFRS-related terms into accounting and management courses at universities and accounting and management schools, and to effectively apply each of these international standards (of course, we are talking about IAS/IFRS or IFRS for SMEs).

1.2.4.4 Impacts on the Economy and Markets

The adoption of IFRS and IFRS for SMEs in Morocco will contribute to better comparability of financial statements, which will promote the smooth functioning of the capital market, while ensuring an optimal balance between the costs incurred and the desired efficiency. In addition, this new framework will establish investor confidence in the financial markets, while ensuring their protection, we are therefore talking about encouraging FDI (Foreign Direct Investment) (Nahmias, 2004)

In this context, Nnadi et al., (2015) confirmed, based on several empirical studies, that the adoption of International Financial Reporting Standards (IFRS) contributes to stimulating FDI.

Moreover, Mita et al., (2018) affirmed that the adoption of IFRS improves the comparability of financial statements, which helps attract more foreign investors, and consequently, the development of the national economy.

1.2.4.5 Impact on the Information System and Financial Communication

The two most important strategic issues in the transition to IFRS are information systems and financial communication. Changing accounting standards is indeed a real strategic and operational challenge for general management.

Given the significant impacts expected from the adoption of IFRS standards, it is important to highlight their widespread global adoption. Indeed, according to a report published by the IFRS Foundation in 2018, 144 jurisdictions require the application of IFRS to all or the majority of companies. This wide dissemination demonstrates the growing importance of international accounting harmonization. (Elhamma, 2023)

Furthermore, Turki et al., (2017) stated that the adoption of IFRS standards (in the Frensh context) has improved the quality of financial information, strengthened communication with analysts, while ensuring high transparency in the accounting information system.

2. RESEARCH METHODOLOGY

At this stage of our work, we will present the methodology adopted to conduct our study. This section will not only justify the methodological choices made, but also highlight the three main hypotheses underlying our research approach. These hypotheses will serve as a guiding thread for the analysis, guiding both data collection and interpretation of the results obtained.

2.1. Formulation of Research Hypotheses

A number of studies (Watts and Zimmerman, 1990; Raffournier, 1995; Hand and Skantz, 1998; Gassen and Sellhorn, 2006) have shown that the size of the company has a strong influence on the choice of a company's accounting policy (Ahsina et al., 2013). Indeed, large companies are supposed to publish more information than smaller ones since they generally have a greater demand for information from the public and are subject to more careful scrutiny from financial analysts (Schipper, 1991).

Similarly, Dye (1985) argued that, since annual reports often represent the main, if not the only, source of information available to competitors, managers of small businesses might be reluctant to disclose a large amount of information (Bessieux-Ollier et al., 2014). Furthermore, Watts and Zimmerman (1990) consider size as an indicator of the political visibility of the firm: "size is a proxy for political attention" (Jeanjean, 1999))

It should be remembered that the size of the company can be determined either by its turnover, or by the number of employees. From the above elements, we can pose as a first hypothesis:

> Hypothesis 1: The size of the company could be a factor for the adoption of IFRS by Moroccan companies.

As noted by Marchal et al. (2007), the first application of IFRS as an accounting policy leads to an increase in financial debt, and therefore to the attraction of more investors at the universal level. On the other hand, a company that needs financial support from its creditors is encouraged to opt for choices that reduce the level of debt. The debt ratio is therefore associated with the risk of failure of the company (Bilodeau et al., 2005). In the same context, Watts and Zimmerman (1990) opted for another ratio, the debt-to-equity ratio, and concluded that the higher this ratio, the more managers will tend to use methods that increase earnings and therefore increase equity. So, to reduce the risk of failure, it is necessary to improve debt capacity, while reducing the level of debt leverage. In addition, Jensen and Meckling (1976) consider that debt gives shareholders the opportunity to increase their wealth at the expense of creditors. Since borrowing costs are based on the current risk of the company, shareholders are encouraged to invest borrowed funds in riskier projects than existing ones, to increase profitability without additional cost. (Bessieux-Ollier et al.,2014)

In turn, Raffounier (1990) indicated that, according to positive accounting theory, accounting choices are generally explained by factors such as the firm's debt, the remuneration and size of managers, as well as by an estimate of "Political visibility".(Avelé, 2013)

Based on the above-mentioned data, we can pose as a second hypothesis:

> Hypothesis 2: The entity's debt as an indicator for the adoption of IFRS by Moroccan companies.

Investors are considered "normally" the first "customers" of the accounting and financial standardization process, so that they can optimize their choices and decisions, while basing themselves on more reliable and clear data. But are companies with activities abroad more likely to adopt IFRS?

A study conducted by Cuijpers and Buijinik (2005) in the European context on annual reports for the 1999 financial year, shows that groups, voluntarily adopting internationally recognized standards, are generally listed abroad and have international activity (Demaria, 2008).

In the same context, Dumontier and Raffournier (1998), El-Gazzar et al. (1999) and Ashbaught et al. (2000) have shown that listing on a US market encourages groups to voluntarily adopt internationally recognized accounting standards, such as US GAAP or IAS/IFRS. In this context, it is reasonable to assume that companies operating outside the Moroccan market would be inclined to opt for the standards closest to those used by European companies.

Indeed, the presence of foreign investors, institutional or individual, could influence the functioning of the boards of directors of companies (El Abbadi, 2011-2012), while encouraging the latter to adopt international standards. The third hypothesis is then:

> Hypothesis 3: The existence of foreign investors and the entity's international exposure is a determinant of the adoption of IFRS by Moroccan companies.

2.2. Methodological Choices

In order to analyze our three hypotheses, we carried out an empirical study at the level of 100 Moroccan companies, scattered throughout the Kingdom of Morocco, in order to present more significant results.

The choice of our sample is made on the basis of non-probabilistic sampling, more particularly snowball, with a normal distribution law. Thus, the methodological approach adopted is hypothetico-deductive with the use of the survey method as a means of data collection. In fact, the response rate reached 82%, and the processing of the information collected was carried out using two software programs: Sphinx and SPSS.

Our study model is presented mathematically in the following form:

$$Y = f(X1, X2, X3)$$

With:

Y = Adoption of IFRS by Moroccan companies (Explained/dependent variable), which can take the two modalities {0;1}

X1= Company size (Explanatory variable 1)

X2= Company debt (Explanatory variable 2)

X3= International exposure (Explanatory variable 3)

Our study model is presented in econometric form as follows:

$$Y = b_0 + b_1X1 + b_2X2 + b_3X3$$

With:

(b_0;b_1; b_2; b_3): estimated coefficients of the independent variables

Y = +: The company will choose to adopt IFRS

Y = −: The company will not choose to adopt IFRS

3. RESULTS

Before proceeding with the analysis of the explanatory variables, it is necessary to check whether the study model is relevant. For this, it is necessary to first study the independence of these explanatory variables in the choice of explanatory factors, while basing on the table 6:

Table 6. Correlation matrix of explanatory variables

		Company size	**Company Debt**	**International Exposure**
Company size	**Correlation**	1,000	**0,020**	**-0,342**
	Signification (bilateral)		0,860	0,002
Company Debt	**Correlation**	**0,020**	1,000	**-0,107**
	Signification (bilateral)	0,860		0,337
International Exposure	**Correlation**	**-0,342**	**-0,107**	1,000
	Signification (bilateral)	0,002	0,337	

Source: SPSS software after entering data

The analysis conducted, based on the correlation matrix, reveals that all the correlation coefficients between the explanatory variables are either close to zero or between 0 and -0.5. This indicated a weak correlation between these variables.

In order to verify the independence between the explanatory variables, a linear regression will be carried out using SPSS software. This approach will make it possible to estimate the values of the Variance Inflation Factor (VIF) as well as its reciprocal, the Tolerance (1/VIF), indicators commonly used to detect potential multicollinearity.

Table 7. Collinearity test of explanatory variables VIF

Explanatory variables	Collinearity statistics	
	Tolerance	VIF
Company size	0,883	1,133
Company Debt	0,988	1,012
International Exposure	0,873	1,145

Source: Developed by the authors using SPSS software

This analysis of the collinearity indicators shown in the table 7 above attests to the relative independence of the explanatory variables.

After applying the two methods: the correlation matrix and the VIF, it appears that there is sufficient independence between the explanatory variables allowing their inclusion in the model without risk of bias in the estimation of the coefficients.

At this level, the realization of three kinds of analyses, namely descriptive, bivariate analysis and explanatory analysis are duly necessary to properly conduct this study.

3.1 Results of the Descriptive Analysis

Descriptive analysis provides information on variables related to the companies surveyed. For example, in our study, very small businesses represent 44%, SMEs 40%, and large companies 16% (as shown in table 8).

Table 8. Size of companies that participated in the survey

Company size	Company workforce	Frequency	Percentage
Very small companies	1-2	13	15,9
	3-9	23	28,0
Small and Medium-sized Enterprises	10-199	33	40,2
Large companies	200 et plus	13	15,9
Total		**82**	**100,0**

Source: Developed by the authors using SPSS software

Figure 2. Size of the companies surveyed

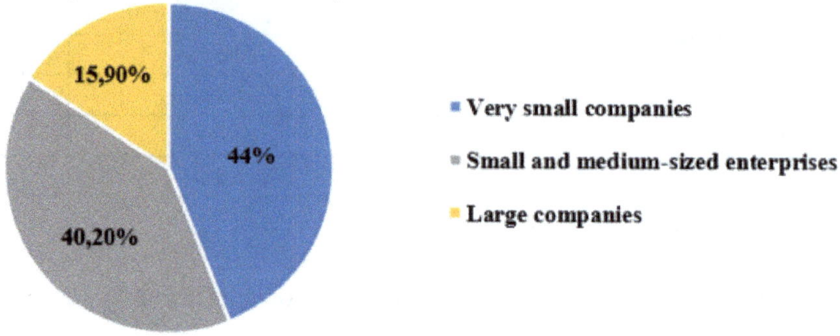

Source: Developed by the authors using SPSS software

According to the comparison of the workforce of the companies surveyed, we find that very small companies and SMEs are the two dominant structures of companies, with percentages of 43.9% and 40.2% respectively; while large companies only represent 15.9%. (Figure 2).

On the other hand, to measure the important mode of financing used by most companies, the different possible financing methods were asked in the distributed questionnaire, and the results are presented in Table 9 as follows:

Table 9. Means of financing businesses

Means of financing	Number	% Observation
Self-funding	57	69,50%
Shareholders' current loans	36	43,90%
Loans from credit institutions	43	52,40%
Leasing	13	15,90%
Bank subsidie	7	8,50%
Total number of companies surveyed	**82**	

Source: Developed by the authors using Sphinx software

Figure 3. Means of financing businesses

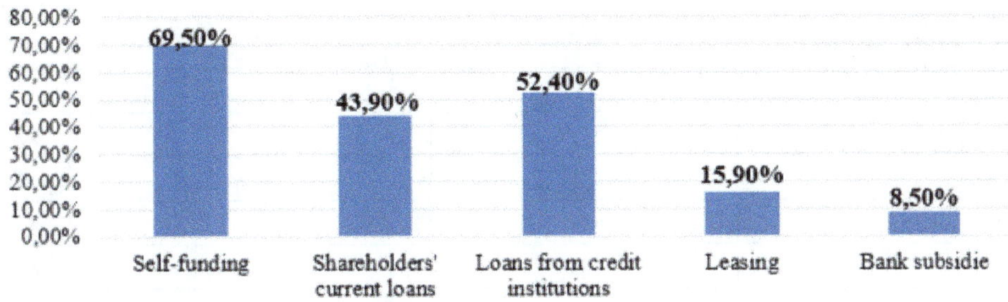

Source: Developed by the authors using Sphinx software

In order to meet their operating or investment needs, companies can use different sources of financing. According to the results of our survey, self-financing appears to be the most commonly used method, representing 69.5% of cases. This is followed by bank loans (52.4%) loans (43.9%), leasing (15.9%) and finally bank subsidies (8.5%). (Figure 3)

3.2 Results of Bivariate Analysis

Bivariate analysis, which is part of descriptive analysis, consists of studying the relationships between two variables, which can be qualitative or quantitative. For this study, the relationships studied will be those linking the qualitative (dependent) variable, which is IFRS adoption, and each explanatory variable in the model, namely: company size, company debt, and the company's international exposure.

3.2.1 Bivariate Analysis of Firm Size and IFRS Adoption by Moroccan Firms

The size of the company is expressed by the number of employees in the company.

The first step in analyzing the relationship between a qualitative and a quantitative variable is graphical representation. To achieve this, it is essential to analyze the values of each variable in order to determine whether a relationship exists between them. (Table 10)

Table 10. Cross-tabulation of company size and IFRS adoption

	Adoption of IFRS by Moroccan companies surveyed		**Total**
Company size (Number of employees)	**No**	**Yes**	
1-2	11	2	13
3-9	17	6	23
10-199	16	17	33
200 and more	5	8	13
Total	**49**	**33**	**82**

Source: Developed by ourselves using Sphinx software

Figure 4. Bar chart that demonstrates the relationship between company size and IFRS adoption by Moroccan companies

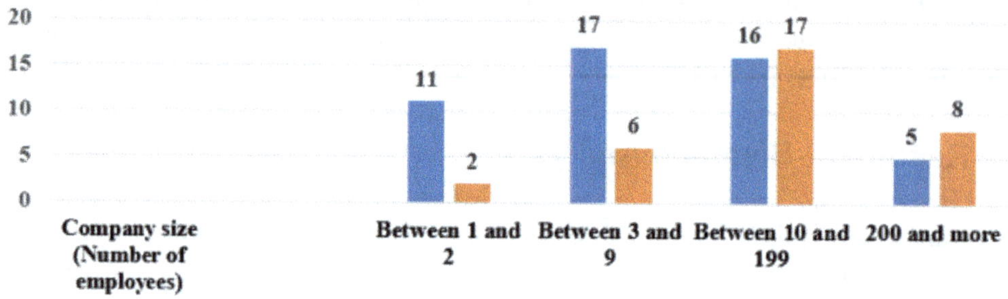

Source: Developed by ourselves using Sphinx software

Based on the cross-tabulation (Table 10) and bar chart (Figure 4) that demonstrate the relationship between company size and IFRS adoption, the decision to adopt IFRS by Moroccan companies varies positively with the size of the company. In other words, the larger the size of the company, the more likely it is to adopt IFRS.

At the bar graph level, we find that, the more the size of the company increases, the more the company intends to adopt IFRS.

The analysis then proves that there is a relationship between the two dependent and independent variables, that is, between size and the adoption of IFRS by Moroccan companies.

3.2.2 Bivariate Analysis of Company Debt and Adoption of IFRS by Moroccan Companies

The analysis of these two so-called qualitative variables involves conducting a cross-tabulation analysis (Table 11). Thus, the calculation of the contingency coefficient will make it possible to indicate the existing relationship between the two variables in question (Table 12). It should be noted that "company debt" for this study is measured by: recourse to loans from credit institutions.

Table 11. Cross-tabulation of the adoption of IFRS by Moroccan companies and loans from banking establishments

	Adoption of IFRS by surveyed companies		
Company debt (Loans from banking establishments)	**No**	**Yes**	**Total**
No	20	17	37
Yes	29	16	45
Total	**49**	**33**	**82**

Source: Developed by the authors using SPSS software

Table 12. Calculation of the contingency coefficient between the adoption of IFRS and the use of bank loans

	Value	**Approximate significance**
Contingency coefficient	**0,105**	**0,340**
Number of valid observations (N)	**82**	

Source: Developed by the authors using SPSS software

Figure 5. Bar graph of the relationship between IFRS adoption and bank loans

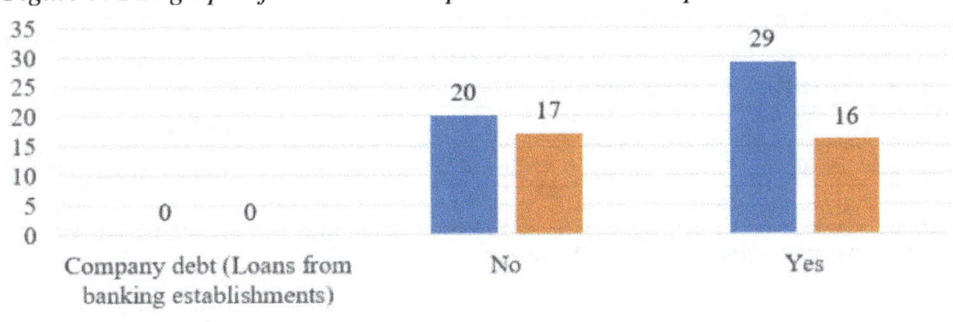

Source: Developed by the authors using SPSS software

The results obtained above demonstrate that among the companies that do not borrow from credit institutions, 20 of them do not plan to adopt IFRS, and only 17 companies are considering doing so. As for the companies surveyed that borrow from banks, 29 of them do not plan to adopt IFRS, and only 16 are considering doing so.

Therefore, the calculation of the contingency coefficient and the significance threshold (Table 12) confirms the absence of a significant link between the adoption of IFRS and debt (the use of bank loans).

3.2.3 Bivariate Analysis of International Exposure and IFRS Adoption by Moroccan Companies

International exposure is expressed by the magnitude of foreign turnover in relation to the company's net turnover.

The study of the relationship between the variable to be explained "the adoption of IFRS by Moroccan companies" and the explanatory variable "international exposure" is expressed in Table 13 as follows:

Table 13. The relationship between IFRS adoption and international exposure

	Probability of IFRS adoption		Total
Company exposure internationally (The magnitude of turnover abroad in relation to the company's net turnover)	**No**	**Yes**	
Weak	5	5	10
Poor	2	1	3
Important	1	4	5
No response	41	23	64
Total	**49**	**33**	**82**

Source: Developed by the authors using SPSS software

Table 14. Symmetrical measures

	Value	Approximate meaning
Contingency coefficient	**0,222**	**0,237**
Number of valid observations	**82**	

Source: Developed by the authors using SPSS software

Figure 6. Relationship between IFRS adoption and international exposure

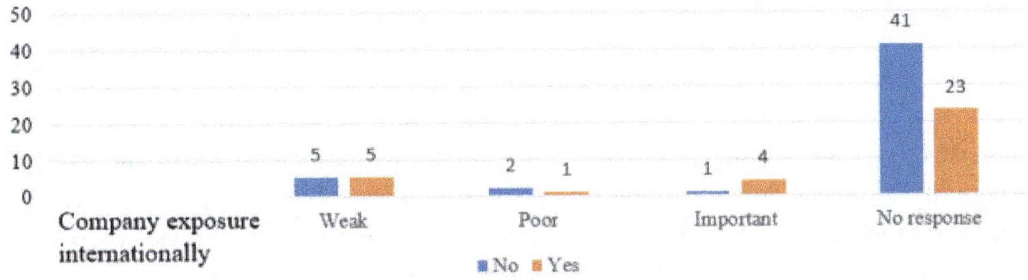

Source: Developed by the authors using SPSS software

The information presented above, more specifically the value of the contingency coefficient (which is equal to 0.222) and the significance threshold (0.237) (as shown in Table 14), confirms that the two variables in question: the adoption of IFRS and international exposure, are two independent variables (Figure 6).

After conducting a descriptive analysis of the links between the qualitative variable to be explained and each of the explanatory variables, it appears that the majority of the observed relationships do not present a statistically significant dependence. Only the variable relating to the size of the company seems to have a significant link with the dependent variable. The first observation raises a particular interest in the role that the size of the company can plan in explaining the phenomenon studied. The next step of our study will therefore consist of integrating all the explanatory variables into a multivariate model, in order to verify whether this relationship remains significant once the other factors are taken into account. If this is the case, a more in-depth analysis will be conducted to evaluate the direction and intensity of this association.

3.3 Results of Logistic Regression Analysis

The formula of our probabilistic model under logistics regression is expressed as:

$$P(Y) = \frac{1}{1 + e^{-(b0+b1X1+b2X2+b3X3)}}$$

With:

- **P(Y)**: The probability that companies will choose to adopt IFRS (Dependent variable).
- **b0** is the constant.

- The coefficients **b1**, **b2**, and **b3** are estimated coefficients of the independent (predictor) variables.
- **X1**, **X2**, and **X3** are the independent variables (X1 (firm size), X2 (firm debt), and X3 (firm international exposure).

In this study, we gradually added our variables explanatory, while trying to judge the quality of the model; and at each stage, we calculated the chi-square test, which represents the statistical indicator of overall significance of the model, as well as the R2 values of Cox and Snell and Nagelkerke, in order to measure at what stage the model is well adjusted. (Table 15)

Table 15. Variables of the equation

	b	E. S	Wald	ddl	Sig.	Exp(b)
Company size	0,831	0,302	7,551	1	0,006	2,295
Company Debt	-0,567	0,490	1,334	1	0,248	0,567
International Exposure	-0,016	0,239	0,004	1	0,948	0,984
Constant	-2,234	1,368	2,664	1	0,103	0,107

Source: Developed by the authors using SPSS software

Thus, based on Table 15 the only significant variable in our logistic regression equation is company size, with:

- A coefficient b1 equal to 0.831;
- A significance level equal to 0.006 (which is less than 5%)
- Expo (b1) or the Odds Ratio = 2.295. This value proves that the more size of the company increases by one unit, the more there is a chance that equal to 2.295 that this same company will adopt IFRS;
- The Wald statistic for b1 = 7.551, which is significantly greater than 0, meaning that this coefficient could contribute to improving the model.

Our logistic regression equation is then presented as follows:

Logit (adopt IFRS)
= - 2.234 + 0.831 Size - 0.567 Debt - 0.016 International Exposure

4. DISCUSSION

This chapter is a theoretical and empirical research project that demonstrates interest in IFRS standards. The objective of this work is to identify the key determinants and factors that can explain the adoption of IFRS standards by Moroccan companies.

In this perspective, a methodology based on an in-depth review if existing literature was adopted. This enabled the identification of three main determinants of the adoption of IFRS standards, namely: the size of the company, its debt and its degree of international exposure.

In this regard, to analyze the validity of these determinants, an empirical study was conducted, including a survey of 100 Moroccan companies, with a response rate of 82%. The collection and processing of data was carried out on the basis of SPSS software, to then be able to carry out three phases of analysis, specifically descriptive analysis which serves to give an overview for each of the determinants; bivariate analysis, which aims to study the relationship between each determinant and the adoption of IFRS standards; and logistic regression analysis, which allows for the best explanation of the variable "Adoption of IFRS standards by Moroccan companies" by the obtained determinants, based on a mathematical model.

Indeed, data analysis reveals that company size may determine a Moroccan entity's choice to adopt IFRS, which confirms the first hypothesis of this research. Generally speaking, based on our empirical study, it appears that the reluctance of the majority of Moroccan companies to adopt an international accounting standard is in fact explained solely by the novelty of the subject for some interviewees, while for others, this reluctance to adopt IFRS/ IFRS for SMEs, is explained by numerous drawbacks presented by this standard, which include: the scarcity of skills proficient in IFRS (Bonito et al. (2018)), the high cost of implementing these standards within companies, and a lack of training for company managers on the subject.

CONCLUSION

Today, businesses worldwide are facing profound upheavals and a dynamic of rapid transformation. These developments are primarily driven by two key factors. First, globalization, which intensifies competition by expanding markets, bringing economies closer together, and requiring companies to comply with international standards to remain competitive. Second, technological progress, which revolutionizing methods of communication, production and management, affecting all sectors of activities.

In this context of global change, accounting has not escaped these transformations. On the contrary, it has found itself at the heart of concerns related to the harmonization of financial reporting. To satisfy the requirements of transparency, comparability and reliability in accounting information, experts in the field have undertaken a comprehensive initiative aimed at standardizing the accounting language. The goal is to enable companies, regardless of their country of establishment, legal status, or sector of activity, to produce financial statement that are understandable and internationally comparable.

It is with this in mind that the International Financial Reporting Standards (IFRS) were developed, along with a version specifically adapted to small and medium-sized enterprises: IFRS for SMSs. These standards aim to standardize accounting practices in a globalized economic environment, thus promoting the fluidity of financial reporting and facilitating access to international markets.

This chapter examines the determinants of the adoption of IFRS standards by Moroccan companies; through a case study conducted among companies located in different regions of the Kingdom of Morocco. The analysis of the collected data highlights a single significant factor influencing this adoption: the size of the company.

In fact, this chapter could have a positive impact on various stakeholders in the accounting and finance field. In fact, researchers and beginners in the field can use this document as a reference and source to introduce themselves to the concept of IFRS, its conceptual framework, and its various contributions. It also offers them the opportunity to discover the factors likely to explain the adoption of IFRS standards by Moroccan companies – a subject little covered in the literature (Elhamma, 2024) – while analyzing and examining the methodology adopted by the authors.

Then, the study carried out can constitute an overview and an inventory of IFRS standards in the Moroccan context, while shedding light on the causes of disapproval of the adoption of these standards by Moroccan companies.

Finally, IFRS standards in the Kingdom of Morocco constitute a young and current topic in the business world, especially since there is little work done on these international accounting standards, whether in terms of documentary research (Elhamma, 2012; Haoudi, 2015; Baghar, 2017; Ghandari, 2018), or in practice (Ahsina, 2012; Taouab et al., 2014; El Hamza, 2018).

In this perspective, and based on the lessons learned from previous theoretical and empirical work, it appears relevant to question the existence of other factors likely to shed light on the process of adopting IFRS standards in the Moroccan context. Furthermore, taking into account the limitations encountered during our own empirical investigation, we propose the following recommendations with a view to enriching future reflections and guiding the actions to be undertaken:

- The need to provide training on international accounting standards for all managers of Moroccan companies in order to popularize them;
- The need to organize seminars and conferences on IFRS, while demonstrating the benefits of adopting these standards, particularly in terms of business competitiveness;
- The need to target Moroccan SMEs, while raising their awareness of the existence of an international accounting framework.

REFERENCES

Ahsina, K. (2012). Implementing IAS-IFRS in the Moroccan context: An explanatory model. *International Journal of Accounting and Financial Reporting, 2*(2), 114–124. DOI: 10.5296/ijafr.v2i2.2524

Ahsina, K., Alaoui,O., Z., & Ellatife, E. (2013). L'adoption des normes comptables internationales IAS/IFRS par les sociétés cotées au Maroc: Un essai d'observation et de modélisation. *Revue Marocaine de Contrôle de Gestion*, N°5

Ahsina, K., Taouab, O., & Cherqaoui, M. B. (2014). L'impact de l'adoption des IFRS sur les sociétés cotées à la Bourse de Casablanca: Une étude exploratoire. *La Revue Gestion et Organisation, 6*(2), 45–57. DOI: 10.1016/j.rgo.2014.09.003

Ahsina, K., Taouab, O., & Daghri, T. (2014). An empirical investigation of adopting IFRS accounting standards: Evidence from Morocco. *Research Journal of Finance and Accounting, 5*(10), 120–131.

Alexander, D., Britton, A., & Jorissen, A. (2007). *International financial reporting and analysis* (3rd ed.). Thomson.

Ashbaugh, H., & Pincus, M. (2000). Domestic accounting standards, international accounting standards, and the predictability of earnings. *Journal of Accounting Research, 39*(3), 417–434. DOI: 10.1111/1475-679X.00020

Avelé, D. (2013). *La théorie positive de la comptabilité: Aspects théoriques et critiques* (Master's thesis). Université de Moncton, Canada.

Baghar, N. (2017). *La normalisation comptable au Maroc: Actualités, enjeux et perspectives* (Master's thesis). École Nationale de Commerce et de Gestion, Université Hassan 1er, Settat.

Belkaoui, A. R. (1995). *The cultural shaping of accounting*. Quorum Books. DOI: 10.5040/9798216187097

Bessieux-Ollier, C., & Walliser, É. (2014). Sur la contingence du référentiel comptable: L'exemple des entreprises françaises cotées sur Alternext. *Revue Française de Comptabilité*, (100), 25–40. DOI: 10.3917/resg.100.0073

Bilodeau, J., Chérief, I., Labelle, R., et al. (2005). Les caractéristiques des contrats de dettes et les clauses restrictives comptables: Quels liens ? *Comptabilité – Contrôle – Audit, 11(2),* 109–133.

Bonito, A., & Pais, C. (2018). The macroeconomic determinants of the adoption of IFRS of SMEs. *Revista de contabilidad-. Revista de Contabilidad, 21*(2), 116–127. DOI: 10.1016/j.rcsar.2018.03.001

Colasse, B. (2000). *Encyclopédie de comptabilité, contrôle de gestion et audit* (Vol. 1). Economica.

Cuijpers, R., & Buijink, W. (2005). Voluntary adoption of non-local GAAP in the European Union: A study of determinants and consequences. *European Accounting Review, 14*(3), 487–524. DOI: 10.1080/0963818042000337132

Demaria, S. (2008). *Le choix d'options comptables lors de la première application des normes IAS/IFRS: Observation et compréhension des choix effectués par les groupes français* (Thèse de doctorat). Groupe de Recherche en Droit, Economie et Gestion. Université Nice Sophia Antipolis.

Doupnik, T. S., & Riccio, E. L. (2006). The influence of conservatism and secrecy on the interpretation of verbal probability expressions in the Anglo and Latin cultural areas. *The International Journal of Accounting, 41*(3), 237–261. DOI: 10.1016/j.intacc.2006.07.005

Dumontier, P., & Raffournier, B. (1998). Why firms comply voluntarily with IAS: An empirical analysis with Swiss data. *Journal of International Financial Management & Accounting, 9*(3), 216–245. DOI: 10.1111/1467-646X.00038

Dye, R. A. (1985). Disclosure of nonproprietary information. *Journal of Accounting Research, 23*(1), 123–145. DOI: 10.2307/2490910

El Abbadi, A. (2011–2012). *L'adoption des normes IFRS par les groupes marocains: Les opportunités et contraintes et leurs apports à la bonne gouvernance: Cas pratique Banque Centrale Populaire* (Mémoire de master). Université My Ismail, Meknès.

El-Gazzar, S. M., Finn, P. M., & Jacob, R. (1999). An empirical investigation of multinational firms' compliance with International Accounting Standards. *The International Journal of Accounting, 34*(2), 239–248. DOI: 10.1016/S0020-7063(99)00005-9

El Hamza, M. (2018). *La convergence du référentiel comptable marocain aux normes IFRS (analyse empirique)* (Thèse de doctorat en sciences de gestion). Groupe ISCAE.

Elhamma, A. (2012). *Comprendre les normes comptables internationales IAS/IFRS au Maroc (1re* (Edition, E. D. G. L., Ed.).

Elhamma, A. (2023). Cinquante ans des normes comptables internationales IAS/IFRS: Adoption, conséquences et où en est-on au Maroc? In R. M'Rabet & M. A. Issami (Eds.), *50 ans de management: Regards croisés d'un demi-siècle du management* (pp. 121–136). Éditions EDISCA.

Elhamma, A. (2023). Impact of mandatory IFRS adoption on economic growth: The moderating role of COVID-19 crisis in developing countries. *Journal of Accounting and Management Information Systems*, *22*(3), 554–568. DOI: 10.24818/jamis.2023.03007

Elhamma, A. (2024). Determinants of national IFRS adoption: Evidence from the Middle East and North Africa region. *International Journal of Accounting. Auditing and Performance Evaluation*, *20*(1-2), 69–90. DOI: 10.1504/IJAAPE.2024.135535

Elhamma, A. (2025a). Impact of mandatory IFRS adoption on foreign direct investment: The moderating role of conflict of interest regulation. *Journal of Financial Reporting and Accounting*, *23*(3), 936–958. DOI: 10.1108/JFRA-04-2022-0145

Elhamma, A. (2025b). Perceived benefits of IFRS adoption in Morocco and French-speaking Sub-Saharan African countries. In F. Albuquerque & P. G. Dos Santos (Eds.), *Contemporary innovations in reporting and analysis* (pp. 183–210). IGI Global. https://doi.org/DOI: 10.4018/979-8-3693-5923-5.ch007

Elhamma, A., & Boutafrout, F. Z. (2025). Examining Creative Accounting as an Explanatory Factor of Taxpayer Behavior: Evidence From Morocco. In B. Alj, L. Alla, & B. Bentalha (Edts), *Modeling and Profiling Taxpayer Behavior and Compliance*, (pp. 165-184), IGI Global Scientific Pubishing. https://doi.org/DOI: 10.4018/979-8-3373-0422-9.ch007

Expert-Comptable, T. P. E. (n.d.). *Ressources pour les petites entreprises*. Retrieved October 10, 2019, from https://www.expert-comptable-tpe.fr/

Falikou Traore, H. (2010). *Enjeux des normes IAS/IFRS pour les comptes consolidés: Cas Omnium Nord-Africain* (Mémoire de fin d'études). Université My Ismail, Meknès.

Focus, I. F. R. S. (n.d.). *Site d'information sur les normes comptables internationales*. Retrieved February 22, 2020, from https://www.focusifrs.com/

Foundation, F. R. S. (n.d.). *IFRS International Financial Reporting Standards*. Retrieved August 1, 2019, from https://www.ifrs.org/

Gassen, J., & Sellhorn, T. (2006). Applying IFRS in Germany: Determinants and consequences. *German Economic Review*, *7*(2), 143–164.

Gray, S. J. (1988). Towards a theory of cultural influence on the development of accounting systems internationally. *Abacus, 24*(1), 1–15. DOI: 10.1111/j.1467-6281.1988.tb00200.x

Hand, J., & Skantz, T. (1998). The economic determinants of accounting choices: The unique case of equity carve-outs under SAB 51. *Journal of Accounting and Economics, 24*(2), 175–203. DOI: 10.1016/S0165-4101(98)00005-6

Haoudi, K. (2015). Passage aux normes IFRS au Maroc: Fondements théoriques, intérêts et enjeux. *International Journal of Innovation and Applied Studies, 10*(4), 1299–1311.

Hofstede, G. (1980). *Culture's consequences: International differences in work-related values.* Sage Publications.

Jeanjean, T. (1999). *La théorie positive de la comptabilité: Une revue de critiques. Cahier 99–12.* CEREG, Université Paris Dauphine.

Jensen, M. C., & Meckling, W. H. (1976). Theory of the firm: Managerial behavior, agency costs and ownership structure. *Journal of Financial Economics, 3*(4), 305–360. DOI: 10.1016/0304-405X(76)90026-X

Koleśnik, K. (2013). The role of culture in accounting in the light of Hofstede's, Gray's and Schwartz's cultural dimensions theories: A literature review. *Journal of Modern Accounting and Auditing, 9*(10), 1365–1375.

Marchal, S., Boukari, M., & Cayssials, J. L. (2007). L'impact des normes IAS/IFRS sur les données comptables des groupes français. *Bulletin de la Banque de France, 163*, 43–54.

Mita, A., Utama, S., Fitriany, F., & Wulandari, E. R. (2018). The adoption of IFRS, comparability of financial statements and foreign investors' ownership. *Asian Review of Accounting, 26*(3), 391–410. DOI: 10.1108/ARA-04-2017-0064

Moukil, A. (2011). *L'impact des normes IFRS sur les banques: Cas du passage aux normes IFRS dans la BMCE Bank* (Master's thesis). Université My Ismail, Meknès.

Nahmias, M. (2004). *L'essentiel des normes IAS/IFRS.* Éditions d'Organisation.

Nnadi, M., & Soobaroyen, T. (2015). International financial reporting standards and foreign direct investment: The case of Africa. *Advances in Accounting, 31*(2), 228–238. DOI: 10.1016/j.adiac.2015.09.007

Nobes, C. (1983). A judgmental international classification of financial reporting practices. *Journal of Business Finance & Accounting, 10*(1), 1–19. DOI: 10.1111/j.1468-5957.1983.tb00409.x

Nobes, C., & Parker, R. (2003). *Comparative international accounting* (7th ed.). Prentice Hall.

Păşcan, I.-D. (2015). Measuring the effects of IFRS adoption on accounting quality: A review. *Procedia Economics and Finance, 32*, 580–587. DOI: 10.1016/S2212-5671(15)01435-5

Raffournier, B. (1995). The determinants of voluntary financial disclosure by Swiss listed companies. *European Accounting Review, 4*(2), 261–280. DOI: 10.1080/09638189500000016

Ramond, O., Paugam, L., Casta, J. F., & Batsch, L. (2012). *Évaluation financière et normes comptables*. Economica.

Schipper, K. (1991). Commentary on earnings management. *Accounting Horizons, 5*(4), 91–102.

Stolowy, H., Lebas, M. J., & Langois, G. (2006). *Comptabilité et analyse financière: Une perspective globale* (1re éd.). Belgique: De Boeck & Larcier.

Turki, H., Wali, S., & Boujelbène, Y. (2017). Adoption obligatoire des IFRS et asymétrie d'information dans le contexte français: effet modérateur de l'endettement. *La revue Gestion et Organisation, Volume 9*, Issue 1, Pages 63-78. https://doi.org/ DOI: 10.1016/j.rgo.2017.01.001

Watts, R. L., & Zimmerman, J. L. (1990). Positive accounting theory: A ten-year perspective. *The Accounting Review, 65*(1), 131–156.

Zouak, H. (2012). *Les normes IFRS dans la mission d'audit: Cas de REDAL.* (Mémoire de master en Finance, Audit et Contrôle de gestion). Université Moulay Ismail, Meknès.

KEY TERMS AND DEFINITIONS

Bivariate analysis: Is a purely statistical method that allows to study the existence of a relationship or correlation between two variables, whatever their type (qualitative, quantitative or mixed).

Conceptual framework: Is a theoretical component that allows the presentation of the main concepts used in a study as well as the presumed relationship between them, with the aim of facilitating the understanding of the phenomenon studied. This concept is used in several disciplines, including in the field of IFRS standards, which serves as a guide for the IASB for the development of these standards.

Determinants: These are the variable and factors likely to explain the occurrence of a phenomenon, based on an empirical study aimed at confirming the existence of a relationship between these variables and the phenomenon studied.

IFRS: These are international accounting and financial standards that allow companies that adopt them to present their financial statements and reporting according to a standardized framework, in order to guarantee transparency, understandability and comparability of data on a global scale.

Logistic regression: Is a statistical method used to model the relationship between a binary dependent variable and one or more independent variables, whether qualitative, quantitative, or both.

The entity's debt: Is a method of financing that a company can use to cover its current activities or to finance its investments. This method of financing is based on external financial resources, mainly in the form of loans of credits.

The entity's international exposure: Defines the degree of integration of a company into the global economy. It reveals the scale and scope of its international activities.

The size of the company: Is one of its fundamental characteristics. It can vary according to several categories, namely: micro-enterprise, small enterprise, medium-sized enterprise, and large enterprise. This classification is mainly based on quantitative criteria, the most commonly used of which are the number of employees and annual revenue.

Chapter 6 Sustainability and Integration of ESG Reporting: Regulatory Frameworks, Standardization, and the Role of the ISSB

Sandra Tenorio-Salgueiro
https://orcid.org/0009-0004-9263-5288
University of Santiago de Compostela, Spain

Milagros Vivel-Búa
https://orcid.org/0000-0002-8829-3746
University of Santiago de Compostela, Spain

Rubén Lado-Sestayo
University of Santiago de Compostela, Spain

Andrea Martínez-Salgueiro
University of Vigo, Spain

ABSTRACT

The growing importance of sustainability information in financial and corporate sectors reflects an increasing focus on assessing risks and opportunities tied to environmental, social, and governance (ESG) factors. However, the lack of a harmonized global framework has hindered the comparability and reliability of this information. This chapter reviews the main regulatory frameworks and sustainability reporting standards, highlighting the role of the International Sustainability Standards Board

DOI: 10.4018/979-8-3373-1902-5.ch006

(ISSB) and its IFRS Sustainability Disclosure Standards S1 and S2, which aim to establish a homogeneous global basis. Despite their initial implementation, these standards must coexist with local regulations such as the Corporate Sustainability Reporting Directive (CSRD) and the European Sustainability Reporting Standards (ESRS), as well as widely accepted voluntary frameworks like the Global Reporting Initiative (GRI). This situation presents a challenge for companies, investors, and regulatory bodies.

1. INTRODUCTION

Over the last few years, interest has increased in the challenges and opportunities generated by environmental, social and governance (ESG) factors in organisations. This situation has led to corporate sustainability information becoming increasingly relevant in the financial sphere. However, there is no harmonised reporting system that allows the incorporation of this information in decision-making, and this has led to difficulties in terms of comparability and reliability.

The rising interest in corporate sustainability reporting has led to the creation of different regulatory frameworks and sustainability standards. This chapter reviews the evolution and current state of these models, with a special focus on the work of the International Sustainability Standards Board (ISSB), which was based in 2021 by the IFRS Foundation to issue sustainability standards, having already published IFRS S1 and IFRS S2. These standards, whose implementation is currently beginning, aim to establish a harmonised sustainability reporting framework at a global level, but their adoption will depend on the regulatory decisions of the countries, so that in practice they will have to coexist with other standards already established or with local regulations. A clear example of this coexistence is the European Union, where a separate regulatory path has been followed through the approval of the Corporate Sustainability Reporting Directive (CSRD) and the creation of the European Sustainability Reporting Standards (ESRS).

In addition, the Global Reporting Initiative (GRI) is the most extensively employed global benchmark for sustainability reporting (KPMG, 2022; IFAC & IACPA, 2023). In the current context, it is foreseeable that IFRS S1 and S2, together with ESRS and the GRI framework, will coexist in business practice.

This context of coexistence of different mandatory regulatory frameworks and voluntary standards generates an increase in complexity, costs and risks for companies and investors. IFRS S1 and S2 aim to provide a global model that facilitates interoperability between the different systems, facilitating the disclosure process for companies and decision-making for investors.

The aim of this chapter is to analyse the main standards and regulatory frameworks for sustainability reporting, with a focus on the work of the ISSB, and the impact of IFRS S1 and S2 on the transparency, comparability and integration of sustainability information in financial decisions. In a context marked by the coexistence of different frameworks, it also reflects on their interoperability and the challenges that this situation poses for the real convergence of financial and non-financial information.

This study has followed a methodology consisting of a descriptive and analytical documentary review, focusing on the main sustainability reporting standards and regulatory frameworks. The aim is to answer the following research question: What is the impact of IFRS S1 and S2 on the transparency, comparability and integration of sustainability information in financial decision-making and how can these standards coexist with other frameworks and standards?

This work has identified a relaxation of regulatory requirements on sustainability disclosure in the European Union, with the incorporation of the Omnibus package in 2025, and an even more pronounced standstill in the United States. In this context, the introduction of IFRS S1 and S2 constitutes a milestone in the standardization of reporting globally. However, differences in the approach to materiality (IFRS applies single materiality, while GRI and ESRS apply double materiality) generate interoperability difficulties between the main frameworks that pose a challenge on the road to harmonisation and real convergence of financial and non-financial reporting.

This paper contributes to academic research by providing an up-to-date and detailed overview of the current sustainability disclosure landscape, with a particular focus on IFRS S1 and S2, and the challenges of harmonisation at the global level.

The chapter is structured in several sections. First, it presents the literature review, which provides a conceptual delineation of key terms in the field of corporate sustainability and reviews previous studies in this field of academic research. This is followed by the methodology of this study. Then, it presents the results achieved and discussion of the work (current state of sustainability disclosures, the impact of IFRS S1 and S2 and analysis of interoperability with the most influential frameworks). Finally, the conclusions are presented, reflecting on the coexistence of the different frameworks and the challenges associated with global harmonisation.

2. LITERATURE REVIEW

2.1. Conceptual Delimitation

Before addressing the literature review, the key concepts that will be used throughout the paper are delimited in order to facilitate their understanding.

The conceptual delimitation of corporate sustainability is sometimes not simple. This is due to the fact that, despite the widespread prominence of corporate sustainability in different forums at the political, economic, social and other levels, there is still some confusion surrounding various key terms linked to it, but which are not strictly equivalent. For example, the terms of 'sustainability' and 'ESG (environmental, social and governance)' are usually used as synonyms, although they are conceptually different. Similarly, the terms 'sustainability regulation' and 'sustainability reporting standards' have different connotations, although they are often used interchangeably. The following is a conceptual delimitation of the main terms in the field of corporate sustainability.

Broadly speaking, *corporate sustainability* involves adopting responsible business strategies and practices that seek to produce positive impacts on the environmental, social and economic environment. The purpose is to guarantee the prosperity of the entity and the communities in which it operates in the long run.

Corporate sustainability reporting, formerly known as non-financial reporting, embodies the current focus on transparency. In these documents companies detail their responsible sustainability practices and strategies. Traditionally, annual reports focused mainly on financial aspects. However, in the last two decades, many companies globally have started to produce corporate sustainability reports, which address three key dimensions (ESG): environmental (the influence of the company's activity on the environment), social (the influence of business activity on society) and governance (how the company articulates its corporate governance).

These reports guide corporations to express their commitment to sustainability and to show how they influence society and the environment, offering a broader perspective of their management, beyond financial indicators.

Today, corporate sustainability reporting is increasingly subject to *sustainability reporting regulations*, especially in Europe, the region where the greatest progress in regulation has been made. These regulations seek to ensure transparency and comparability of the data disclosed, as well as to delimit the companies obliged to disclose sustainability information.

The surge in corporate sustainability reporting, driven in large part by the above-mentioned legislative efforts, has led to the development of a number of *sustainability reporting standards*. These frameworks provide clear guidelines "to help companies measure, manage and communicate their sustainability performance" (de Arriba-Sellier, 2023) in an effective and consistent manner. In contrast to mandatory regulations imposed by public bodies, these standards are initiatives developed by private bodies and partnerships, which makes them voluntary. However, their adoption by companies has been so significant that they have influenced the creation of formal sustainability disclosure regulations. Indeed, the widespread acceptance and application of these standards has led regulators to consider their guidelines and principles when developing sustainability regulations. This is because these frameworks offer proven methodologies and best practices that facilitate the measurement and communication of sustainability performance.

ESG refers to metrics that evaluate a corporation's sustainability and "are used by investors, analysts and other stakeholders to analyse its environmental, social and governance performance" (Ding et. al, 2025). Because they are developed by an external party, they provide valuable insight into the company's sustainability performance.

2.2. Previous Studies

Several authors have addressed the analysis of sustainability reporting in academic research to date. Globally, the work of van der Lugt et al. (2020) stands out, who examined the state of current sustainability reporting internationally, including mandatory systems, i.e. regulatory frameworks, and voluntary systems, i.e. reporting standards. In particular, they reviewed the reporting model in 84 countries and the main trends, challenges and policy views at the international level. Their results showed a considerable increase in the number of regulatory measures, but also in the complexity of the system, and highlighted the lack of coordination between different issuers and the urgent need to harmonise the reporting process.

In the European Union, the leadership of this region in the issuance of sustainability reporting standards has been emphasized. Castilla et. al (2021) highlighted the transparency that characterises European companies in the publication of their sustainable practices. Fernández-Feijóo et. al (2014) concluded that European countries lead the ranking in the disclosure of information on corporate social responsibility.

In particular, some authors have analysed the coexistence of IFRS S1 and S2 with existing reporting models (del Olmo & López, 2024; Macías & Fico, 2023). This research highlights the complexity of the current landscape and the difficulties in the interoperability of existing systems.

In addition, some studies have been carried out that specifically explore the influence of IFRS on certain economic variables. Elhamma (2023) analysed the impact of mandatory IFRS on economic growth, examining the moderating effect of the COVID-19 crisis in developed countries. The same author, in 2025, conducted a study of the impact on foreign direct investment, taking into account the dampening effect of conflict-of-interest regulation.

Finally, the adoption of IFRS in specific regions has also been studied. Elhamma (2024) analysed the determinants of IFRS adoption in the Middle East and North Africa. The same author, in 2025, analysed the benefits of IFRS adoption in Morocco and French-speaking sub-Saharan countries.

Few studies have addressed corporate sustainability reporting in a comprehensive manner, analysing both mandatory and voluntary frameworks together. This study aims to present a comparative study of the different models from an up-to-date perspective, with a focus on IFRS S1 and S2, and their impact on the transparency, comparability and integration of financial and non-financial information at a global level.

3. METHODOLOGY

The methodology of this study consists of a descriptive and analytical documentary review, which focuses on the outstanding sources of sustainability reporting standards and regulation. Thus, the research is based on official documents issued by voluntary standard issuing bodies and regulatory bodies that are the main actors in the current landscape of sustainability disclosure.

In particular, documents such as drafts, standards, technical guides and institutional communiqués published between 1997 and 2025 were collected and reviewed. A detailed reading of official documents was carried out, complemented by academic articles on the subject under study.

The objective is to identify convergences and divergences between the frameworks analysed, with a particular focus on IFRS S1 and S2, in order to conclude on their interoperability.

4. RESULTS AND DISCUSSION

4.1. Current Status of Corporate Sustainability Disclosures

Managing sustainability challenges and opportunities has become a key factor for investors and their investment strategies. A survey conducted by PWC in 2021 revealed that 79% of investors consider sustainability issues to be essential to their decision-making (Chalmers et. al, 2021). In addition, another survey by the Task Force on Climate-related Financial Disclosures (TCFD) in 2022 revealed that 90% of investors and other stakeholders use climate-related information to guide financial decisions, and 66% take this data into account when valuing financial assets (TCFD, 2022).

Disclosure of sustainability information is increasing, although it is mainly concentrated in large companies in developed markets, with variations by sector and company.

A 2022 KPMG study revealed that 79% of the 5,800 corporations with highest revenue in 58 countries report on sustainability, up from 64% in 2012. Taking into account the 250 largest corporations globally, 96% report on sustainability. However, the growth is mostly seen in companies with more than $10 billion in market capitalisation. High disclosure rates, exceeding 85%, have been found in Asia-Pacific and Western Europe, and even exceeding 95% in North America. Eastern Europe and Latin America show moderate rates of close to 70%, while the Middle East and Africa show a much lower rate of around 50% (KPMG, 2022).

The content of sustainability reporting varies significantly by company: 64% focus on environmental risks, 49% on social risks and 44% on governance. Moreover, these differences depend on industry sectors. For example, the energy, mining, technology and automotive industries tend to report more frequently on climate risks, while biodiversity is more commonly addressed in the mining, forestry, food and beverage, energy, utilities and chemicals sectors (KPMG, 2022).

The Carrots & Sticks 2020 document distinguish a total of 266 voluntary sustainability reporting systems, including reporting standards and others, as well as 348 mandatory systems, mainly regulations developed by public bodies, covering a total of 60 countries (van der Lugt et. al, 2020).

4.2. Sustainability Reporting Standards

Sustainability reporting standards are voluntary, but they have had a substantial effect on the evolution of regulatory frameworks for mandatory application. This is the case of the European Union, which has opted for the implementation of its own regulations, a process that has culminated in the approval of the CSRD and the issuance of the ESRS in 2023. Throughout the elaboration phase of the ESRS, the European Financial Reporting Action Group (EFRAG) and the European Commission have relied on renowned international organizations such as the ISSB, the GRI and the TCFD.

The purpose of this section is to examine the evolution and current status of the main sustainability reporting standards. It looks in depth at the work of the ISSB and the IFRS S1 and S2 standards, which are expected to be implemented as mandatory standards by different jurisdictions and to contribute to the harmonisation of the global reporting state.

4.2.1. Current Situation

Currently, the most extensively employed sustainability reporting standards globally are the models developed by the GRI, the Sustainability Accounting Standards Board (SASB) and the TCFD.

Research conducted by the International Federation of Accountants (IFAC) and the International Association of Certified Professional Accountants (IACPA) in 2023 showed that, out of a pool of 1,350 companies, 999 used the GRI, 851 the TCFD and 662 the SASB model (IFAC & IACPA, 2023).

A KPMG report in 2022 identified that considering the top 100 corporations in 58 countries (with a global sample of 5,800), 68% used the GRI, 34% the TCFD and 33% the SASB model. These figures increased to 78%, 61% and 49%, respectively, among the 250 largest companies globally (KPMG, 2022).

4.2.2. Factors Hindering Comparability

An international survey conducted in 2021 by PwC revealed that 33% of investors rated the quality of disclosures as "poor", indicating a lack of rigour on key aspects related to sustainability and its relevance to the business model (Chalmers et. al, 2021). Similarly, the Global Investor Survey 2022 indicated that 87% of respondents believe that corporate reporting includes unsubstantiated information about companies' sustainable practices (Chalmers et. al, 2022).

KPMG's 2022 work revealed that less than half of the companies had any assurance system on sustainable reporting, making it difficult for investors to rely on the quality of the information. In addition, this work also showed that many organizations used several frameworks simultaneously in their disclosure: 68% the GRI model, 34% the TCFD model, 33% the SASB model and 23% the stock exchange guidance (KPMG, 2022).

The deficiencies in the quality of information identified by users of the reports, coupled with the use of several frameworks by companies, lead to difficulties in comparing information and using it in decision-making. Companies also suffer from inefficiencies and additional costs in the reporting process.

In this context, IFRS S1 and S2 aim to provide an international harmonised framework to enable companies to prepare their information efficiently and investors to use transparent and comparable information for decision-making.

4.2.3. Evolution of the Main Reporting Standards

Global Reporting Initiative (GRI)

It was established in the US in 1997, in the wake of the environmental crisis following the Exxon Valdez oil spill, as a collaborative project developed by non-profit organisations, with the backing of the United Nations Environment Programme (UNEP) (GRI, n.d.).

It is a non-profit organisation that aims to facilitate the disclosure of sustainability information at an international level. To this end, it issued its first guidelines in 2000, which in 2016 became the first global sustainability reporting standards. They are currently used by more than 14,000 companies in over 100 countries (GRI, n.d.).

A KPMG study in 2022 showed that they are the most extensively used standards internationally (KPMG, 2022). Another EFRAG study revealed that they are also the most widely used standards at the European level (EFRAG, 2021).

Carbon Disclosure Project (CDP)

It was established in the UK in 2000 by institutional investors. It is a non-profit organisation that aims to enhance transparency and accountability in the field of corporate sustainability (Depoers et al., 2016).

Annually, the CDP collects data on the emissions, climate risks and sustainable strategies of large international companies. It is aligned with the TFCD and in 2021 was used by more than 14,000 companies to disclose their sustainable information (CDP, 2022).

Climate Disclosure Standards Board (CDSB)

It was established in the UK in 2007. It is an international grouping of environmental and business organisations, which aims to establish a model for environmental information disclosure. The CDP is represented in the internal bodies of the CDSB, which is aligned with the TCFD (CDSB, n.d.).

Sustainability Accounting Standards Board (SASB)

It was founded in 2011 in the US. It is a non-profit organisation that was created with the aim of facilitating the communication of sustainability information (IFRS, n.d.).

It provides standards available for 77 sectors, which identify challenges and opportunities most likely to impact on companies' financial variables and disclose the most useful measures for investors (IFRS, n.d.).

International Integrated Reporting Council (IIRC)

It was established in the UK in 2011 by "a coalition of regulators, investors, businesses, standards regulators, standard setters, accountancy professionals and non-governmental organisations" (IR, 2013).

In 2014 it issued the International Integrated Reporting (IR) Framework, with the aim of promoting the quality of sustainability reporting to aid decision-making (Medisoa, 2023).

In 2020, five of the major international organisations in the area of sustainability disclosure announced their collaboration through the publication of the "Statement of Intent to Work Together Towards Comprehensive Corporate Reporting" (CDP et al., 2020), with the support of the European Commission, the IFRS Foundation, the International Organisation of Securities Commissions (IOSCO) and the International Business Council of the World Economic Forum (WEF).

In 2021 the IIRC merged with the SASB and formed the Value Reporting Foundation (VRF). In 2022, the VRF and the CDSB consolidated into the IFRS Foundation, which had founded the ISSB in 2021 (IFRS, n.d.).

Task Force on Climate-related Financial Disclosures (TCFD)

It was founded in 2015 by The Financial Stability Board (TSB). It is an international organisation that aims to facilitate the dissemination of climate information (IBM, n.d.).

The TCFD recommendations, published in 2017, can be integrated with existing organisational performance reports. By November 2022, more than 4,000 organisations in 101 jurisdictions endorsed the TCFD, representing total capital of US$27 trillion. Between 2017 and 2021, the number of companies reporting under the TCFD grew by 26% (IBM, n.d.). Although initially voluntary guidelines, these recommendations have been adopted as part of mandatory regulations in various regions (IBM, n.d.).

In the EU context, the creation and revision of the ESRS was supported by several international organisations, including the TCFD. The structure of the ESRS, which were adopted in 2024, is organised around four main pillars modelled on the TCFD. This alignment facilitates harmonisation between the two standards and allows companies already familiar with the TCFD framework to more easily integrate ESRS requirements into their disclosure practices.

In 2023, the US Securities and Exchange Commission (SEC) approved "The Enhacement and Standardization of Climate-Related Disclosures for Investors", climate risk disclosure legislation, which incorporates elements of the TCFD framework.

World Economic Forum (WEF)

It was founded in 1971 in Switzerland as a non-profit organisation with the aim of promoting cooperation between various stakeholders (WEF, 2020).

In 2020, it published its sustainability reporting model, the document "Measuring Stakeholder Capitalism - Towards common metrics and consistent reporting of sustainable value creation", which is aligned with the GRI and the TCFD.

International Sustainability Standards Board (ISSB)

The IFRS Foundation Consultation

In 2020, the IFRS Foundation launched a public consultation to assess whether there was a need for it to engage in standard setting in the area of sustainability. This consultation revealed that stakeholders needed more transparent and comparable sustainability information for decision-making (IFRS, 2020). In particular, both investors and international bodies, such as the G20, G7 and IOSCO, saw an urgent need for the IFRS Foundation to issue sustainability standards (IFRS, 2020).

Establishment of the ISSB

It was founded in 2021 by the IFRS Foundation, in response to the public consultation launched in 2020. It is a global sustainability standard-setting body that operates in parallel with the International Accounting Standards Board (IASB), which focuses on financial reporting standards (IFRS, 2020).

Work of the ISSB

The work of the ISSB is to elaborate the IFRS Sustainability Disclosure Standards, a sustainability disclosure framework that promotes transparency and comparability of sustainability information globally, and facilitates interoperability with other reporting models (IFRS, n.d.).

To ensure the connection between IFRS and sustainability standards, the ISSB works closely with the IASB. Although they are independent boards, they work in continuous coordination to ensure the compatibility of their standards (IFRS, n.d.).

ISSB Standards Development Process

A rigorous process was followed to satisfy the needs of an extensive group of global stakeholders (IFRS, 2023).

First, draft standards were published in March 2022, which were based on accepted reporting standards. Second, a consultation was launched in which dissemination events were held and through which comments and responses were received on the draft standards (IFRS, 2023). Finally, through a thorough analysis of the feedback received, which involved the preparation of documents and additional meetings, the revision of the definitive release of IFRS S1 and S2 was completed (IFRS, 2023).

ISSB Support on Sustainability Reporting Standards

The ISSB builds on initiatives of various global bodies - CDSB, IIRC, SASB, VRF, TCFD and WEF - and works closely with the GRI.

In 2021 the IIRC merged with the SASB and formed the VRF. In 2022, the VRF and the CDSB consolidated into the IFRS Foundation, which had founded the ISSB in 2021 (IFRS, n.d.).

Both the TCFD and the WEF have supported the foundation of the ISSB. Companies implementing IFRS S1 and S2 will comply with the TCFD's model, as this is integrated into the ISSB Standards (IFRS, n.d.).

In addition, as of March 2022, the GRI and the IFRS Foundation have entered into a collaboration to cooperate in their sustainability-related labour and standards development programmes, with the aim of ensuring compatibility between ISSB's investor-focused reporting and the GRI's reporting to a wider audience (IFRS, n.d.).

Dissemination of ISSB Standards

In June 2023, the ISSB published IFRS S1, which sets out "general requirements for sustainability-related financial disclosures", and IFRS S2, which focuses on "climate-related disclosures" (IFRS, n.d.). These standards are effective for the fiscal year 2024 (IFRS, n.d.).

IFRS S1, *"General Requirements for Financial Information Related to Sustainability"*, "sets out requirements for companies to disclose decision-useful information for investors about sustainability-related risks and opportunities in the short, medium and long term" (IFRS n.d.). IFRS S2, *"Climate-related Disclosures"*, "sets out requirements for companies to disclose information on their climate risks and opportunities, building on IFRS S1" (IFRS, n.d.). This standard integrates the TCFD model (IFRS n.d.).

Given the authority of the IFRS Foundation, the ISSB standards leave a number of decisions to the local jurisdiction, including whether the standard is mandatory (IFRS n.d.).

Forthcoming ISSB Areas of Work

In the two years after the enforcement of the standards, the ISSB's main focus will be on facilitating adoption.

In addition, it has initiated projects to investigate the divulge of challenges and opportunities related to "biodiversity, ecosystems and human capital" (IFRS n.d.). Also, it has been decided that the improvement of the SASB Standards will be a priority. Currently, the ISSB Standards only cover general requirements and climate, without addressing in depth other areas, for which companies need to take into account the SASB Standards. Improving these standards is therefore an appropriate approach to support the implementation of IFRS S1 (IFRS n.d.).

4.3. Sustainability Reporting Regulation

In recent years, a very considerable grow has been observed in sustainability-related regulation, especially in the context of the European Union.

Europe is considered to be at the forefront of the transformation towards a sustainable economic model for two main reasons: firstly, because sustainability is projected as the engine of future growth; and secondly, because it is addressed as a cross-cutting policy that affects all other areas, rather than being treated as an isolated initiative (Castilla et. al, 2021). European companies lead the ranking in the disclosure of information on corporate social responsibility (Fernández-Feijóo et. al, 2014), and the transparency that characterises companies in this region in the disclosure of their sustainable practices stands out (Castilla et. al, 2021).

The European Union has chosen to issue its own sustainability disclosure regulations, publishing ESRS in 2023. In addition, other regions have also implemented or plan to implement mandatory regulations in this area, such as Brazil, Canada, Egypt, New Zealand, Singapore, Switzerland, the United Kingdom and the United States (IFRS, 2023).

The objective of this section is to examine the regulatory state for sustainability disclosure, differentiating between the EU and the US.

4.3.1. EU Corporate Sustainability Disclosure Regulations

Non-Financial Reporting Directive (NFRD) (2014)

In October 2014, the European Parliament and the European Council adopted the Non-Financial Reporting Directive 2014/95/EU (NFRD), which extended the non-financial disclosure requirements introduced by Directive 2013/34/EU.

The NFRD aims to improve the transparency and responsibility of large entities relative to their social and environmental impacts. It requires some large entities to communicate non-financial information, thereby providing stakeholders - including investors, consumers and civil society - with relevant data that they can consider in their decision-making. Specifically, it applies to "large public interest entities with more than 500 employees, including listed companies, banks, insurance companies and other public interest entities" (European Parliament and Council, 2014).

The Directive promotes a standardised approach to non-financial reporting across all EU members and aims to ensure comparability and reliability of disclosures. In paragraph 9 of the introduction, the Directive gives some examples of national, European or international frameworks that corporations may use to communicate their non-financial information, such as the GRI. In any case, companies should indicate which model they have used.

To complement the NFRD, the European Commission published, in 2017, the Guidelines on Non-Financial Reporting (2017/C 215/01), and, in 2019, the Supplement on Climate-related Reporting (2019/C 209/01).

Corporate Sustainability Reporting Directive (CSRD) (2022)

In 2021, through an evaluation process of the NFRD issued in 2014, the European Commission concluded that the comparability and accessibility of the information was insufficient, and the scope of coverage was narrow, which drive to the issuance of a new Corporate Sustainability Reporting Directive (CSRD), approved by the European Parliament and European Council in December 2022, whose primary objective is to address these shortcomings of the previous regulation.

In particular, the CSRD aims to increase the transparency, comparability and consistency of reporting, to close the divergence between the information needs of users and the sustainability data that companies provide, and to reinforce the shift to a sustainable economic and social model in the European Union (Andreu et al., 2024).

The main new feature of the CSRD compared to the NFRD is the introduction of the ESRS, developed by the EFRAG and published in July 2023.

Another of the most relevant changes with respect to the previous Directive is the extension of the scope of application, in a progressive and staggered manner over time:

- In 2025 (fiscal year 2024), it will apply to companies that were already subject to the NFRD, "i.e. large public interest companies with more than 500 employees" (European Parliament and Council, 2014).
- In 2026 (tax year 2025), it will affect companies that meet two of these criteria: "more than 250 employees, turnover of more than EUR 40 million and/or a balance sheet total of EUR 20 million" (European Parliament and Council, 2014).
- In 2027 (tax year 2026) it will apply to "listed SMEs, small and non-complex financial institutions and captive insurance and reinsurance undertakings" (European Parliament and Council, 2014).

- o Finally, in 2028 (tax year 2027), the Directive will reach third country companies "turnover of more than €150 million and at least one branch or subsidiary with a turnover of more than €40 million" (European Parliament and Council, 2014).

The CSRD replaces, in paragraph 8 of its introduction, the term 'non-financial information' used hitherto, and in particular taken over by the previous NFRD, with the term 'sustainability information'. It considers that the former is inaccurate, as the reality is that such information is increasingly important from a financial point of view.

The new Directive attaches considerable importance to the concept of dual materiality. Organizations will be required to conduct a dual materiality analysis, evaluating the influence of the entity's practices on people, society and the environment, and sustainability challenges and opportunities that impact the company's results (Scheel, 2024).

In addition, the CSRD introduces the obligation to present the data in a united electronic format (XHTML language), for its easy incorporation into the Single European Access Point, which will favour the accessibility of the information and contribute to European digitalisation. Finally, the new Directive requires corporations to have their sustainability information verified by an independent third party, initially through a limited verification commission, but with the expectation of moving towards reasonable assurance as of 2028 (Andreu et al., 2024).

European Sustainability Reporting Standards (ESRS) (2023)

ESRS were published by the European Commission in July 2023, through a delegated act that complements the requirements established by the CSRD. They have been developed by the EFRAG, an independent organisation appointed by the European Commission "to provide technical advice on the development of the standards" (EFRAG, n.d.).

Currently, 12 sustainability reporting standards have been published, which are grouped into two main blocks: cross-cutting and thematic standards. The cross-cutting standards serve as a reference and should be consulted when interpreting the thematic standards. The thematic standards, also known as sector-agnostic, are applicable to all companies and are distributed into three sub-blocks: environment, social and governance. Each thematic standard contains a set of disclosure requirements (DRs), complemented by implementation requirements (ARs), which have the same authority as the disclosure requirements (Andreu et al., 2024).

One of the most important new features introduced by these standards is the requirement to conduct a dual materiality analysis ("financial materiality" and "impact materiality")" (European Commission, 2023).

As for the sectoral standards, the European Commission has decided to postpone their entry into force by two years, now setting June 2026 as the new date.

Throughout the process of developing and revising the ESRS, EFRAG and the European Commission have worked closely with various international organisations, such as ISSB, GRI and TCFD. This joint effort seeks to guarantee a top level of interoperability between sustainability reporting models.

The structure of the ESRS, in terms of reporting areas, is organised around four main pillars that replicate that of the TCFD. This alignment facilitates harmonisation between standards and allows companies already familiar with other reporting frameworks to more easily integrate ESRS requirements into their disclosure practices.

By promoting this interoperability, the aim is not only to simplify the process for corporations to report their sustainability information, but also to improve comparability and transparency for investors and other stakeholders. This is essential to foster greater confidence in the information disclosed and to promote the evolution to a more sustainable economy.

Given the level of difficulty some companies may face in complying with certain issues required by the standards, a number of transitional exemptions have been provided to facilitate their implementation.

Proposal for the Simplification of Key Corporate Sustainability Regulations (Omnibus Package) (2025)

On 26 February 2025, the European Commission issued two proposals for directives aimed at simplifying the main corporate sustainability regulations in the EU. The first amends several key directives - "auditing, accounting, sustainability reporting and corporate due diligence"- (European Commission, 2025), while the second suggest to postpone the implementation of certain reporting requirements (European Commission, 2025).

These initiatives are part of the Omnibus package, which aims to reduce regulatory burdens, foster a more favourable business environment and strengthen EU competitiveness and growth. It is estimated that they could generate annual administrative savings of around €6.3 billion and mobilise around €50 billion in public and private investment (European Commission, 2025).

The main changes proposed to the CSRD include the following:

- Reduced scope: It would be limited to "large companies with more than 1,000 employees, reducing the number of companies subject to the standard by 80% and aligning the thresholds with the Corporate Sustainability Due Diligence Directive (CSDDD)" (European Commission, 2025).

- o Revision of the ESRS: ESRS will be revised to reduce data points, clarify requirements, improve consistency with other legislation and simplify implementation.
- o Abolition of sector-specific rules: The possibility of adopting sector-specific rules will be eliminated.
- o Removal of reasonable warranty: The option to require a reasonable warranty in lieu of a limited warranty is removed.
- o Deferral of requirements: It is proposed to defer the adoption of the CSRD by two years for large corporations that do not yet report and for listed SMEs.

This new proposal aims to alleviate the excessive administrative burden that the CSRD places on SMEs and medium-sized companies. In this way, the revised Directive only applies to large companies, with more than 1,000 employees and with specific financial criteria. Smaller companies will be able to opt for more simplified voluntary reporting.

4.3.2. U.S. Corporate Sustainability Disclosure Regulations

Comparison: European Union vs United States

The European regulatory framework for sustainability is stricter and more specific, while the United States has maintained a more relaxed approach and lacks an equivalent regulation in this area.

This disparity is also reflected in the regulation of corporate sustainability-related disclosures. In Europe, we have seen a significant evolution in the requirements for companies, starting with the publication of the NFRD in 2014, followed by the CSRD in 2022, and culminating in 2023 with the issuance of the ESRS.

In the US, regulatory progress was virtually non-existent until 2024, when the SEC published its first rule on sustainability disclosures, entitled "The Enhancement and Standardization of Climate-Related Disclosures for Investors". However, following litigation in the Eighth Circuit, the SEC suspended the climate disclosure rule and, on 27 March 2025, after the change of Administration in the US, decided to withdraw its advocacy of the rules as costly and intrusive (SEC, 2025).

The lack of a strong regulatory framework in sustainability, especially in terms of disclosure, has led to weaker sustainability practices among US companies. Environmental scores are notably higher in Europe, with an upward trend, while in the US the increase is less pronounced (Peiró & Segarra, 2013). In the social dimension, European companies also score better, while in corporate governance, North American companies stand out more (Peiró & Segarra, 2013). European companies lead in sustainability disclosure and are more committed to reporting, while

North American companies show lower levels of disclosure and a less systematic approach to sharing this information (Hartman et al., 2007).

The Enhacement and Standardization of Climate-Related Disclosures for Investors (2024)

On 6 March 2024, the SEC approved " The Enhacement and Standardization of Climate-Related Disclosures for Investors", a rule aimed at improving public communication of climate-related risks and impacts by corporations.

This new regulation requires entities to communicate climate risk management and how they oversee these risks. It also requires disclosure of "the financial effects of extreme weather events and other natural conditions in audited financial statements" (PWC, 2024). For larger companies it also demands disclosure on "their greenhouse gas emissions, which will be subject to a phased-in verification requirement" (PWC, 2024).

The US regulation is based on the TCFD model, which also serves as a reference for other recent reporting regulation worldwide. However, the SEC's rules differ significantly from other frameworks, such as the CSRD or the IFRS Sustainability Disclosure Standards. The SEC has indicated that it will "monitor how reporting evolves under international requirements and practices before deciding whether this approach would provide consistent, reliable and comparable information for investors" (PWC, 2024).

The new rules were scheduled to take effect in 2026 (fiscal year 2025), with extended deadlines for smaller companies and for disclosures related to greenhouse gas emissions. Nevertheless, the rules were temporarily suspended by the SEC due to challenges to the rules by several states and individuals, which resulted in consolidated litigation before the Eighth Circuit. On 27 March 2025, following the change in government in the US, the SEC voted to withdraw its support of these new rules, arguing that they were costly and overly intrusive (SEC, 2025).

The withdrawal of the SEC's defence does not automatically mean that the rules are invalidated. The Eighth Circuit has yet to rule on the legal challenges and could resolve to maintain them in whole or in part, or relegate them to the SEC for reconsideration. Nevertheless, this decision marks a clear shift in the agency's approach to climate disclosure under the new Trump administration (Sidley, 2025).

4.4. The Sustainability Disclosure Standards: IFRS S1 and S2

4.4.1. IFRS Standard S1: General Requirements for Financial Disclosures Related to Sustainability

IFRS S1 "requires companies to disclose information about sustainability risks and opportunities that is relevant to investors' decision-making" (IFRS, 2023). To meet this requirement, it develops general requirements on how to divulge this data and how to integrate it into a full set of sustainability-related financial information (IFRS, 2023).

It is based on the International Integrated Reporting Framework, developed by the IIRC, currently part of the IFRS Foundation (IFRS, 2023).

The most relevant information on the standard is presented below:

Main Content of IFRS S1

The standard requires disclosure in four key areas, aligned with the TCFD model, but extended to "sustainability risks and opportunities beyond climate change: governance, strategy, risk management, and metrics and targets" (IFRS, 2023).

Conceptual Basics of IFRS S1

Material or Relevant Information

IFRS S1 "is designed to meet the information needs of investors and it requires disclosure of material information about sustainability risks and opportunities that could reasonably affect the company's prospects" (IFRS, 2023). Information is material "if its omission, inaccuracy or bias could influence the decisions of primary users of financial information" (IFRS, 2023).

Reasonable Presentation

Sustainability reporting should accurately represent "the material risks and opportunities that could reasonably be expected to affect an enterprise's prospects", providing a full, neutral and accurate description (IFRS, 2023).

Reporting Entity

The entity disclosing sustainability information must be the same entity reporting the financial statements. Thus, a parent company that presents consolidated statements under IFRS should also present sustainability information for the whole group (IFRS, 2023).

Connected Information

The company should disclose the connections between "sustainability risks and opportunities; areas of governance, strategy, risk management, metrics and targets; and sustainability information and financial statements" (IFRS, 2023).

General Requirements of IFRS S1

Location of information

The data requested by the ISSB Standards must be included in general purpose financial reports along with the financial statements. Additional sustainability information may be added as long as it does not distort or hinder the understanding of the material disclosures required by IFRS S1 and S2 (IFRS, 2023).

Frequency of publication

Sustainability information should be presented at identical moment and cover identical period as the financial statements. Related to the first year of application, companies will be able to present this information in the next half-yearly financial report (IFRS, 2023).

Comparative information

Comparative information must be presented for all amounts, unless otherwise stated in another standard. Comparatives are not required to be included in the first year of application, nor for non-climatic sustainability risks in the second year if only climatic risks were initially reported (IFRS, 2023).

Declaration of compliance

Firms should "make an explicit and unreserved declaration of compliance with the ISSB Standards" (IFRS, 2023), provided that they meet all ISSB requirements. They are exempt from disclosing information prohibited by law or regulation, or information about opportunities whose disclosure would be commercially sensitive (IFRS, 2023).

Current and expected financial effects

Disclose how sustainability challenges and opportunities "affect, and are expected to affect, the financial position and financial variables results and cash flows in the short, medium and long term, integrating it into financial planning" (IFRS, 2023).

Judgements, uncertainties and errors

Companies should disclose significant judgements employed in the formulation of sustainability information, report the key uncertainties that affect the amounts reported and restate comparative information if errors are detected, unless impracticable (IFRS, 2023).

4.4.2. IFRS Standard S2: Climate-related Disclosures

IFRS S1 requires "companies to apply IFRS S2 to identify and disclose material information about climate-related risks and opportunities that may reasonably affect their prospects" (IFRS, 2023). IFRS S2 establishes specific disclosure requirements around "governance, strategy, risk management, as well as companies' climate metrics and objectives" (IFRS, 2023).

Climate-related risks are threats that can negatively affect an entity's operations, financial performance or strategy due to the influence of climate change. Climate change can impact businesses through both physical risks - such as a raise in the occurrence of unusual weather conditions - and transitional risks, related to changes in policies, regulations or technological advances (IFRS, 2023).

In turn, climate opportunities are related to efforts to reduce or adapt to climate change, offering businesses possibilities for innovation, expansion into new markets or sustainable product development (IFRS, 2023).

The most relevant information on the standard is presented below:

Scope of Disclosures Required by IFRS S2

Governance

According to IFRS S2, companies must disclose information explaining how their governance processes, internal controls and oversight mechanisms address climate change risks and opportunities, thereby facilitating investor understanding.

The company should disclose how its governance structure oversees climate-related risks and opportunities.

This includes identifying the responsible bodies or individuals, detailing how responsibilities are assigned within mandates and functions, how the competencies required to oversee the climate strategy are assessed, and the role of managers in its implementation.

Strategy

Companies should describe (IFRS, 2023):

- Climate risks and opportunities that could affect their prospects.
- How these factors influence "their strategy, business model and decision-making processes".
- Current and planned transformations in its business model and how it allocates the necessary resources to implement these strategies.
- Current and predicted impacts of climate risks and opportunities on its financial situation and financial variables in the short, medium and long term.
- Resistance of its strategy and business model to different climate scenarios and its capacity to adapt.

Risk Management

IFRS S2 requires the company to report "on the processes used to identify, assess, prioritise and monitor climate-related risks and opportunities" (IFRS, 2023). The standard requires that the company must also communicate "how these processes are integrated into its overall risk management system" (IFRS, 2023).

Metrics and Targets

IFRS S2 mandates the disclosure of data that assist investors in assessing how their performance is affected by the risks and opportunities relative to climate change. Companies are expected to disclose (IFRS, 2023):

- Data related to cross-sector metrics and sector-specific metrics.
- The climate targets they are obliged to meet, as well as the metrics used to measure and communicate progress towards those targets.

4.4.3. Entry Into Force And Enforceability of Standards 1 and 2

Standards come into force for annual periods starting on or after 1 January 2024, so investors could access information prepared in accordance with these standards from 2025. Companies must apply both standards together. However, the ISSB has provided for temporary exemptions to facilitate initial adoption (e.g. during the first-year companies can limit their reporting to climate-related risks and opportunities) (IFRS, 2023).

The adoption of these standards is voluntary, so the ISSB does not mandate their application. It is left to jurisdictional authorities to decide whether to require or permit their use. Companies may implement them regardless of whether their financial statements follow IFRS Accounting Standards or any other set of generally accepted accounting principles (IFRS, 2023).

The ISSB works actively with jurisdictions to encourage adoption and ensure compatibility and interoperability of regulatory frameworks. To support this process, the IFRS Foundation created the Sustainability Standards Advisory Forum and maintains the Jurisdictional Working Group and, in 2024, published supporting guidance for jurisdictions and preparers.

4.4.4. Implementation of IFRS S1 and S2: Proportionate Approach, Exemptions and Supportive Remedies

The development of IFRS S1 and S2 has followed a pragmatic approach, incorporating principles of proportionality, flexibility and transitional measures, to facilitate global application. The ISSB is aware of the difficulties that companies face in integrating sustainability into their corporate reporting, so this approach seeks to reduce the operational burden on companies without harming their quality and usefulness to investors (IFRS, 2023).

During the first year of application, these standards provide for transitional exemptions, including: reporting only on climate risks and opportunities, excluding other sustainability aspects; deferring the joint presentation of sustainability-related financial information and financial statements; temporarily exempting disclosure of Scope 3 GHG emissions, especially for sectors such as asset management, banking and insurance; allowing the use of the GHG Protocol to measure emissions in certain cases; and not requiring comparative information (IFRS, 2023).

To facilitate practical implementation, the ISSB has published Basics of the Conclusions, implementation guides, materials and illustrative examples. As part of its ongoing commitment to effective implementation, it has also established the Transition Implementation Group (TIG) and will continue to develop additional training materials.

4.4.5. Effects of the Application of IFRS S1 and S2

The adoption of these standards on sustainability reporting involves both costs and benefits for companies and investors. While the costs are often immediate and visible, the benefits tend to unfold over the longer term and may be more subtle. This analysis summarises the main expected impacts, benefits and costs, as well as steps taken to reduce implementation costs.

The most important information on the review of the benefits and costs of the application of these standards, according to the document "Effects Analysis" published by the IFRS Foundation in 2023, is presented below:

Benefits of Implementation

The implementation of IFRS S1 and S2 offers important benefits for both investors and companies. For investors, the availability of more consistent, comparable and verifiable information is a significant improvement over the manual and dispersed collection of sustainability data. This improved quality of information helps to optimise risk and opportunity analysis, reduce uncertainties and facilitate more informed and efficient investment decisions. Greater transparency on sustainability-related risks is also expected to contribute to overall financial stability by better reflecting the true cost of risk (IFRS, 2023).

From a business perspective, the benefits focus on improving the quality of internal and value chain data, strengthening governance, corporate strategy, access to capital and reputation. The implementation of IFRS S1 and S2 could as well facilitate the streamlining of sustainability reporting processes, enabling companies to respond more efficiently to investor demands for information. In the longer term, it is anticipated that the adoption of the standards will drive better identification of sustainability-related risks and opportunities, thereby increase organisational resilience and support sustainable value creation.

Market studies, as well as the experiences of voluntary issuers of previous standards, support these benefits, which also include the reduction of regulatory fragmentation and the development of more efficient and transparent capital markets.

Implementation Costs

Despite these benefits, the implementation of IFRS S1 and S2 entails certain costs, particularly in the initial stages. For investors, the main costs would be associated with the adaptation or creation of internal systems to process and analyse the new information. For companies, the most relevant costs include hiring specialised staff, modifying or installing data collection and analysis systems, and designing or adapting internal control and reporting processes.

Many preparers anticipate that initial costs will be significant, particularly in developing and implementing new systems and training internal teams. However, these costs are expected to progressively decrease as organisations gain experience, consolidate their processes and take advantage of economies of scale in managing sustainability information.

Cost Reduction Efforts

Recognising these challenges, the ISSB has taken actions to mitigate the economic effect of adopting the standards. First, standards are based on widely used sustainability models, such as the TCFD recommendations, which facilitates their adoption by companies that already apply these standards.

In addition, the ISSB has worked to improve interoperability with jurisdictional regulations, such as the ESRS and the GRI standards. It has also issued application guides and examples to help companies interpret and comply with the standards more efficiently.

To facilitate a gradual transition, temporary exemptions have been introduced, such as the possibility to disclosure only climate risks in the first year or to postpone the disclosure of Scope 3 greenhouse gas emissions. In addition, proportionality measures are foreseen for smaller companies and those located in developing economies, recognising the diversity of resources and capabilities in different economic contexts.

Finally, the ISSB has created a body to support entities and investors in preparing to implement the new standards, thus ensuring a more inclusive and effective adoption across all regions.

4.4.6. Assurance under IFRS S1 and S2

The IFRS Foundation has no mandate to require a specific level of assurance or to develop standards in this area. It is for each jurisdiction to "determine whether assurance on sustainability information is required, although it is expected that regulators will require certain levels of assurance, as both standards are designed to facilitate this objective" (IFRS, n.d.).

Although the IFRS Foundation does not develop assurance standards or make them mandatory, it recognises their role in improving the quality of investor information (IFRS, 2023).

4.5. Interoperability Between IFRS, Standards and Regulatory Frameworks

The ISSB Standards are being considered for adoption by many regulators outside the European Union because of the IFRS Foundation's authority and experience in issuing international standards. Countries such as Canada, Japan and Singapore have initiated public consultations to incorporate these standards into their regulatory frameworks. Australia and Malaysia have also recently concluded similar processes (IFRS, 2024). In total, more than 30 jurisdictions are moving towards the introduction of ISSB Standards into their regulatory systems (IFRS, 2024).

In contrast, the European Union has chosen to develop its own standards, the ESRS, which reflect specific political and social priorities of the bloc. Both the ISSB Standards and the ESRS will have to coexist with the GRI framework, which remains the most extensively employed voluntary sustainability standard globally (KPMG, 2022; IFAC & IACPA, 2023).

4.5.1. Materiality or Relative Importance Approach: Single or Dual Materiality

The approach of the ISSB Standards in terms of materiality is simple materiality, i.e. the target audience of the sustainability standards are investors and therefore the objectives are focused on the information necessities of them. Financial materiality is kept at the core, so external events that may affect the economic-financial situation of the entity and its results (external to internal impact) are reported (del Olmo and López, 2024). This information is more closely connected to financial reporting, because of the current focus of the IASB.

The EU approach in the ESRS and the GRI, however, is that of double materiality. The double materiality approach implies that the target audience of sustainability reporting encompasses multiple stakeholders, thus including not only financial materiality, but also impact materiality, which comprises the influence of the entity on the environment and society (del Olmo and López, 2024).

The ISSB has recognised in the "Sustainability Reporting Consultation Paper" that "disclosures that focus on a company's impact on the environment are increasingly important to investors" (IFRS, 2020). This approach has been called for by various stakeholders, but the ISSB opted for a progressive approach to simplify and facilitate implementation in the initial phase (IFRS, 2020).

4.5.2. Interoperability

One of the ISSB's priorities is to "simplify the sustainability reporting environment, easing the reporting burden for companies and increasing the efficiency of the disclosure system" (IFRS 2023). To this end, it actively collaborates with regulatory authorities and international bodies, such as the European Commission, EFRAG and the GRI, through the Jurisdictional Working Group (IFRS 2023).

One of its main priorities is to achieve interoperability between its standards (IFRS S1 and S2), ESRS, GRI Standards and other relevant regulatory frameworks. Specific efforts have been made to identify common requirements - for example between IFRS and ESRS - to avoid duplication and facilitate more harmonised reporting. In addition, the ISSB works closely with GRI to improve compatibility between the two reporting frameworks (IFRS, 2023).

However, convergence towards a single global framework faces a major challenge: the difference in approach between single materiality (prioritised by the ISSB) and dual materiality (adopted by the EU and the GRI).

In the field of accounting, the European Union had already opted, in 2002, for the adoption of a pre-existing international framework - IFRS - through Regulation (EC) No 1606/2002. The adoption of an international standard favoured greater comparability of financial statements, an achievement that today is reflected in its application in more than 160 countries, being mandatory for listed entities and groups in 144 of them, including the Member States of the EU (IFRS, 2018).

In contrast, regarding sustainability, the EU has decided to develop its own standards, prioritising the dual materiality approach, which considers both the effect of sustainability on financial performance and the effect of the organization on the environment and society. For its part, the IFRS Foundation recognises that fully adopting this approach would imply fundamental changes in its governance structure, given that it would be necessary to formally integrate the representation of non-governmental organisations, civil society and other non-financial groups (del Olmo and López, 2024).

While the ISSB maintains its current approach based on single materiality, it does not rule out in the future extending its framework to include dual materiality considerations, as reflected in its recent consultative document.

5. CONCLUSIONS

The integration of sustainability into the scope of IFRS is one of the main challenges for the future of corporate reporting. The rising relevance of sustainability has highlighted the necessity for robust, comparable and globally harmonised reporting frameworks. However, the current landscape remains fragmented, increasing cost, complexity and risk for corporations and investors alike.

This chapter has focused on the analysis of the main sustainability disclosure standards and regulatory frameworks, with an in-depth analysis of the impact of IFRS S1 and S2. Through a descriptive and analytical documentary review of official sources, we have examined the coexistence between reporting systems and their impact on the convergence of financial and non-financial information.

Although the EU had positioned itself as a leader in sustainability regulation with the development of the ESRS, the presentation of the Omnibus package in 2025 marked a significant change of direction. With this initiative, the European Commission seeks to simplify and make regulatory requirements more flexible, reducing their scope and postponing implementation deadlines. This decision reflects, in part, recognition of the limits of regulation and the disproportionate burdens that regulation imposed, especially on small and medium-sized enterprises. On balance, Europe appears to have moderated its regulatory momentum on sustainability.

In the US, the setback has been even more drastic. Following the publication in 2024 of its first meaningful climate disclosure rule ("The Enhancement and Standardization of Climate-Related Disclosures for Investors"), the SEC cancelled its implementation due to opposition from several states and individuals, which led to consolidated litigation. In 2025, under a new administration, the SEC decided to withdraw its defence of the regulation, highlighting the fragility of regulatory progress on sustainability and the profound political influence on regulatory development in this area.

In this context, the foundation of the ISSB in 2021 represented a crucial step towards global harmonisation of sustainability reporting. IFRS S1 and IFRS S2 aim to raise transparency and comparability of information and facilitate its integration into financial decision-making. Currently, more than 30 jurisdictions are in the process of or have already adopted these standards in their regulatory frameworks, highlighting their relevance as the main global reference.

Nevertheless, fundamental differences between the regulatory approaches remain. The ISSB adopts the principle of single materiality, focusing exclusively on information that is relevant to the value of the company from an investor's perspective. In contrast, the ESRS and the GRI - the most extensively employed sustainability reporting standard worldwide – use the approach of dual materiality, which incorporates both the financial effects of sustainability on the company and the influence of the entity on the environment and society. This divergence is not limited to technical differences, but reflects competing views on the purpose of sustainability reporting, which could make it difficult, at least in the short term, to achieve international convergence similar to that previously achieved in the accounting field with IFRS.

To conclude, the integration of sustainability into global corporate reporting is an evolving process, with progress, setbacks and differences in approach. Success will depend on the ability of international bodies and national jurisdictions to foster interoperability and to strike a balance between quality reporting and reducing regulatory burdens, with the ultimate purpose of establish a model that responds effectively to the needs of both financial markets and society as a whole.

This paper has some limitations that are important to note. First, it is based on an analysis of documentary sources without incorporating empirical evidence on their actual application. Secondly, it focuses on a review of the content of the main disclosure standards and norms, without gathering the perspectives of key players such as regulators, companies or users of financial information. Finally, this is a constantly evolving topic, due to the dynamic nature of the regulatory context and, although the most recent and relevant updates are included, it is possible that there may be further developments that may qualify some of the conclusions.

Possible future lines of research include exploring the actual implementation of IFRS S1 and S2 in different jurisdictions, including sector-specific analyses, and examining co-existence with other regulatory frameworks, as well as exploring the practical implications of divergences between single and dual materiality approaches.

REFERENCES

Andreu, A., Castilla, A., Gálvez, M., & García, I. (2024). Sustainability. The coming regulatory tsunami (III). *EY Rethinking Sustainability.* https://www.ey.com/es_es/insights/rethinking-sustainability/sostenibilidad-tsunami-regulatorio-iii

Castilla, A., Andreu, A., & García, I. (2021). Sustainability. The Coming Regulatory Tsunami. *EY Rethinking Sustainability.* https://www.ey.com/es_es/insights/rethinking-sustainability/sostenibilidad-tsunami-regulatorio

CDP. CDSB, GRI, IIRC, SASB (2020). Statement of Intent to Work Together Towards Comprehensive Corporate Reporting. 11 September 2020. https://www.globalreporting.org/media/bixjk1ud/statement-of-intent-to-work-together-towards-comprehensive-corporate-reporting.pdf

CDP. (2022). Disclosing through CDP. The business benefits. https://cdn.cdp.net/cdp-production/comfy/cms/files/files/000/006/049/original/CDP_Benefits_of_Disclosure_brochure_2022.pdf

Chalmers, J., Picard, N., Eastman, H., & Wilkinson, G. (2021). PwC`s Global investor survey 2021: The economic realities of ESG. PWC https://www.pwc.com/gx/en/corporate-reporting/assets/pwc-global-investor-survey-2021.pdf

Chalmers, J., Picard, N., Eastman, H., & Wilkinson, G. (2022). PwC`s Global investor survey 2022: The ESG execution gap. PWC https://www.pwc.com/gx/en/global-investor-survey/PwC-Global-Investor-Survey-2022.pdf

Commission Delegated Regulation (EU) 2023/2772 of 31 July 2023 supplementing Directive 2013/34/EU of the European Parliament and of the Council as regards sustainability reporting standards. 31 July 2023. https://eur-lex.europa.eu/legal-content/EN/TXT/HTML/?uri=OJ:L_202302772

de Arriba-Sellier, N. (2023). The International Regulation and Coordination of Sustainable Finance. In: Dam-de Jong, D., Amtenbrink, F. (eds) Netherlands Yearbook of International Law 2021. Netherlands Yearbook of International Law, vol 52. T.M.C. Asser Press, The Hague. https://doi.org/DOI: 10.1007/978-94-6265-587-4_8

del Olmo, J., & López, F. (2024). Sustainability reporting standards, international harmonisation or global entanglement. *La Ley* https://dialnet.unirioja.es/servlet/articulo?codigo=9250447

Depoers, F., Jeanjean, T., & Jérôme, T. (2016). Voluntary Disclosure of Greenhouse Gas Emissions: Contrasting the Carbon Disclosure Project and Corporate Reports. *Journal of Business Ethics*, *134*(3), 445–461. DOI: 10.1007/s10551-014-2432-0

Ding, T., Jona, J., Potter, B., & Soderstrom, N. (2025). Are climate scenario analysis disclosures valued by investors? *Journal of Accounting and Public Policy*, *51*, 107313. DOI: 10.1016/j.jaccpubpol.2025.107313

Directive 2014/95/EU of the European Parliament and of the Council of 22 October 2014 amending Directive 2013/34/EU as regards disclosure of non-financial and diversity information by certain large undertakings and groups. 22 October 2014. OJEU n. 330. https://eur-lex.europa.eu/legal-content/EN/TXT/PDF/?uri=CELEX:32014L0095

Directive (EU) 2022/2464 of the European Parliament and of the Council of 14 December 2022 amending Regulation (EU) No 537/2014, Directive 2004/109/EC, Directive 2006/43/EC and Directive 2013/34/EU, as regards corporate sustainability reporting. 14 December 2022. OJEU n. 322. https://eur-lex.europa.eu/legal-content/EN/TXT/PDF/?uri=CELEX:32022L2464

EFRAG. (2021). Current Non-Financial Reporting Formats and Practices 2021. European Reporting Lab. https://www.efrag.org/sites/default/files/2024-07/EFRAG_PTF-NFRS_A6_FINAL%5B1%5D.pdf

EFRAG. (n.d.). EFRAG Sustainability Reporting Technical Group (EFRAG SR TEG). https://www.efrag.org/en/about-us/governance/efrag-sustainability-reporting-technical-expert-group-efrag-sr-teg

Elhamma, A. (2023). Impact of mandatory IFRS adoption on economic growth: The moderating role of COVID-19 crisis in developing countries. *Journal of Accounting and Management Information Systems*, *22*(3), 554–568. DOI: 10.24818/jamis.2023.03007

Elhamma, A. (2024). Determinants of national IFRS adoption: Evidence from the Middle East and North Africa region. *International Journal of Accounting. Auditing and Performance Evaluation*, *20*(1-2), 69–90. DOI: 10.1504/IJAAPE.2024.135535

Fernández-Feijóo, B., Romero, S., & Ruiz, S. (2014). Commitment to corporate social responsibility measured through global reporting initiative reporting: Factors affecting the behaviour of companies. *Journal of Cleaner Production*, *81*, 244–254. DOI: 10.1016/j.jclepro.2014.06.034

GRI. (2024). About GRI. https://www.globalreporting.org/about-gri/

Hartman, L. P., Rubin, R. S., & Dhanda, K. K. (2007). The Communication of Corporate Social Responsibility: United States and European Union Multinational Corporations. *Journal of Business Ethics*, *74*(4), 373–389. DOI: 10.1007/s10551-007-9513-2

IBM. (n.d.). TCFD. https://www.ibm.com/es-es/topics/tcfd

ICAC. (2023). Sustainability Information. https://www.icac.gob.es/sostenibilidad/informacionsostenibilidad

IFAC & AICPA & CIMA. (2023). State of play: Sustainability Disclosure & Assurance 2019-2020. IFAC https://ifacweb.blob.core.windows.net/publicfiles/2023-12/IFAC_State%20of%20Play_Sustainability%20Disclosure%20%26%20Assurance%202019-2021_ES_Secure.pdf

IFRS. (2018). IFRS Foundation updates jurisdiction profiles to reflect decision by 17 African countries to adopt IFRS Standards from 2019. https://www.ifrs.org/news-and-events/news/2018/01/ifrs-foundation-updates-jurisdiction-profiles-to-reflect-decision-by-17-african-countries /

IFRS. (2020). Consultation Paper on Sustainability Reporting. *IFRS Foundation.* https://www.ifrs.org/content/dam/ifrs/project/sustainability-reporting/consultation-paper-on-sustainability-reporting.pdf

IFRS. (2023). Effects Analysis: IFRS Sustainability Disclosure Standards. *IFRS Foundation.* https://www.ifrs.org/content/dam/ifrs/project/general-sustainability-related-disclosures/effects-analysis.pdf

IFRS. (2023). Feedback Statement. IFRS Sustainability Reporting Standards. *IFRS Foundation.* https://www.ifrs.org/content/dam/ifrs/project/general-sustainability-related-disclosures/feedback-statement.pdf

IFRS. (2023). IFRS S1: General Requirements for Disclosure of Sustainability-related Financial Information. *IFRS Foundation.* https://www.ifrs.org/content/dam/ifrs/publications/pdf-standards-issb/english/2023/issued/part-a/issb-2023-a-ifrs-s1-general-requirements-for-disclosure-of-sustainability-related-financial-information.pdf

IFRS. (2023). IFRS S2: Climate-related Disclosures. *IFRS Foundation.* https://www.ifrs.org/content/dam/ifrs/publications/pdf-standards-issb/english/2023/issued/part-a/issb-2023-a-ifrs-s2-climate-related-disclosures.pdf

IFRS. (2023). Project Summary: IFRS Sustainability Disclosure Standards. *IFRS Foundation.* https://www.ifrs.org/content/dam/ifrs/project/general-sustainability-related-disclosures/project-summary.pdf

IFRS. (2024). New report sets out global progress towards both mandated and voluntary corporate climate-related disclosures. https://www.ifrs.org/news-and-events/news/2024/11/new-report-global-progress-corporate-climate-related-disclosures/?utm_source=chatgpt.com

IFRS. (2024). Progress towards adoption of ISSB Standards as jurisdictions consult. https://www.ifrs.org/news-and-events/news/2024/04/progress-towards-adoption-of-issb-standards-as-jurisdictions-consult/

IFRS. (n.d.). International Sustainability Standards Board. https://www.ifrs.org/groups/international-sustainability-standards-board/

IFRS. (n.d.). International Integrated Reporting. https://integratedreporting.ifrs.org/

IFRS. (n.d.). ISSB: Frequently Asked Questions. https://www.ifrs.org/groups/international-sustainability-standards-board/issb-frequently-asked-questions/

IR. (2013). The International IR Framework. Integrated Reporting. https://integratedreporting.ifrs.org/wp-content/uploads/2015/03/13-12-08-THE-INTERNATIONAL-IR-FRAMEWORK-SPANISH-1.pdf

KPMG. (2022). Big shifts, small steps. Survey of Sustainability Reporting 2022. *KPMG.* https://assets.kpmg.com/content/dam/kpmg/xx/pdf/2022/10/ssr-small-steps-big-shifts.pdf

Medisoa (2023). Key sustainability reporting standards. https://medisoa.com/principales-estandares-para-el-reporte-de-sostenibilidad/

PWC. (2024). SEC adopts climate-related disclosure rules. https://viewpoint.pwc.com/dt/us/en/pwc/in_briefs/2024/2024-in-brief/ib202402.html

Scheel, P. (2024). The potential of dual materiality in CSRD. *Magnus Commodities.* https://magnuscmd.com/es/el-potencial-de-la-doble-materialidad-en-la-csrd/

Securities and Exchange Commission. The Enhacement and Standardization of Climate-Related Disclosures for Investors. March 6, 2024. https://www.sec.gov/files/rules/final/2024/33-11275.pdf

Sidley (2025). SEC Ends Defense of Climate-Related Disclosure Rules. https://www.sidley.com/en/insights/newsupdates/2025/04/sec-ends-defense-of-climate-related-disclosure-rules

TCFD. (2022) Task Force on Climate-related Financial Disclosures. 2022 Status Report. *TCFD.* https://assets.bbhub.io/company/sites/60/2022/10/2022-TCFD-Status-Report.pdf

van der Lugt, C., van de Wijs, P., & Petrovics, D. (2020). Carrots & Sticks. Sustainability reporting policy: Global trends in disclosure as the ESG agenda goes mainstream. *Global Reporting Initiative (GRI) and the University of Stellenbosch Business School (USB).* https://www.carrotsandsticks.net/media/zirbzabv/carrots-and-sticks-2020-june2020.pdf

WEF. (2020). Explore from metrics. https://www.weforum.org/stakeholdercapitalism/our-metrics/

KEY TERMS AND DEFINITIONS

Corporate sustainability report: A document in which a company communicates its sustainability actions and results.

Corporate sustainability: Integration of responsible practices that seek a positive impact on the environment, society and the economy.

Dual or double materiality: An approach that considers both the sustainability risks and opportunities that affect investor value and the impact of the company on its environment.

ESG: Indicators that measure a company's environmental, social and governance performance, used by investors and analysts.

Interoperability: Ability to use sustainability reports produced under different frameworks interchangeably, ensuring compliance with the requirements of each framework.

Simple materiality: Focus on sustainability risks and opportunities that affect investor value.

Sustainability regulation: Mandatory rules created by public bodies to regulate the disclosure of sustainability information.

Sustainability reporting standards: Voluntary guidelines that help companies to report sustainability information.

Chapter 7

The Impact of Mandatory IFRS Adoption on Foreign Direct Investment:

Evidence From Jordan, Morocco, and the United Arab Emirates

Azzouz Elhamma
https://orcid.org/0000-0003-3382-0278
Ibn Tofaîl University, Morocco

ABSTRACT

This article examines the impact of the mandatory adoption of International Financial Reporting Standards (IFRS) on foreign direct investment (FDI) in three selected countries from the Middle East and North Africa (MENA) region (Jordan, Morocco, and the United Arab Emirates-UAE) over the period 1980–2019. Using descriptive statistics and fixed-effects panel regression analysis, the findings indicate that mandatory IFRS adoption is positively and significantly associated with FDI inflows in the three MENA countries. This significant relationship is statistically confirmed in Jordan and the UAE, where IFRS is required for all companies (both listed and unlisted). However, the relationship is not statistically significant in Morocco, where IFRS is mandated only for specific entities, such as banks and other financial institutions. The findings of this research offer significant theoretical and practical contributions for academics and policymakers.

DOI: 10.4018/979-8-3373-1902-5.ch007

1. INTRODUCTION

For many years, Foreign Direct Investment (FDI) has been regarded as a key solution for sustaining economic growth (Iamsiraroj and Ulubaşoğlu, 2015) and improving the quality and development of human resources (Nam and Ryu, 2023; Simionescu and Naros, 2019), especially in emerging and developing countries (Mahmoodi and Mahmoodi, 2016). According to the World Bank (2021), FDI flows have reached significant levels, exceeding 2.38 trillion US dollars in 2021. The World Trade Organization (WTO, 1996) defines FDI as follows: "foreign direct investment (FDI) occurs when an investor based in one country (the home country) acquires an as-set in another country (the host country) with the intent to manage that asset". The French National Institute of Statistics and Economic Studies (*Institut National de la Statistique et des Études Économiques*, INSEE) defines FDI as "investments made by an institutional unit residing in one economy with the aim of acquiring a lasting interest in an institutional unit residing in another economy, and of exercising significant influence over its management within the framework of a long-term relationship".

In the 21st century, many developing countries have removed barriers on inward FDI and adopted policies to enhance their business environments, transitioning from a government-controlled model to a market-oriented approach (Contractor et al. 2021). However, FDI inflows to emerging and developing economies vary significantly. In this context, many studies have attempted to address the following question: How do regulatory and institutional factors in the host country influence the attraction or repulsion of FDI? Bayraktar (2013) showed that "countries which have better records of doing business tend to attract more FDI". Contractor et al. (2021) demonstrated "that countries with more efficient start-up regulations, stronger protection of minority investment, and better procedures and infrastructure for international trade across their borders attract more FDI". Tag and Degirmen (2022), using panel data from 127 countries over 19 years, found that "foreign direct investment increases in countries with institutions that ensure the rule of law, expand trade freedoms, and reduce regulatory barriers to investing and doing business" (Tag and Degirmen, 2022, p. 737). One institutional reform that could enhance foreign investor confidence is the adoption of an accounting system that provides reliable, comparable, and relevant financial information. In this regard, implementing IFRS could attract more FDI, particularly in developing and emerging countries.

With the aim of generating reliable, relevant, and comparable high-quality accounting and financial information, nine countries came together in 1973 to create the IASC "International Accounting Standards Committee", which became the IASB "International Accounting Standards Board" in 2001. Its purpose was to develop and publish "International Accounting Standards" (IAS), which were later renamed "International Financial Reporting Standards" (IFRS) in 2001, with the goal of achieving global acceptance. During the past two decades, especially following the EU's adoption in 2005 of Regulation No. 1606/2002, IFRS adoption has spread significantly worldwide (Elhamma, 2025c). In 2018, 87% of countries required the adoption of IFRS for all or most companies (IFRS Foundation report, 2018).

In the academic and research world, several research studies have been carried out to highlight the key determinants of IFRS adoption (Alon and Dwyer, 2014; Elhamma, 2024a; etc.), its effect on the quality of accounting and financial information (Mensah, 2020; Oluwagbemiga, 2021; Ebaid, 2024; Elhamma, 2025b; Oubahou et al. 2025); etc. Nevertheless, empirical research on the potential effects of IFRS adoption on FDI inflows remain limited (Elhamma, 2025a; Owusu et al., 2017). In this context, the objective of our research is to investigate the impact of the mandatory adoption of IFRS on FDI inflows in three MENA countries: Jordan, Morocco, and the United Arab Emirates. The selection of these countries aims to cover different economic and geographical contexts within the MENA region, giving a broader perspective on the potential effect of the mandatory adoption of IFRS on FDI flows. The data was collected from 1980 to 2019, covering a period of over 40 years. Following the results of the stationarity test of variables and the Hausman test, the panel data were analyzed using the "fixed-effects model". The main results indicate a positive and significant impact of the mandatory adoption of IFRS on FDI inflows. However, this relationship was not observed in Morocco.

The results of this study make several important theoretical and managerial contributions for academics and policymakers. Theoretically, the results provide new insights that enrich the accounting and economic literature on the effects of mandatory IFRS adoption on macroeconomic metrics, particularly in the MENA region. Managerially, the study suggests that adopting IFRS can enhance financial transparency, which significantly boosts FDI inflows into the MENA region.

The chapter is structured as follows. The section 2 is theoretical framework and hypotheses development, which is followed by our methodological choices. Section 4 is empirical results and discussion. The section 5 is summary and conclusion.

2. THEORETICAL FRAMEWORK AND HYPOTHESES DEVELOPMENT

Before examining the potential effect of IFRS adoption on FDI inflows (2.2), it is important to briefly highlight the main economic and demographic characteristics and accounting systems of the three countries selected for this study (2.1).

2.1. Key Economic and Demographic Indicators and IFRS Adoption in the Three Selected Countries

In this subsection, we begin by presenting key economic and demographic statistics for the three MENA countries selected for this study (2.1.1), followed by an overview of the status of IFRS adoption in each country (2.1.2).

2.1.1. Key Economic and Demographic Indicators of the Three Selected Countries

The three countries selected for this study are part of the MENA region, comprising one North African country (Morocco) and two Middle Eastern countries (Jordan and the United Arab Emirates). The main economic and demographic indicators of these countries are summarized in the Table 1.

Table 1. Major economic and demographic indicators for selected MENA countries (1980–2020)

		1980	1990	2000	2010	2020
Population (in millions)	Jordan	2.23	3.62	5.37	7.29	10.86
	Morocco	19.45	24.37	28.42	32.46	36.58
	The UAE	1.01	1.89	3.49	6.86	9.40
GDP (current USD) (in billions)	Jordan	3.91	4.16	8.46	27.13	43.7
	Morocco	21.73	30.18	43.02	100.87	121.35
	The UAE	43.6	50.7	104.34	300.19	349.47
FDI net inflows (million, current USD)	Jordan	33.83	37.6	913.25	1,688.39	760.28
	Morocco	89.41	165.12	426.55	1,240.62	1.42 billion
	The UAE	97.64	-115.82	-506.33	8,796.76	19.88 billions

Source: World Bank (https://data.worldbank.org/)

Figure 1. Total Population of Selected MENA Countries (1980-2020)

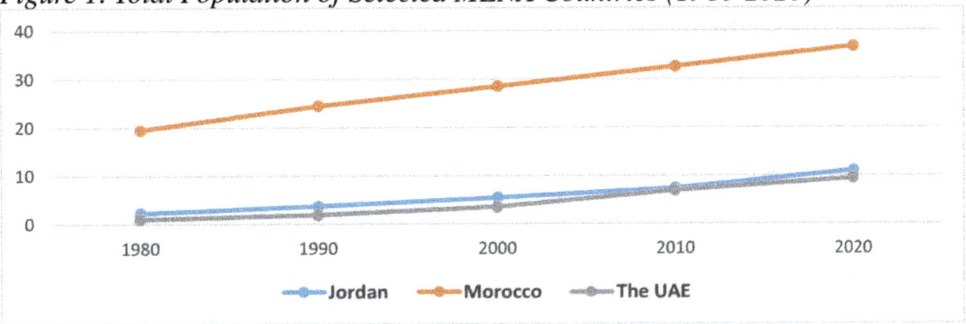

Source: WDI

Figure 2. GDP (Current USD) Trends in Three Selected MENA Countries (1980–2020)

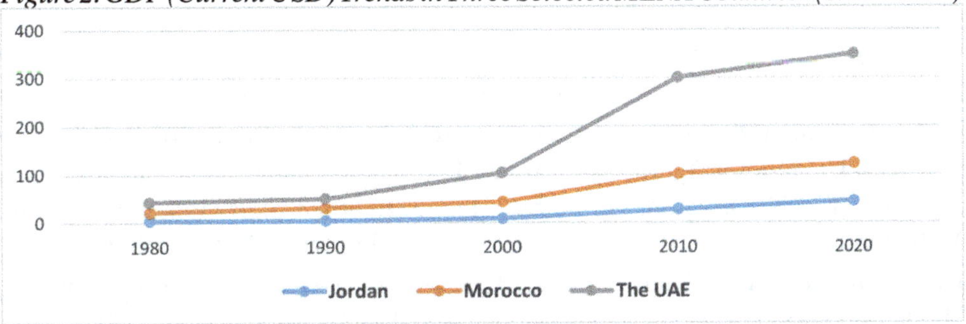

Source: WDI

Figure 3. Foreign Direct Investment (FDI) Net Inflows for Three Selected MENA Countries (1980–2020)

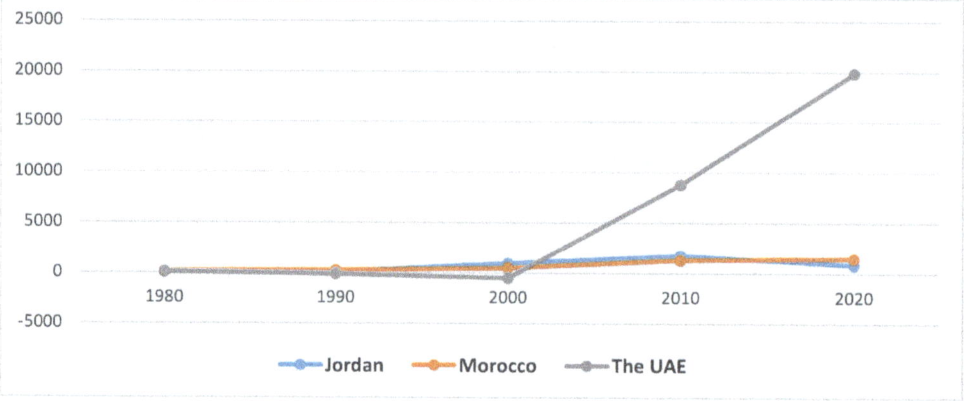

Source: WDI

Between 1980 and 2020, all three MENA selected countries experienced significant demographic and economic growth. In Jordan, the population grew from 2.23 million to 10.86 million (Figure 1), with GDP rising from USD 3.91 billion to USD 43.7 billion (Figure 2). However, FDI inflows fluctuated, reaching USD 1.69 billion in 2010, before falling back to USD 760.28 million in 2020 (Figure 3). In Morocco, the population grew from 19.45 million to 36.58 million (Figure 1), and GDP increased from USD 21.73 billion to USD 121.35 billion (Figure 2). FDI net inflows continued to increase, reaching USD 1.42 billion in 2020 (Figure 3). In the UAE, the population grew from 1.01 million to 9.40 million (Figure 1), with GDP rising from USD 43.6 billion to USD 349.47 billion (Figure 2). FDI net inflows showed wide variations, but increased sharply after 2010, reaching USD 19.88 billion in 2020 (Figure 3).

2.1.2. An Overview of IFRS Adoption in the Three Selected Countries

In Jordan, the adoption of the full IFRS Standards began in 1997 (Masoud, 2017). The corporate financial reporting framework is governed by the "Companies Law 22/1997". This law "requires public shareholding companies, general partnerships, limited partnerships, limited liability companies, private shareholding companies, and foreign companies operating in Jordan to present annual financial statements in accordance with internationally recognized accounting and auditing principles" (International Monetary Fund, ROSC AA, 2004). In addition, and according to the law 23/1997 of the JSC (Jordanian Securities Commission), "all entities subject to JSC's supervision are required to use IFRS standards".

During the last years, some research has tried to explain the national IFRS adoption in Jordan. Tahat et al. (2018) demonstrated that "the national IFRS adoption is influenced by the government of Jordan (regulatory frameworks), pressures from international donors and large economic organizations (politico-economic factors), education and training/development (cultural inputs), and the efforts to attract foreign investments and getting access into the international fund and trade (economic factors)" (Tahat et al., 2018, p. 464). In the same vein, Al-Htaybat (2018) found that the Gulf War was an external factor driving IFRS adoption, while the need for new regulations to protect the Jordanian economy and attract foreign investment were the internal factors.

In Morocco, management tools and practices were traditionally based on French models (Elhamma and Moalla, 2015). However, in recent years, companies have started using more modern and innovative approaches (Elhamma 2015, 2023c, 2025d). The French protectorate has largely influenced the Moroccan accounting standards. The Moroccan financial accounting is primarily based on the French model (Elhamma, 2023b). The "Code Général de la Normalisation Comptable" (CGNC: General Code of Accounting Standardization) is largely drawn on the "Plan Comptable Général" (PCG: French General Chart of Accounts). The CNC (National Accounting Council), created by decree n° 2-88-19 in 1989, is considered by "law 15-89 of January 1993" as the national and official producer of the standard accounting. Since January 2008, the Moroccan central bank has required banks and other financial institutions to adopt IFRS ("circular 56/G/2007"). For other types of listed companies, the use of IFRS is permitted ("Circular No. 06/05 of 2007 of the Moroccan Stock Exchange").

In 2003, the Moroccan accounting framework was criticized by the IMF and the World Bank in their report ROSC ("Report on the Observance of Standards and Codes") on accounting and auditing (AA) (International Monetary Fund, ROSC AA, 2003). This report showed that the Moroccan framework for the preparation and presentation of financial statements presents a fundamental difference compared to the framework approved by the IASC. Empirically, this situation was confirmed recently by Khlif et al. (2020). These authors found that "Algeria has higher IFRS convergences than Morocco and Tunisia". In front of this situation, the World Bank and the Moroccan CNC initiated an IFRS Conversion Project in 2020. The project aims to converge the Moroccan CGNC with IFRS standards and IFRS for SME. Alnaas and Rashid (2019) examined the influence of some firm characteristics on harmonization of companies listed on three North African countries, namely Egypt, Morocco and Tunisia. These researchers found that "the level of compliance with

IFRS increases with company size, institutional ownership, industry and language of disclosure".

In the UAE, since 2003, all companies listed on UAE stock exchanges, as well as all banks have been required to adopt IFRS. On 25 March 2015, the requirement to use IFRS was expanded by the "new UAE Commercial Companies Law (UAE Federal Law No. 2 of 2015)". This new CCL requires "all companies to use full IFRS as developed and issued by the IASB". However, "small and medium-sized entities can use either the IFRS for SMEs or full IFRS". Sharairi (2018) studied the factors that influence the IFRS adoption decision by Islamic banks in the UAE. The researcher demonstrated that "factors, such as religion, culture and local investors, may have limited influence on the current adoption of accounting standards in the Islamic banks".

2.2. The Potential Effects of IFRS Adoption on FDI Inflows

The macroeconomic implications of IFRS adoption remain largely underexplored in the existing literature (Elhamma, 2023a). Empirical research in this area is limited, especially in the context of developing and emerging countries. In general, the majority of existing studies indicate that the adoption of IFRS positively influences FDI inflows into host countries. In this context, Márquez-Ramos (2008) examined a sample of 27 EU countries from 1999 to 2007 and demonstrated a positive effect of IFRS adoption on FDI inflows. According to this author, "the adoption of a high quality set of harmonised accounting standards fosters trade and FDI since the improvement of accounting information, in turn, fosters financial transparency and comparability, and reduces information asymmetries and unfamiliarity among agents in different countries". In a similar vein, Gordon et al. (2012) tested the effect of IFRS adoption on FDI inflows using a sample of 1,300 observations across 124 countries from 1996 to 2009. Employing an ordinary least squares (OLS) approach, they found a positive and statistically significant relationship between the adoption of IFRS and FDI inflows.

In a study of 12 Latin American countries covering the period from 1997 to 2010, Akisik (2014) found that IFRS adoption had a positive effect on foreign direct investment inflows. Jayeoba et al. (2016) investigated the effects of IFRS adoption on FDI inflows in six African countries over the period 1980-2015. The researchers concluded that adopting IFRS had a strong positive effect on FDI inflows. Similarly, using data from 26 emerging countries between 1996 and 2014, Lungu et al. (2017) found that "the countries adopting IFRS are more likely to benefit from a higher increase in FDI inflows than the non-adopters". They also demonstrated that IFRS adoption led to an increase in FDI inflows, particularly "for listed companies and in non-European Union countries".

Pricope (2017), using a sample of 38 low-income countries between 2008 and 2014, demonstrated that IFRS adoption positively affected FDI flows in this group of countries. Similarly, Nejad et al. (2018) found a positive and significant relationship between the adoption of IFRS and FDI flows in 10 ASEAN countries from 2001 to 2016. Their results also revealed a positive association between IFRS adoption and FDI inflows. Likewise, Musah et al. (2020) found that IFRS adoption boosted FDI inflows in 20 African countries between 1980 and 2015.

Akisik (2020) examined "the effects of financial development, International Financial Reporting Standards (IFRS), and the rule of law on foreign investments in 51 advanced and developing countries from 1997 to 2017". The results highlight the important role of IFRS, financial development, and the rule of law in foreign investment. In the same vein, Golubeva (2020) analyzed 493 FDI observations from Swedish firms in 73 countries between 2007 and 2014. The study found that adopting IFRS had a significant impact on both FDI and the profits from foreign investments. In the MENA region, Mameche and Masood (2021) investigated the impact of IFRS adoption on FDI inflows in the "Gulf Cooperation Council" (GCC) countries from 1980 to 2017 using the ARDL model. Their findings indicated that, in the short term, IFRS adoption increases FDI flows by 3%, while in the long term, it has a negative effect of 10.4% on FDI.

Despite the findings mentioned above, not all researchers agree on the relationship between IFRS adoption and FDI flows, as other studies have found different outcomes. Nnadi and Soobaroyen (2015), using data from 34 African countries over a 20-year period, demonstrated that full IFRS adoption negatively impacted net FDI inflows. According to these researchers, key institutional factors, including "the rule of law, the legal systems, and the level of corruption" play a more important role than IFRS adoption in maintaining or increasing FDI in these countries. In a similar vein, Owusu et al. (2017) tested the relationship between IFRS adoption and FDI inflows in 116 developing countries from 1996 to 2013. Their findings showed that IFRS adoption by itself does not have a significant impact on FDI inflows to these countries. Recently, Ehamma (2025a) studied how conflict of interest regulations (CIR) influence the relationship between IFRS adoption and FDI inflows in 15 MENA countries from 2008 to 2020. Using the "Generalized Method of Moments" (GMM) estimation technique, the main findings indicate that both "mandatory of IFRS adoption and CIR do not have a significant effect on FDI inflows in MENA region; however, their interaction has a positive and significant effect on FDI inflows". This indicates that the continued development of the CIR further strengthens the positive effect of mandatory IFRS adoption on FDI inflows.

Drawing on the literature reviewed above, the following hypotheses can be proposed:

- *Hypothesis 1: "Mandatory IFRS adoption has a positive and significant impact on FDI inflows in the three selected MENA countries".*
- *Hypothesis 2: "Mandatory IFRS adoption has a positive and significant impact on FDI inflows in Jordan".*
- *Hypothesis 3: "Mandatory IFRS adoption has a positive and significant impact on FDI inflows in Morocco".*
- *Hypothesis 4: "Mandatory IFRS adoption has a positive and significant impact on FDI inflows in the United Arab Emirates".*

3. METHODOLOGY

This section begins by presenting the study variables and their data sources (3.1), followed by an overview of the econometric model employed in the study (3.2).

3.1. Measurement of Variables and Data Sources

In the fields of economics and management, researchers typically choose between qualitative and quantitative methodological approaches (Elhamma, 2024b). In this research, we have adopted a quantitative approach, relying on secondary data primarily sourced from the "World Bank's World Development Indicators" (WDI).

In this study, we chose five variables: FDI inflows (dependent variable), mandatory IFRS adoption (independent variable), and economic growth, inflation rate, and persistence to the last grade of primary education (control variables).

3.1.1. Foreign Direct Investment

Generally, various measures have been used in previous research to assess Foreign Direct Investment (FDI) across countries, such as the value of FDI (typically in US dollars), the natural logarithm of FDI values, or FDI as a percentage of GDP (%GDP). For the present study, given the significant differences in economic wealth among the three countries analyzed, we have chosen to use the latter measure. The data were collected from the "World Bank's World Development Indicators" (WDI).

3.1.2. Level of the Mandatory IFRS Adoption

Following prior studies (e.g., Alon and Dwyer, 2014; Judge et al., 2010), this study uses the Deloitte website as the primary source of information on IFRS adoption status across jurisdictions. Unlike previous studies, the score for this variable depends on the level of the mandatory adoption of IFRS for both listed and unlisted companies. In this research, we have chosen the following scores: "0" if IFRS are not required; "1" if IFRS are required for some listed or unlisted companies; and "2" if IFRS are required for all listed or unlisted companies.

The scores for this variable (IFRSADOP) across the three MENA countries studied are summarized in the Table 2.

Table 2. Extent of Mandatory IFRS Adoption and Corresponding Scores in the Three Selected MENA Countries (1980–2019)

<table>
<tr><th></th><th colspan="2">Listed companies</th><th colspan="2">Unlisted companies</th></tr>
<tr><th></th><th>Some companies</th><th>All companies</th><th>Some companies</th><th>All companies</th></tr>
<tr><td rowspan="2">The United Arab Emirates (UAE)</td><td>-</td><td>"Since 2003, IFRS are required".</td><td>"Since 2003, IFRS are required for all banks. IFRS are not required for unlisted companies other than banks".</td><td>"Since 2015, The new CCL IFRS require IFRS for all companies. Small and medium-sized entities can use the IFRS for SMEs or full IFRS".</td></tr>
<tr><td colspan="4">Scores of the variable IFRSADOP
• 1980-2003: IFRS are not required yet, score=0
• Between 2003 and 2015: score=2 (all listed companies)+1 (some unlisted companies)=3
• After 2015: score =2 (all listed companies)+2 (all unlisted companies)=4</td></tr>
<tr><td rowspan="2">Morocco</td><td>"Since 2008, IFRS are requires for all banks and similar financial institutions periods starting 1 January 2008"</td><td>.</td><td>"IFRS are requires for all banks and similar financial institutions periods starting 1 January 2008".</td><td></td></tr>
<tr><td colspan="4">Scores of the variable IFRSADOP
• 1980-2008: IFRS are not required yet, score =0
• After 2008: score =1 (some listed companies)+1 (some unlisted companies)=2</td></tr>
<tr><td rowspan="2">Jordan</td><td></td><td>"The Companies Law 22/1997 requires all companies regulated by the Jordanian Securities Commission to use IFRS (full IFRS)".</td><td></td><td>"The Companies Law 22/1997 requires all companies to use the full IFRS or the IFRS for SMEs".</td></tr>
<tr><td colspan="4">Scores of the variable IFRSADOP
• 1980-1997: IFRS not required yet, score =0
• After 1997: score =2 (all listed companies) + 2 (all unlisted companies)=4</td></tr>
</table>

Source: Author according to https://www.iasplus.com/

3.1.3. Control Variables

To gain a deeper understanding of FDI attractiveness, we selected three key control variables: market size, proxied by GDP growth; macroeconomic stability, measured by inflation; and the quality of human capital, proxied by the level of education (Table 3). These elements are crucial for evaluating the appeal of countries to foreign investors.

Table 3. The three control variables of the study

Variables	Measurement	Acronym	Sources of data
Market size	GDP growth	GDPGROW	"GDP growth annual (world bank)" (WDI)[REMOVED HYPERLINK FIELD]
Macroeconomic stability	Inflation rate	INFLRAT	"Inflation consumer prices (% annual)" (WDI)[REMOVED HYPERLINK FIELD]
Human capital	Persistence to last grade of primary	PERSPRIM	"Persistence to last grade of primary, total (% of cohort)" (WDI)

Source: Authors

3.2. Econometric Model

The objective of this research is to investigate the potential effect of IFRS adoption on FDI flows in three selected MENA countries. Panel data from 1980 to 2019 will be utilized, and the model is presented as follows:

$$FDI_{it} = \beta_0 + \beta_1 IFRSADOP_{it} + \beta_2 GDPGROW_{it} + \beta_3 INFLRAT_{it} + \beta_4 PERSPRIM_{it}$$

Where: FDI represents "Foreign Direct Investments Inflows". IFRSADOP represents" mandatory IFRS adoption". GDPGROW represents "the Annual Economic Growth". INFLRATE represents "the Annual Inflation rates". PERSPRIM represents "Persistence to last grade of primary". "i" represents individual countries. "t" is "the time period". "β*i*" is "the coefficient related to different types of variables" and "ε_{it}" is "the error term".

4. RESULTS AND DISCUSSION

This section begins with the presentation of descriptive statistics and correlation results (4.1), followed by the stationarity test results for the variables used in the study (4.2), and concludes with the regression analysis results and discussion (4.3).

4.1. Descriptive Statistics and Correlation Matrix

The table 4 summarizes the main descriptive statistics for the study variables.

Table 4. Data Descriptive Statistics

		Mean	St.Deviation	Min	Max	Obs
FDI	The 3 MENA countries	2.53	3.52	-1.17	23.54	120
	Jordan	4.32	5.19	-0.59	23.54	40
	Morocco	1.78	1.46	0.03	7.15	40
	UAE	1.48	1.94	-1.17	6.77	40
IFRSADOP	The 3 MENA countries	1.43	1.73	0	4	120
	Jordan	2.3	2.00	0	4	40
	Morocco	0.6	0.92	0	2	40
	UAE	1.4	1.67	0	4	40
GDPGROW	The 3 MENA countries	4.03	5.03	-14.95	23.87	120
	Jordan	4.12	4.54	-10.72	17.17	40
	Morocco	4.07	3.78	-5.4	12.37	40
	UAE	3.91	6.50	-14.95	23.87	40
INFLRATE	The 3 MENA countries	4.11	3.90	-1.9	25.71	120
	Jordan	4.65	5.00	-0.87	25.71	40
	Morocco	3.76	3.4	0.3	12.49	40
	UAE	3.93	3.06	-1.9	12.3	40
PERSPRIM	The 3 MENA countries	87.97	9.71	63	98	120
	Jordan	95	2.75	83	98	40
	Morocco	78.17	9.31	63	95	40
	UAE	90.75	6.02	75	98	40

Notes. FDI represents "Foreign Direct Investments Inflows". IFRSADOP represents "the extent of mandatory IFRS adoption". GDPGROW represents "the Annual Economic Growth". INFLRATE represents "the Annual Inflation rates". PERSPRIM represents "Persistence to last grade of primary".

The mean value of FDI is 2.53, with a standard deviation of 3.52, indicating significant variation in FDI levels, suggesting that FDI inflows are volatile over the period studied. However, this average is 4.32 for Jordan, 1.78 for Morocco, and 1.48 for the UAE. The extent of mandatory IFRS adoption (IFRSADOP) has a mean of 1.43, with a standard deviation of 1.73, highlighting significant differences in IFRS adoption among the countries sampled. The highest mean is for Jordan (2.3), and the lowest is for Morocco (0.6). Regarding GDPGROW, the mean value was 4.03%, with a high standard deviation of 5.03%, indicating that economic growth fluctuates widely, ranging from negative growth to a maximum of 23.87%.Inflation (INFLRAT) has a mean value of 4.11%, with a standard deviation of 3.90%, indicating that inflation is relatively volatile across countries. Finally, persistence to the last year of elementary school (PERSPRIM) has the highest average at 88.21%, with a relatively low standard deviation of 9.81%. These statistics reveal considerable variability in the factors influencing FDI, such as the level of mandatory IFRS adoption, economic conditions, inflation, and educational outcomes, which may provide insights into the attractiveness of these countries to foreign investors.

The results of the correlation between the variables are summarized in Table 5 below.

Table 5. Correlation Matrix

	FDI	**IFRSADOP**	**GDPGROW**	**INFLRATE**	**PERSPRIM**
FDI	1				
IFRSADOP	0.62* 0.62* (1) 0.32** (2) 0.77*(3)	1			
GDPGROW	0.17 0.29***(1) 0.03 (2) 0.13 (3)	0,02 0.03 (1) -0.05 (2) 0.02 (3)	1		
INFLRATE	-0.05 -0.06 (1) -0.59*(2) 0.16 (3)	-0.23 -0.35**(1) -0.46*(2) -0.10 (3)	-0.06 -0.26***(1) 0.04 (2) 0.08 (3)	1	
PERSPRIM	0.25** -0.04 (1) 0.36**(2) 0.33**(3)	0.52* 0.29**(1) 0.87*(2) 0.29**(3)	-0.01 -0.11 (1) -0.19 (2) 0.017 (3)	-0,06 -0.36**(1) -0.38**(2) 0.25 (3)	1

Notes. FDI represents "Foreign Direct Investments Inflows". IFRSADOP represents "the extent of mandatory IFRS adoption". GDPGROW represents "the Annual Economic Growth". INFLRATE represents "the Annual Inflation rates". PERSPRIM represents "Persistence to last grade of primary". Stars indicate statistical significance: *p < 0.01; **p < 0.05; ***p < 0.10. (1)Jordan (2) Morocco (3) The UAE.

FDI is significantly and positively correlated with IFRSADOP (0.62; p < 0.01), suggesting that wider mandatory IFRS adoption is associated with greater FDI inflows. This may be explained by foreign investors' preference for harmonized, transparent, and high-quality accounting standards. However, the weak and insignificant correlation (0.17) between FDI and GDP growth suggests that there is no strong direct relationship between economic growth (market size) and foreign investment in these countries. Similarly, the negative and insignificant correlation (-0.05) between inflation and FDI indicates that inflation does not have a clear impact on FDI flows, or at least that this impact is not statistically significant. On the other hand, the positive and significant correlation (0.25; p < 0.05) between educational persistence and FDI suggests that stronger performance in primary education could improve a country's attractiveness to foreign investors, although the effect is relatively moderate. There are no issues of multicollinearity in our study, as all correlations are below 0.8.

4.2. Stationarity Test Results

Results of the IPS (Im–Pesaran–Shin) and ADF (Augmented Dickey–Fuller) stationarity tests are summarized in Table 6.

Table 6. IPS and ADF stationarity tests results

"Im–Pesaran–Shin (IPS)" unit-root test results				
	t-bar	**t-tilde-bar**	*Z-t-tilde-bar*	*p-value*
FDI	-2.8471	-2.5187	-2.2874	0.0111**
GDPGROW	-7.5751	-4.4569	-6.4870	0.0000*
INFLRATE	-3.0984	-2.7749	-2.8425	0.0022*
PERSPRIM	-3.2519	-2.7271	-2.7389	0.0031*
"Fisher-type unit-root test based on Augmented Dickey–Fuller (ADF)"				
	Inverse chi-squared (p-value)	Inverse normal (p-value)	Inverse logit t (p-value)	Modified inv. chi-squared (p-value)
FDI	0.0011*	0.0032*	0.0015*	0.0000*

continued on following page

Table 6. Continued

"Im–Pesaran–Shin (IPS)" unit-root test results				
	t-bar	**t-tilde-bar**	*Z-t-tilde-bar*	*p-value*
GDPGROW	0.0000*	0.0000*	0.0000*	0.0000*
INFLRATE	0.0009*	0.0004*	0.0008*	0.0000*
PERSPRIM	0.0000*	0.0002*	0.0000*	0.0000*

*Significant at 1% **Significant at 5%

The Im-Pesaran-Shin (IPS) unit root test results show that all variables (FDI, GDPGROW, INFLRATE, and PERSPRIM) are stationary, as their p-values are below the 0.05 significance level. In other words, we reject the null hypothesis of a unit root for each variable, meaning that these variables are not affected by long-term trends or structures. The results of Fisher's ADF test also confirm stationarity, with p-values close to zero for all variables, further reinforcing this conclusion.

4.3. Regression Results and Discussion

The Hausman test is typically used to choose between the "random effects" and "fixed effects" models. However, random effects estimation requires a large number of cross-sections. In this study, we determine that the "fixed effects model" is more appropriate for the regression analysis. The following table summarizes the results of the empirical model used to test the research hypotheses.

Table 7. Results of the fixed effects regression model

	Coefficient	**Std. Error**	**t-Statistic**	**Prob.**
IFRSADOP	1.364098	0.17	8.05	0.000
GDPGROW	0.1115401	0.04	2.34	0.021
INFLRATE	0.0789266	0.06	1.22	0.226
PERSPRIM	-0.0552511	0.04	-1.39	0.167
Constant	4.661257	3.46	1.34	0.182
R-squared	0.44			

Notes. FDI represents "Foreign Direct Investments Inflows". IFRSADOP represents "the extent of mandatory IFRS adoption". GDPGROW represents "the Annual Economic Growth". INFLRATE represents "the Annual Inflation rates". PERSPRIM represents "Persistence to last grade of primary".

The effect of mandatory IFRS adoption (IFRSADOP) on foreign direct investment inflows (FDI) is positive and statistically significant at the 1% level ($\beta = 1.36$; $p < 0.01$), suggesting that wider adoption of IFRS is associated with increased FDI inflows in the three selected MENA countries. These results validate the Hypothesis

H1, which asserts that "Mandatory IFRS adoption has a positive and significant impact on FDI inflows in the three selected MENA countries". These findings are consistent with those of previous studies (Márquez-Ramos, 2008; Gordon et al., 2012; Akisik, 2014; Jayeoba et al., 2016; Lungu et al., 2017; Nejad et al., 2018; Musah et al., 2020; Golubeva, 2020; etc.), which demonstrate that IFRS adoption improves financial transparency and facilitates increased foreign investment. Research conducted across various contexts including Africa, ASEAN, Latin America, emerging economies, the MENA region, etc. reaches similar conclusions.

In addition, our results show that GDPGROW has a positive and statistically significant effect on FDI inflows ($\beta=0.11$, $p < 0.05$), indicating that economic growth (the market size) has a positive and significant impact on FDI inflows. This result confirms findings from several researchers. Walsh and Yu (2010) examine the macroeconomic factors influencing foreign direct investment (FDI) using data from 27 high- and middle-income countries over the period 1985-2008. The macroeconomic variables considered in their analysis include "trade openness", "exchange rate", "GDP growth", "inflation", and "GDP per capita". Their findings highlight a significant association between the identified variables and the total volume of FDI. In a similar vein, Asongu et al. (2018) examine the determinants of FDI in the "BRICS (Brazil, Russia, India, China, and South Africa)" and "MINT (Mexico, Indonesia, Nigeria, and Turkey)" countries. Using data spanning from 2001 to 2011 and employing a fixed-effects regression model, their findings indicate that FDI flows to these countries are mainly influenced by market size, as measured by GDP. Recently, Lee et al. (2024), using data from 1996 to 2019 for 178 countries, found that "the results of fixed and random effects models indicate the effect of economic index on FDI is positive and significant in both developed and developing economies". However, the impact of inflation and the quality of human resources do not have statistically significant effects on FDI in the countries and years studied.

After testing the first research hypothesis (H1), which examines the potential impact of the mandatory adoption of IFRS on FDI inflows across the three countries collectively, it is crucial to test this relationship for each country separately (H2, H3, and H4). Table 8 summarizes these results.

Table 8. Effect of mandatory IFRS adoption on FDI inflows by country

	Jordan (Number of obs.=40)	**Morocco (Number of obs.=40)**	**UAE (Number of obs.=40)**
IFRSADOP	1.896619*	-0.549025	0.9124153*
GDPGROW	0.3633265**	0.0519306	0.0271036
INFLRATE	0.2382472***	-0.250818*	0.1492517**

continued on following page

Table 8. Continued

	Jordan (Number of obs.=40)	Morocco (Number of obs.=40)	UAE (Number of obs.=40)
PERSPRIM	-0.2577332	0.0728949	0.0084439
Constant	21.84052	-2.854115	-1.250271
R-squared	0.53	0.41	0.67
Adjusted R-squared	0.48	0.34	0.63

The results for the three countries studied (Jordan, Morocco, and the UAE) reveal varying effects of the extent of mandatory IFRS adoption, economic growth, inflation, and the quality of primary education on FDI inflows. The extent of mandatory IFRS adoption (IFRSADOP) has a significant and positive effect on FDI inflows in Jordan (β=1.89, p <1%) and the UAE (β=0.91, p <1%). However, this impact is not significant in Morocco. These results confirm Hypothesis H2, which posits that "mandatory IFRS adoption has a positive and significant impact on FDI inflows in Jordan", as well as Hypothesis H4, which suggests a similar effect in the United Arab Emirates. However, the findings do not support Hypothesis H3, which asserts that "mandatory IFRS adoption has a positive and significant impact on FDI inflows in Morocco". These results may be attributed to the varying degrees of IFRS adoption across the three countries. In both Jordan and the United Arab Emirates, IFRS adoption is more extensive compared to Morocco. In Jordan, since 1997, IFRS has been mandatory for all listed companies, while unlisted companies may choose between full IFRS and IFRS for SMEs (Deloitte, www.iasplus.com). In the UAE, IFRS became mandatory for listed companies and certain unlisted entities, such as banks, beginning in 2003. Following the enactment of the new Commercial Companies Law (CCL) in 2015, IFRS adoption was extended to all companies (Deloitte, www.iasplus.com). On the other hand, the mandatory adoption of IFRS in Morocco remains limited to a select group of entities, particularly banks and other financial institutions, a requirement in place since 2008. Other types of companies, including those listed on the stock exchange, retain the option to adopt either IFRS or local accounting standards (Deloitte, www.iasplus.com).

Based on these results, three recommendations can be made. First, strengthen the mandatory adoption of IFRS in Morocco. The absence of a significant effect of mandatory IFRS adoption on FDI inflows in Morocco suggests that policymakers, especially accounting standard-setters, should reinforce the implementation of international financial reporting standards. Improved enforcement and compliance can enhance financial transparency and potentially attract more foreign investment. Second, the adoption of IFRS in Jordan and the UAE should be continued and further consolidated. The significant positive effects observed in Jordan and the

UAE indicate that further expanding and consolidating the mandatory adoption of IFRS can help sustain and possibly increase foreign direct investment inflows in these countries. Third, it is essential to offer strong institutional support and invest in professional training. To promote wider adoption of IFRS, particularly in developing countries such as Morocco, it is important to establish training programs for accounting professionals and to strengthen the capacity of regulatory institutions to support and monitor IFRS implementation.

5. CONCLUSION

The aim of this research was to examine the effect of mandatory IFRS adoption on FDI inflows in three selected MENA countries: Jordan, Morocco, and the UAE. Data were gathered over a 40-year period, from 1980 to 2019. The main findings reveal a significant positive impact of mandatory IFRS adoption on FDI inflows, although this relationship was not significant in Morocco.

The results of this study provide valuable contributions to both theoretical understanding and practical application. Theoretically, they provide new insights and knowledge that enhance the economic and accounting literature. In the economic literature, these results highlight an important factor influencing the attractiveness of FDI to MENA countries. In accounting, they highlight a key aspect of the macroeconomic impact of IFRS adoption. Practically, the results offer policymakers and national accounting standard setters significant evidence of the positive impact of IFRS adoption on FDI inflows.

However, the results of this research should be interpreted with caution due to some limitations. The first limitation is the generalizability of the findings. The results are based on just three countries (Jordan, Morocco, and the UAE) which may not apply to all MENA countries. The economic and institutional differences between these countries could affect how widely these results can be applied. The second primary limitation of this study lies in focusing solely on the direct relationship between mandatory IFRS adoption and FDI inflows. Furthermore, the analysis does not consider potential moderating or mediating variables such as institutional quality, the strength of business law and governance frameworks, or political stability that could provide deeper insights into the nature of the IFRS–FDI relationship.

Given the limitations presented above, several avenues for future research can be identified. First, studies could be conducted within the MENA region or extended to other regions such as Latin America, ASEAN countries, or other emerging and developing economies, to enhance the generalizability of the findings. Second, future research could incorporate moderating or mediating variables, such as infrastructure quality, tax incentives, or access to financing sources, etc. In general, the adoption of

IFRS is frequently accompanied by broader strategic initiatives designed to attract higher levels of FDI.

REFERENCES

Akisik, O. (2014). *Financial reporting and foreign direct investments in Latin America. Accounting in Latin America*. Emerald Group Publishing.

Akisik, O. (2020). The impact of financial development, IFRS, and rule of law on foreign investments: A cross-country analysis. *International Review of Economics & Finance*, *69*, 815–838. DOI: 10.1016/j.iref.2020.06.015

Al-htaybat, K. A. (2018). IFRS adoption in emerging markets: The case of Jordan. *Australian Accounting Review*, *28*(1), 28–47. Advance online publication. DOI: 10.1111/auar.12186

Alnaas, A., & Rashid, A. (2019). Firm characteristics and compliance with IAS/IFRS: Evidence from North African companies. *Journal of Financial Reporting and Accounting*, *17*(3), 383–410. DOI: 10.1108/JFRA-06-2018-0052

Alon, A., & Dwyer, P. (2014). Early adoption of IFRS as a strategic response to transnational and local influences. *The International Journal of Accounting*, *49*(3), 348–370. DOI: 10.1016/j.intacc.2014.07.003

Asongu, S., Akpan, U. S., & Isihak, S. R. (2018). Determinants of foreign direct investment in fast-growing economies: Evidence from the BRICS and MINT countries. *Financial Innovation*, *4*(26), 26. Advance online publication. DOI: 10.1186/s40854-018-0114-0

Bayraktar, N. (2013). Foreign direct investment and investment climate. *Procedia Economics and Finance*, *5*, 83–92. DOI: 10.1016/S2212-5671(13)00013-0

Contractor, F. J., Nuruzzaman, N., Dangol, R., & Raghunath, S. (2021). How FDI inflows to emerging markets are influenced by country regulatory factors: An exploratory study. *Journal of International Management*, *27*(1), 100834. DOI: 10.1016/j.intman.2021.100834

Ebaid, I. E.-S. (2024). Does the implementation of IFRS improve transparency regarding the company's financial conditions?: Evidence from an emerging market. *PSU Research Review*, *8*(2), 498–513. DOI: 10.1108/PRR-11-2021-0063

Elhamma, A. (2015). The relationship between budgetary evaluation, firm size and performance. *Journal of Management Development*, *34*(8), 973–986. DOI: 10.1108/JMD-06-2014-0053

Elhamma, A. (2023a). Impact of mandatory IFRS adoption on economic growth: The moderating role of COVID-19 crisis in developing countries. *Journal of Accounting and Management Information Systems*, *22*(3), 554–568. DOI: 10.24818/jamis.2023.03007

Elhamma, A. (2023b). Cinquante ans des normes comptables internationales IAS/IFRS: Adoption, conséquences et où en est-on au Maroc? In R. M'Rabet & M. A. Issami (Eds.), *50 ans de management: Regards croisés d'un demi-siècle du management* (pp. 121–136). Éditions EDISCA.

Elhamma, A. (2023c). The relationship between organisational decentralisation, balanced scorecard and its perceived benefits in Moroccan SMEs. International Journal of Accounting. *Auditing and Performance Evaluation*, *19*(2), 185–202. DOI: 10.1504/IJAAPE.2023.132384

Elhamma, A. (2024a). Determinants of national IFRS adoption: Evidence from the Middle East and North Africa region. *International Journal of Accounting. Auditing and Performance Evaluation*, *20*(1–2), 69–90. DOI: 10.1504/IJAAPE.2024.135535

Elhamma, A. (2024b). Participant observation as a qualitative research method in management sciences: Interests, conditions, and limitations. In Bentalha, B., & Alla, L. (Eds.), *Applying qualitative research methods to management science* (pp. 75–91). IGI Global., DOI: 10.4018/979-8-3693-5543-5.ch004

Elhamma, A. (2025a). Impact of mandatory IFRS adoption on foreign direct investment: The moderating role of conflict of interest regulation. *Journal of Financial Reporting and Accounting*, *23*(3), 936–958. DOI: 10.1108/JFRA-04-2022-0145

Elhamma, A. (2025b). Perceived benefits of IFRS adoption in Morocco and French-speaking Sub-Saharan African countries. In F. Albuquerque & P. G. Dos Santos (Eds.), *Contemporary innovations in reporting and analysis* (pp. 183–210). IGI Global. https://doi.org/DOI: 10.4018/979-8-3693-5923-5.ch007

Elhamma, A. (2025c). A half-century of international accounting standards (IAS/IFRS): Assessing the mandatory adoption, impact, and Morocco's position in the convergence process. In Vardari, L., & Qabrati, I. (Eds.), *Aligning financial reporting standards with global trade needs* (pp. 185–204). IGI Global., DOI: 10.4018/979-8-3373-0887-6.ch007

Elhamma, A. (2025d). Digitalization of management control: Case of Moroccan companies. In Khalil, A., Bousselmi, H. E. W., & Ben Slimene, I. (Eds.), *Digital technologies for sustainability and quality control* (pp. 33–52). IGI Global., DOI: 10.4018/979-8-3693-4373-9.ch002

Elhamma, A., & Moalla, M. (2015). Impact of uncertainty and decentralization on activity-based costing use. *International Journal of Accounting and Economics Studies*, *3*(2), 148–155. DOI: 10.14419/ijaes.v3i2.4817

Golubeva, O. (2020). Maximising international returns: Impact of IFRS on foreign direct investments. *Journal of Contemporary Accounting & Economics*, *16*(2), 100200. DOI: 10.1016/j.jcae.2020.100200

Gordon, L. A., Loeb, M. P., & Zhu, W. (2012). The impact of IFRS adoption on foreign direct investment. *Journal of Accounting and Public Policy*, *31*(4), 374–398. DOI: 10.1016/j.jaccpubpol.2012.06.001

Iamsiraroj, S., & Ulubaşoğlu, M. A. (2015). Foreign direct investment and economic growth: A real relationship or wishful thinking? *Economic Modelling*, *51*, 200–213. DOI: 10.1016/j.econmod.2015.08.009

IFRS Foundation. (2018). *Use of IFRS standards around the world: Overview*. https://www.ifrs.org/content/dam/ifrs/around-the-world/adoption/use-of-ifrs-around-the-world-overview-sept-2018.pdf

International Monetary Fund. (2003). *Morocco: Report on the observance of standards and codes (ROSC)—Data module*. https://www.imf.org/en/Publications/CR/Issues/2016/12/30/Morocco-Report-on-the-Observance-of-Standards-and-Codes-ROSC-Data-Module-16468

International Monetary Fund. (2004). *Jordan: Report on the observance of standards and codes—Data module—Update*. https://www.imf.org/external/pubs/ft/scr/2004/cr0432.pdf

Jayeoba, O. O., Ajibade, A. T., Olayinka, I. M., Ogundajo, G. O., & Kwarbai, J. D. (2016). Accounting standards and foreign direct investment inflows in selected African countries (1980–2015). *International Journal of Advanced Academic Research/Social and Management Sciences*, *2*(10), 17–25.

Judge, W., Li, S., & Pinsker, R. (2010). National adoption of international accounting standards: An institutional perspective. *Corporate Governance*, *18*(3), 161–174. DOI: 10.1111/j.1467-8683.2010.00798.x

Khlif, H., Kamran, A., & Manzurul, A. (2020). Accounting regulations and IFRS adoption in francophone North African countries: The experience of Algeria, Morocco, and Tunisia. *The International Journal of Accounting*, *55*(1), 2050004. Advance online publication. DOI: 10.1142/S1094406020500043

Lee, S. J., Kang, S. J., & Lee, S. (2024). Economic, social and institutional determinants of FDI inflows: A comparative analysis of developed and developing economies. *Transnational Corporations Review*, *16*(3), 200074. DOI: 10.1016/j.tncr.2024.200074

Lungu, C. I., Caraiani, C., & Dascălu, C. (2017). The impact of IFRS adoption on foreign direct investments: Insights for emerging countries. *Accounting in Europe*, *14*(3), 331–357. DOI: 10.1080/17449480.2017.1374546

Mahmoodi, M., & Mahmoodi, E. (2016). Foreign direct investment, exports and economic growth: Evidence from two panels of developing countries. *Ekonomska Istrazivanja*, *29*(1), 938–949. DOI: 10.1080/1331677X.2016.1164922

Mameche, Y., & Masood, A. (2021). Macroeconomic evidence on the impact of mandatory IFRS adoption on FDI in the Gulf Cooperation Council (GCC) countries. *Journal of Accounting in Emerging Economies*, *11*(4), 610–631. DOI: 10.1108/JAEE-04-2020-0084

Marquez-Ramos, L. (2008). The effect of IFRS adoption on trade and foreign direct investments. *International Trade and Finance Association Conference Papers*, 19.

Masoud, N. (2017). The effects of mandatory IFRS adoption on financial analysts' forecast: Evidence from Jordan. *Cogent Business & Management*, *4*(1), 1290331. Advance online publication. DOI: 10.1080/23311975.2017.1290331

Mensah, E. (2020). The effect of IFRS adoption on financial reporting quality: Evidence from listed manufacturing firms in Ghana. *Ekonomska Istrazivanja*, *34*(1), 2890–2905. DOI: 10.1080/1331677X.2020.1860109

Musah, A., Adjeib, E., & Ahmed, I. A. (2020). The effect of IFRS adoption on foreign direct investment in Africa. *Journal of Applied Accounting and Taxation*, *5*(2), 117–126. DOI: 10.30871/jaat.v5i2.1481

Nam, H.-J., & Ryu, D. (2023). FDI and human development: The role of governance, ODA, and national competitiveness. *Journal of International Financial Markets, Institutions and Money*, *85*, 101769. DOI: 10.1016/j.intfin.2023.101769

Nejad, M. Y., Ahmad, A., Salleh, M. F. M., & Rahim, R. A. (2018). International financial reporting standards foreign direct investment in ASEAN countries. *Gadjah Mada International Journal of Business*, *20*(3), 303–329.

Nnadi, M., & Soobaroyen, T. (2015). International financial reporting standards and foreign direct investment. *Advances in Accounting*, *31*(2), 228–238. DOI: 10.1016/j.adiac.2015.09.007

Oluwagbemiga, O. E. (2021). The influence of IFRS adoption on the quality of financial reporting in Nigerian listed companies. In Lee, C.-F., & Yu, M.-T. (Eds.), *Advances in Pacific Basin Business, Economics and Finance* (Vol. 9, pp. 137–160). Emerald Publishing Limited., DOI: 10.1108/S2514-465020210000009005

Oubahou, Y., El Ouafa, K., & Bengrich, M. (2025). The impact of IFRS adoption on the relevance of financial reporting in emerging markets: The case of Moroccan listed companies. *EuroMed Journal of Business*. Advance online publication. DOI: 10.1108/EMJB-05-2024-0128

Owusu, G., Yaw, M., Saat, N. A. M., Suppiah, S. D., & Hook, L. S. (2017). Do accounting standards matter for foreign direct investment in developing countries? *International Journal of Economics & Management, 11*(S3), 891–915.

Pricope, C. F. (2017). The implications of IFRS adoption on foreign direct investment in poor countries. *Audit Financiar, 15*(146).

Sharairi, M. H. (2018). Factors that influenced the adoption of IFRS by Islamic banks in the UAE. *Accounting Research Journal, 33*(1), 75–91. DOI: 10.1108/ARJ-11-2017-0185

Simionescu, M., & Naros, M. S. (2019). The role of foreign direct investment in human capital formation for a competitive labour market. *Management Research and Practice, 11*(1), 5–14.

Tag, M. N., & Degirmen, S. (2022). Economic freedom and foreign direct investment: Are they related? *Economic Analysis and Policy, 73*, 737–752. DOI: 10.1016/j.eap.2021.12.020

Tahat, Y., Omran, M. A., & AbuGhazaleh, N. M. (2018). Factors affecting the development of accounting practices in Jordan: An institutional perspective. *Asian Review of Accounting, 26*(4), 464–486. DOI: 10.1108/ARA-01-2017-0010

Walsh, J. P., & Yu, J. (2010). Determinants of foreign direct investment: A sectoral and institutional approach. *IMF Working Paper, 10*(187), 1. Advance online publication. DOI: 10.5089/9781455202218.001

World Bank. (2021). *World development indicators*. https://databank.worldbank.org/source/world-development-indicators

World Trade Organization. (1996). *Trade and foreign direct investment*,57. https://www.wto.org/english/news_e/pres96_e/pr057_e.htm

KEY TERMS AND DEFINITIONS

IFRS (International of Financial Reporting Standards): IFRS are international accounting standards developed and published by the IASB, aiming to ensure the comparability, transparency, and reliability of financial information.

Mandatory IFRS adoption: Mandatory adoption of IFRS occurs when a country requires some or all companies to apply IFRS in their financial reporting.

FDI (Foreign Direct Investments): FDI occurs when an investor from one country (the home country) invests in a business in another country (the host country), either by acquiring an existing company or creating a new one, with the intention of managing it.

Jordan: Jordan is a Middle Eastern country located at the crossroads of Asia, Africa, and Europe, with Amman as its capital. It has a diversified economy, primarily based on services, tourism, and remittances from expatriates.

Morocco: Morocco is a North African country located at the westernmost part of the continent, bordered by the Atlantic Ocean to the west and the Mediterranean Sea to the north. The capital city is Rabat. Morocco has a diversified economy, with key sectors including agriculture, tourism, industry, services, and remittances from Moroccans living abroad.

The United Arab of Emirates (The UAE): The United Arab Emirates (UAE) is a country located in the southeastern part of the Arabian Peninsula. Its capital is Abu Dhabi. The UAE's economy is diversified, with key sectors including oil, trade, tourism, and financial services.

Chapter 8
Macroeconomic and Institutional Determinants of IFRS Adoption:
Evidence From Developing Countries

Aya El Ayachi
https://orcid.org/0009-0006-0184-491X
International University of Rabat, Morocco

Ayoub Jroundi
https://orcid.org/0009-0006-5270-9611
National School of Business and Management, Ibn Tofail University, Kenitra, Morocco

ABSTRACT

This study examines the macroeconomic and institutional determinants of International Financial Reporting Standards (IFRS) adoption in seven developing countries: Morocco, South Africa, Egypt, Tunisia, Algeria, Qatar, and Jordan. Utilizing panel data from 2010 to 2022 and a binary logistic regression model, it analyzes the impact of GDP per capita, foreign direct investment, trade openness, rule of law and regulatory quality on IFRS adoption. The findings demonstrate that institutional factors—particularly regulatory quality—are critical drivers of IFRS adoption. These results highlight the importance of institutional development over economic size in enabling effective accounting reforms. The study provides valuable insights for academics and policymakers seeking to better understand the

DOI: 10.4018/979-8-3373-1902-5.ch008

IFRS adoption process in developing country contexts.

1. INTRODUCTION

The changing global economic landscape has a large impact on the international harmonization of accounting standards. These standards are intended to improve commonality, comparability and high-quality financial reporting which are essential to global financial stability and investor confidence (De George et al, 2016 and Nguyen et al., 2023). The discussion about the adoption of International Financial Reporting Standards (IFRS) provided a common framework for developing reliable and relevant financial information to support investment and economic integration globally (Mensah, 2021).

The International Financial Reporting Standards (IFRS) have slowly developed since 1973 and were initially developed by the International Accounting Standards Committee (IASC), and are currently administered by the International Accounting Standards Board (IASB), and IFRS 'is a set of accounting standards intended to be applied on a consistent worldwide basis that is, in developed, transitional and emerging economies' (Bengtsson, 2022). After encouragement from the World Bank and the International Monetary Fund (IMF), IFRS were widely promoted as a tool to achieve financial transparency and support economic development by international bodies (Elhamma, 2023, 2025).

Previous research has found various macroeconomic and institutional factors driving IFRS adoption. Countries with better economic indicators, solid legal frameworks and strong regulatory systems tend to adopt IFRS more readily (Klish et al., 2022; Bengtsson, 2021). Adoption is not uniform and features wide variability in developing and emerging economies where institutional and governance capabilities differ widely.

This study examines the macroeconomic and institutional drivers of IFRS adoption in seven developing countries; specifically Morocco, South Africa, Egypt, Tunisia, Algeria, Qatar and Jordan. The research question is: What are the macroeconomic and institutional drivers of a country's decision to adopt IFRS? Research on the factors influencing IFRS adoption in developing countries remains limited and underexplored (Elhamma, 2024).

To investigate the research question, we use a quantitative research design utilizing panel data from 2010-2022. The analyses included descriptive statistics, correlation and a binary logistic regression. The dependent variable was IFRS status adoption, and the independent variables were GDP per capita, foreign direct investment (FDI), trade openness, rule of law and regulatory quality.

The evidence emphasizes the importance of institutional quality, especially regulatory quality, in determining whether IFRS will be adopted. While there are positive relationships with trade openness and the rule of law, GDP per capita and FDI have no statistically significant impact. These results suggest that institutional development may be a more enabling factor for accounting reform than size or wealth of an economy.

This research makes a contribution to the literature by providing current empirical evidence in a largely neglected area with the Middle East and North Africa (MENA) region and Sub-Saharan Africa. It has also highlighted the implications for national governance structures and regulatory frameworks that need to be in place before successful convergence to IFRS is possible.

The remainder of the paper is structured as follows: Section 2 discusses the principles and literature; Section 3 outlines the methodology and data sources used; Section 4 describes and discusses the empirical results; and Section 5 concludes with issues of study limitations and suggested future research directions.

2. LITERATURE REVIEW AND HYPOTHESES FORMULATION

2.1 IFRS Worldwide

The global diffusion of the International Financial Reporting Standards (IFRS) has reshaped the financial reporting regulation landscape in countries worldwide in a significant way, as countries desire improvements with transparency, investor confidence, and in the alignment to global markets (De George et al., 2016; Nobes & Zeff, 2016). As reported by the IFRS Foundation (2020), of the 166 jurisdictions that were surveyed, 144 require/ allow IFRS for some domestic publicly accountable entities, showing serious commitment to financial harmonization.

Since 2005, IFRS adoption in the European Union has been mandatory for all listed entities, effectively making the EU the forerunner in global convergence (Camfferman & Zeff, 2017). While private entities from many states still use their respective national GAAPs, the IFRS requirement for audit capital market entities is the same. The IFRS adoption was primarily in reaction to the progress a goal of increasing foreign direct investment and understanding between various foreign jurisdiction financial statements existed (Ball, 2006).

Approximately 30 countries have fully or partially adopted IFRS in Sub-Saharan Africa. IFRS adoption has most often been in part to conditional aid programs, and with technical assistance from large international organizations and/or because of wider institutional reforms (Albu et al., 2014; Boolaky et al., 2020). Although impediments still exists, such as limited technical capacity and weak institutional structures, the general trend reveals progress toward greater regulatory convergence to IFRS standards.

In the MENA region, the situation is more heterogeneous: Gulf countries such as the UAE and Qatar have progressed to a significant degree in complying with IFRS largely due to their involvement in global financial markets; north African countries such as Morocco, Tunisia, and Algeria, on the other hand, have chosen a phased or partial adoption (Hassan et al., 2014; Khlif et al., 2020). Research suggests that the adoption decisions are affected by external donor pressure, regulatory reform initiatives, and the intention of attracting foreign direct investment (Elhamma, 2025; Tahat et al., 2018).

The Asia-Pacific has a wide range of adoption behaviors. Countries such as Australia, Hong Kong, and the Philippines are fully compliant with IFRS but major economies such as China and India keep standards with national adaptations that converge with IFRS through the Chinese Accounting Standards (CAS), and Indian Accounting Standards (Ind AS) (Bengtsson, 2021; Nobes & Zeff, 2016). These national adaptations reflect regulatory autonomy while also producing some international comparisons.

Latin America has emerged as one of the most committed regions to IFRS. Countries such as Brazil, Chile, and Mexico have adopted full IFRS for all listed companies, motivated by a desire to improve capital market access and gain credibility with international investors (Alon & Dwyer, 2014). Regional institutions, such as the Inter-American Development Bank, have supported this convergence through technical assistance and policy guidance.

North America remains an outlier. Canada adopted IFRS in 2011 for publicly accountable enterprises, whereas the United States continues to rely on US GAAP, showing little intention of transitioning. Despite earlier convergence efforts, the FASB and the IASB have since diverged on several accounting principles (Bengtsson, 2021).

This comparative global overview is synthesized in the table below:

Table 1. Comparative Global Overview of IFRS Adoption by Region

Region	*Countries Using IFRS*	*Approach*	*Notes*
European Union	All 27	Mandatory for listed companies	Adopted in 2005; some national GAAP still used for private firms.
Sub-Saharan Africa	~30	Mixed (some full, some partial)	Adoption driven by donors, IMF, and institutional reforms.
MENA	~10	Partial and selective	Mixed approaches based on economic openness and donor influence.

continued on following page

Table 1. Continued

Region	*Countries Using IFRS*	*Approach*	*Notes*
Asia-Pacific	>20	Diverse (IFRS + local rules)	China and India use locally adapted standards (e.g., Ind AS, CAS).
Latin America	>15	Mostly full IFRS	Strong regional push via development banks and market integration.
North America	1 (Canada)	Limited	USA continues to use US GAAP. Canada adopted IFRS in 2011 for public entities.

Source: IFRS Foundation (2020); EY (2022); World Bank (2021); PwC (2023); IMF (2022).

2.2. Determinants of IFRS adoption

This section presents the main macroeconomic and institutional variables that are expected to influence the adoption of International Financial Reporting Standards (IFRS). Based on prior studies and cross-country data trends, four determinants are examined: economic development (GDP per capita), foreign direct investment (FDI), trade openness, and institutional quality (rule of law and regulatory quality). The goal is to link these drivers directly to IFRS adoption, avoiding excessive theoretical framing.

2.2.1 Impact of GDP on IFRS Adoption

Economic development is widely recognized as a core determinant of IFRS adoption. Countries with higher levels of gross domestic product (GDP) per capita typically have greater financial and human resources to support complex regulatory changes such as the transition to IFRS. In practical terms, economic readiness reflects the availability of capital for reform, investment in digital infrastructure, and the training of qualified accounting professionals—elements that are fundamental to a successful implementation process (Shima & Yang, 2012; Zeghal & Mhedhbi, 2006).

Empirical studies confirm this linkage. For example, Bonito & Pais, 2018 and Nguyen et al., 2023 show that nations with robust macroeconomic profiles are more likely to adopt international standards, and tend to report higher post-adoption improvements in financial transparency. In the African context, Mensah (2021) identifies a positive correlation between GDP and financial reporting quality, suggesting that economically stronger nations are also better equipped to enforce IFRS at both the legal and operational levels.

However, GDP alone may not fully capture the institutional complexity required for IFRS implementation. Irvine (2008) argues that macroeconomic indicators should be examined alongside other factors such as governance and professional infrastructure. Outellou et al. (2023), studying Morocco's experience, show that financial limitations—particularly the costs of IT upgrades, staff training, and regulatory alignment—often delay or weaken the process of IFRS harmonization. In line with these findings, Elhamma (2025) notes that even in middle-income countries, financial constraints can result in symbolic rather than substantive convergence.

Furthermore, macroeconomic indicators interact with institutional elements to shape IFRS trajectories. Daskalopoulos et al. (2016) stated that economic development may mitigate the impact of governance indicators and credit ratings, particularly in attracting foreign capital based on the promise of complying with IFRS.

For these reasons, GDP per capita is used in this study as a proxy for a country's economic and infrastructural preparedness. Not only does GDP serve as a measure of financial capability but it also represents the wider environment to successfully absorb and internalize IFRS reforms.

> ***Hypothesis H1.*** Countries with higher GDP per capita are more likely to adopt IFRS.

2.2.2 Impact of Foreign Direct Investment (FDI) on IFRS Adoption

Foreign direct investment (FDI) is increasingly recognized as a significant factor influencing the adoption of IFRS in developing countries or emerging economies. Countries interested in attracting international capital will often adopt more well-established accounting standards that are recognized worldwide to increase transparency, reduce information asymmetry, and establish reliability with external stakeholders. Thus, IFRS adoption can be perceived as an indicator of regulatory reliability and financial openness (Hope et al., 2006; Shima & Yang, 2012).

The link between FDI inflows and IFRS adoption has been empirically supported in multiple studies. For example, Khlif et al. (2020) showed that IFRS adoption leads to better quality financial reporting which subsequently improves decision making for investors and increases capital inflows as a result. In Morocco, the move toward IFRS had some decision-making links to bettering the investment climate and greater integration into the larger global financial markets (Outellou et al., 2023). Similar trends have been seen in Gulf countries, who have adopted IFRS also as part of the larger initiative to modernize with a view to attract international capital (Morshed, 2024).

FDI represents not only a flow of capital but also the introduction of foreign expectations about governance, accountability and regulatory convergence. Many development-focused multilateral institutions, and multinational corporations, endorse IFRS as a condition to enter the market or fund projects and encourage the countries to adopt international practices as part of their wider agenda of internationalizing policies.

However, some countries adopted IFRS on a proactive basis prior to any substantial FDI arriving, hence, the timing and levels of IFRS can also be considered as a political strategy than reactively responding to demands from the investors (Zahid & Simga-Mugan, 2019). Similarly, we view FDI as a primary consideration of IFRS adoption, as a form of both opportunity and installed pressure for the state to be considered as more integrated within the global investment environment.

> ***Hypothesis H2.*** Higher amounts of foreign direct investment are positively correlated with the probability of IFRS adoption.

2.2.3 Impact of Trade Openness on IFRS Adoption

Scholars generally regard trade openness, which refers to the extent of cross-border trade navigated through the principles and rules regulating trade relative to the size of an economy, as a significant driver of IFRS adoption. Countries that are more opened to trade will often have higher expectations to align their financial reporting systems with the dictates of international standards, because such alignment can help facilitate cross-border transactions and relationships, improve transparency, lower information asymmetry (Judge, et al. 2010; Shima & Yang 2012).

In empirical studies, a positive association is consistently documented between trade openness and the propensity of IFRS adoption. Akisik, et al. (2020) find that countries with a higher trade-to-GDP ratio are more compelled to adopt IFRS, particularly in the African region where export-oriented strategies comprise a critical credible component for continuing economic development. The legitimization of financial reporting with international norms assists in establishing credibility among foreign suppliers, customers, and investors.

Moreover, trade openness raises the demand for comparability among financial statements. International partners general require partners be transparent and provide standardized accounting information to assess financial vitality and operational capacity. Adoption of IFRS enhances the quality of these disclosures and further reduces international commerce transaction and financial risk (Nguyen, et al., 2023).

In addition, the presence of regional economic agreements and trade arrangements contributes to convergence. For example, countries in Oman have different governance structures but they often harmonize regulatory codes in order to promote integration and diminish barriers to trade within the regional bloc. IFRS adoption is often seen as a pathway to regulatory harmonization, and hence, economic legitimacy.

Nonetheless, adoption results are mediated by local capacity to implement IFRS. According to Doan et al. (2020), there is limited scope in practice for IFRS implementation in countries with weak institutional readiness or professional infrastructure even if the incentive to trade is present.

In this study, trade openness is considered as an important variable in that it represents the globalization of economic activity and the implications for the domestic regulatory landscape.

> ***Hypothesis H3.*** Countries with a greater degree of trade openness are more inclined to adopt IFRS.

2.2.4 Impact of Rule of Law on IFRS Adoption

The rule of law is a governing imperative of the successful adoption of International Financial Reporting Standards (IFRS). Rule of law illustrates the extent of enforcement that is un-biased to legal frameworks, in addition to, whether or not actors in a particular country are held under a transparent and reliable legal framework. This institutional dimension influences the formal adoption of IFRS and its practice level.

Numerous studies have verified that the enforcement of legal structures assists in furthering compliance with IFRS. Judge et al. (2010) state that countries with strong legal structures are likely to move from symbolic convergence- where IFRS is adopted in the legislation but has no influence or is not practiced- to a substantive convergence where IFRS is enforced in everyday accounting.

Elhamma (2025) shows that with their judicial system and validity of contingence between taxation and accounting regulations, Morocco has failed to influence its implementation of IFRS despite formal endorsement. Similarly, in Tunisia, Ben Slama and Klibi (2017) describe how weak enforcement structures and political interference have obstructed IFRS convergence, despite legislative progress.

The rule of law also shapes stakeholders' trust in accounting information. In jurisdictions where contracts are enforced and corruption is minimal, companies are more likely to perceive IFRS as a credible and useful standard (Mensah, 2021). Conversely, where courts are inefficient or political capture is high, IFRS adoption risks being limited to cosmetic compliance without meaningful reform.

In light of these findings, we propose the following hypothesis:

> ***Hypothesis H4.*** Countries with higher levels of a rule of law are more likely to adopt, and implement IFRS effectively.

2.2.5 Impact of Regulatory Quality on IFRS Adoption

Regulatory quality—defined as the government's ability to formulate and implement effective policies and regulation that allow and stimulate development by the private sector— is a fundamental driver of IFRS adoption. It reflects the efficiency, transparency, and coherence of the regulation frameworks and the ability of institutions to enhance compliance, adapt to change, and coordinate regulations across sectors.

Within IFRS, regulatory quality serves two key functions. One is to provide the administrative and legal infrastructure to transpose international standards into local accounting practice. The second function is to provide consistency and clarity in the implementation of IFRS, which is vital to avoid regulatory fragmentation between fiscal, financial and professional authorities.

A number of empirical studies provide evidence of this connection. Outellou et al. (2023) note that in their study of Morocco, weak coordination of regulatory authorities have led to delays in implementing IFRS as they have hinted at their commitments to adopting IFRS. Similarly, Elhamma (2023, 2025) have detailed the lack of an overseeing body alongside regulatory actors, which has created institutional bottlenecks that prevent IFRS from being operationalized.

Bengtsson (2021) reaffirms the notion that ineffective regulatory harmonization is likely to undermine the credibility of reforms, especially in regimes where the central bank, ministries of finance, and professional accounting organizations perform in discrete domains for good or ill. In such thickets of institutions, legitimate attempts to modernize reporting practices are essentially creating redundant concurrent systems, or at best poorly aligned. In contrast, jurisdictions demonstrating good regulatory quality generally demonstrate greater coherence in implementing IFRS, as well as clearer processes, unambiguous mandates, and more robust monitoring efforts (Klish et al., 2022; Morshed, 2024).

In addition, regulatory quality is closely linked to the normative pillar of neo-institutional theory. It conditions how professional norms are institutionalized, whether through accounting education, certification, or audit supervision. According to Zeghal and Mhedhbi (2006), the presence of an active accounting profession and qualified oversight institutions significantly enhances the sustainability of IFRS reforms.

In this regard, regulatory quality not only determines the formal capacity to adopt IFRS, but also the actual ability to enforce it meaningfully across sectors and actors. Based on this reasoning, the following hypothesis is formulated:

Hypothesis H5. Countries with higher regulatory quality are more likely to adopt and effectively implement IFRS.

3. RESEARCH METHODOLOGY

3.1 The Study Sample

In scientific research, researchers and academics generally choose between qualitative and quantitative methods to conduct their studies (Elhamma, 2024). The present study adopts a quantitative approach, utilizing secondary data published by international organizations. In our study, we examine the process of seven countries in the MENA and Sub-Saharan Africa regions adopting IFRS, starting from 2010 to 2022. As the 7 selected countries each have their own economies and institutions, we can examine the adoption of IFRS from a wide angle. The selection of countries depended on their importance to the region, the availability of data and their degree of adoption of IFRS. The selected countries are: Morocco, South Africa, Jordan, Qatar, Egypt, Tunisia, and Algeria.

An effort was made to include countries that use IFRS to different degrees. "1" stands for Morocco, South Africa, Jordan and Qatar, where all or nearly all listed firms must follow IFRS. Countries such as Algeria, Tunisia and Egypt (coded as "0") tend to use IFRS rules only part of the time, mostly limited to consolidated reports.

Every country's IFRS assessment was based on their official rules, important international accounting textbooks and relevant regional financial documents. Because of this issue, IFRS adoption is understood only in black-or-white terms: it has either begun or not started. The study records how companies operating in economies of different sizes and levels of trade adoption use guidelines set by IFRS. Clocking in at seven countries over a 13-year period (2010–2022), there are 91 country-year observations ($7 \times 13 = 91$). Each observation corresponds to a specific country in a certain year, thereby presenting its macroeconomic and institutional situation along with IFRS adoption status. This panel structure allows for both across countries and through time comparison, strengthening the analysis.

The table below (table 2) presents IFRS adoption status in the discussed countries, the year of adoption, and the main regulators in each country.

Table 2. IFRS Adoption Status by Country

Country	*IFRS Adoption*	*Year*	*Scope*	*Regulator*
Morocco	Full (Consolidated Statements)	2008	Listed companies and financial institutions	Moroccan Capital Market Authority (AMMC)
South Africa	Full	2005	All listed firms	Johannesburg Stock Exchange Board
Egypt	Hybrid (EAS/IFRS)	2007	Major listed companies and financial institutions	Egyptian Financial Supervisory Authority
Tunisia	Sectoral	2012	Banks and insurance companies. Public enterprises and banks post-2020	Tunisian Financial Market Council
Algeria	Partial	2018	Public enterprises and banks	Ministry of Finance
Qatar	Full	2009	Listed companics and financial institutions	Qatar Financial Markcts Authority
Jordan	Full	2005	Listed companies and large private enterprises	Jordan Securities Commission

Source: based on www.ifrs.org

3.2 Data and Variables

The study combines two types of indicators, which means it also combines two datasets.

The period studied covers from 2010 to 2022 and focuses on a dataset including macroeconomic and institutional factors. The macroeconomic indicators study the economic level, while the institutional indicators study governance quality and how it significantly affects IFRS adoption.

This dataset allows us to study IFRS adoption. These 13 years allow us to see what influenced MENA countries and South Africa to adopt or not adopt IFRS. Analyzing the factors over a longer period, makes us avoid the short-term fluctuations that can falsify the findings.

This study includes macroeconomic indicators to study the economic development and financial openness of a country. These last two things influence accounting reforms. Additionally, a country with a strong economy and more active markets, is more likely to adopt global standards like IFRS.

A country's governance structure impacts significantly the adoption and implementation of IFRS. The complexity of IFRS requires a strong governance structure. That's the main reason why this study includes institutional indicators as well.

All of these indicators were obtained from the World Bank, which ensures that the data is reliable (table 3).

Table 3. Country Level Data (2010-2022)

Indicator	*Definition*	*Source*
GDP per capita	Gross domestic product divided by mid-year population.	World Bank
FDI net inflows	Foreign direct investment, net inflows (% of GDP).	World Bank
Trade openness	A country's economic integration with global markets.	World Bank
Regulatory quality	Index measuring perceptions of the government's ability to formulate and implement sound policies.	World Bank
Rule of law	Index measuring confidence in and adherence to the rule of law.	World Bank

- ***The dependent variable***

In this study, the dependent variable is the success of the adoption of IFRS . The main purpose is to present the different macroeconomic and institutional factors that may have influenced the countries' decision to implement IFRS. Additionally, the reason why this analyzes is made across a long period is that the implementation of IFRS wasn't sudden but rather as gradual process. So, observing the variables for several years will reflect that progression.

IFRS Adoption Success (IAS): A successful implementation can be reached by other available economic indicators, when their values are "healthy". The healthy values that are necessary for an effective IFRS adoption include a high GDP per capita, strong FDI growth, low and stable inflation rate, larger equity market, strong regulatory performance, and higher rule of law score.

- ***The independent variables***

The variables applied in this study have been carefully decided on and categorized into two main factors: institutional factors and macroeconomic factors. These two main variables aim to investigate which determinants have a significant relationship with the adoption of IFRS. The macroeconomic indicators reflect the economic landscape of the countries. They help analyze how the implementation of IFRS may have been encouraged. These variables were chosen based on their availability over the 2010-2022 period.

The table below (Table 4) represents a detailed overview on the main independent variables used in this study, including their definitions and sources.

Table 4. Independent Variables and their Influence on IFRS

Category	*Variables*	*Expected sign*
Macroeconomic	GDP per capita	Positive
	FDI net inflows	Positive
	Trade openness	Positive
Institutional	Regulatory quality	Positive
	Rule of law	Positive

The table above shows the direction of the relationship we anticipate between each variable and the adoption of IFRS. These signs are based on findings from previous studies and logical reasoning about how these factors typically influence accounting reforms.

- A **positive sign** means that we expect the variable to have an encouraging influence on IFRS adoption. Which means, if the variable increases, IFRS implementation is also expected to improve.
- A **negative sign** means that we expect the variable to have a limiting effect on IFRS adoption. If the variable increases, IFRS implementation may not be effective or just reduces the chance of adoption.

3.3. The Econometric Model

In this study, the dependent variable (IFRS adoption) is binary; therefore, logistic regression (Logit model) is the suitable method for analyzing the statistical relationship between IFRS adoption and the five independent variables. The following equation represents the model:

$$Logit(p) = Log\,[\,p/(1-p)] = \beta_0 + \beta_1 GDP + \beta_2 FDI + \beta_3 TO + \beta_4 RL + \beta_5 RQ$$

- p / (1-p) is called the "odds ratio".
- log [p / (1-p)] is "log odds ratio" or "logit".

- "p" is the probability that a country adopts IFRS.

We can calculate "p" as follows: $p = 1/ \left[1 + e \left(\beta_0 + \beta_1 GDP + \beta_2 FDI + \beta_3 TO + \beta_4 RL + \beta_5 RQ + \varepsilon t\right)\right]$

With: IFRS is IFRS adoption; GDP is the GDP per Capita (GDP); FDI is FDI net inflows (FDI); TO is Trade Openness (TO); RL is Rule of Law, and RQ is Regulatory Quality.

4. RESULTS AND DISCUSSION

4.1. Descriptive Statistics and matrix correlations

Descriptive statistics for the five main variables used in this study - GDP per capita, Foreign Direct Investment (FDI), Trade Openness (TO), Rule of Law (RL), and Regulatory Quality (RQ) - are displayed in Table 5. The descriptive statistics included minimum, maximum, mean, and standard deviation, giving a broad view of how the data varies across countries over time. These descriptive statistics were based on 91 observations, utilizing 13 years of annual data (2010-2022) from 7 countries provide a reasonable basis to move into the econometric analysis. The range of values suggests a high level of economic and institutional heterogeneity characteristics of the selected countries which can provide valuable insight and appreciation for the distinctive backgrounds and evolution of IFRS adoption for MENA and Sub-Saharan Africa.

Table 5. Main Descriptive Statistics

	N	Minimum	Maximum	Mean	Std. Deviation
GDP	91	271	4767	1840	1282
FDI	91	-1.69	9.66	1.78	1.71
TO	91	29.86	118.70	73.30	24.08
RL	91	-0.94	0.98	-0.06	0.50
RQ	91	-1.39	0.87	-0.19	0.59

GDP per capita refers to income per person and should be expressed in USD, not USD billion. Suggested revision: "GDP per capita varies from USD 271 to USD 4,767, highlighting the significant disparity among the sample. South Africa and Qatar exhibit higher GDP per capita values, indicating greater financial capacity to meet the multiple and complex demands of IFRS conversion, including infrastructure investment, staff training, and regulatory overhaul. Nguyen et al. (2023) also observe that a higher GDP per capita is generally associated with favorable conditions for introducing accounting reforms, as economic development facilitates the transition to international standards.

FDI inflows, ranging from -1.69% to 9.66% of GDP, with a mean of 1.78%, reveal moderate foreign investment engagement across the sample. The presence of negative values in certain years points to volatility in investor confidence, potentially driven by political instability or lack of financial transparency. Although high levels of FDI are generally viewed as indicators of either legitimacy or at least the potential for legitimacy through acceptance of global standards (Elhamma, 2023), the irregularity of the data highlights governance and risk factors that may ultimately impact the diffusion of IFRS, even though the statistics provide optimism about economic viability.

The trade openness values range from 29.86% to 118.70% of GDP with an average value of 73.30%. Once again, trade openness indicates different levels of global economic integration, with countries that have higher trade intensity typically adopting IFRS, to facilitate cross border transactions and in response to external stakeholder demands for comparability (Boolaky et al., 2018). However, given the high standard deviation, it is clear that trade openness alone cannot universally predict IFRS adoption, as will be explored in the regression section. This raises broader questions about trade-relating institutional learning or donor imposition and whether either of those are being adequately conditionally supported by domestic governance ability.

The mean Rule of Law (RL) index for the sample was -0.06, with a range from -0.94 to 0.98, which indicates weaknesses in legal systems, to include poorly functioning contract law and property rights. Similarly, the Regulatory Quality (RQ) index has a mean of -0.19 (ranging from -1.39 to 0.87), suggesting a generally low capacity of governments to design and enforce effective policies. These findings are consistent with Klish et al. (2022), who emphasized that poor institutional infrastructure is a significant constraint on IFRS implementation.

The table below (Table 6) presents the correlation matrix of this study.

Table 6. Correlation Matrix

	IFRS	GDP	FDI	TO	RL	RQ
IFRS	1	-.023	.134	.368**	.633**	.792**
GDP	-.023	1	-.211*	-.742**	-.207*	-.078
FDI	.134	-.211*	1	.204	.018	.008
TO	.368**	-.742**	.204	1	.664**	.545**

continued on following page

Table 6. Continued

	IFRS	GDP	FDI	TO	RL	RQ
RL	.633**	-.207*	.018	.664**	1	.911**
RQ	.792**	-.078	.008	.545**	.911**	1

**Significant at level 1% *Significant at level 5

The correlation matrix in Table 5 outlines some meaningful relationships between IFRS adoption and the selected macroeconomics and institutional variables. There are strong and statistically significant correlations with IFRS use, including Rule of Law ($r = .633, p < 0.01$) and Regulatory Quality ($r = .792, p < 0.01$). These findings support that stronger institutional structures are more likely to adopt international standards, which has been clearly articulated by Judge et al., (2010) and Khlif et al. (2020) expressed how legal and regulatory quality reflect coercive and normative pressures in the institutional environment, fundamental to realizing a successful convergence to IFRS.

Trade Openness ($r = .368, p < 0.01$) also represents a moderate and positive association with IFRS adoption, confirming Boolaky et al., (2018) where increased exposure to international trade means there is more demand for consistent financial reporting internationally, and particularly as governments and firms response to expectations from their foreign stakeholders and global investors.

In the opposite dimension, the correlation from Foreign Direct Investment (FDI) to IFRS adoption is weak and statistically insignificant ($r = .134$). This indicates that foreign capital inflows alone are not an adequate predictor for IFRS adoption. As stated in Mensah (2021) and Judge et al. (2010), institutional readiness and governance have oftentimes mediated the effect of economic factors like FDI. This explains why countries might have high levels of FDI, but still not get proper levels of alignment with IFRS, when institutional capacities are weak, or when compliance is simply symbolic.

Likewise, GDP has a correlation of near-zero with IFRS use ($r = -.023$), further indicating that economic size or wealth is not a direct driver of accounting reform unless regulatory features, as well as state capacity, are in place. This builds on the prior work of Nguyen et al. (2023), who argue that economic indicators cannot be analyzed on their own and must account for legal and political constraints in order for reforms like IFRS to succeed. These correlations highlight the central role of institutional factors in explaining IFRS adoption patterns, a trend further explored in the regression analysis that follows.

4.2. Logistic Regression Results

The binary logistic regression results estimating the probability of IFRS adoption are presented in Table 7, based on the same panel dataset and evaluating the same predictors, plus additionally controlling for GDP per capita, FDI, Trade Openness, Rule of Law, and Regulatory Quality.

Table 7. Binary Logistic Regression Results

	B	S.E.	Wald	df	Sig.	Exp(B)
GDPUS$	0.00	0.00	2.26	1.00	0.13	1.00
FDI	0.64	0.87	0.54	1.00	0.46	1.90
TO	0.15	0.11	1.82	1.00	0.18	1.16
RL	-19.06	12.19	2.44	1.00	0.12	0.00
RQ	46.11	21.98	4.40	1.00	0.04	105
Constant	-11.17	9.90	1.27	1.00	0.26	0.00

Table 7 shows that the only predictor that was statistically significant at the 5% level ($p = 0.04$) was Regulatory Quality (RQ), which had a very large coefficient (B = 46.11) and odds ratio (Exp(B) = 105). A positive and strong relationship existed between RQ and the adoption of IFRS. The size of the coefficient suggested that, relative to the other index measures, countries with more effective and credible regulatory quality were over a hundred times more likely to adopt IFRS. Our conclusion is consistent with institutional theory as discussed by Klish et al. (2022), in that the existence of effective governance infrastructures aid the adoption of global standards. This also supports Judge et al. (2010) and Khlif et al. (2020) whose cast coercive and normative types of institutional pressures (such as regulation and professional) from the time of adoption as instrumental pressures to facilitate IFRS convergence outcomes.

While GDP per capita, Trade Openness and Rule of Law had coefficients in the expected direction, none were statistically significant at any conventional level of alpha. The lack of significance in these variables could be due to the small sample size for this research design, or the fact that RL and RQ seem to correlate with each other (see earlier correlation matrix). Regardless, the direction of these estimates provides empirical evidence to expectations of theory, as more open and developed economies may adopt IFRS, if institutional foundations are strong enough.

In particular, the effect of Trade Openness ($\beta = 0.15$, $p = 0.18$) was positive but insignificant. This finding adds complexity to prior literature. For instance, Akisik et al. (2020) argue that a higher level of trade openness facilitates the uptake of IFRS in Africa due to the higher likelihood of interaction between countries that adopted IFRS and various international stakeholders. Conversely, Zahid and Simga-Mugan (2019) conducted a study of 145 countries and found that countries that were early adopters of IFRS tended to have lower levels of trade openness. The authors used trade integration from neighbouring countries as criteria for adoption and focus was more on motivations for IFRS adoption that may differ depending on the institutional maturity of specific regions or donor influence. The mixed evidence in the literature justifies the inconclusive result depicted in the present model.

Regarding Foreign Direct Investment (FDI), despite the indication of a direct relationship ($B = 0.64$) it remains statistically insignificant ($p = 0.46$). Mensah (2021) and Elhamma (2023) both note that FDI alone does not necessarily invoke meaningful changes related to improving an institutional setting with symbolic adoption displacing meaningful implementation. The finding aligns with the notion of FDI inflows often occurring for short-term profit opportunities without leading to improved systems for their own entities' accounting infrastructure.

In conclusion, the logistic regression reaffirms that Regulatory Quality is by far the most solidly founded and consistent driver of IFRS adoption in any jurisdiction. Overall, we can conclude that economic variables, while useful, do not provide adequate explanatory resources on their own — we must understand the quality of institutional governance to draw more meaningful insights. The results are a useful empirical contribution to the fundamental assumptions of neo-institutional theory: for institutional convergence with IFRS to be meaningful, there must be more than economic preparation — there must also be strong, credible, functional institutions, for sustainability to be verified.

5. CONCLUSION

This chapter analyzed the determinants influencing IFRS adoption in seven selected developing countries, drawing upon neo-institutional theory and empirical analysis. Specifically, it examined three critical dimensions: economic readiness, global connectivity, and institutional quality, to explain cross-country variations in IFRS implementation.

The logistic regression analysis, covering 91 country-year observations from seven countries between 2010 and 2022, highlighted regulatory quality as the strongest and most consistent determinant of IFRS adoption. On the other hand, while conventional economic variables such as GDP per capita and foreign direct investment (FDI) are conceptually important, they did not provide statistically significant results on their own. This seems in line with recent literature (Mensah, 2021; Elhamma, 2023, 2025) which also highlights that a meaningful IFRS adoption depends more on the nature and quality of institutional governance rather than the strength of economic capacity and international economic ties.

Furthermore, trade openness proved to have a favorable, even if statistically insignificant, relationship with IFRS adoption suggesting globalizations role as a facilitator of harmonization, but not with the externality alone as strong institutional environments are required for convergence to be effective. The results confirmed the theoretical argument laid out in this chapter and the point that IFRS adoption is a political and institutional process driven internally, and not solely as a reaction to external economic contexts.

In conclusion, this research makes an important contribution to the literature by drawing attention to the importance of institutional environments to achieve robust IFRS or standards implementation. In practice, policymakers should prioritize building regulations, governance transparency, and institutional consistency to promote substantive compliance, rather than symbolic forms of compliance.

Future research might expand on these insights by exploring the role of political factors, donor influences, and targeted capacity-building initiatives in facilitating IFRS convergence, especially in regions that remain underexplored, such as Africa and the MENA region.

REFERENCES

Akisik, O., Gal, G., & Mangaliso, M. P. (2020). IFRS, FDI, economic growth and human development: The experience of Anglophone and Francophone African countries. *Emerging Markets Review*, *45*, 100725. DOI: 10.1016/j.ememar.2020.100725

Albu, C. N., Albu, N., & Alexander, D. (2014). When global accounting standards meet the local context-Insights from an emerging economy. *Critical Perspectives on Accounting*, *25*(6), 489–510. DOI: 10.1016/j.cpa.2013.03.005

Alon, A., & Dwyer, P. D. (2014). Early adoption of IFRS as a strategic response to transnational and local influences. *The International Journal of Accounting*, *49*(3), 348–370. DOI: 10.1016/j.intacc.2014.07.003

Ball, R. (2006). International Financial Reporting Standards (IFRS): pros and cons for investors. *Accounting and Business Research, 36*(sup1), 5–27. https://doi.org/ DOI: 10.1080/00014788.2006.9730040

Ben Slama, F., & Klibi, M. F. (2017). Accounting development in a changing environment: The case of Tunisia. *International Journal of Law and Management. Scopus.*, *59*(5), 756–775. Advance online publication. DOI: 10.1108/IJLMA-03-2016-0034

Bengtsson, M. (2022). *National Adoptions of IFRS: Accounting Perspectives*. InterchOpen., DOI: 10.5772/intechopen.103679

Bengtsson, M. M. (2021). Determinants of de jure adoption of international financial reporting standards: A review. *Pacific Accounting Review*, *34*(1), 156–173. DOI: 10.1108/PAR-10-2020-0193

Bonito, A., & Pais, C. (2018). The macroeconomic determinants of the adoption of IFRS for SMEs. *Revista de Contabilidad-Spanish Accounting Review. Revista de Contabilidad*, *21*(2), 116–127. Advance online publication. DOI: 10.1016/j.rcsar.2018.03.001

Boolaky, P. K., Omoteso, K., Ibrahim, M. U., & Adelopo, I. (2018). The development of accounting practices and the adoption of IFRS in selected MENA countries. *Journal of Accounting in Emerging Economies*, *8*(3), 327–351. DOI: 10.1108/JAEE-07-2015-0052

Boolaky, P. K., Tawiah, V., & Soobaroyen, T. (2020). Why Do African Countries Adopt IFRS? An Institutional Perspective. *The International Journal of Accounting*, *55*(1), 2050005. Advance online publication. DOI: 10.1142/S1094406020500055

Camfferman, K., & Zeff, S. A. (2017). The Challenge of Setting Standards for a Worldwide Constituency: Research Implications from the IASB's Early History. *European Accounting Review*, *27*(2), 289–312. DOI: 10.1080/09638180.2017.1296780

Daskalopoulos, E., Evgenidis, A., Tsagkanos, A., & Siriopoulos, C. (2016). Assessing variations in foreign direct investments under international financial reporting standards (IFRS) adoption, macro-socioeconomic developments and credit ratings. *Investment Management and Financial Innovations. Scopus.*, *13*(3), 328–340. Advance online publication. DOI: 10.21511/imfi.13(3-2).2016.05

De George, E. T., Li, X., & Shivakumar, L. (2016). A review of the IFRS adoption literature. *Review of Accounting Studies. Review of Accounting Studies*, *21*(3), 898–1004. Advance online publication. DOI: 10.1007/s11142-016-9363-1

Doan, D.-T., Nguyen, L.-N. T., & Phan, H. T. (2020). Factors affecting the application of IFRS through the perceptions of business managers and auditors in Vietnam. *Problems and Perspectives in Management. Problems and Perspectives in Management*, *18*(1), 371–384. Advance online publication. DOI: 10.21511/ppm.18(1).2020.32

Elhamma, A. (2023). Cinquante ans des normes comptables internationales IAS/IFRS: Adoption, conséquences et où en est-on au Maroc? In R. M'Rabet & M. A. Issami (Eds.), *50 ans de management: Regards croisés d'un demi-siècle du management* (pp. 121–136). EDISCA.

Elhamma, A. (2023). Impact of mandatory IFRS adoption on economic growth: The moderating role of COVID-19 crisis in developing countries. *Journal of Accounting and Management Information Systems*, *22*(3), 554–568. DOI: 10.24818/jamis.2023.03007

Elhamma, A. (2024). Determinants of national IFRS adoption: Evidence from the Middle East and North Africa region. *International Journal of Accounting. Auditing and Performance Evaluation*, *20*(1-2), 69–90. DOI: 10.1504/IJAAPE.2024.135535

Elhamma, A. (2024). Participant Observation as a Qualitative Research Method in Management Sciences: Interests, Conditions, and Limitations. In Bentalha, B., & Alla, L. (Eds.), *Applying Qualitative Research Methods to Management Science* (pp. 75–91). IGI Global., DOI: 10.4018/979-8-3693-5543-5.ch004

Elhamma, A. (2025). A half-century of international accounting standards (IAS/IFRS): Assessing the mandatory adoption, impact, and Morocco's position in the convergence process. In Vardari, L., & Qabrati, I. (Eds.), *Aligning financial reporting standards with global trade needs* (pp. 185–204). IGI Global., DOI: 10.4018/979-8-3373-0887-6.ch007

Elhamma, A. (2025). Perceived benefits of IFRS adoption in Morocco and French-speaking Sub-Saharan African countries. In F. Albuquerque & P. G. Dos Santos (Eds.), *Contemporary innovations in reporting and analysis* (pp. 183–210). IGI Global. https://doi.org/DOI: 10.4018/979-8-3693-5923-5.ch007

Elhamma, A. (2025). Impact of mandatory IFRS adoption on foreign direct investment: The moderating role of conflict of interest regulation. *Journal of Financial Reporting and Accounting*, *23*(3), 936–958. DOI: 10.1108/JFRA-04-2022-0145

Hassan, E. A., Rankin, M., & Lu, W. (2014). The development of accounting regulation in iraq and the IFRS adoption decision: An institutional perspective. *The International Journal of Accounting*, *49*(3), 371–390. DOI: 10.1016/j.intacc.2014.07.001

Hope, O.-K., Jin, J., & Kang, T. (2006). Empirical evidence on jurisdictions that adopt IFRS. *Journal of International Accounting Research*, *5*(2), 1–20. DOI: 10.2308/jiar.2006.5.2.1

IFRS Foundation (Ed.). (2020). *Due process handbook* (August 2020). IFRS Foundation Publications Department.

Irvine, H. (2008). The global institutionalization of financial reporting: The case of the United Arab Emirates. *Accounting Forum*, *32*(2), 125–142. DOI: 10.1016/j.accfor.2007.12.003

Judge, W., Li, S., & Pinsker, R. (2010). National adoption of international accounting standards: An institutional perspective. *Corporate Governance*, *18*(3), 161–174. DOI: 10.1111/j.1467-8683.2010.00798.x

Khlif, H., Ahmed, K., & Alam, M. (2020). Accounting Regulations and IFRS Adoption in Francophone North African Countries: The Experience of Algeria, Morocco, and Tunisia. *The International Journal of Accounting*, *55*(1), 2050004. Advance online publication. DOI: 10.1142/S1094406020500043

Klish, A. A., Shubita, M. F. S., & Wu, J. (2022). IFRS adoption and financial reporting quality in the MENA region. *Journal of Applied Accounting Research*, *23*(3), 570–603. DOI: 10.1108/JAAR-08-2020-0155

Mensah, E. (2021). The effect of IFRS adoption on financial reporting quality: Evidence from listed manufacturing firms in Ghana. *Ekonomska Istrazivanja*, *34*(1), 2890–2905. DOI: 10.1080/1331677X.2020.1860109

Morshed, A. (2024). Assessing the Economic Impact of IFRS Adoption on Financial Transparency and Growth in the Arab Gulf Countries. *Economies. Scopus.*, *12*(8), 209. Advance online publication. DOI: 10.3390/economies12080209

Nguyen, H. T. T., Nguyen, H. T. T., & Nguyen, C. V. (2023). Analysis of factors affecting the adoption of IFRS in an emerging economy. *Heliyon*, *9*(6), e17331. DOI: 10.1016/j.heliyon.2023.e17331 PMID: 37389083

Nobes, C. W., & Zeff, S. A. (2016). Have Canada, Japan and Switzerland Adopted IFRS? *Australian Accounting Review*, *26*(3), 284–290. DOI: 10.1111/auar.12131

Outellou, S., Taouab, O., & Abdelbaki, N. (2023). Les Déterminants de l'Adoption des IFRS par les Entreprises: Cas du Maroc. *European Scientific Journal*, *19*(13), 13. Advance online publication. DOI: 10.19044/esj.2023.v19n13p158

Shima, K. M., & Yang, D. C. (2012). Factors affecting the adoption of IFRS. *International Journal of Business*, *17*(3), 276–298.

Tahat, Y., Omran, M. A., & AbuGhazaleh, N. M. (2018). Factors affecting the development of accounting practices in Jordan: An institutional perspective. *Asian Review of Accounting*, *26*(4), 464–486. DOI: 10.1108/ARA-01-2017-0010

Zahid, R. M. A., & Simga-Mugan, C. (2019). An Analysis of IFRS and SME-IFRS Adoption Determinants: A Worldwide Study. *Emerging Markets Finance & Trade*, *55*(2), 391–408. https://ideas.repec.org//a/mes/emfitr/v55y2019i2p391-408.html. DOI: 10.1080/1540496X.2018.1500890

Zeghal, D., & Mhedhbi, K. (2006). An analysis of the factors affecting the adoption of international accounting standards by developing countries. *The International Journal of Accounting*, *41*(4), 373–386. DOI: 10.1016/j.intacc.2006.09.009

KEY TERMS AND DEFINITIONS

IFRS: A collection of accounting standards that are known worldwide to increase the uniformity, clarity and usefulness of financial reports from different countries.

Macroeconomic determinants: They are broad economic factors, such as gross domestic product (GDP), foreign direct investment (FDI), and trade openness, that influence a country's economic performance and decision-making. These factors play an important role in the adoption of IFRS.

Institutional quality: Institutional quality refers to the effectiveness of a country's governing structures and rules, encompassing transparency, legal stability, anti-corruption measures, and regulatory capacity.

GDP: An important measure of a nation's economy, it is used to demonstrate how much the country can produce on average per person and how effective the economy can be with reforms.

FDI: When foreign investors bring in capital to our markets, many believe this represents openness in the economy and shows trust in it.

Rule of Law: This measurement reflects if people trust the rules and stick to agreements or laws in the society.

Regulatory Quality: The capacity of the government to set helpful regulations that improve financial reporting and business activity.

Trade Openness: How much a country takes part in international trade, usually measured by a percentage of its GDP, goes along with globalization and open policies.

Chapter 9
The Impact of IPSAS on the Quality of Financial Reporting in Public Sector Organizations: An Empirical Study

Rajae El-Moumane
https://orcid.org/0009-0001-9737-7706
Ibn Tofaîl University, Morocco

ABSTRACT

The Kingdom's General Treasury's accession to the IPSAS board in 2012 represents a significant advancement in public sector accounting reform in Morocco. This initiative aligns with the principles of the Moroccan Constitution of 2011 regarding transparency and accountability, as well as with the requirements of Organic Law No. 130-13 on finance, which mandates the State to maintain comprehensive accounts alongside budgetary accounts. This move aims to enhance good governance and improve the management of public finances. Our research is based on a quantitative study involving a sample of 84 respondents, aimed at assessing the level of IPSAS adoption among Moroccan public sector practitioners and analyzing its impact on the comparability, reliability, relevance, and intelligibility of financial information. The results indicate that, despite increasing awareness, the level of IPSAS adoption remains low in Morocco. Nevertheless, respondents unanimously acknowledge that these standards significantly enhance the quality of financial information.

DOI: 10.4018/979-8-3373-1902-5.ch009

INTRODUCTION

In accordance with the New Public Management approach focused on objectives and results, and driven by the broader trend toward reforming financial information systems (Christiaens et al, 2014), notably through the application of "New Public Management" (NPM) principles, also referred to as "New Public Financial Management" (NPFM) (Guthrie et al, 1999), the production of clear, intelligible, reliable, and relevant information has become essential, particularly for reporting to the State and citizens on outcomes in relation to the strategic orientations implemented.

Indeed, public administrations around the world, including those in developing countries, have undergone profound reforms in recent decades, leading to fundamental changes in public accounting systems, notably the shift from "cash-based accounting" to "accrual accounting". Anglo-Saxon countries were the first to reform their public finances (Pollitt & Bouckaert, 2011), followed by European countries, with the aim of improving accountability and efficiency in their public administrations. According to Chan (2004), the shift to accrual accounting was a necessity rather than a luxury, as cash-based accounting is plagued by various shortcomings: it does not provide a true and fair view of the State's asset management, only considers revenues and expenditures (cash inflows and outflows), does not address commitment accounting, and does not track changes in the State's asset value.

Consequently, as part of these financial reforms, governments have begun implementing the "International Public Sector Accounting Standards" (IPSAS) to enhance the credibility, quality and reliability of financial information, with the aim of gaining citizens' trust and attracting foreign investment (SAFA, 2006).

In Africa, many countries have proposed incorporating IPSAS into their public financial management reforms, while others—such as Algeria, Ghana, Liberia, Mauritania, Morocco, Nigeria, Rwanda, South Africa, Tanzania, Uganda and Zambia—have already adopted them (Ademola, 2020). The implementation of these standards represents a significant milestone in the modernization process (Stutcliffe, 2003), aimed at meeting increasing demands for transparency, accountability, and efficiency in the management of public funds.

Morocco, as part of this major reform effort, undertook an accounting modernization by adopting the IPSAS standards in 2008, to improve public financial management and increase accountability of public sector entities for their performance (Ayachi, 2018). In 2012, the Kingdom's General Treasury (TGR) joined the IPSAS Board "International Public Sector Accounting Standards". This step constitutes a major advancement in the reform of Morocco's public sector accounting, enabling the adoption of international accounting standards in a context where accrual accounting is the cornerstone of these standards. This initiative is also aligned with the principles of the 2011 Moroccan Constitution regarding transparency and accountability, as well as with the requirements of Organic Law No. 130-13 on public finance, which mandates the State to maintain general accounts in addition to budgetary accounts to foster good governance and enhance the management of public finances.

In this article, we conduct a quantitative empirical investigation based on a sample of 84 respondents to examine the impact of IPSAS on the comparability, reliability, relevance, and intelligibility of public financial information in the Moroccan context. This research aims to address the following questions:

- Do Moroccan public sector practitioners have sufficient knowledge of IPSAS standards?
- Are IPSAS standards widely applied in the Moroccan public sector?
- According to respondents' perceptions, which qualitative characteristics of public financial information are most influenced by the application of IPSAS in Morocco?

Our article is structured in two main sections. Following the introduction, the first section presents a literature review on the implementation of IPSAS. The second section details our empirical study, outlining the research objectives and methodology, come after a discussion of the key findings, their implications, and the main conclusions.

1. LITERATURE REVIEW

1.1. Public Sector Accounting System Reform

Over the past 25 years, numerous reforms inspired by "New Public Management" (NPM) have significantly shaped the public sector in many countries, notably through the adoption of accrual accounting (also referred to as commitment or double-entry accounting) (Christiaens et al., 2014). The literature highlights that this accounting approach serves as a key lever for public sector reforms, aiming to enhance the performance and responsiveness of public services while strengthening accountability in the use of public resources (Ouda, 2007).

Several previous studies have supported this approach to public accounting reform (Alshujairi, 2014). Indeed, according to members of the European Commission, the shift to accrual accounting has helped manage the debt and deficit crisis, as the financial information generated by accrual accounting enables comparability and accountability at the micro-accounting level (Lüder, 2000).

For Pina and Torres (2003), the transition from a cash-based accounting system to an accrual-based system is essential for the effective and successful implementation of reforms inspired by New Public Management (NPM). According to these authors, this accounting approach, as outlined in NPM reforms, provides comprehensive and more accurate information on the state's solvency, its asset position, and the costs of services provided to the public (Pina and Torres, 2003). Christiaens et al. (2014) argue that the shift from cash to accrual accounting in the public sector is a key element in modernizing financial information systems. Similarly, Chan (2004) asserts that reforming public accounting directly contributes to improving public financial management. Roje et al. (2012) emphasize that quality information is crucial for decision-making, and that a complete and reliable accounting information system is vital for effective public management. The priority given to financial integrity in public reforms, combined with the implementation of accrual accounting, is a critical lever for making IPSAS fully operational and effective in the context of public accounting modernization.

1.2. IPSAS: International Public Sector Accounting Standards in Public Sector

IPSAS, based on private-sector IFRS, were issued by the "International Public Sector Accounting Standards Board" (IPSASB) with the goal of enhancing government accountability, improving the reliability and quality of financial reporting, and enhancing the relevance of financial information (IPSASB, 2018). IPSAS have played a crucial role in public sector accounting reform efforts worldwide (Adhikari and Mellemvik, 2010; Christiaens et al., 2010, 2015; Jensen and Smith, 2013). According to Christiaens et al. (2015), "*IPSAS have become the international benchmark for the development of public sector accounting systems worldwide. For this reason, IPSAS deserve the attention of decision-makers in the accounting field, as well as practitioners and researchers*".

IPSAS are international accounting standards adapted to the public sector. These standards are equivalent to the "International Financial Reporting Standards" (IFRS) used in the private sector (Toudas et al., 2013; Jensen, 2018). They aim to modernize public accounting by employing the fundamental principles and methods of accrual accounting.

Reforms of state financial systems led to the development of the IPSAS standards (El Hachimi & Benthami, 2024). Their adoption by the European Union in 2005 contributed to their global dissemination, including in developing countries (Trabelsi, 2017). Today, many countries apply these standards, such as Australia, Morocco, Canada, Argentina, Mexico, New Zealand, Germany, South Africa, the Netherlands and the United States. According to Des Robert and Colibert (2008), "*not a week went by without a government announcing its decision to adopt IPSAS standards*". Over the years, these standards have become increasingly widespread and are now considered the main international reference in public sector accounting (Brusca & Martinez, 2016). This evolution has led several international public organizations, including the UN, the OECD, and various United Nations agencies, to adopt them (Grossi & Soverchia, 2011). Subsequently, other international bodies—such as the "World Bank", "the International Monetary Fund" (IMF), and the "Asian Development Bank"—have also supported their adoption.

Figure 1. The actors in the process of IPSAS

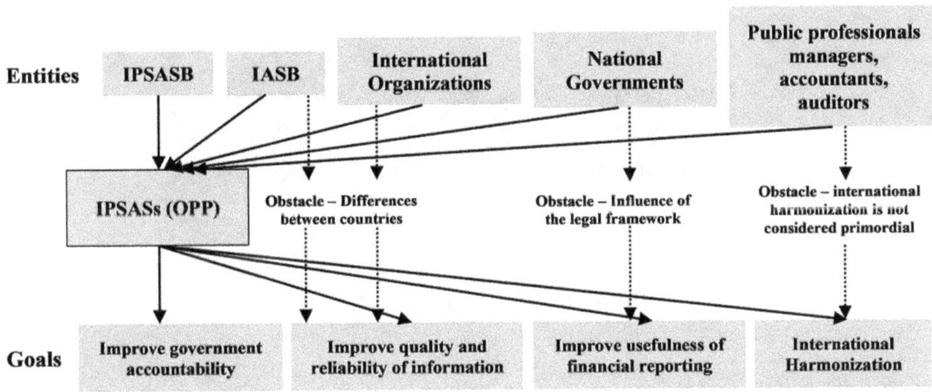

Source: Jorge et al, (2019). P. 5

IPSAS standards aim to promote the international harmonization and convergence of financial statements (Humphrey et al., 2009). Indeed, if each state implements an accrual accounting system tailored to its own needs, reforms based on this approach will be heterogeneous, leading to divergence in public sector financial information systems on three levels: the content, the timeline for adoption, and the methods of applying accrual accounting (Brusca and Condor, 2002; Lüder and Jones, 2003; Pina and Torres, 2003; Benito, Brusca and Montesinos, 2007; Carvalho et al., 2007). Therefore, the adoption of IPSAS enables the integration of international standard criteria into local accounting regulations (Pacter, 2005).

Overall, there are numerous aims associated with IPSAS implementation:

- The harmonization of public sector accounting at the international level (Christiaens et al., 2015);
- The improvement of the quality of financial statements (in terms of relevance, reliability, etc.);

- The introduction of accrual-based accounting practices to better reflect the economic and financial situation of adopting countries;
- The enhancement of accountability and transparency in the management of public resources;
- The provision of relevant and comprehensive financial information (including costs, revenues, assets, liabilities, etc.).

Figure 2. The Scope of the IPSAS

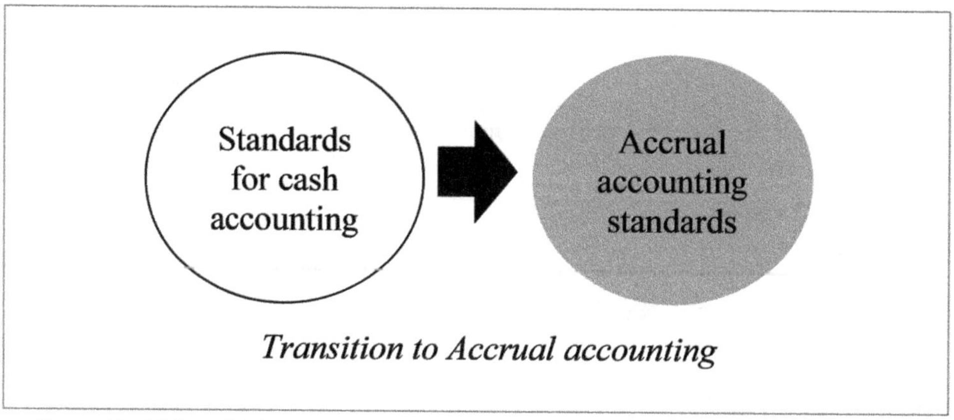

Source: Ilie & Miose (2012). P. 37

1.3. Theories on the Adoption of IPSAS Standards For The Modernization Of Public Accounting Management

In the literature, several theories are used to analyze and explain the adoption of IPSAS standards as part of public accounting management reforms:

Table 1. Theoretical Frameworks Mobilized for IPSAS Standards

Theory	Authors	Principles
NPM theory	Hood (1995)	This approach focuses on reforming and modernizing public administration by drawing from private sector management practices. IPSAS standards help reform financial management systems and enhance the quality of public financial information.
Neo-institutional theory	Di Maggio & Powell (1983)	Organizations with similar characteristics generally tend to imitate and conform to each other, becoming more alike to gain institutional legitimacy. Adopting IPSAS as "myths" can strengthen states' legitimacy in an international environment.
Theory of public value	Moore (1995)	Public organizations generate public value for citizens and stakeholders. IPSAS can be seen as a strategic lever for creating public value by promoting transparency, communication, performance, and accountability in public organizations.

Source: prepared by the authors.

1.4. IPSAS Implementation in Moroccan Public Sector

As part of a broader effort to modernize public management, Morocco initiated a reform of its public accounting system in 2008 through the adoption of the International Public Sector Accounting Standards (IPSAS), with the objective of enhancing public financial management and strengthening the accountability of public sector entities for their performance (Ayachi, 2018). In 2012, the General Treasury of the Kingdom (TGR) became a member of the IPSAS Board, positioning Morocco as the first Arab and the third African country to join this Board (Khattabi & Elmallouki, 2023). This initiative represents a significant step in the modernization of the Moroccan public sector's accounting framework, characterized by the progressive implementation of international standards grounded in the accrual accounting basis.

Furthermore, Morocco's membership in the IPSAS Board provides an opportunity to align its financial statements with those of other member countries and to benefit from enhanced financial transparency. This membership also facilitates the optimization of processes related to the preparation, execution, and oversight of the state budget, thereby contributing to a substantial improvement in financial reporting for the benefit of all stakeholders, including the government, parliament, the Court of Auditors, and citizens.

This approach aligns with the principles set forth in the Moroccan Constitution of 2011, which served as the foundation for a series of reforms aimed at enhancing accountability and transparency. It also corresponds to the provisions of Organic Law No. 130-13 relating to the Finance Law, which mandates the State to adopt accrual accounting in addition to budgetary accounting, with the goal of promoting good governance and improving the management of public finances. The reform of state accounting has been identified as a priority project within the broader efforts to modernize and optimize Morocco's public financial management system (Khattabi & Elmallouki, 2023). According to the Ministry of Economy and Finance: "*Conceptually, the reform of State accounting is not merely a change in the accounting framework; rather, it entails a comprehensive overhaul and reconstruction of state accounting in accordance with international standards, specifically the International Public Sector Accounting Standards (IPSAS), which are modeled on business practices*"[1].

The reform of the accounting system in Morocco was primarily led by:

- **The introduction of general accounting** in accordance with Article 31 of Organic Law 130.13 relating to the Finance Law states: "*The State shall keep budgetary accounts of revenue and expenditure. It shall also keep general accounts of all its operations*". This law provides that the State's general accounting must adopt the same principles as those applied in private companies and requires that the State's accounts be sincere, regular, and faithful. General accounting serves as the tool for evaluating the State's assets, liabilities, and commitments, and enhances the transparency of financial data through consolidated financial statements (Guthrie, 1998);
- **Aligning government accounting with international standards**, specifically the International Public Sector Accounting Standards (IPSAS)—aims to strengthen control and transparency in public sector accounts (Guthrie, 1998), provide clearer and more detailed financial information, and promote enhanced consistency and comparability of financial statements across time and among various public organizations. (Belanca & Vandernoot, 2013);
- **The development of the accounting framework** by the General Treasury of the Kingdom, in compliance with IPSAS standards while taking into account the specific characteristics of the Moroccan State. This framework includes the creation of a conceptual framework, the adoption of 13 core accounting standards, the establishment of a chart of accounts, the definition of account operating procedures, and the formulation of specific instructions for each category of State accountants;
- **The introduction of financial control and auditing** aims to ensure the regularity, sincerity, and legality of the Moroccan State's financial operations and statements. The Court of Auditors is the body responsible for the external oversight of public finances. Its mission is to examine the accounts and operations of public entities to ensure compliance with the applicable legislative and regulatory provisions;
- **The development of the State Accounting Plan (PCE)**, adopted during the 12th plenary session of the National Accounting Council in 2008, reflects budgetary, asset, and cost analysis dimensions in line with IPSAS standards.

The measures undertaken by the State go beyond the mere control of funds, extending to the assessment of its assets, expenditures and revenues, financial results, cash flows, debts and receivables, costs, and commitments, with the aim of providing a more comprehensive analysis of its financial position.

Figure 3. Objectives of the State Accounting Plan

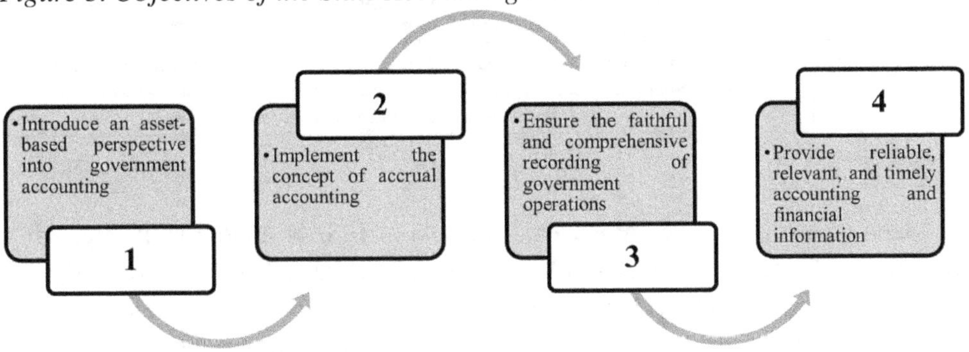

Source: The Kingdom's General Treasury's (TGR), 2011

1.5. Advantages of IPSAS Implementation In The Public Sector

The adoption of IPSAS offers many practical benefits, as evidenced by countries that have implemented them and view them as a lever for reforming their public accounting systems. These standards also enhance the comparability of accounting information while strengthening the accountability and transparency of public finances (Brusca & Martínez, 2016).

The qualitative characteristics of the information presented in general purpose financial statements are essential for producing high-quality, useful information for users. According to IFAC (2018), these characteristics include understandability, relevance, faithful representation, reliability, and comparability. Financial information that meets these criteria contributes to the production of high-quality financial statements, thereby enhancing the decision-making process within public organizations.

Table 2. Qualitative Characteristics of Financial Information

Intelligibility	**Financial information is intelligible when users can comprehend its meaning. It must be sufficiently clear, precise, and structured to be easily understood by users. Information related to complex elements Should not be omitted from financial statements solely due to its complexity for certain users.**
Relevance	Information is relevant when it is likely to influence users' decisions by providing useful insights to assess a past, present, or future situation, or to confirm or correct previous evaluations.
Reliability	Reliable information is information free from significant errors or bias, upon which users can rely to faithfully reflect the reality it is intended to represent.
Comparability	Comparability requires that financial information is presented consistently over time and across different public entities, allowing for cross-analysis and relevant assessments of performance and financial position.

Source: IFAC, 2018

Many researchers have emphasized the role of IPSAS standards in improving the quality of financial reporting. According to Rechka & Kabbaj (2019), IPSAS enhance the comparability, clarity, and understandability of public financial reporting, particularly regarding the use of public financial resources and the execution of annual budgets in accordance with the provisions of the Finance Act. Accounts prepared in accordance with IPSAS provide a true and fair view of financial performance (Rechka & Kabbaj, 2019). Similarly, Ball (2015) asserts that IPSAS facilitate the preparation of high-quality reports in the public sector, thereby promoting more rigorous tax control. The transparency they introduce into financial statements contributes to strengthening government accountability.

The results of the work conducted by Brusca & Martínez (2016) highlight that IPSAS significantly improve comparability between governments, a finding also confirmed by Christiaens et al. (2015). Indeed, the comparability of financial information relies on the consistent application of similar accounting standards and procedures over time and across different organizations (IASB, 2010). The willingness of public entities to prepare harmonized financial statements will enable consistent and aligned reporting with that of other similar entities (Okoh & Ohwoyibo, 2010). Therefore, the IPSASB (2012) encourages the implementation of IPSAS standards to achieve high comparability in the public sector. In this regard, Atu, Atu, and Okoye (2013) argue that the application of these standards facilitates the harmonization of financial statements, thereby ensuring high comparability of financial information at the international level.

Other researchers, such as Oduware (2012) and Bellanca & Vandernoot (2013), have also highlighted that IPSAS facilitate the comparability and transparency of financial information. Furthermore, Christiaens, Manes-Rossi, Vanhee and Aversano (2013) found that these standards contribute not only to strengthening comparability but also to improving the consolidation of financial statements by integrating international best practices within public organizations globally.

Other research has highlighted the benefits of adopting IPSAS. Bergmann (2012) demonstrated that accrual accounting based on IPSAS has proven useful in supporting decision-making in the Swiss public sector. Idrissi (2019) emphasized that these standards promote the transparency and relevance of public accounts. Similarly, Ofoegbu (2014), Mhaka (2014) and Chan (2010) showed that adopting IPSAS strengthens the credibility of public entities' financial statements.

The Association of Chartered Certified Accountants (ACCA, 2017) presents nine (9) benefits related to the adoption of IPSAS standards in the public sector:

Figure 4. Benefits of IPSAS adoption in the public sector

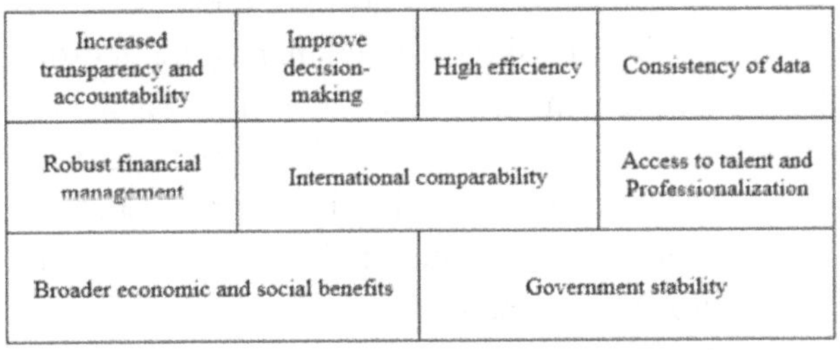

Source: ACCA, 2017

2. APPROACH AND METHODOLOGY

Our empirical investigation aims to study the impact of IPSAS standards on the comparability, reliability, relevance, and understandability of public financial information in the Moroccan context. We seek to answer the following questions:

- Do Moroccan public sector practitioners have sufficient knowledge of IPSAS standards?
- Are IPSAS standards widely applied in the Moroccan public sector?
- According to respondents' perceptions, which qualitative characteristics of public financial information are most influenced by the application of IPSAS in Morocco?

2.1. Study Sample

In the social sciences, researchers can choose between quantitative and qualitative methods (Elhamma, 2024). In this study, a quantitative research approach was employed, and data were collected from accounting professionals in Morocco. Morocco was selected as the focus of this study due to the increasing adoption of modern management tools by Moroccan companies in recent years. These include the implementation of IFRS standards (Elhamma, 2024, 2025), contemporary management control systems (Elhamma, 2015, 2023), and reforms aimed at modernizing the public sector (Elhamma & El-Moumane, 2025).

This study is based on a questionnaire survey administered to accounting professionals in Morocco, either in paper format during professional meetings or electronically to facilitate data collection. The choice of these professionals is justified, on the one hand, by their role in public financial management processes, as they are directly involved in the implementation of accounting reforms. On the other hand, their technical expertise, familiarity with IPSAS, and practical experience enable the collection of reliable data on the level of adoption of these standards and support a relevant assessment of their impact on the quality of financial information and the efficiency of public sector management.

Due to the lack of precise information on the total population of accounting practitioners, we opted for simple random sampling. In total, the responses of 84 Moroccan participants were retained. The table below presents the composition of our sample.

Table 3. The sample according to the profession of respondents

Profession	*N*	%
University Professor in Accounting, Control, and Auditing	14	17%
Auditor	14	17%
Accountant	8	10%
Charted accountant	14	17%
Management controller	16	19%
Chief Financial officers	6	7%
Financial Manager	12	14%
TOTAL	**84**	**100%**

Our sample consists of 84 respondents working in accounting-related professions within the Moroccan public sector: university professors in accounting, financial control, and auditing (17%), auditors (17%), accountants (10%), charted accountants

(17%), management controllers (19%), chief financial officers (7%), and financial managers (14%).

Figure 5. Distribution of respondents by the public institution in which they work

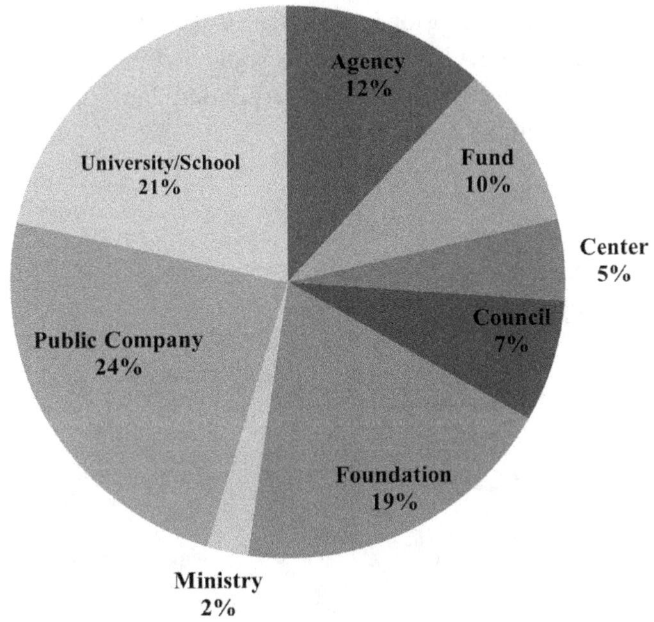

The graph above shows the distribution of respondents according to the public institution in which they carry out their professional activities. A concentration of respondents can be observed in certain public institutions, notably public companies (24%), universities/schools (21%), and foundations (19%). Other institutions are also represented, including agencies (12%), funds (10%), centers (5%), councils (7%), and ministries (2%).

2.2. Measurement of Variables: Benefits of IPSAS Adoption in the Moroccan Public Sector

In order to evaluate the perceived benefits of adopting IPSAS standards, four essential qualitative characteristics of financial information were selected: comparability, reliability, relevance, and Intelligibility.

To measure the impact of this adoption, we proposed a five-point rating scale ranging from "very low improvement" to "very high improvement".

3. RESULTS AND DISCUSSION

3.1. Prior knowledge levels of respondents regarding IPSAS standards

To assess the respondents' prior knowledge of IPSAS, we asked the question: "Have you ever heard of IPSAS?" The results show that 95% of the sample reported being aware of the standards, while 5% responded "no" (including 3 financial managers and 1 management controller).

Figure 6. Level of Knowledge of IPSAS

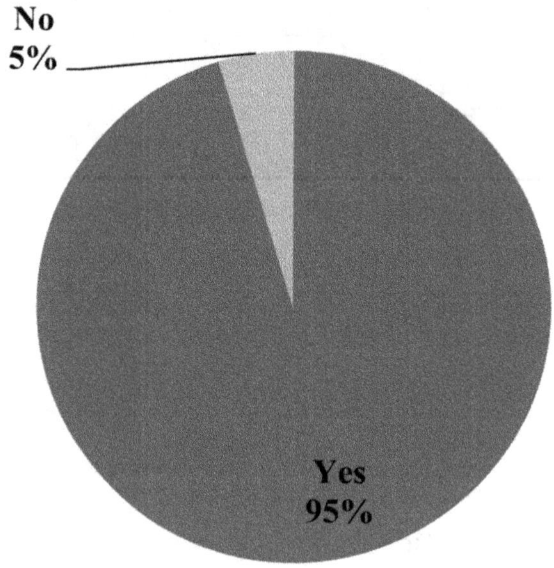

Table 4. Level of Knowledge of IPSAS by Profession

Profession	No	Yes
Auditor		14
Accountant		8
Management controller	1	15
Chief Financial officers		6
Charted accountant		14

continued on following page

Table 4. Continued

Profession	No	Yes
University Professor in Accounting, Control, and Auditing		14
Financial manager	3	9
TOTAL	**4**	**80**

These results show that IPSAS standards are widely known by practitioners performing accounting-related functions in the Moroccan public sector. Therefore, this familiarity can be considered a favorable prerequisite for the effective adoption of these standards in the Moroccan public sector.

3.2. Level of IPSAS Standards Adoption in Moroccan Institutions

To study the level of institutional adoption of IPSAS standards in the Moroccan public sector, the following question was asked: "Does your organization apply IPSAS standards?" The results reveal that only 12% of our sample reported having adopted IPSAS (10 respondents), while 88% answered "no" (74 respondents).

Figure 7. Level of IPSAS Standards Adoption in Moroccan Institutions

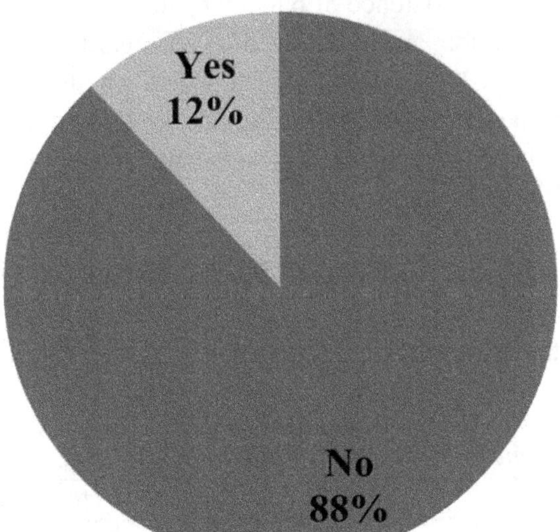

Table 5. Level of IPSAS Standards Adoption in Moroccan Institutions

Public institution	**No**	**Yes**
Agency	10	
Fund	8	
Center	4	
Council	6	
Foundation	12	4
Ministry	2	
Public company	14	6
University/School	18	
TOTAL	**74**	**10**

Within our sample, some public organizations, including foundations and public companies, have initiated the process of adopting IPSAS standards. However, other categories of public organizations have yet to take such a step.

This discrepancy may be explained by the significant costs associated with implementing these standards, notably in terms of staff training, the adoption of new technologies, and the need for specialized expertise (Ademola et al., 2020). According to Brusca and Martínez (2016), key obstacles to IPSAS adoption include criticism of their alignment with private-sector accounting models, concerns over national control and the persistence of budgetary illusion, the high cost of training required for implementation, and unresolved issues regarding IPSASB governance. In the case of Morocco, IPSAS adoption faces several challenges, particularly legal constraints, as implementation requires a clear and well-structured regulatory framework with sufficiently detailed legal texts—a mechanism that remains inadequately defined to date (Idrissi Chouahdi, 2019).

3.3. Perceived Benefits of the IPSAS Adoption

The following table summarizes the main results:

Table 6. Perceived benefits of the IPSAS adoption of Moroccan respondents

	Comparability	**Reliability**	**Relevance**	**Intelligibility**
Very low improvement	2 (2%)	2 (2%)	2 (2%)	2 (2%)
Low improvement	2 (2%)	2 (2%)	0 (0%)	4 (5%)
Moderate improvement	10 (12%)	4 (5%)	8 (10%)	6 (7%)

continued on following page

Table 6. Continued

	Comparability	Reliability	Relevance	Intelligibility
High improvement	34 (41%)	32 (38%)	38 (45%)	28 (33%)
Very high improvement	36 (43%)	44 (53%)	36 (43%)	44 (52%)
TOTAL	**84 (100%)**	**84 (100%)**	**84 (100%)**	**84 (100%)**

Figure 8. Moroccan Respondents' Perceptions of the Benefits of IPSAS Adoption

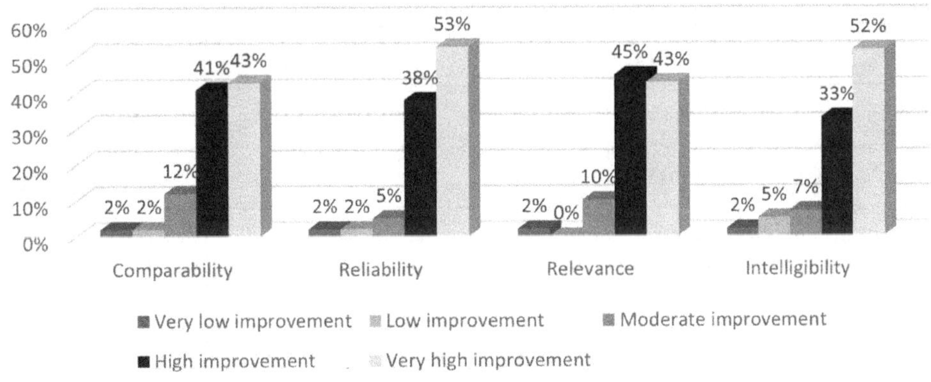

More than 80% of respondents believe that the adoption of IPSAS standards improves the comparability (84%), reliability (91%), relevance (88%), and intelligibility (85%) of financial information produced by Moroccan public sector organizations. These results are consistent with previous research, which highlights that the adoption of IPSAS standards has significant and positive effects on the comparability, relevance, reliability, and intelligibility of public sector financial statements. Chan (2010) states that the adoption of IPSAS improves comparability and transparency, allowing public organizations to make more informed decisions based on reliable and relevant information. Deloitte (2013) confirms that information produced according to IPSAS standards is useful and enables users to assess the financial situation, performance, and cash flows in order to make effective decisions. According to Colibert and Des Robert (2008): "IPSAS standards guarantee the reliability and relevance of financial information, essential conditions for ensuring meaningful comparisons over time or between different public organizations. By promoting transparency, these standards meet a fundamental objective of establishing a climate of trust among all stakeholders: citizens and national or international institutions to which the financial statements produced by these organizations are addressed".

To further analyze the responses collected, the results will be presented separately according to the professional categories of the respondents, as illustrated in the following tables:

Table 7. Perception of the improvement in the comparability of financial information by respondents' professions

Profession	Very low improvement	Low improvement	Moderate improvement	High improvement	Very high improvement	TOTAL
University Professor in Accounting, Control, and Auditing	2 (14%)	2 (14%)	0 (0%)	4 (29%)	6 (43%)	**14** (100%)
Auditor	0 (0%)	0 (0%)	4 (29%)	4 (29%)	6 (43%)	**14** (100%)
Accountant	0 (0%)	0 (0%)	0 (0%)	6 (75%)	2 (25%)	**8** (100%)
Charted accountant	0 (0%)	0 (0%)	0 (0%)	6 (43%)	8 (57%)	**14** (100%)
Management controller	0 (0%)	0 (0%)	2 (13%)	10 (63%)	4 (25%)	**16** (100%)
Chief Financial officers	0 (0%)	0 (0%)	2 (33%)	0 (0%)	4 (67%)	**6** (100%)
Financial manager	0 (0%)	0 (0%)	2 (17%)	4 (33%)	6 (50%)	**12** (100%)

According to our sample, 100% of accountants and chartered accountants, 88% of management controllers, 83% of financial managers, 71% of university professors and auditors, and 67% of chief financial officers believe that the adoption of IPSAS standards significantly, or even very significantly, improves the comparability of financial statements produced in the public sector.

Table 8. Perception of the improvement in the reliability of financial information by respondents' professions

Profession	Very low improvement	Low improvement	Moderate improvement	High improvement	Very high improvement	TOTAL
University Professor in Accounting, Control, and Auditing	2 (14%)	2 (14%)	0 (0%)	2 (14%)	8 (57%)	**14** (100%)
Auditor	0 (0%)	0 (0%)	0 (0%)	10 (71%)	4 (29%)	**14** (100%)
Accountant	0 (0%)	0 (0%)	0 (0%)	2 (25%)	6 (75%)	**8** (100%)
Charted accountant	0 (0%)	0 (0%)	0 (0%)	6 (43%)	8 (57%)	**14** (100%)

continued on following page

Table 8. Continued

Profession	Very low improvement	Low improvement	Moderate improvement	High improvement	Very high improvement	TOTAL
Management controller	0 (0%)	0 (0%)	0 (0%)	2 (12%)	14 (88%)	**16** (100%)
Chief Financial officers	0 (0%)	0 (0%)	0 (0%)	2 (33%)	4 (67%)	**6** (100%)
Financial manager	0 (0%)	0 (0%)	4 (33%)	8 (67%)	0 (0%)	**12** (100%)

According to our sample, all accountants and chartered accountants, auditors, chief financial officers, and management controllers, as well as the majority of university professors (71%) and financial managers (67%), consider that the adoption of IPSAS standards significantly, or even very significantly, improves the reliability of financial information in the public sector.

Table 9. Perception of the improvement in the relevance of financial information by respondents' professions

Profession	Very low improvement	Low improvement	Moderate improvement	High improvement	Very high improvement	TOTAL
University Professor in Accounting, Control, and Auditing	2 (14%)	0 (0%)	2 (14%)	6 (43%)	4 (29%)	**14** (100%)
Auditor	0 (0%)	0 (0%)	0 (0%)	10 (71%)	4 (29%)	**14** (100%)
Accountant	0 (0%)	0 (0%)	0 (0%)	2 (25%)	6 (75%)	**8** (100%)
Charted accountant	0 (0%)	0 (0%)	0 (0%)	6 (43%)	8 (57%)	**14** (100%)
Management controller	0 (0%)	0 (0%)	2 (12%)	6 (38%)	8 (50%)	**16** (100%)
Chief Financial officers	0 (0%)	0 (0%)	0 (0%)	0 (0%)	6 (100%)	**6** (100%)
Financial manager	0 (0%)	0 (0%)	4 (33%)	8 (67%)	0 (0%)	**12** (100%)

According to our sample, 100% of auditors, accountants, chartered accountants, and chief financial officers, 88% of management controllers, and 67% of financial managers believe that IPSAS standards have a significant, or even very significant, impact on the relevance of financial statements produced in the public sector.

Table 10. Perception of the improvement in the intelligibility of financial information by respondents' professions

Profession	Very low improvement	Low improvement	Moderate improvement	High improvement	Very high improvement	TOTAL
University Professor in Accounting, Control, and Auditing	2 (14%)	2 (14%)	0 (0%)	2 (14%)	8 (57%)	**14** (100%)
Auditor	0 (0%)	0 (0%)	2 (14%)	8 (57%)	4 (29%)	**14** (100%)
Accountant	0 (0%)	0 (0%)	0 (0%)	2 (25%)	6 (75%)	**8** (100%)
Charted accountant	0 (0%)	0 (0%)	2 (14%)	4 (29%)	8 (57%)	**14** (100%)
Management controller	0 (0%)	0 (0%)	0 (0%)	4 (25%)	12 (75%)	**16** (100%)
Chief Financial officers	0 (0%)	0 (0%)	0 (0%)	2 (33%)	4 (67%)	**6** (100%)
Financial manager	0 (0%)	2 (17%)	2 (17%)	6 (50%)	2 (17%)	**12** (100%)

According to our sample, all accountants, management controllers, and chief financial officers, as well as the majority of auditors (86%), university professors (71%), and financial managers (67%), consider that the adoption of IPSAS standards can have a significant, or even very significant, impact on the intelligibility of financial information in the public sector.

Table 11. Average % of respondents who believe that IPSAS improve the characteristics of financial reporting "significantly" or "very significantly".

	Comparability	Reliability	Relevance	Intelligibility	Average
Accountant	100%	100%	100%	100%	**100%**
Charted accountant	100%	100%	100%	86%	**96.4%**
management controller	88%	100%	88%	100%	**93.9%**
Chief Financial officers	67%	100%	100%	100%	**91.8%**
Auditor	71%	100%	100%	86%	**89.3%**
University Professor in Accounting, Control, and Auditing	71%	71%	71%	71%	**71,4%**
Financial manager	83%	67%	67%	67%	**70.8%**

The results show that accountants are the professionals most convinced of the benefits of IPSAS, unanimously believing that these standards significantly improve the quality of financial information in the public sector, in terms of comparability, reliability, relevance, and intelligibility. This favorable perception is also strongly shared by charted accountants (96.4%), management controllers (93.9%), Chief

Financial officers (91.8%), and auditors (89.3%). On the other hand, university professors and financial managers are more moderate in their level of support, with rates of 71.4% and 70.8%, respectively.

CONCLUSION

This research aims to examine the impact of IPSAS adoption on the qualitative characteristics of financial information, namely: comparability, reliability, relevance, and intelligibility. The results of our empirical investigation, based on a sample of 84 respondents from various public sector organizations in accounting-related professions, indicate that IPSAS standards have a significant positive impact on improving comparability (84%), reliability (91%), relevance (88%), and intelligibility (85%) of financial information in the public sector. Indeed, over 80% of respondents believe that the adoption of IPSAS enhances these characteristics in financial information produced by Moroccan public sector organizations. Furthermore, our results highlight that professional such as accountants, chartered accountants, management controllers, financial directors, and auditors are particularly convinced of the benefits of IPSAS standards, emphasizing their positive influence on these aspects of financial information. In contrast, university professors and financial managers express a more cautious level of support.

This study has shown a high level of awareness of IPSAS within Moroccan public sector entities, and that these standards are widely known among practitioners involved in accounting-related functions. This familiarity can therefore be considered a favorable prerequisite for promoting the effective adoption of IPSAS and ensuring their sustainable integration into public sector accounting practices in Morocco.

However, our study indicates that the transition to IPSAS in Morocco requires a relatively long implementation period. In fact, regarding the level of institutional adoption of IPSAS in the Moroccan public sector, only 12% of respondents stated that they had effectively adopted the standards, compared to 88% who reported that they had not yet implemented them. According to Ademola et al. (2020), *"the cost of implementation, staff training, technological factors, knowledge and awareness of IPSAS, and the availability of expertise have a significant influence on IPSAS implementation"*. Similarly, Brusca and Martínez (2016) highlight several obstacles to IPSAS adoption, including criticism of their alignment with the corporate accounting model, the desire of some countries to retain control and maintain budgetary illusions, the high cost of training required, and concerns about IPSASB governance. In the Moroccan context, Idrissi Chouahdi (2019) notes that IPSAS adoption faces several challenges, particularly legal constraints. Their implementation requires a clear and structured regulatory framework supported by precise legal texts—a mechanism that, to date, remains insufficiently defined.

Finally, this study has two methodological limitations. The first relates to the relatively small sample size, which limits the generalizability of the results. The second concerns the exclusive use of a perceptual approach based on a questionnaire, which may introduce a bias in the analysis of the results. In order to enrich this study, the integration of other explanatory variables (organizational, institutional or technical), and the broadening of the sampling base to include a larger number of public organizations, will be relevant to reinforce the robustness of the analyses and the external validity of the results.

REFERENCES

Ademola, A. O., Ben-Caleb, E., Madugba, J. U., Adegboyegun, A. E., & Eluyela, D. F. (2020). International public sector accounting standards (IPSAS) adoption and implementation in Nigerian public sector. *International Journal of Financial Research, 11*(1), 434–444.

Adhikari, P., & Mellemvik, F. (2010). The adoption of IPSASs in South Asia: A comparative study of seven countries. *Research in Accounting in Emerging Economies, 10*, 171–201. DOI: 10.1108/S1479-3563(2010)0000010012

Alshujairi, M. H. (2014). Government accounting system reform and the adoption of IPSAS in Iraq. *Research Journal of Finance and Accounting, 5*(24), 1–20. https://www.iiste.org/Journals/index.php/RJFA/article/download/18490/19035

Atu, O. E. O. K., Atu, O. G., & Okoye, A. F. (2013). International Public Sector Accounting Standards (IPSAS): Challenges and Way Forward in Nigeria. *Quarterly Journal of Associational of National Accountants of Nigeria, 21*(1), 26–32.

Ayachi, G. (2018). La convergence de la comptabilité de l'État avec les normes IPSAS: Le cas du Maroc [MPRA Paper No. 90039]. University Library of Munich. https://mpra.ub.uni-muenchen.de/90039/

Ball, I. (2015). Debate: Would IPSAS help Greece? *Public Money & Management, 35*(6), 397–398. DOI: 10.1080/09540962.2015.1076954

Bellanca, S., & Vandernoot, J. (2013). Analysis of Belgian public accounting and its compliance with International Public Sector Accounting Standards (IPSAS) 1, 6, and 22. *International Journal of Business and Management, 8*(9), 122–133. DOI: 10.5539/ijbm.v8n9p122

Bellanca, S., & Vandernoot, J. (2013). Belgian public accounting: Evolution and compliance with IPSAS. *International Advances in Economic Research, 19*(1), 79–81. DOI: 10.1007/s11294-012-9386-8

Benito, B., Brusca, I., & Montesinos, V. (2007). L'harmonisation des systèmes gouvernementaux d'information financière: Le rôle des IPSAS. *Revue Internationale des Sciences Administratives, 73*(2), 323–350. DOI: 10.3917/risa.732.0323

Benito, B., Brusca, I., & Montesinos, V. (2007). The harmonization of government financial information systems: The role of the IPSASs. *International Review of Administrative Sciences, 73*(2), 293–317. DOI: 10.1177/0020852307078424

Bergmann, A. (2012). The influence of the nature of government accounting and reporting in decision-making: Evidence from Switzerland. *Public Money & Management, 32*(1), 15–20. DOI: 10.1080/09540962.2012.643050

Brusca, I., & Condor, V. (2002). Towards the harmonisation of local accounting systems in the international context. *Financial Accountability & Management, 18*(2), 129–162. DOI: 10.1111/1468-0408.00148

Brusca, I., & Martínez, J.-C. (2016). L'adoption des IPSAS: Un défi pour la modernisation et l'harmonisation de la comptabilité du secteur public. *Revue Internationale des Sciences Administratives, 82*(4), 761–781. DOI: 10.3917/risa.824.0761

Carvalho, J. B. da C., Camões, P. J., Jorge, S. M., & Fernandes, M. J. (2007). Conformity and diversity of accounting and financial reporting practices in Portuguese local government. *Canadian Journal of Administrative Sciences / Revue Canadienne des Sciences de l'Administration*. Advance online publication. https://doi.org/DOI: 10.1002/cjas.1

Chan, J. L. (2004). Une révolution mondiale dans la comptabilité publique? Une analyse des IPSAS et quelques recommandations. *Revue Française de Comptabilité*, (janvier), 27–31.

Chan, J. L. (2010). *Government adoption of accounting standards, especially IPSAS*. http://www.jameslchan.com/papers/ChanPhDSem6.pdf

Christiaens, J., Reyniers, B., & Rollé, C. (2010). Impact of IPSAS on reforming governmental financial information systems: A comparative study. *International Review of Administrative Sciences, 76*(3), 537–554. DOI: 10.1177/0020852310372449

Christiaens, J., Reyniers, B., & Rollé, C. (2010). Les conséquences des IPSAS sur la réforme des systèmes d'information financière publique: Étude comparative. *Revue Internationale des Sciences Administratives, 76*(3), 563–581. DOI: 10.3917/risa.763.0563

Christiaens, J., Vanhee, C., Manes-Rossi, F., Aversano, N., & Van Cauwenberge, P. (2014). The effect of IPSAS on reforming governmental financial reporting: An international comparison. *International Review of Administrative Sciences, 81*(1), 158–177. DOI: 10.1177/0020852314546580

Christiaens, J., Vanhee, C., Manes-Rossi, F., Aversano, N., & Van Cauwenberge, P. (2015). Les conséquences des IPSAS sur la réforme des rapports financiers du gouvernement: Comparaison internationale. *Revue Internationale des Sciences Administratives, 81*(1), 171–191. DOI: 10.3917/risa.911.0171

Colibert, J., & Des Robert, J.-F. (2008). *Les normes IPSAS et le secteur public: Normes comptables applicables aux États et municipalités, établissements publics, organisations internationales*. Dunod. (Collection Management Public).

DiMaggio, P. J., & Powell, W. W. (1983). The iron cage revisited: Institutional isomorphism and collective rationality in Organizational Fields. *American Sociological Review*, *48*(2), 147–160. DOI: 10.2307/2095101

El Hachimi, C., & Benthami, A. (2024). La modernisation des systèmes comptables de l'État marocain à la lumière des normes IPSAS. *European Scientific Journal*, *20*(7), 155–170. DOI: 10.19044/esj.2024.v20n7p155

Elhamma, A. (2015). The relationship between budgetary evaluation, firm size, and performance. *Journal of Management Development*, *34*(8), 973–986. DOI: 10.1108/JMD-06-2014-0053

Elhamma, A. (2023). The relationship between organisational decentralisation, balanced scorecard, and its perceived benefits in Moroccan SMEs. *International Journal of Accounting. Auditing and Performance Evaluation*, *19*(2), 185–202. DOI: 10.1504/IJAAPE.2023.132384

Elhamma, A. (2024). Determinants of national IFRS adoption: Evidence from the Middle East and North Africa region. *International Journal of Accounting. Auditing and Performance Evaluation*, *20*(1-2), 69–90. DOI: 10.1504/IJAAPE.2024.135535

Elhamma, A. (2024). Participant observation as a qualitative research method in management sciences: Interests, conditions, and limitations. In Bentalha, B., & Alla, L. (Eds.), *Applying qualitative research methods to management science* (pp. 75–91). IGI Global., DOI: 10.4018/979-8-3693-5543-5.ch004

Elhamma, A. (2025). Impact of mandatory IFRS adoption on foreign direct investment: The moderating role of conflict of interest regulation. *Journal of Financial Reporting and Accounting*, *23*(3), 936–958. DOI: 10.1108/JFRA-04-2022-0145

Elhamma, A. (2025). Perceived benefits of IFRS adoption in Morocco and French-speaking Sub-Saharan African countries. In F. Albuquerque & P. G. Dos Santos (Eds.), *Contemporary innovations in reporting and analysis* (pp. 183–210). IGI Global. https://doi.org/DOI: 10.4018/979-8-3693-5923-5.ch007

Elhamma, A., & El-Moumane, R. (2025). The role of strategic planning in resilience and crisis management: A case study of a public organization in Morocco. In Dias Rouco, J. C., & Nunes Figueiredo, P. C. (Eds.), *Enhancing resilience in business continuity management* (pp. 433–460). IGI Global., DOI: 10.4018/979-8-3693-8809-9.ch015

Grossi, G., & Soverchia, M. (2011). European Commission adoption of IPSAS to reform financial reporting. *Abacus, 47*(4), 525–552. DOI: 10.1111/j.1467-6281.2011.00353.x

Guthrie, J. (1998). Application of accrual accounting in the Australian public sector – Rhetoric or reality. *Financial Accountability & Management, 18*(2), 117–140. DOI: 10.1111/1468-0408.00047

Guthrie, J., Olson, O., & Humphrey, C. (1999). Debating developments in new public financial management: The limits of global theorizing and some new ways forward. *Financial Accountability & Management, 15*(3–4), 209–228. DOI: 10.1111/1468-0408.00082

Hood, C. (1995). The "New Public Management" in the 1980s: Variations on a theme. *Accounting, Organizations and Society, 20*(2-3), 93–1009. DOI: 10.1016/0361-3682(93)E0001-W

Humphrey, C., Loft, A., & Woods, M. (2009). The global audit profession and the international financial architecture: Understanding regulatory relationships at a time of financial crisis. *Accounting, Organizations and Society, 34*(6-7), 810–825. DOI: 10.1016/j.aos.2009.06.003

Idrissi Chouahdi, A. (2019). *Les conditions d'applications des normes IPSAS au Maroc en comparaison avec la Belgique* [Doctoral thesis, Université de Liège]. ORBi. https://orbi.uliege.be/handle/2268/235459

Ilie, E., & Miose, N.-M. (2012). IPSAS and the application of these standards in Romania. *Procedia: Social and Behavioral Sciences, 62*, 35–39. DOI: 10.1016/j.sbspro.2012.09.008

International Federation of Accountants (IFAC). (2018). *Handbook of the International Code of Ethics for Professional Accountants.* https://www.ifac.org

Jensen, G. R. (2018). International Public Sector Accounting Standards (IPSAS). In Farazmand, A. (Ed.), *Global Encyclopedia of Public Administration, Public Policy, and Governance*. Springer., DOI: 10.1007/978-3-319-20928-9_2280

Jorge, S., Brusca, I., & Nogueira, S. P. (2019). Translating IPSAS into national standards: An illustrative comparison between Spain and Portugal. *Journal of Comparative Policy Analysis, 21*(5), 445–462. Advance online publication. DOI: 10.1080/13876988.2019.1579976

Khattabi, L., & Elmallouki, L. (2023). Le passage aux normes IPSAS au Maroc: Vers un nouveau mode de gestion des finances publiques. *International Journal of Accounting, Finance, Auditing, Management and Economics, 4*(3–1), 466–480. https://doi.org/DOI: 10.5281/zenodo.8064041

Lüder, K. (2000). National accounting, governmental accounting and cross-country comparisons of government financial condition. *Financial Accountability & Management, 16*(2), 117–128. DOI: 10.1111/1468-0408.00100

Lüder, K., & Jones, R. (2003). *Reforming governmental accounting and budgeting in Europe*. Fachverlag Moderne Wirtschaft.

Mhaka, C. (2014). IPSAS, a guaranteed way of quality government financial reporting? A comparative analysis of the existing cash accounting and IPSAS-based accounting reporting. *International Journal of Finance & Economics, 3*(3), 134–141.

Moore, M. H. (1995). *Creating public value: Strategic management in government*. Harvard University Press.

Oduware U. (2012), IFRS Adoption in Nigeria and Optimizing the Gains of Global Investment Climate Akintola Williams Deloitte, 1-15.

Ofoegbu, G. N. (2014). New public management and accrual accounting basis for transparency and accountability in the Nigerian public sector. *IOSR Journal of Business and Management, 16*(7), 104–113. DOI: 10.9790/487X-1673104113

Okoh, L., & Ohwoyibo, O. (2010). Public Accountability: Vehicle for Socio- Economic Development of Nigeria. *International Journal of Investment and Finance, 3*(1&2), 145–149.

Pacter, P. (2005). What exactly is convergence? *International Journal of Accounting. Auditing and Performance Evaluation, 2*(1/2), 67–83. DOI: 10.1504/IJAAPE.2005.006893

Pina, V., & Torres, L. (2003). Reshaping public sector accounting: An international comparative view. *Canadian Journal of Administrative Sciences, 20*(4), 334–350. DOI: 10.1111/j.1936-4490.2003.tb00709.x

Pollitt, C., & Bouckaert, G. (2011). *Public management reform: A comparative analysis—New Public Management, governance, and the Neo-Weberian State* (3rd ed.). Oxford University Press.

Rechka, F., & Kabbaj, S. (2019). Les normes IPSAS et le passage d'une comptabilité de caisse à une comptabilité d'exercice au Maroc. *Revue du contrôle, de la comptabilité et de l'audit, 3*(4), 649–678.

Roje, G., Vasiček, V., & Hladika, M. (2012). The perspectives of IPSASs introduction in Croatian public sector. *International Journal of Public Sector Performance Management*, *2*(1), 25–43. DOI: 10.1504/IJPSPM.2012.048742

SAFA (South Asian Federation of Accountants). (2006). *A study on accrual-based accounting for governments and public sector entities in SAARC countries*. South Asian Federation of Accountants.

Toudas, K., Poutos, E., & Balios, D. (2013). Concept, regulations and institutional issues of IPSAS: A critical review. *European Journal of Business and Social Sciences*, *2*(1), 43–54.

Trabelsi, A. (2017). *Application des normes IPSAS en Tunisie*. Al Manhal.

KEY TERMS AND DEFINITIONS

Accounting reform: refers to the process of modernizing, adapting, and strengthening a country's accounting systems, standards, and practices in response to evolving economic, legal, institutional, and governance needs. Its primary objective is to optimize the management of public resources and rationalize government expenditures.

Accrual accounting: is an accounting approach whereby financial transactions are recorded when they occur, regardless of when cash flows are received or paid. Thus, public revenues are recognized when earned, and expenses when incurred, providing a more accurate and comprehensive view of a public organization's financial position. This approach enables better management of public resources and enhances transparency in the oversight of public finances.

Cash accounting: is a method of accounting in which financial transactions are recorded only when actual receipts or disbursements occur. Thus, government revenues are recorded when funds are received, and expenditures when payments are made, regardless of when the commitments were incurred. Although simpler to apply, this system provides a limited and incomplete view of the financial position of public organizations, as it does not always capture all available resources or future obligations.

IPSAS: refers to a set of accounting standards developed by the International Public Sector Accounting Standards Board (IPSASB), operating under the oversight of the International Federation of Accountants (IFAC). These standards aim to enhance the quality, comparability, reliability, relevance, and clarity of financial reporting by public sector entities across the globe.

ENDNOTE

1 Ministry of Economy and Finance, Reform of State Accounting. Quarterly Review.

Chapter 10
IFRS S1 and S2 Adoption in a Non-Mandatory Environment:
Institutional Drivers and Insights From Air Canada

Ayoub Jroundi
https://orcid.org/0009-0006-5270-9611
Ibn Tofail University, Morocco

ABSTRACT

This chapter examines the early adoption of IFRS S1 and S2 within a non-mandatory regulatory environment, using a qualitative case study of Air Canada. Guided by neo-institutional theory, it investigates how institutional dynamics influence the voluntary implementation of sustainability disclosure standards. The chapter draws on insights from a semi-structured interview with Air Canada's Director of Corporate Sustainability Reporting, offering a detailed view of the internal motivations, operational challenges, and strategic considerations that underpin early engagement with the ISSB framework. The findings show that IFRS S2 is more readily integrated due to its alignment with existing climate disclosure practices, whereas IFRS S1 presents interpretive and practical difficulties. In the absence of regulatory obligation, the decision to adopt is shaped by investor expectations, peer influence, and professional norms. This study contributes to the literature by offering grounded evidence on how organizations internalize and operationalize ESG standards in a voluntary setting.

DOI: 10.4018/979-8-3373-1902-5.ch010

1. INTRODUCTION

Over the past twenty years, sustainability concerns have become a central issue in discussions around corporate accountability and transparency. Investors, regulators, and civil society alike have pushed for greater visibility on how firms address environmental, social, and governance (ESG) risks. This growing pressure has led to a proliferation of voluntary ESG disclosure frameworks — among them the Global Reporting Initiative (GRI), which adopts a stakeholder-oriented approach and encourages disclosures about the wider impact of an organization on society and the environment, the Task Force on Climate-related Financial Disclosures (TCFD), which lays out reporting recommendations for climate-related financial risks and governance ecosystems; and the Sustainability Accounting Standards Board (SASB), which focuses on financially material ESG issues that are relevant for investors, and across a variety of sectors. While these initiatives marked an important step, their coexistence has resulted in inconsistencies that limit cross-sector comparability and investor confidence (Ed-Dafali et al., 2025; Zaid & Issa, 2023).

Recognizing this gap, the IFRS Foundation moved to develop a global standard that would consolidate ESG disclosures within the financial reporting architecture. In 2021, it established the International Sustainability Standards Board (ISSB), and later published IFRS S1 and S2. These standards aim to introduce a coherent, investor-oriented sustainability reporting framework with global reach (IFRS Foundation, 2023). However, adopting these new frameworks is far from straightforward. Recent literature has identified both conceptual and operational challenges, including vague guidance in IFRS S1, difficulties in aligning with pre-existing data systems, and varying interpretations of materiality across jurisdictions (Gebhardt et al., 2024; Simnett et al., 2025). These issues are even more pronounced in developing economies, where institutional readiness, organizational design, and absorptive capacity shape how firms respond (Benhayoun et al., 2025; Boolaky et al., 2020).

Canada presents an interesting case in this regard. Although no mandatory sustainability reporting regime is currently in place, firms are nonetheless facing rising expectations from stakeholders, including institutional investors, proxy advisory firms, and ESG rating agencies (Albu et al., 2014). This creates a situation where voluntary adoption becomes strategically motivated, not just regulatory-driven.

Air Canada, as one of Canada's largest publicly listed firms, offers a valuable case to explore how companies are responding to IFRS S1 and S2 in the absence of regulatory compulsion. Drawing on insights from neo-institutional theory (DiMaggio & Powell, 1983), the study aims to examine the institutional drivers and internal organizational practices influencing voluntary adoption. Specifically, it explores how internal readiness, stakeholder pressure, and strategic motivation interact to facilitate or hinder the integration of these standards.

Methodologically, the study employs a qualitative single-case study design based on a semi-structured interview with Air Canada's Director of Corporate Sustainability Reporting. Neo-institutional theory serves as the analytical lens to interpret the coercive, mimetic, and normative pressures that shape ESG disclosure behavior. This approach enables a context-sensitive exploration of how organizations navigate emerging sustainability standards under non-mandatory conditions.

The findings reveal that IFRS S2, due to its alignment with the TCFD, was perceived as easier to operationalize, whereas IFRS S1 presented more significant challenges stemming from its broader scope and limited technical guidance. The case also highlights the enabling role of cross-functional collaboration, ESG program maturity, and digital infrastructure. These results provide empirical insights into the practical challenges and strategic considerations of early IFRS S1 and S2 adopters.

This chapter contributes to the limited body of qualitative research on IFRS sustainability standards by offering evidence from a non-mandatory environment. It sheds light on how institutional logics, internal capabilities, and stakeholder expectations interact in shaping ESG reporting practices. The study also offers reflections on how organizations interpret and adapt global standards in contextually specific ways.

Following this introduction, the next section reviews the existing literature and theoretical framework, before turning to the research methodology and findings. Section 2 outlines the research methodology, including the case study design. Section 3 presents the empirical findings from the Air Canada case. Section 4 discusses these findings through the lens of neo-institutional theory. The chapter concludes with a summary of key implications, limitations, and recommendations for future research.

2. LITERATURE REVIEW

2.1 IFRS in Sustainability Reporting: from ESG Emergence to Standardization Via ISSB

2.1.1 The Institutional Trajectory and Global Role of IFRS Standards

Prior to exploring the arrival of IFRS S1 and S2, it is important to consider the historical and institutional context of the IFRS framework itself. We first know that IFRS was created by the International Accounting Standards Committee (IASC) in 1973 and transitioned to the International Accounting Standards Board (IASB) in 2001 to address inconsistent practices that were leading to disparate accounting treatment and consequential inefficiencies in comparability around the world, which weakened investor confidence (Benhayoun et al., 2025; IFRS Foundation, 2023).

The objective was clearly focused on the creation of a high quality, understandable, enforceable and globally accepted set of accounting standards based on principles, not rules (Defond, 2019; Street & Gordon, 2023). The principles-based nature has been effective in giving IFRS space to be flexible across jurisdictions, promoting responsiveness to multiple economic situations. IFRS now has more than 140 jurisdictions that require or permit IFRS for use including all G20 economies - this highlights the Institutional context (Boolaky et al., 2020; IFRS Foundation, 2023).

On an analytical basis, the global spread of IFRS reflects ideas of neo-institutionalism whereby organizations follow widely legitimated norms and structures (DiMaggio & Powell, 1983). Countries and organizations adopt IFRS as a process of legitimation, it is not only about technical efficiency as countries may also adopt IFRS as a study of symbols to demonstrate membership in the international community and high degree of professionalism - a collective of coercive (regulatory), mimetic (if peers are doing it, we must too), and normative (the profession is using it) pressures (Boolaky et al., 2020; Meyer & Rowan, 1977).

There have also been several empirical studies that show the economic benefits of adopting IFRS. For example, in emerging markets it has been shown that IFRS adoption yields higher levels of foreign direct investment, increasing access to global capital markets, and increase quality in financial reporting (Bakr & Napier, 2022; Benhayoun et al., 2025; Elhamma, 2023c, 2024). However, these reported benefits are not systematic and depend on domestic institutional quality, enforcement or readiness of the market. For instance, in Morocco, introduction or adoption of IFRS began with sectors to which the economy themselves had international interests, first with banking and insurance followed by the other sectors of the economy (Benhayoun et al., 2025; Elhamma, 2023c, 2023a).

While the IFRS Foundation historically focused on financial reporting, it has provided new standards and guidance to meet the recent stakeholder demand for a different type of accountability associated with sustainability. The establishment of the ISSB in 2021 represents the next stage growth when combining ESG reporting with financial reporting (IFRS Foundation, 2023; Zaid & Issa, 2023).

The move towards sustainability accountability is no coincidence. In recent years, institutional pressures on firms to be more credible and transparent about corporate ESG risks have only intensified. The recent crises from the 2008 financial collapse to the crisis of climate change (Benhayoun et al., 2025; Liu & Lee, 2024) have meant ESG risks and opportunities have become business critical. Thus, bringing together sustainability and financial reporting read together as part of the IFRS architecture is an important milestone on the road towards a harmonized global disclosure regime that aligned financial performance within long-term social and environmental risks.

This understanding of the institutional nature and history of IFRS is important to comprehend the rational and intended considerable impact of IFRS S1 and S2. Rather than emerging from thin air, these sustainability-related standards are the outcome of several decades of institutional investigatory learning, prior attempts at global convergence and convergence, and a growing demand from stakeholders for integrated accountability systems and practices (Caputo & Pizzi, 2024; de Villiers et al., 2022; Ed-Dafali et al., 2025).

Although there is now a strong and organized system for financial reporting support because of the institutionalization of IFRS, socially and environmentally related dimensions are increasingly being brought to bear in recent years. The next subsection examines this progression from traditional financial reporting to the incorporation of ESG.

2.1.2 The Shift From Traditional Financial Reporting to ESG Integration

Traditionally, corporate financial reporting was primarily focused on indicators of financial performance (in particular, revenue, profitability, and asset valuation) and did not consider environmental and social issues, which were neither reported nor played an important role in corporate deliverables (Devi et al., 2025). Environmental and social concerns, on the other hand, were often overlooked or considered peripheral. Traditional accounting standards such as IFRS and GAAP typically treated sustainability disclosures as optional and external to core financial reporting, which led to a fragmented and inconsistent portrayal of ESG-related risks and their implications (Liu & Lee, 2024).

Over the last twenty years, corporate reporting practices have seen a significant change, much of which is being fuelled by the growing acceptance of ESG as a financial material (Suta et al., 2025). Incidents like the 2008 global financial crisis and the heightened climate-related economic shocks have increased the appetite of investors to more transparency over corporate sustainability risks (Benhayoun et al., 2025). In parallel, regulatory changes in areas such as the EU's Sustainable Finance Disclosure Regulation (SFDR) have solidified the requirement for standardized ESG reporting frameworks (Roy & Vasa, 2025).

In response, there have been a number of voluntary ESG reporting frameworks, but their rapid increase has resulted in disparate practices and limited comparability across jurisdictions (Ed-Dafali et al., 2025). For instance, while the Global Reporting Initiative (GRI) embraces a stakeholder-based lens to undertake ESG disclosure, the Task Force on Climate-Related Financial Disclosures (TCFD) focuses on management of climate risk within the financial services sector, and the Sustainability

Accounting Standards Board (SASB) offers better industry-specific standards addressing financially material ESG issues (Rani et al., 2025; Suta et al., 2025).

Although the development of these frameworks has greatly improved ESG reporting, there continues to be a lack of a global, uniform standard, resulting in ongoing inconsistencies in the materiality assessments and alignment of disclosures within and across countries and sectors (Liu & Lee, 2024). This fragmentation has highlighted the need for a globally accepted framework, in the stewardship of the IFRS Foundation, to establish a level of consistency in reporting ESG information within financial disclosure systems (Benhayoun et al., 2025).

In response to these changes in the reporting expectations, the IFRS Foundation undertook structural reforms and limited activities to formalize and consolidate the disclosures of sustainability. These reforms led to the establishment of the ISSB, which is examined below.

2.1.3 The Role of the IFRS Foundation and ISSB in Standardizing Sustainability Disclosures

In addressing the problems stemming from fragmented ESG reporting approaches, the IFRS Foundation established the International Sustainability Standards Board (ISSB) in 2021 to create a global set of sustainability disclosure standards that is investor grade (IFRS Foundation, 2023). The ISSB is not starting afresh, as its recent standards draw upon previous efforts and commit to inclusively building on them. The ISSB has indicated that it sees the existing major standards including GRI, SASB, and TCFD as part of a unified sustainability disclosure structure (Liu & Lee, 2024).

The mission of the ISSB is to ensure sustainability-related risks and opportunities are reported in the same framework as financial information to enhance comparability/usefulness of ESG-related data within and across capital markets (Benhayoun et al., 2025). An important feature of ISSB standards is to be aligned with existing IFRS accounting standards to facilitate incorporation within the financial reporting system of corporations (Ed-Dafali et al., 2025).

To meet both general and climate-specific disclosure requirements, the ISSB released two flagship standards in IFRS S1 and IFRS S2 (IFRS Foundation, 2023).

- IFRS S1 (General Sustainability-Related Disclosures) requires disclosures on material sustainability risks and opportunities that may affect a company's cash flows, financial position or strategic direction. It also requires disclosures on governance, risk management, and ESG performance disclosures (Rani et al., 2025; Suta et al., 2025).

- IFRS S2 (Climate-Related Disclosures) focuses on climate-related risks and builds on the TCFD structure by requiring disclosures on GHG emissions (Scopes 1, 2 and 3), climate resilience strategies, and transition plans to allow investors to assess a company's exposure to climate risks (Benhayoun et al., 2025; Ed-Dafali et al., 2025).

IFRS S1 and S2 represent a critical development in global sustainability reporting, as they bring together a single framework under IFRS, focused on investors, that increases the transparency, comparability, and reliability of ESG disclosures across jurisdictions (Suta et al., 2025). The ISSB is connecting sustainability-related information to the IFRS reporting framework and changing the historical gap between financial and non-financial reporting(Liu & Lee, 2024).

With the institutional context established, the focus will now shift to the two main standards published by the ISSB (IFRS S1 and S2), their purpose, design principles and implementation difficulties.

2.2 IFRS S1 & S2: Development, Objectives, and Practical Implications Compared to Other Frameworks

The creation of IFRS S1 and IFRS S2 by the International Sustainability Standards Board (ISSB) is a critical moment in the global standardization of sustainability-related financial disclosures (Benhayoun et al., 2025; de Villiers et al., 2022; IFRS Foundation, 2023). These standards were developed to combat the shortcomings of existing ESG reporting frameworks, with a specific emphasis on comparability, lack of enforcement, and alignment with financial reporting (Blessing, 2024; Ed-Dafali et al., 2025; Nielsen, 2023). IFRS S1 outlines general requirements for sustainability disclosures regarding enterprise value, while IFRS S2 focuses exclusively on climate-related disclosures around risks, metrics, governance, and resilience (Gebhardt et al., 2024; IFRS Foundation, 2023; Pratama et al., 2024).

IFRS S1 established the building blocks of using ESG information in the larger context of reporting on unused information, including notions of materiality, connectivity of information, and consistency across all reports and entities (Caputo & Pizzi, 2024; IFRS Foundation, 2023). Furthermore, IFRS S2 builds off the recommendations provided by the Task Force on Climate-related Financial Disclosures (TCFD), which introduces significant disclosures related to governance, strategy, risk management, and climate-related metrics (i.e. Scope 1, 2, and 3 emissions) (IFRS Foundation, 2023; Suta et al., 2025).

Empirical literature indicates that there are numerous challenges with respect to implementation, particularly in developing and emerging economies. In Morocco, for instance, organizational absorptive capacity, institutional support, and internal mechanisms will constrain the implementation of IFRS S1 and S2 (Benhayoun et al., 2025). Similar issues have been documented in Southeast Asia, where metrics and target disclosures are observed to lag behind the other dimensions such as governance and risk assessment (Choy, 2023; Mou & Ma, 2023; Pratama et al., 2022).

In comparison with existing ESG frameworks, IFRS S1 and S2 have a decidedly more investor and financially material focus than many of the stakeholder-orientated approaches (Zaid & Issa, 2023). For example, the Global Reporting Initiative (GRI) propagates the need for double materiality, with the organization's impact on society and the environment as its main priority (de Villiers et al., 2022; Rani et al., 2025). While the GRI is the most widely used and broad-based framework, the issue for reported information compared across jurisdictions is that the whole system is predicated on voluntary reporting and inconsistency in its application (Benhayoun et al., 2025; Ed-Dafali et al., 2025).

While TCFD is impactful, endures conceptual tensions and is globally influential and a basis for IFRS S2, TCFD, like SASB, are non-mandatory and been incorporated with little attachment to financial statements and therefore raises concerns over enforceability and mitigated consistency (IFRS Foundation, 2023; Roy & Vasa, 2025; Suta et al., 2025). The SASB framework, once again, with regard to that it is aligned to financial materiality and sector specific, has limited utilitarian stature, as even under SASB's uncomplicated framework, there has been inconsistent implementation and engagement in emerging market economies (Abhayawansa, 2022; IFRS Foundation, 2023; Rani et al., 2025).

Even with the various conceptual tensions, there is a conscious effort to nurture convergence. The GRI and ISSB have a collaboration agreement, this signals that there is some regard for interoperability and harmonization (Caputo & Pizzi, 2024; de Villiers et al., 2022).

Further, there are some indications from corporate practice that we can make some reasonable deductions, related to IFRS S1 and S2 aligned disclosures, to increase ESG transparency and comparability (Bentley-Goode et al., 2024; Simnett et al., 2025). However, adoption is not yet complete, and there are still challenges related to assurance, climate metrics, and industry relevant indicators (Gebhardt et al., 2024). Also, in some regional regulatory environments, such as the EU corporate sustainability reporting directive (CSRD) these requirements can support the global adoption of IFRS S1 and S2 and in turn are in some context verifying as a baseline framework (Caputo & Pizzi, 2024; Ed-Dafali et al., 2025; Vishnu Nampoothiri et al., 2024).

In conclusion, IFRS S1 and S2 represent an important step for a consistent, investor-oriented ESG reporting approach. GRI, TCFD, and SASB have started the sustainability disclosure journey, yet IFRS provides a consistent and measurable approach in conjunction with financial accounting standards. The experience of IFRS will depend on regulatory support, where each party is at in terms of institutional capacity, and how ESG standards can be reconciled to present financial relevance with broader sustainability initiatives (Benhayoun et al., 2025; Blessing, 2024; Ed-Dafali et al., 2025).

In order to consider how standards are interpreted and adopted by firms, we need to use a theoretical framework. The next section introduces neo-institutional theory, which is a useful lens to examine the adoption patterns of standards.

2.3 Theoretical Framework: Neo-Institutional Theory and Adoption of IFRS S1 & S2

Adoption of IFRS S1 and S2 sustainability standards require an understanding of the institutional processes that help shape and influence corporate reporting behaviours. Neo-institutional theory (DiMaggio & Powell, 1983) can inform an understanding of how coercive, mimetic, and normative pressures impact the reporting behaviours of organizations, especially as there is some worldwide demand for ESG disclosures that are consistent across organizations (Benhayoun et al., 2025; Meyer & Rowan, 1977).

Coercive pressures arise extensively from regulation at the government and global levels that force organizations to adopt standards like IFRS S1 and S2, to comply with international expectations (Bakr & Napier, 2022; Kholeif, 2010). Mimetic pressures occur for organizations which have insufficient institutional or industry guidance and peer organizations have been successful in achieving some first mover advantage; therefore some may copy their peers using sustainability practices to gain financial legitimacy (Oliveira et al., 2016). Normative pressures may also drive the adoption of how firms view their status in the professional organizations, like IFAC, which provides guidance and structure through professional standards and education (Boolaky et al., 2020).

Despite all these pressures, it is common for developing economies to face practical impediments to normative, mimetic, and coercive pressures, which translate into decoupling of symbolic adoption versus operational uptake of these (Albu et al., 2014). In addition, critics have limitations as a framework: it does not seem to allow for localized resistance or the complexity of operationalizing institutions into practice (Botzem et al., 2017).

In sum, neo-institutional theory is well suited for the adoption of IFRS S1 and S2, and provides a richer understanding of the institutional processes, adoption processes and implementation challenges, especially from the perspective of diverse emerging institutional contexts.

The application of this theoretical framework can be further illuminated by using more current empirical evidence. The following section synthesizes important findings from the literature on the adoption of IFRS S1 and S2, especially in emerging markets.

2.4 Empirical Studies on IFRS S1 & S2 and ESG Reporting: Evidence and Gaps

Studies conducted evidentially have produced substantial research about the potential outcomes, implications, benefits, and disadvantages of adopting IFRS S1 and S2. For example, Benhayoun et al. (2025) found that Moroccan companies' organisational absorptive capacity, structure, and culture will determine the extent of the ISSB standard readiness (i.e., IFRS S1 and S2) adoption process.

Following the above studies, Gaviria et al. (2023) identified several significant logistical challenges to adopting IFRS S1 and S2 within SMEs in Colombia. These challenges included poor internal controls and absent standardized indicators. Relatedly, studies conducted in Southeast Asia reinforce the challenges of implementation; Pratama et al. (2024) reported lack of consistency between governance disclosures and ESG matters, which may signify uneven levels of progress toward the other ESG components.

Additionally, Gebhardt et al. (2023) argued that even companies with strong strategic intent for ESG reporting have not effectively aligned their technical infrastructures and internal processes with the complexities of integrated ESG reporting processes. They concluded that their research suggested the barriers to IFRS S1 based sustainability disclosures are compounded by fragmented IT systems and varied cross functional familiarity with sustainable practices and their reporting requirements.

Investor based-inquiries have signified the positive investor outcomes associated with credible and aligned IFRS S1 and S2 disclosures; Hewa et al. (2025) and Shao & Xue (2024), found a connection between better aligned disclosures, increased investor confidence, and subsequent investment decisions. Nevertheless, assurance practices remain limited and inconsistent globally, as documented by Bentley-Goode et al. (2024) .

Elhamma (2023a, 2024, 2025) highlights that in developing economies, the positive impact of IFRS adoption on macroeconomic outcomes, such as foreign direct investment, remains contingent on institutional quality and governance safeguards. His findings reinforce the view that standard-setting alone is insufficient in the absence of strong regulatory support.

Despite substantial insights, gaps remain notably underexplored:

- Limited qualitative research capturing professional experiences in implementing IFRS standards, especially within emerging economies and francophone contexts.
- Sparse understanding of practical applications of 'materiality' under IFRS S1.
- Insufficient exploration of internal organizational and audit processes impacting ESG disclosure practices.

Addressing these gaps through qualitative approaches, such as semi-structured interviews, this research seeks deeper insights into real-world adoption experiences and practical challenges, thus enriching the existing empirical landscape.

3. RESEARCH METHODOLOGY

3.1 Research Design and Case Selection

This chapter adopts a case study research design as proposed by Yin (2009), focusing on exploring the initial stages of adoption of IFRS S1 and S2 sustainability standards within Air Canada. Given the emerging and complex nature of these standards, employing a qualitative case study method is particularly appropriate for gaining deep insights into organizational practices, motivations, and barriers associated with their implementation. Eisenhardt (1989) emphasizes that case studies are suitable for exploring dynamic processes in depth, particularly when dealing with relatively unexplored phenomena. Siggelkow (2007) further suggests that a single, illustrative case can provide significant theoretical and practical insights, especially when the area of inquiry is new or evolving, such as sustainability reporting frameworks.

Air Canada was chosen for this case study due to its initiative-taking approach toward ESG (Environmental, Social, and Governance) practices and its explicit efforts to align reporting practices with international sustainability standards. Operating within a highly regulated and publicly accountable industry, Air Canada presents an ideal context for examining the dynamics involved in transitioning to IFRS S1 and S2. The company's unique position as a leading international airline, combined with investor expectations and regulatory pressures, offers valuable perspectives on adopting global sustainability disclosure frameworks.

3.2 Data Collection, Analysis, and Methodological Considerations

The primary data for this study was obtained through a semi-structured interview conducted with Meryem Baskoun, Director of Corporate Sustainability Reporting and Communications at Air Canada. Ms. Baskoun was selected because of her extensive expertise and practical experience in ESG reporting, spanning over 13 years, including roles in ESG ratings, consultancy, and currently corporate ESG implementation. To accommodate her professional schedule and encourage thoughtful, reflective responses, the interview was conducted via email using a semi-structured format. This method is consistent with accepted qualitative research practices and enabled a flexible, context-sensitive data collection process.

The interview was structured around key themes identified in the existing literature: organizational readiness, drivers, and motivations for IFRS adoption, preparation steps undertaken, implementation challenges faced, comparison with other ESG frameworks (GRI, TCFD), and practical recommendations. Follow-up email correspondence allowed the participant to clarify and expand on her responses in her own timeframe. This asynchronous exchange enabled the collection of nuanced, experience-based information that could have been lost in more time-constrained or rigid interview settings.

The collected interview data was systematically analyzed through thematic analysis, as described by Braun & Clarke (2006). Thematic analysis involved coding responses into defined categories derived both from the interview data and relevant literature, helping to identify recurring patterns and key themes.

To uphold methodological rigor, the study followed guidelines recommended by established qualitative research authorities (Eisenhardt, 1989; Yin, 2009). Methodological transparency was ensured by articulating each research step clearly, maintaining alignment between research objectives, empirical approach, and theoretical framing. The case was further strengthened through triangulation with the literature, supporting the reliability and relevance of insights drawn. Although the single-case approach limits generalizability, the study's primary objective is exploratory rather than confirmatory. The depth and contextual relevance of this case offer valuable preliminary insights. Future research could broaden these findings by including more cases across different contexts.

4. RESULTS

This section presents the main empirical findings from the case study conducted with Air Canada's Director of Corporate Sustainability Reporting. The purpose is to document how IFRS S1 and S2 are being approached at an early stage by a large, complex organization operating in a non-mandatory regulatory environment. Rather than aiming for generalization, the focus is on capturing context-specific insights that reflect organizational readiness, implementation efforts, and practitioner perspectives. The findings are organized in relation to five themes identifiable in the interview data: (1) the drivers and motivators to adopt the standards, (2) the internal preparation process, (3) the practical and structural challenges faced, (4) the comparative positioning of IFRS to other ESG frameworks, and (5) recommendations from practitioners on implementation.

4.1 Drivers and Motivations

Air Canada's intention to adopt IFRS-based sustainability disclosures is specifically related to the fragmentation in the area of reporting. The respondent made it clear that the standards will "put some structure into the reporting," while noting that they now report alongside their peers, and that "the issuer community certainly needs to convey the expectations of the social bond issuer ultimate shareholder and that to get in alignment with the respective institutions." These motivations relate to larger trends outlined in the literature that suggest organizations adopt sustainability standards not only from a compliance perspective, but to establish credibility (Benhayoun et al., 2025; Caputo & Pizzi, 2024).

Internally, the reporting process based on sustainability reporting standards utilizes the same cross-functional approach. It includes ESG teams, investor relations, internal audit, finance and risk, and the external auditor. This cross-functional coordination reflects the growing maturity of sustainability reporting, highlighting that it is no longer viewed as a compliance requirement, but as a strategic organizational process (Pratama et al., 2024).

Still, challenges persist. Fragmented IT systems, inconsistent language, and limited internal awareness hinder progress. These issues echo those seen in other contexts, especially where readiness is high but systems and culture lag behind (Mou & Ma, 2023). While the respondent acknowledged the strategic importance of IFRS adoption, she expressed doubts about its short-term benefits, particularly regarding IFRS S1, which remains vague and difficult to operationalize (Simnett et al., 2025).

While internal motivations and external stakeholder pressures are the factors that facilitate initial adoption of an innovation, the implementation process generates a different set of challenges. These are presented in the next subsection.

4.2 Implementation Challenges and Organizational Realities

The absence of regulatory enforcement in Canada remains a critical barrier. Without a legal mandate, Air Canada must weigh the cost and timing of adoption amid regulatory uncertainty. This aligns with the concept of partial or symbolic adoption in contexts of legal ambiguity (Albu et al., 2014; Kholeif, 2010).

The issue of technological fragmentation adds additional complications to implementation. The financial and non-financial systems are disconnected, which makes the consolidation of disclosures difficult and, at the same time, crucial for complying with the integrated reporting requirements of IFRS S1 and S2. Additionally, while Air Canada pursues selective assurance of its KPIs, these efforts remain limited and illustrate the broader implementation gap (Bentley-Goode et al., 2024).

More than technical limitations, the process demands cultural change. A shared understanding of the purpose and language of sustainability reporting is still developing across departments, reflecting the social nature of reporting and the role of institutional learning (Boolaky et al., 2020).

In addition to navigating thcsc opcrational considerations, companies find themselves having to work through an incredibly complicated environment of existing ESG frameworks. The following section explores the relative positioning of IFRS S1 and S2 in comparison to the typical use of other frameworks.

4.3 Positioning IFRS S1 and S2 in Relation to Other ESG Frameworks

Air Canada's prior use of GRI, TCFD, CDP, UNGC, and SDGs reflects a mature, stakeholder-oriented ESG approach. Transitioning to IFRS shifts the focus toward investor materiality, requiring a redefinition of audiences and disclosure priorities. While IFRS S2, which aligns with TCFD, was easier to adopt, IFRS S1 presented challenges due to its generality and limited guidance (Gebhardt et al., 2024; Nielsen, 2023).

Though IFRS is intended to enhance comparability and transparency, the respondent noted these benefits remain theoretical. Like many early adopters, the company awaits broader industry application before evaluating these claims (Simnett et al., 2025).

Most importantly, not interpreted as a rupture, the practitioner suggested cooperation and congruence between frameworks. This perspective lines up with current efforts to promote new interoperability between ISSB and other standards (de Villiers et al., 2022). Therefore, the transition is one of recalibration; to re-align existing practices under new disclosure logics.

The respondent emphasized the need for support tools rather than standard revisions. Practical examples, clearer guidance, and interoperability are key to meaningful implementation. This reflects a growing consensus that barriers are often operational, not conceptual (Simnett et al., 2025).

Her advice to peers was straightforward: avoid starting from nothing. Instead, conduct a gap analysis and leverage existing disclosures. This incremental approach, grounded in adaptation rather than reinvention, mirrors what literature recommends for effective adoption in complex organizations (Pratama et al., 2024).

5. DISCUSSION

The case of Air Canada offers insight into how early-stage adoption of IFRS S1 and S2 involves not only technical and regulatory considerations but also institutional logics and internal interpretations. Evaluated through the neo-institutional theory perspective, the patterns described are indicative of coercive, mimetic, and normative institutional pressures as described by DiMaggio & Powell (1983). Air Canada expressed expectation of future regulations; by aligning their practices with peer practices, and by responding to professionals (like auditors), represent a multi-faceted area of influence, while legitimacy considerations may come ahead of regulatory compliance to inform disclosure decisions.

This interpretation of institutional pressures is similar to findings from recent studies whereby organizations tend to weigh a combination of anticipated regulation, peer benchmarking and professional norms regardless of direct legislative requirements (Albu et al., 2014; Boolaky et al., 2020). Air Canada's early adoption of IFRS sustainability standards represents this. Although coercive regulatory forces are limited in Canada, the mimetic and normative pressures appear to shape internal decision making for sustainability disclosures.

Internally with their processes, the firm confirms the findings reported by Gebhardt et al. (2023) and Pratama et al. (2024) that successful implementation is contingent on cross-functional coordination. Sustainability reporting is no longer the exclusive domain of communications teams: Air Canada's ESG professionals, finance, investor relations, and auditors are connected to reporting against internal strategic priorities and external expectations. However, while the reporting system is interconnected, there are structural gaps. Disjointed information technology (IT) systems, overlapping data streams, and varied levels of familiarity with the standards limit report effectiveness and efficiency. These problems reaffirm the findings outlined by Mou & Ma (2023), which show how often technical readiness and cultural readiness are out of sync during regulatory change.

The respondent's commentary about IFRS S1 and S2 is revealing. IFRS S2, which closely tracked TCFD was seen as relatively easy to adopt, whereas IFRS S1 was viewed as abstract, and not particularly operationalizing. The respondent's comment evokes concerns expressed by Simnett et al. (2025) and Nielsen (2023) in terms of how the overly general nature of IFRS S1 creates unclear pathways for how to operationalize principles into verifiable disclosures. In this respect, the respondent's cautious perspective is not unique, and instead represents a shared uncertainty amongst early adopters, who were hesitant to implement these position and processes until they had sufficient examples, templates, and benchmarking before taking full opportunities presented by the standards.

The idea that IFRS should complement and not replace existing frameworks is consistent with the interoperability agenda pursued by the ISSB and discussed by de Villiers et al. (2022). The respondent did not suggest abandoning GRI or TCFD for a clean set of IFRS standards, but sees this as a practical recalibration of systems, not a severance. Ultimately, this reinforces the viewpoint that sustainability reporting is more appropriately viewed as a developing ecosystem, not a standardized regulatory checklist.

In construction of the discussion, it is important to keep in mind that the barriers to adoption are most often operational rather than conceptual. As observed, many companies endorse the goals of IFRS in principle, but do not practical method to approach them. Air Canada's experience exemplifies this gap, with the informant highlighting the need for clearer guidance, industry examples, and an incremental approach. These suggestions highlight what Simnett et al. (2025) refer to as the "missing infrastructure" of ESG reporting, in terms of not only systems, but also knowledge and interpretative support.

The results align with Elhamma's (2023) research, which demonstrates that IFRS adoption in developing countries has limited influence on economic outcomes (like foreign direct investment) without well-designed institutional safeguards, including some regulation of conflicts of interest. His analysis supports the contention that simply adopting standards is meaningless without an appropriate institutional and governance framework.

The study has some limitations, particularly as it was single-case in design and focused solely on a preparatory phase of IFRS S1 and S2 adoption, and not a fully operationalized implementation. Even though the data are rich and context-specific, we do not claim that they are generalizable across all sectors or jurisdictions. However, the case provides some meaningful contributions to understand how leading firms interact with early-stage sustainability reporting in voluntary circumstances. This study reinforces the notion that sustainability standards compliance is not simply a linear or technical compliance process, and is instead based on strategic and legitimacy considerations, institutional pressures, and organizational capability. In this way, the Air Canada case illustrates how a global standard is interpreted, adapted, and integrated into local corporate realities through a process of progressive and incremental institutionalization.

Future research could adopt several complementary paths to deepen our understanding of IFRS S1 and S2 implementation. First, cross-country comparative studies could reveal how institutional, cultural, or legal contexts influence firms' interpretations of materiality and sustainability risk. Second, longitudinal analyses may track how organizations evolve their reporting practices over time, moving from symbolic to substantive adoption. Third, sector-specific investigations would help determine whether certain industries face unique barriers or accelerators to ESG standard integration. Fourth, the role of intermediaries—such as auditors, ESG consultants, and standard-setters—deserves closer attention for their influence on implementation quality. Finally, further research could examine how assurance practices, digital infrastructures, and board-level governance structures interact to support or hinder IFRS S1/S2 alignment.

6. CONCLUSION

This chapter sought to investigate voluntary adoption of IFRS S1 and S2 in a non-prescriptive regulatory environment, illustrated using Air Canada. The aim is to learn about how companies manage an early embrace of sustainability disclosure standards when regulatory requirements do not demand them. This was accomplished through a qualitative case study design utilizing semi-structured interviewing which was analyzed using a neo-institutional theoretical framework. Utilizing Neo-institutional theory as a conceptual lens, this chapter has demonstrated via Air Canada's case that institutional pressures, and especially mimetic and normative mechanisms, drive early voluntary adoption, even without coercive regulation. The Air Canada case highlights how the desire to align with evolving global norms and satisfy what investors require as a response to material issues can be a significant force in voluntary adoption, where legitimacy-seeking is a key strategic drive.

Empirical findings evidenced that IFRS S2, compared to IFRS S1, which closely resembles TCFD, was both easier to operationalize and integrate into existing reporting systems. In contrast, IFRS S1 was more challenging to implement, in part due to its broad scope and the flexibility it allows in interpretation based on the reporting company's discretion. Importantly, internal organizational readiness reflected through cross-functional activity, ESG maturity, and digital enablement emerged as interdependent enablers in addressing the complexities embedded in the standards.

This study contributes to the body of literature in at least two important ways. First, it extends applications of neo-institutional theory to sustainability reporting, providing valuable insights into mimetic and normative mechanisms in voluntary adoption settings. Second, it provides insight on a practical level where firms can build internal readiness for their ESG reporting using digital enablement and cross functional coordination.

However, key limiting barriers remain outside of Air Canada-style ESG reporting, notably the lack of integrated IT systems and the ongoing ambiguity surrounding the conceptual framing and expectations of materiality in climate-related disclosures. The chapter reaffirms the explanatory power of neo-institutional theory in understanding how norms and standards are adopted and adapted in different institutional contexts. The findings also confirmed previous research arguing that the adoption of ESG standards is not a technical, rational decision-making process, but one that is socially constructed and enacted through interpretation, organization culture, and changing norms and expectations.

The research design does have some limitations. The findings are not generalizable beyond a single firm and a single interview. Furthermore, the analysis only contemplates the early adoption interest and does not evaluate longer-term implementation effects or the views of investors. Although this study is limited by its single-case scope, it provides valuable insights to our understanding of how sustainability disclosure works at the micro-level when operating under a voluntary regime. Future research should build on this exploration using comparative case studies across different sectors and jurisdictions to examine how varied institutional settings moderate the adoption of the IFRS standards for the board. As noted in the previous section, several potential research avenues were identified, especially around materiality interpretation, cross-national implementation, and assurance characteristics under IFRS S1 and S2. Ultimately, the extent to which organizations adopt the standardized ESG reporting will depend not just on regulatory compliance but also on the ability for organizations to internalize, interpret, and implement these global standards in practice.

REFERENCES

Abhayawansa, S. (2022). Swimming against the tide: Back to single materiality for sustainability reporting. *Sustainability Accounting. Management and Policy Journal, 13*(6), 1361–1385. DOI: 10.1108/SAMPJ-07-2022-0378

Albu, C. N., Albu, N., & Alexander, D. (2014). When global accounting standards meet the local context-Insights from an emerging economy. *Critical Perspectives on Accounting, 25*(6), 489–510. DOI: 10.1016/j.cpa.2013.03.005

Bakr, S. A., & Napier, C. J. (2022). Adopting the international financial reporting standard for small and medium-sized entities in Saudi Arabia. *Journal of Economic and Administrative Sciences, 38*(1), 18–40. DOI: 10.1108/JEAS-08-2018-0094

Benhayoun, I., El Amrani, M., Barhdadi, A., & Azzaoui, W. (2025). Adoption of ISSB standards in emerging markets – insights from Moroccan companies' organizational readiness. *Journal of Financial Reporting and Accounting*. DOI: 10.1108/JFRA-07-2024-0468

Bentley-Goode, K. A., Simnett, R., Thompson, A., & Trotman, A. J. (2024). Choice of assurance provider and impact on quality of sustainability reporting: Evidence from sustainability reporting restatements. *Accounting and Finance*. https://www.scopus.com/inward/record.uri?eid=2-s2.0-85209989086&doi=10.1111%2facfi.13367&partnerID=40&md5=fe10fc893e605511235a86093e3a6733

Blessing, J. (2024). ESG frameworks and regulatory convergence: A global review. *Corporate Governance Journal, 28*(1), 11–35.

Boolaky, P. K., Tawiah, V., & Soobaroyen, T. (2020). Why Do African Countries Adopt IFRS? An Institutional Perspective. *The International Journal of Accounting, 55*(1), 2050005. Advance online publication. DOI: 10.1142/S1094406020500055

Botzem, S., Quack, S., & Zori, S. (2017). International Accounting Standards in Africa: Selective Recursivity for the 'Happy Few'? *Global Policy, 8*(4), 553–562. DOI: 10.1111/1758-5899.12514

Braun, V., & Clarke, V. (2006). Using thematic analysis in psychology. *Qualitative Research in Psychology, 3*(2), 77–101. DOI: 10.1191/1478088706qp063oa

Caputo, F., & Pizzi, S. (2024). Bridging the gap between financial and sustainability reporting. What are the implications for sustainable development? In *The Routledge Handbook of Accounting for the Sustainable Development Goals*. Taylor and Francis; Scopus. DOI: 10.4324/9781003404118-20

Choy, L. Y. (2023). Climate disclosures and sustainability regulation in Southeast Asia. *Asian Journal of Accounting Research, 8*(3), 210–227.

de Villiers, C., La Torre, M., & Molinari, M. (2022). The Global Reporting Initiative's (GRI) past, present and future: Critical reflections and a research agenda on sustainability reporting (standard-setting). *Pacific Accounting Review, 34*(5), 728–747. DOI: 10.1108/PAR-02-2022-0034

Defond, M. L. (2019). Why accounting matters: Evidence from accounting's ""big bang."" *Journal of International Accounting Research, 18*(3), 87–96. Advance online publication. DOI: 10.2308/jiar-52568

Devi, R., Firoz, M., & Saravanan, R. (2025). Unveiling redundancy in environmental, social, and governance reporting framework in India: An exploratory study. *Sustainability Accounting. Management and Policy Journal, 16*(2), 551–582. DOI: 10.1108/SAMPJ-10-2023-0786

DiMaggio, P. J., & Powell, W. W. (1983). The Iron Cage Revisited: Institutional Isomorphism and Collective Rationality in Organizational Fields. *American Sociological Review, 48*(2), 147. DOI: 10.2307/2095101

Ed-Dafali, S., Adardour, Z., Derj, A., Bami, A., & Hussainey, K. (2025). A PRISMA-Based Systematic Review on Economic, Social, and Governance Practices: Insights and Research Agenda. *Business Strategy and the Environment, 34*(2), 1896–1916. DOI: 10.1002/bse.4069

Eisenhardt, K. M. (1989). Building Theories from Case Study Research. *The Academy of Management Review, 14*(4), 532–550. JSTOR. DOI: 10.2307/258557

Elhamma, A. (2023a). *Cinquante ans des normes comptables internationales IAS/IFRS: Adoption, conséquences et où en est-on au Maroc?* (pp. 121–136).

Elhamma, A. (2023b). Impact of mandatory IFRS adoption on economic growth: The moderating role of Covid-19 crisis in developing countries. *Journal of Accounting and Management Information Systems, 22*(3). Advance online publication. DOI: 10.24818/jamis.2023.03007

Elhamma, A. (2023c). Impact of mandatory IFRS adoption on foreign direct investment: The moderating role of conflict of interest regulation. *Journal of Financial Reporting and Accounting*. DOI: 10.1108/JFRA-04-2022-0145

Elhamma, A. (2024). Determinants of national IFRS adoption: Evidence from the Middle East and North Africa region. *International Journal of Accounting, Auditing and Performance Evaluation, 20*(1–2), 69–90. *Scopus.* Advance online publication. DOI: 10.1504/IJAAPE.2024.135535

Elhamma, A. (2025). Perceived Benefits of IFRS Adoption in Morocco and French Speaking Sub-Saharan African Countries. In *Contemporary Innovations in Reporting and Analysis* (pp. 183–210). IGI Global Scientific Publishing.

Gaviria, D. A. G., Martínez, E. M. C., Polo, O. C. C., & Arcila, J. O. S. (2023). Accounting mechanism to measure the environmental impact of industries in the ABURRÁ VALLEY and its application of the general disclosure requirements related to financial information on sustainability (IFRS S1) and climate-related disclosures (IFRS S2). *Revista de Gestao Social e Ambiental, 17*(5), e03639. Advance online publication. DOI: 10.24857/rgsa.v17n5-013

Gebhardt, M., Schneider, A., Siedler, F., Ottenstein, P., & Zülch, H. (2024). Climate reporting in the fast lane? The impact of corporate governance on the disclosure of climate-related risks and opportunities. *Business Strategy and the Environment, 33*(7), 7253–7272. DOI: 10.1002/bse.3852

Hewa, S., Mala, R., Chen, J., & Dumay, J. (2025). Climate related disclosures and investor behaviour: An Australian study. *Advances in Accounting, 68*, 100809. https://www.scopus.com/inward/record.uri?eid=2-s2.0-85218249704&doi=10.1016%2fj.adiac.2025.100809&partnerID=40&md5=70355b38f822282169b52235d05ca203. DOI: 10.1016/j.adiac.2025.100809

IFRS Foundation. (2023). *IFRS S1 and S2: Sustainability disclosure standards.* IFRS Foundation Publications. https://www.ifrs.org

Kholeif, A. (2010). A new institutional analysis of ifrss adoption in egypt: A case study of loosely coupled rules and routines. In *Research in Accounting in Emerging Economies* (Vol. 10). https://doi.org/DOI: 10.1108/S1479-3563

Liu, H., & Lee, H. (2024). The Role of Ownership Structure in the Relationship Between Environmental, Social, and Governance Practices and Financial Reporting Quality: Evidence from China. *Sustainability (Basel), 16*(23), 10687. Advance online publication. DOI: 10.3390/su162310687

Meyer, J. W., & Rowan, B. (1977). Institutionalized Organizations: Formal Structure as Myth and Ceremony. *American Journal of Sociology, 83*(2), 340–363. DOI: 10.1086/226550

Mou, R., & Ma, T. (2023). A Study on the Quality and Determinants of Climate Information Disclosure of A-Share-Listed Banks. *Sustainability (Basel), 15*(10), 8072. Advance online publication. DOI: 10.3390/su15108072

Nielsen, C. (2023). ESG Reporting and Metrics: From Double Materiality to Key Performance Indicators. *Sustainability (Basel), 15*(24), 16844. Advance online publication. DOI: 10.3390/su152416844

Oliveira, M. C., Ceglia, D., & Filho, F. A. (2016). Analysis of corporate governance disclosure: A study through BRICS countries. *Corporate Governance (Bradford), 16*(5), 923–940. DOI: 10.1108/CG-12-2015-0159

Pratama, A., Dewi, N., Sofia, P., Muhammad, K., & Megawati, L. R. (2024). Sustainability Reporting Ecosystem and IFRS S1 and S2: How Accounting Research Can Assist its Implementation. *Journal of Ecohumanism, 3*(4), 3101–3168. DOI: 10.62754/joe.v3i4.3830

Pratama, A., Jaenudin, E., & Anas, S. (2022). Environmental, Social, Governance-Sustainability Disclosure Using International Financial Reporting Sustainability Standards S1 in Southeast Asian Companies: A Preliminary Assessment. *International Journal of Energy Economics and Policy, 12*(6), 456–472. DOI: 10.32479/ijeep.13581

Rani, R., Vasishta, P., Singla, A., & Tanwar, N. (2025). Mapping ESG and CSR literature: A bibliometric study of research trends and emerging themes. *International Journal of Law and Management.* DOI: 10.1108/IJLMA-09-2024-0301

Roy, J. K., & Vasa, L. (2025). Financial technology and environmental, social and governance in sustainable finance: A bibliometric and thematic content analysis. *Discover Sustainability, 6*(1), 148. Advance online publication. DOI: 10.1007/s43621-025-00934-2

Shao, M., & Xue, M. (2024). Firms' voluntary climate action disclosures and stock market reaction: A BERT-based analysis of earnings conference calls in China. *Journal of Climate Finance, 8*, 100047. DOI: 10.1016/j.jclimf.2024.100047

Siggelkow, N. (2007). Persuasion with case studies. *Academy of Management Journal, 50*(1), 20–24. DOI: 10.5465/amj.2007.24160882

Simnett, R., Tan, Y., You, J., & Zhou, S. (2025). Australian Listed Entities' Preparedness for Mandatory Reporting and Assurance of Climate-related Disclosures. *Abacus.* https://www.scopus.com/inward/record.uri?eid=2-s2.0-85219160823&doi=10.1111%2fabac.12363&partnerID=40&md5=e4e09238299c6eadf40fe895aea27427

Street, D. L., & Gordon, E. A. (2023). An interview with IASB Chair Dr. Andreas Barckow. *Journal of International Financial Management and Accounting. 34*(2), 358–377. Advance online publication. DOI: 10.1111/jifm.12171

Suta, A., Molnár, P., Limbach, Z., & Tóth, Á. (2025). Dictionary-based assessment of European Sustainability Reporting Standard (ESRS) disclosure topics. *Discover Sustainability*, *6*(1), 146. Advance online publication. DOI: 10.1007/s43621-025-00930-6

Vishnu Nampoothiri, M., Entrop, O., & Annamalai, T. R. (2024). Effect of mandatory sustainability performance disclosures on firm value: Evidence from listed European firms. *Corporate Social Responsibility and Environmental Management*, *31*(6), 5220–5235. DOI: 10.1002/csr.2860

Yin, R. K. (2009). *Case Study Research: Design and Methods*. SAGE Publications. https://books.google.co.ma/books?id=k0WrN3rBz_sC

Zaid, M. A. A., & Issa, A. (2023). A roadmap for triggering the convergence of global ESG disclosure standards: Lessons from the IFRS foundation and stakeholder engagement. *Corporate Governance (Bradford)*, *23*(7), 1648–1669. DOI: 10.1108/CG-09-2022-0399

KEY TERMS AND DEFINITIONS

ESG Integration: The process of embedding environmental, social, and governance factors into corporate strategy, decision-making, and reporting, particularly to align with stakeholder and investor expectations.

IFRS S1 (General Sustainability-related Disclosures): A standard issued by the ISSB that requires companies to disclose material sustainability-related risks and opportunities relevant to enterprise value, focusing on governance, risk management, and strategy.

IFRS S2 (Climate-related Disclosures): A standard aligned with the TCFD framework that mandates the disclosure of climate-related risks, Greenhouse gas emissions, and resilience strategies to inform investor decisions.

Institutional Isomorphism: A concept from neo-institutional theory describing how organizations conform to similar practices due to regulatory (coercive), peer-driven (mimetic), and professional (normative) pressures.

Materiality (Single vs. Double): Materiality in sustainability reporting refers to the process of determining what information is relevant or material for stakeholders. IFRS S1 takes a single materiality approach, focusing on information that influences investor decisions, as opposed to double materiality which also considers broader societal impact.

Organizational Readiness: The level to which a company is internally prepared (i.e. structurally, culturally, and technology-wise) to accept and implement new frameworks (e.g. IFRS S1 & S2), including personnel capacity, data systems, and governance arrangements.

Voluntary Adoption: The implementation of standards such as IFRS S1 and S2 without regulatory mandate, often driven by legitimacy concerns, investor expectations, or peer influence.

Chapter 11
Accounting Harmonization in French-Speaking African Countries: Dynamics and Prospects

Abdessamad Dibi
https://orcid.org/0009-0001-8691-5337
ENSEM, Hassan 2 University of Casablanca, Morocco

Ali Ouarab
Mouloud Maammeri University of Tizi, Ouzou, Algeria

Abdennasser Elfigha
https://orcid.org/0009-0008-1683-4890
ENSET, Hassan 2 University, Morocco

Hamdi Amifi
ENSET, Hassan 2 University, Morocco

ABSTRACT

The aim of this paper is to situate the process of harmonizing the accounting system in French-speaking African countries within the general context of the dissemination of international IAS-IFRS standards, in order to understand its dynamics and define its perspective. Based on a historical approach and an analysis of various documentary sources, this study shows that while international IAS-IFRS standards are currently global in scope, the harmonization of the accounting system in French-speaking African countries cannot be deterministic. Rather, it should be aligned

DOI: 10.4018/979-8-3373-1902-5.ch011

with the cultural and economic specificity of these nations, while taking into account the various options available.

INTRODUCTION

Over the last few decades, Africa has been facing a number of political, economic, social and cultural challenges which have had a destabilizing impact both on the cycles of production and distribution of wealth and on the various initiatives and discussions aimed at overcoming this context of uncertainty. One of these issues was the role of accounting in supporting and reinforcing the various strategies for emerging from the crisis. It is in this context that reform programmers aimed at modernizing accounting standards have been put in place in various African countries. These reforms, carried out under the aegis of international financial institutions such as the World Bank and the International Monetary Fund, have all been wholly or partially inspired by IAS-IFRS. These standards, drawn up by the IFRS Foundation (IFRSF), have become the global language of financial statements, trusted by investors the world over, and their use is currently required or recommended by more than 169 jurisdictions across five continents, including no fewer than thirty African countries.

In addition, the various accounting reforms carried out in Africa have been the subject of a number of research studies on their relevance and technical consequences (Elhamma, 2025; Waweru et al, 2023; Jayasinghe et al., 2021; Oluwagbemiga, 2021; Boolaky et al., 2020; Osinubi, 2020; Degos et al., 2019; Hopper et al., 2017; Sellami & Fendri, 2017; Zori, S. G., & Seny Kan, K., 2017; Khoutra, 2014). Nevertheless, much of this work has focused on English-speaking African countries, notably South Africa, Ghana, Kenya and Nigeria, revealing a large gap in understanding the evolution of the accounting system in a large part of this continent made up of French-speaking countries, in particular the countries of the Maghreb, Central, Equatorial and West Africa (Elhamma, 2025; 2024; 2023c).

The purpose of this paper is to situate the process of harmonizing the accounting systems of French-speaking African countries within the general context of the dissemination of international IAS-IFRS standards in order to understand its dynamics and define its perspective.

By accounting harmonization we mean the institutional process whose purpose is to bring national accounting standards and practices into line with each other and, consequently, to facilitate the comparison of accounting statements produced by companies in different countries (Colasse, 2004), or the political process aimed at reducing differences in national accounting practices in order to increase their compatibility and comparability with international standards (Hoarau, 1995). By 'IAS/IFES' we mean the generic notion of International Financial Reporting Standards as adopted by the International Accounting Standards regulation. According to the foundation's official website, the ultimate objective of adopting these standards is to improve the intelligibility, relevance, reliability, comparability and transparency of financial information in order to reduce information asymmetry between the various parties (iasb.org).

Historically, the accounting standards in force in French-speaking African countries were essentially inspired by continental doctrine based on the 4th and 7th European directives. The foundations of this system were based on written and codified law, detailed accounting rules and a strong link to taxation and the commercial code (Raffournier, 2007). This is particularly true of the General Accounting Plan (Plan Comptable Général or PCG) of the OCAM, which came into force in 1970 and was replaced in 1998 by the West African Accounting System (Système Comptable Ouest African or SYSCOA) of the Organization for the Harmonization of Business Law in Africa (OHADA)[1]. These include the Algerian Chart of Accounts of 1975, the Tunisian Chart of Accounts of 1967, the Ivory Coast Chart of Accounts of 1972, the Senegalese Chart of Accounts of 1975 and the Moroccan Code Général de Normalisation Comptable (CGNC), which has been in force since 1990.

As the capital of local companies continues to be opened up to foreign investors, the privatization process and the free trade agreements signed with the industrial powers (European Union, United States of America, China, Russia, Turkey), it is becoming increasingly important for entities and countries in French-speaking Africa to convert to the IAS-IFRS international accounting standards (Ramanna & Sletten, 2014). The global spread of IAS-IFRS has become a reality, and there is a growing gap between the accounting systems of French-speaking African countries and their main economic and trading partners (Dibi & Amifi, 2024).

However, while most of the qualitative characteristics retained in the international standards, in terms of intelligibility, relevance and comparability, seem to be compatible with the general environment in French-speaking African countries, the practical application of some of them seems to pose real difficulties. Indeed, the harmonization of accounting standards is not limited to a purely technical project, which concerns a few accounting or valuation rules, but constitutes a real conceptual, doctrinal and philosophical gap (Dibi & Amifi, 2024; Degos et al., 2019; Bampoky, 2019; Zori, S. G., & Seny Kan, K., 2017).

Adopting a historical approach informed by the study of various documentary sources, our reflection is driven by the following research question: How has the accounting system in French-speaking African countries evolved in the global context of the spread of IAS-IFRS?

To answer this central question, we propose the following five sub-questions:

- What is the current state of international adoption of IAS-IFRS?

- What are the factors influencing the adoption of IFRS worldwide?
- In this context, what has been the trend towards accounting harmonization in French-speaking African countries?
- What is at stake in the transition to IAS-IFRS for entities and governments in general, and in French-speaking Africa in particular?
- What is the outlook for accounting harmonization in French-speaking Africa?

The aim of our work is to enrich research in terms of understanding the evolution of the accounting system in this large part of the African continent, which is made up of French-speaking countries. Our main results indicate that accounting harmonization in these countries cannot be deterministic, but should rather be aligned with the cultural and economic specificity of these nations, while taking into account the various options available.

We will begin by mapping the adoption of IAS-IFRS in order to highlight their widespread adoption worldwide. The factors influencing the adoption of IFRS worldwide will then be presented. We will then analyse the dynamics of accounting harmonization in the various countries of French-speaking Africa, presenting in particular the main reform projects underway in these countries. We will then explain the challenges of the transition to IAS-IFRS for companies and governments in French-speaking Africa. Finally, we will highlight, from a cost-benefit perspective, the prospect of accounting harmonization in these countries and our policy recommendations.

1. INTRODUCTION TO IAS-IFRS AND THEIR GLOBAL IMPORTANCE

The purpose of this section is to map the adoption of IAS-IFRS in order to highlight their widespread adoption worldwide.

Inspired by Anglo-Saxon doctrine, IAS-IFRS are based on an economic approach to reality that favors investors. The foundations of this system are based on customary law that leaves a large place to case law, accounting standards drawn up by professional organizations, accounting that is disconnected from taxation and financial information geared towards the financial markets.

IAS-IFRS are drafted by a group of experts using a deductive 'top-down' method that is related to the 'Due Process' accounting standard-setting process used in the United States (Khoutra, 2014).

Based on a conceptual framework whose main mission is to create a single "language" for financial reporting on a global scale, IFRS form a coherent and exhaustive set of standards for the preparation of financial statements, encompassing

fundamental concepts such as the definition of assets and liabilities, their valuation methods and the conditions for their recognition. The aim of these standards is to provide accurate, exhaustive and transparent financial information, and they currently support the process of convergence with local standards in different countries around the world, with a view to improving existing practice. IAS-IFRS are now the global language of financial reporting, widely used in developed, emerging and developing economies. Nevertheless, while some countries have adopted IAS-IFRS outright, others have evolved their accounting systems to incorporate IAS-IFRS, while others continue to prohibit the application of IAS-IFRS to their domestic companies. Currently, there are over 169 jurisdictions that require the use of IFRS accounting standards for all or most listed companies. According to the IASB website[2], the benefits sought through this adoption are threefold. Firstly, to provide transparency by improving the quality of financial information, thereby enabling investors and other market participants to make informed economic decisions. Secondly, to strengthen accountability by reducing the information gap between investors and companies. Third, to improve economic efficiency, by helping investors to evaluate potential investments around the world, thereby allocating capital to the most promising opportunities and reducing the cost of capital for companies.

Figure 1. Jurisdictions where IFRS are required for all or most listed companies by region and percentage

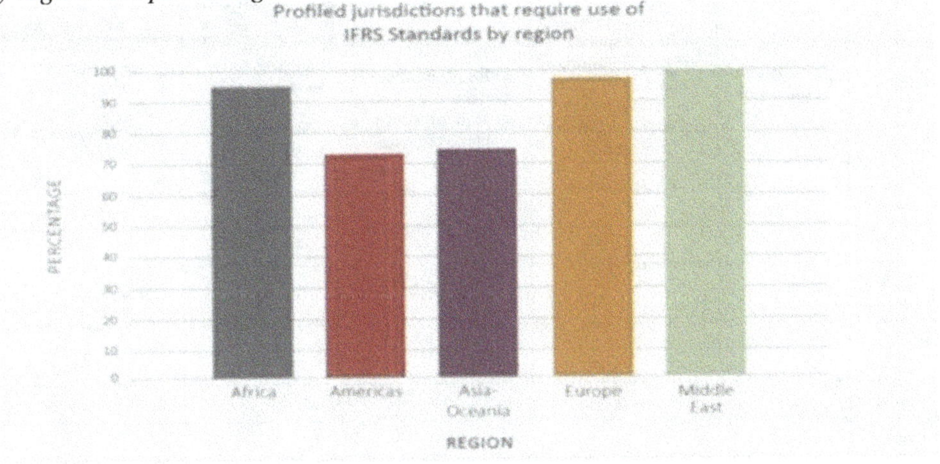

Source: www.ifrs.org

Figure 1 shows that the percentage of jurisdictions in which IFRS are required for all or most listed companies is 100% in the Middle East, 97% in Europe, 95% in Africa and over 70% in Asia-Oceania and the Americas.

According to the specialist literature, several factors may explain this widespread adoption of IAS-IFRS across the world. Firstly, factors linked to the standards themselves. Companies may consider switching to IAS-IFRS because it seems irreversible, particularly given the convergence of the standards of the main economic and financial partners with these international standards (Dibi & Amifi, 2024; Feudjo et al., 2021; de Brebisson et alphonse, 2018). Such harmonization would provide local entities with a high-quality accounting framework recognised by international financial centres (Elhamma, 2025; Waweru et al., 2023; Degos et al., 2018). Then there are factors linked to the international context. Countries may consider switching to IAS-IFRS in response to recommendations from international bodies, in particular the World Bank and the International Monetary Fund (Elhamma, 2024; Zori, S. G., & Seny Kan, K., 2017; Judge et al., 2010). Such an approach is likely to improve the comparability of financial statements in relation to partners, make it easier to obtain credit from financial institutions and promote local companies' access to foreign capital markets (Musah et al., 2020; Boolaky et al., 2020; Yousefinejad et al., 2018; Jayeoba et al., 2016).

The following table (Table 1) analyses the use of IFRS accounting standards in the 168 jurisdictions profiled by the IFRS Foundation (Updated in September 2023):

Table 1. Profile of IFRS accounting jurisdictions

Region	Jurisdictions in the region	Jurisdictions that require IFRS Accounting Standards for all or most domestic publicly accountable entities	Jurisdictions that require IFRS Accounting Standards as % of total jurisdictions in the region	Jurisdictions that permit or require IFRS Accounting Standards for at least some (but not all or most) domestic publicly accountable entities	Jurisdictions that neither require nor permit IFRS Accounting Standards for any domestic publicly accountable entities
Europe	44	43	98%	1	0
Africa	39	37	95%	1	1
Middle East	13	12	92%	1	0
Asia-Oceania	35	28	80%	2	5
Americas	37	26	70%	9	2
Totals	168	147	87.5%	13	8
As % of 168	100%	87.5%		7.7%	4.8%

Based on IFRS.org

As Table 1 shows, the rate of adoption of IAS-IFRS varies considerably from country to country, with some countries having fully adopted the standards, while others are still in the early stages of implementation. For example, of the 147 jurisdictions that impose IFRS accounting standards on all or most domestic listed companies, around 65% also impose IFRS accounting standards on some domestic unlisted companies, typically financial institutions and large unlisted companies. Furthermore, of these 147 jurisdictions, 19 do not have a stock exchange, but impose IFRS accounting standards on all financial institutions. However, six of these jurisdictions, which do have a stock exchange, impose IFRS accounting standards on other listed companies, but not on listed financial institutions. In total, therefore, more than 169 countries around the world currently apply IAS-IFRS, either directly or through reconciliation. Of these countries, 86 also require or permit the IFRS accounting standard for SMEs, and 12 are currently studying it. Finally, it should be noted that the African countries that have partially or fully adopted IFRS are mainly English-speaking African countries.

Two major findings emerge from this mapping of the adoption of IAS-IFRS: on the one hand, international accounting standards are widely used throughout the world, but with varying adoption policies, and on the other, the total adoption of IAS-IFRS is concentrated in English-speaking African countries. These two observations lead us to analyse the factors influencing the adoption of IFRS worldwide.

2. FACTORS INFLUENCING THE ADOPTION OF IAS-IFRS WORLDWIDE

This section describes the various policies for adopting IFRS and the factors influencing their adoption.

Accounting standard setting is the process of developing common rules to harmonize and improve accounting practices. Whether at national, continental or global level, accounting standard-setting involves adopting both substantive and procedural rules. In terms of substance, it involves adopting accounting principles, procedures, conventions and formulations based on a source of thought and in line with the spirit on which each State bases its economic and social development. In terms of form, the aim is to adopt, in a manner consistent with the previous system, models and presentations to be respected when recording and processing transactions in the accounts, as well as in the preparation and presentation of summary accounting and financial documents. This process of accounting standardization is dynamic and evolves according to the national, continental and global environment. It also reflects the economic power of each state, group of states or professional organizations (Feudjo, 2010). In addition, the legal framework, the economic system, the level of development and the links between accounting and taxation are all contingent factors that can explain the differences in accounting standards between countries (Zori, S. G., & Seny Kan, K., 2017; Colasse, 2004). And it is precisely this diversity of accounting standard-setting systems that makes harmonization necessary on a continental and international scale (Khoutra, 2005).

The adoption of an accounting standard is therefore the result of the conflicting interests of hierarchical players, as well as their position and real power in the profession. Historically, the standard-setting of accounting practices in the continental European system has been the responsibility of the State, whereas in the Anglo-Saxon system, it is more the responsibility of professional organizations. The current context of IAS-IFRS dissemination reflects the hegemony and economic power of the major industrialized countries.

From this point of view, the international experience of accounting harmonization offered these countries a choice between various options, in particular adoption, adaptation and convergence. These policies are independent of each other and are generally based on stable country characteristics (de Brebisson et alphonse, 2017). While outright adoption of IFRS is the simplest, most straightforward and least costly option (Ramanna & Sletten, 2014), it is generally of interest to less developed countries seeking to adopt a quality standard, even if it is not well used due to a lack of sufficient authority. However, the choice of adopting IFRS is determined by the official languages of each country, with the English language favoring strong adoption of these standards (Zori, S. G., & Seny Kan, K., 2017; de Brebisson et alphonse, 2017). Convergence by stages, which consists of introducing IFRS into the local reference framework while risking ambiguities for investors, seems to be better suited to developed countries that target specific applications where IFRS are a complementary tool to the standards. Finally, convergence by component, which consists of amending local standards to bring them into line with IFRS, is more time-consuming and costly. In this case, IFRS are used for all the financial statements of the targeted entities, whereas standardization of practices will require eventual convergence of local standards, based on experience and the dissemination of best practices, the timing of which remains uncertain (de Brebisson et alphonse, 2017).

The figure below (Figure 2) summarize the advantages and limitations of these three accounting harmonization options.

Figure 2. Different IFRS adoption policies

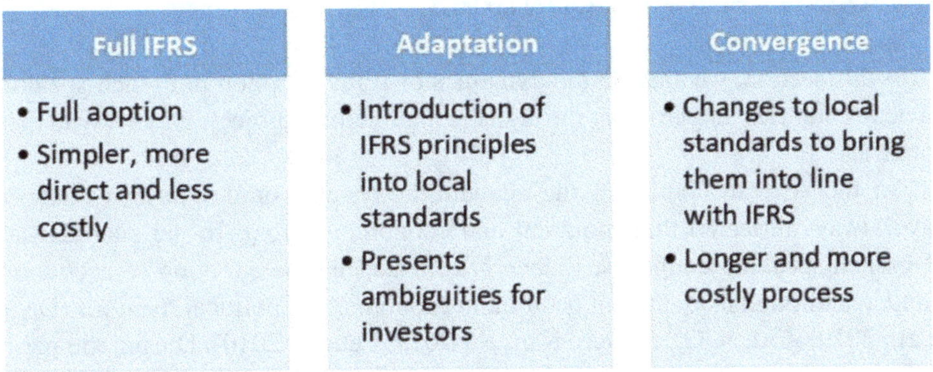

Based on the literature

In seeking to explain the factors influencing IFRS adoption policies around the world, de Brebisson et alphonse (2017) concluded that, on the one hand, policy choices are made independently of possible options and, on the other hand, these choices are strongly influenced by the cultural characteristics and development status of countries. According to the results obtained by the authors, IFRS seem to be of interest to less developed countries seeking to adopt a quality standard, whereas more developed countries are positioning themselves for targeted applications, where IFRS are a complementary tool to local standards. Furthermore, the English language plays a positive role in the adoption of IFRS, whereas the French language is an obstacle to this adoption (de Brebisson et alphonse, 2017).

For their part, Boolaky et al (2020), in seeking to explain these factors influencing IFRS adoption policies in the African context, concluded that this adoption is linked more to the coercive, mimetic and normative pressures exerted in particular by the World Bank and the IMF than to the substantial economic benefits of this adoption. Indeed, the results obtained by the authors reveal that while the adoption of IFRS seems to constitute a strong legitimizing signal for an African country and for its entire accounting community, the immediate benefits of a rapid and unsupported adoption would benefit, almost exclusively, a relatively small group of local IAF representatives and entities affiliated with multinationals that comply with IFRS (Boolaky et al., 2020).

It goes without saying that while the adoption of IAS-IFRS is a global phenomenon, its implementation and impact vary considerably from region to region. In particular, French-speaking African countries face unique challenges and opportunities in adopting these standards.

3. ADOPTION OF IAS-IFRS IN FRENCH-SPEAKING AFRICAN COUNTRIES

In this section, we analyse the dynamics of IFRS adoption in French-speaking African countries, in particular through the main reform projects underway in these countries.

On the African continent, the accounting systems of the various countries have always reflected their political and economic history. In the singular case of French-speaking countries, France has influenced the adoption of accounting standards through its dominant position in economic and political relations (Degos et al., 2019; Zori, S. G., & Seny Kan, K., 2017; Feudjo, 2010). During the period of French colonization, various countries in West Africa, Equatorial Africa, the Maghreb and Madagascar successively used the French charts of accounts of 1947 and 1957. After gaining independence in the 1960s, these countries continued to apply the 1957 chart of accounts. Subsequently, even though some of these countries chose to draw up their own national chart of accounts, it was basically based on the French chart of accounts. This was the case for Tunisia in 1967, Algeria in 1975, the OCAM countries in 1970, Ivoiry Coast in 1972, Senegal in 1975 and Morocco in 1990. These different local accounting systems have provided the profession with an accounting framework, a terminology and a chart of accounts leading to the presentation of annual financial statements known as summary documents (balance sheet and general operating account), which apply to all companies, whatever their size or sector of activity, with the exception of financial companies.

However, since the beginning of the twenty-first century, the limitations of the local accounting system in the various countries of French-speaking Africa have begun to be felt, particularly for aspects related to consolidated accounts and group operations (Elhamma, 2024; Boolaky et al., 2020). The opening up of capital to foreign investors, the privatization process and free trade agreements with industrialized countries are all factors that explain the interest of local companies in adopting IAS-IFRS (Dibi & Amifi, 2024; Degos et al., 2019; Zori, S. G., & Seny Kan, K., 2017). The latter, in addition to providing comparability, neutrality and transparency to the financial statements, can help reduce the cost and effort of publishing them. French-speaking African countries will thus see the emergence of a process of accounting harmonization with IFRS.

In 2001, OHADA member countries adopted the new 'SYSCOHADA' accounting system for personal accounts, and in 2002 for consolidated and combined accounts. The latter was developed in continuity with the OCAM chart of accounts and the 1982 chart of accounts in France, which are its main sources of inspiration and experience (Degos et al., 2019; Feudjo, 2010). Since 1 January 2019, these countries have been applying IFRS for their consolidated accounts (Moussa, 2020) et allowing their use for unlisted companies. However, although it adopts new accounting standards for the valuation and presentation of financial statements derived from IAS-IFRS, this new 'SYSCOHADA' accounting system remains faithful to the principles of the continental school (Wamba et al., 2023; Degos et al., 2019). In Madagascar, the standard-setter adopted a new reference framework in 2005, entitled 'General Chart of Accounts consistent with IFRS'. However, this new framework includes a second part dealing with the organisation of accounting, nomenclature and the operation of accounts (Khouatra, 2005). In Morocco, in 2007 the Central Bank required all banks and similar financial institutions to use IAS-IFRS for financial years beginning on or after January 2008. It has also authorized companies listed on the Casablanca Stock Exchange, with the exception of banks and similar financial institutions, to use IAS-IFRS to publish their consolidated financial statements. Nevertheless, CGNC continues to be used for individual financial statements. In Algeria, the Financial Accounting System (FAS), which came into force in 2010, was designed through a partial adoption of IFRS, insofar as transactions resulting from the entity's activities are recorded in accounts whose nomenclature, content and operating rules are defined by regulation (Khouatra & Merhoum, 2017).

Figure 3. Summary of the various reforms introduced in the local accounting system of different countries in French-speaking Africa

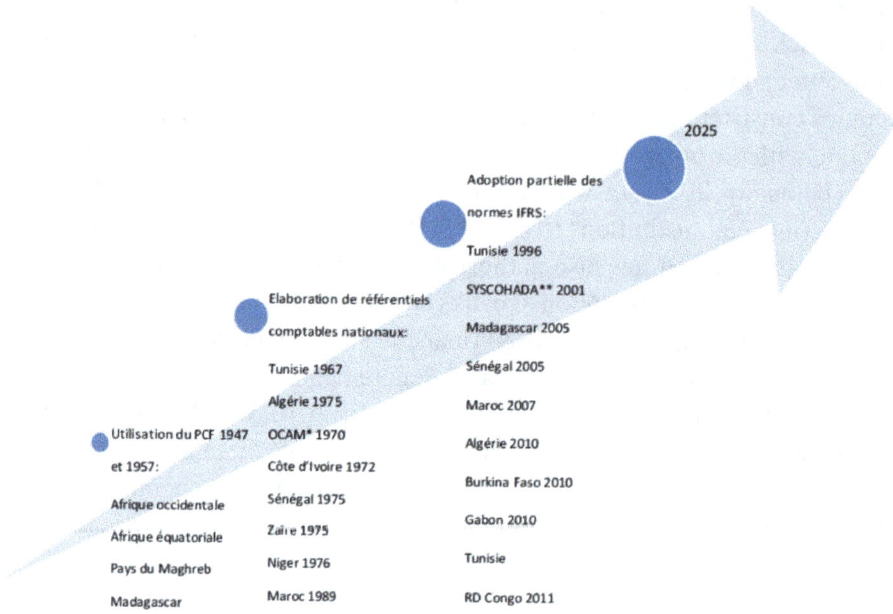

*Organisation Commune Africaine, Malgache et Mauricienne (OCAM) created in 1966 brought together the following countries: Benin, Burundi, Cameroon, Central African Republic, Chad, Congo, Ivory Coast, Dahomey (now Togo), Gabon, Upper Volta (now Burkina Faso), Niger, Rwanda, Senegal and Zaire (now the Democratic Republic of Congo). The OCAM chart of accounts was introduced in 1970.

** The SYSCOHADA accounting system common to 17 countries in West Africa, Central Africa and the Indian Ocean has been in force since January 2001.

Based on the Literature

As can be seen from Graph N°3, if the full adoption of the IAS-IFRS standard for all "full IFRS" companies seems to have been ruled out in order to avoid obstacles encountered by countries that have implemented it, the "degree" of convergence remains a major obstacle to be managed with caution (El Quortobi, 2013). For example, the adoption of IAS-IFRS for publicly traded companies and public-interest corporations has been considered in most reforms carried out in different countries in French-speaking Africa. However, for non-listed companies, the general trend has been to use them rather than adopt them. Thus, the evolution of local accounting standards in different countries of French-speaking Africa was made to meet the limits of the current framework, while remaining quite simple and within the scope of the economic fabric of these countries, which consists mainly of SMEs. Therefore, the IAS-IFRS standard is more considered as an objective to be achieved, insofar as the "full IFRS" option does not seem realistic or feasible for the social accounts (Zori, S. G., & Seny Kan, K., 2017).

Two major findings emerge from the review of the main accounting reform projects in the different countries of French-speaking Africa. On the one hand, the state is the main promoter of economic development and the main actor in the institutional framework for accounting standards. On the other hand, the evolution of the local accounting system in these different countries has been guided by the limits of the current reference framework, while remaining fairly simple and within the scope of the economic fabric of these countries, which consists mainly of SMEs.

4. CHALLENGES AND OPPORTUNITIES OF ACCOUNTING HARMONIZATION IN FRENCH-SPEAKING AFRICA

In this section, we discuss the challenges of the transition to IAS-IFRS for companies and governments in French-speaking African countries.

It goes without saying that, in the different countries of French-speaking Africa, the existing accounting system has already reached its limits and its harmonization has become a pressing need (El Quortobi, 2013). In practice, local companies use IAS-IFRSs when seeking solutions to problems that are not addressed by the local system or are addressed incompletely. However, the nature of economic transactions has changed and continues to change, raising new accounting questions that the normalizer is called upon to adequately address. Admittedly, it partly satisfies this demand, but this is often done with deadlines that do not correspond to the pace of working life, and sometimes by questioning the very basis of the system.

The countries of francophone Africa are then faced with a double challenge. First, there is a need to improve the quality of the accounting and financial information produced and provide clear answers to new issues raised by practice. For this, it is necessary for these countries to have a recognized analysis grid, of the type "conceptual framework" of IAS-IFRSs, in order to be able to answer the various questions posed by accounting practice. The IFRS seem to be of interest for those less developed countries that are looking for a quality standard (Brebisson et alphonse, 2018). Secondly, it is necessary for these countries to move towards a reference framework that is easy to use and would not require significant reprocessing in case of reporting or consolidation according to IFRS standards.

Accounting harmonization in the countries of francophone Africa could then allow to develop economic growth (ElHamma, 2023). As can be seen in Figure 4, this opportunity stems from the legal and regulatory simplification that would facilitate international economic integration and transactions.

Figure 4. Economic opportunity of accounting harmonization in the countries of French-speaking Africa

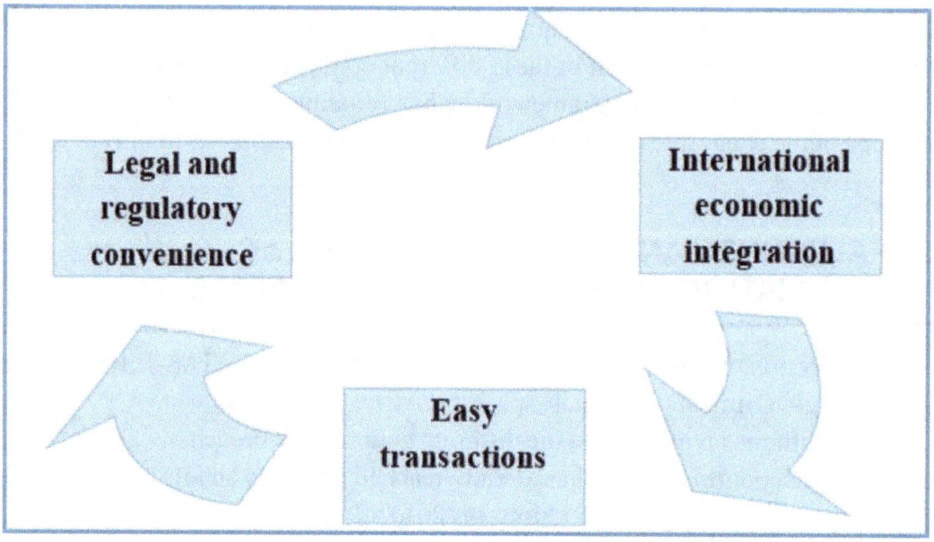

Based on the literature

Generally speaking, the transition to IAS-IFRSs offers several opportunities for entities and countries. Among the benefits for businesses, the initial objective of the standard is to promote international comparability of accounts (Waweru et al., 2023; Jayasinghe et al., 2021; Degos et al., 2019; Hopper et al., 2017; Watts & Zimmerman, 1978). This point is indeed fundamental in the eyes of investors, because the IAS-IFRS standards will eventually lead to standardized valuation and presentation rules for the financial statements of different entities. Secondly, IAS-IFRSs allow for the standardization of the calculation of sometimes complex elements such as turnover or treatment of goodwill (Casta, 2009). In addition, the implementation of these standards allows for a break with the traditional accounting system, which consists of recording transactions at historical cost, and to migrate to the preeminence of substance over form, in a way that best reflects the economic reality of the social accounts. Finally, in addition to the content and technical aspect of the standards, companies will have to adapt, evaluate their assets and find solutions to effectively manage the implementation of these new standards, which will enable them to go beyond the strict regulatory framework and optimize their operation (Degos et al., 2019). Companies will indeed be led to demonstrate a better understanding of risks through this work of leveling, assessment and, more generally, reflection. This would improve the perception of the company by investors, especially foreign investors (FDI).

For countries, the transition to IAS-IFRSs is a much more important issue than simply changing the standard. These new standards reject assessments based on convention or appearance and aim to better reflect economic reality. Their adoption should help to enhance the efficiency of the local domestic market, reduce the cost of raising capital for companies, restore investor confidence and ultimately improve the competitiveness and growth of the national economy (ElHamma, 2023; Soulaymano, 2023; Hniche, 2009). For public organizations, the transition to IAS-IFRSs allows them to comply with an accounting framework that is recognized as being rational by the companies with which they may be required to collaborate (Khouatra, 2014). Indeed, the new accounting practices resulting from IAS-IFRS can help to give legitimacy to the organizations that develop them, through the construction of an appearance of rationality and efficiency (Degos et al., 2019; Plane, 2013; Carruthers, 1995; DiMaggio & Powell, 1983).

It therefore appears that the gradual anchoring of the accounting system of the countries of francophone Africa will be a guarantee of credibility in front of the major political and economic groupings present as well as on the world financial places, but also a factor of economic attractiveness likely to attract players of higher power, Encourage foreign direct investment and promote effective solutions to financing problems that hinder business growth and development in Africa.

Numerous research studies have shown that the objectives of the relevance of accounting information and its comparability have been validated as motivations for international accounting harmonization, especially in France (Ouarab & Kaci, 2024; Lenormand & Touchais, 2009), the United Kingdom (Iatridis, 2010), the European Union (Chai et al., 2010) and Nigeria (Oluwagbemiga, 2021; Osasere & Ilaboya, 2018). Other studies have also shown a positive relationship between IFRS adoption and FDI inflows, particularly in the African (Musah et al., 2020) and Asian (Yousefinejad et al., 2018) contextes. Nevertheless, research based on sociological Neo-institutionalist theory (DiMaggio & Powell, 1983; Meyer & Rowan, 1977) has noted that for developing countries, the transition to IAS-IFRS was made rather by mimicry (Boubakary & Zerbib, 2019), under joint pressure from the World Bank (WB) and the International Monetary Fund (IMF) (Judge et al., 2010) or to facilitate access to foreign aid (Boolaky et al., 2020).

In addition, IAS-IFRSs are still the subject of conceptual and technical debate among academics and practitioners of accounting and auditing, particularly with regard to the so-called "fair value" method (Khouatra, 2014). Indeed, conceptually, the choice to favour current or potential shareholders as well as lenders amounts to adopting a reductive and short-term vision of value creation. In addition, human capital is reduced to a source of burdens (wages) and debts (pensions), instead of being considered as an intangible investment and a value-creating asset (Colasse, 2011). On the technical side, successive financial crises in the global economy have already demonstrated the pro cyclical effects of fair value valuation (Colasse, 2011).

This analysis of the issues involved in the transition to IAS/IFRS for entities and states in French-speaking Africa allows us to make two major findings. First, from a theoretical point of view, the adoption of IFRSs would have economic and social benefits for entities and states in francophone Africa. Second, the empirical validity of these benefits depends on the cultural characteristics and development situation of individual countries adopting IFRSs.

5. FUTURE DIRECTIONS AND POLICY RECOMMENDATIONS

In this section, we highlight, from the perspective of a cost-benefit balance, the prospect of accounting harmonization in French-speaking African countries as well as our policy recommendations in this area.

It is clear that the competent authorities in the various countries of French-speaking Africa are aware that a project for convergence of the local accounting system to IAS-IFRS standards does not depend solely on technique (Zori, S. G., & Seny Kan, K., 2017; Colasse, 2011), but also includes political, economic, legal and cultural aspects. Indeed, the gap between the two systems, local and international, is not limited to accounting or valuation rules, but rather resembles a conceptual and doctrinal, even philosophical discrepancy.

This general context of the dissemination of IAS-IFRS, with all its historical, political, economic, legal and cultural dimensions, offers us a reading grid that allows us to better understand the prospects of accounting harmonization in these countries, particularly in terms of benefits and costs (Degos et al., 2019; Zori, S. G., & Seny Kan, K., 2017).

When it comes to accounting standards, the Anglo-Saxon countries favour a «technocratic» approach, while the countries of French-speaking Africa opt for a partnership tradition. In the latter case, the state assumes a leading role in the process of accounting standardization and regulation. Indeed, in these different countries, the power of accounting regulation is held by the State, although the national accounting standards body is extended to the various stakeholders of the accounting profession, the Financial Market Council and the College of Accountants. In addition, accounting harmonization in the countries of French-speaking Africa is carried out by hybridization, that is to say in an approach aimed at preserving a distinct accounting identity and specificity. Notable features of this approach include the existence of a General Accounting Plan and a framework for accounting standardization and regulation, conferring on the state a leading role in the management of public finances (Khouatra, 2018). As a political normalizer, it would favour accounting regulations limiting the level of information published, while the professional normalizer (accounting profession or financial market) would push for richer publications (Bertomeu & Cheynel, 2013). In addition, in accounting systems where the tax and distributable income are closely linked to the accounting result, as is the case in francophone Africa, the regulator will resist the generalization of IFRS standards (Nobes, 2010). Moreover, at the institutional level, language and legal system can promote or hinder the adoption of IFRS. Indeed, it was observed that English-speaking countries have a more favourable approach to adopting the international standard than French-speaking countries (Degos et al., 2019; Zori, S. G., & Seny Kan, K., 2017; Nobes, 2006; Alexander, 2010).

In terms of the cost of accounting information, it is established that compliance with international standards entails additional costs. This is due to the requirement for additional disclosures and the waiver of the high level of discretion in local accounting practices (Giuletti et al., 2000; Brigham & Waterson, 2003; Dumontier & Raffournier, 2005). Consequently, the evolution of the accounting system in the countries of francophone Africa is guided by a philosophy that adopts only those provisions not likely to increase the cost of accounting information, based on the overall philosophy of the IAS-IFRS. As an illustration, the various accounting provisions adopted met three criteria respecting the cost/benefit balance recommended by the IFRS standard itself: to allow for improved quality of accounting information, be feasible and not generate excessive costs for the business.

With regard to the recipients of accounting information, the objective of accounting harmonization in the countries of French-speaking Africa is to establish an accounting system that is both calculable and readable for foreign investors, while retaining the power of standardization at national level (Degos et al., 2019). In order to achieve this goal, the harmonization process is structured around the following four guidelines: first of all, placing the investor at the centre of the target group of accounting information recipients, in accordance with the general philosophy of the IAS-IFRS. Secondly, implement all the provisions of the IAS-IFRS framework considered relevant for improving the quality of financial information produced in the current economic context of these countries. Third, ensure that the provisions adopted are feasible and do not represent a significant cost to local businesses. Fourth, it is imperative that the new provisions are translated into each country's national reference document in a clear and understandable way.

Moreover, the harmonization of the accounting system in French-speaking African countries with IAS-IFRS has economic, social and political consequences (Plihon, 2007). This process of accounting harmonization could indeed have three significant consequences for these countries. First, the production of accounting information, which would now be primarily carried out by the IASB, a private institution representing the interests of shareholders and investors, would lead to an audit of accounting by this same institution, at the expense of political and social control in different countries (Burlaud & Colasse, 2010). Second, national accounts and GDP could be affected by the classification of costs by function as defined by these standards. As a result, it may become impossible to calculate and share the added value between different stakeholders of the company (Michaïlesco & Rougès, 2012). In addition, the application of the fair value principle could have a destabilizing effect due to its volatility. This volatility could lead to a significant deterioration in the quality of information relating to the valuation of companies and their results (Christensen et al., 2008).

Table 2. Cost-benefit balance of the adoption of IFRSs by countries in French-speaking Africa

	Benefits of adopting IFRS		**Costs associated with adopting IFRS**	
In economic terms	Reducing the cost of preparing financial statements for international companies	Daske, 2006	Cost of implementing the standards	Jermakowy et al., 2012 ; Giuletti et al.,2000 ; Brigham and Waterson, 2003 ; Dumontier and Raffournier, 2005
	Attracting foreign direct investment into the local economy	Musah et al., 2020 ; Gordon et al., 2012	Cost of revising the legislation	George et al, 2013
	Improving the competitiveness of companies	Soulaymano, 2023 ; Franco, Kothari and Verdi, 2011 ; Hniche, 2009	Deterioration in the quality of information following the application of 'fair value'.	Christensen et al., 2008
	Promoting comparability of financial statements	Waweru et al., 2023 ; Jayasinghe et al., 2021 ; Degos et al., 2019 ; Hopper et al., 2017 ; Watts and Zimmerman, 1978	Cost of applying IFRS and monitoring compliance	

continued on following page

Table 2. Continued

	Benefits of adopting IFRS		Costs associated with adopting IFRS	
In political terms	Give public organizations greater legitimization	Khouatra, 2014 ; Plane, 2013 ; Carruthers,1995 ; DiMaggio and Powell, 1983	Loss of sovereignty in setting national accounting standards	Burlaud and Colasse, 2010
	Access to investor-friendly status through the application of international best practice	Waweru et al., 2023 ; Jayasinghe et al., 2021, Degos et al., 2019	Loss of external legitimacy	
	Strengthening relations with international organizations (WB, IMF)	Judge et al., 2010		
	More access to foreign aid	Boolaky et al., 2020		

Based on the literature

As shown in Table N°2, an analysis of the costs and benefits of adopting IFRSs by French-speaking African countries reveals a general trend towards adopting these standards. However, the choice of a specific accounting policy by a country is determined by its ability to establish a normative balance that responds to its particular situation. This multi factorial approach allows us to understand the existence of several options. These include the application of a single reference or several references, either mandatory or optional. The choice of one or the other of these options is strongly influenced by the cultural characteristics and development situation of different countries (Brebisson et alphonse, 2018).

CONCLUSION

This research work aimed to situate the process of harmonization of the accounting system in the countries of francophone Africa, in the general context of the dissemination of IAS-IFRS, in order to understand its dynamics and define its perspective. To meet this objective, we have adopted a historical reflexive approach nourished by the study of various documentary sources.

It follows from this work that the adoption of IAS-IFRS by entities and states in francophone Africa can significantly improve their visibility on international markets. However, the transition to these standards is a complex project that goes beyond the technical aspect and extends to the legal, economic, political and cultural aspects. Indeed, the IAS-IFRS not only lead to changes and accounting implications, but also to the harmonization of local accounting standards with international standards. This involves the mobilization of technical, human and financial resources, both from the standardization body and from the company itself. In addition, modern developments related to accounting harmonization such as the role of digital accounting systems, the introduction of sustainable development reporting (ESG) and IFRS issues for SMEs should also be taken into account.

The analysis of the dynamics and prospects of accounting harmonization in the countries of francophone Africa leads us to the following findings:

- International accounting standards have been widely used worldwide, but their adoption has varied across regions and national contexts. In Africa, the full adoption of IAS-IFRSs is mainly limited to countries with Anglo-Saxon culture.
- In the countries of French-speaking Africa, the state plays a leading role as the main vector of economic development. As a result, it is the main actor in the institutional framework governing accounting standards. The evolution of the local accounting system in these countries has been guided by the limitations inherent to the current framework, while remaining relatively simple and the scope of the economic fabric of these countries, mainly composed of SMEs.
- In the event of adoption of IAS-IFRSs, it is theoretical that economic and social benefits are observed at the level of the entities and states of these countries. However, the empirical validity of these benefits is conditioned by the cultural characteristics and the development situation of different countries adopting IFRS.
- In the countries of francophone Africa, harmonization policies reflect a normative balance that takes into account the cultural specificity and development situation of each country or group of countries. This perspective reflects a movement that gives a major role to the state, while preserving a certain identity and national accounting specificity.

Although the IAS-IFRS standards currently enjoy a global scope, the harmonization of the accounting system within the countries of French-speaking Africa cannot be done in a deterministic way. Rather, it must be aligned with the cultural and economic specificity of these nations, while taking into account the various options available. It is also essential to identify the real needs of these countries and to assess beforehand to what extent the potential of the major international financial centers can be a definite advantage for their businesses and economic development. Furthermore, we recommend that the reflection on the harmonization of accounting practices in the countries of francophone Africa should be redirected towards optimizing accounting information for those entities that have a clear need for it, to enable them to produce coherent information.

Our work has two main limitations: the lack of empirical data and the lack of analysis of the role of different stakeholders. The use of these two elements is likely to offer our study on accounting harmonization in French-speaking Africa a more complete and practical contribution. Despite these limitations, we hope that our work has contributed to the enrichment of research in understanding the evolution of the accounting system in this large part of the African continent made up of francophone countries.

In our future research, we are therefore planning to carry out comparative case studies of some key countries in the francophone area of Africa (Algeria, Madagascar, Morocco, Senegal) to highlight differences in the implementation strategy, institutional support and local stakeholder engagement.

REFERENCES

Bampoky, B. (2019). Les difficultés de normalisation comptable dans l'espace OHADA. *ACCRA*, (2), 25–59. DOI: 10.3917/accra.005.0025

Boolaky, P. K., Tawiah, V., & Soobaroyen, T. (2020). Why do African countries adopt IFRS? An institutional perspective. *The International Journal of Accounting*, *55*(1), 2050005. DOI: 10.1142/S1094406020500055

Boubakary, B., & Zerbib, R. (2019). Influence des modes managériales sur la culture d'entreprise: Une approche exploratoire dans le contexte camerounais. *La Revue des Sciences de Gestion*, (297–298), 33–44. DOI: 10.3917/rsg.297.0033

Burlaud, A., & Colasse, B. (2010). Normalisation comptable internationale: Le retour du politique? *Comptabilité Contrôle Audit*, *16*(3), 153–176. DOI: 10.3917/cca.163.0153

Casta, J. F. (2009). Théorie positive de la comptabilité. In Colasse, B. (Ed.), *Encyclopédie de comptabilité, contrôle de gestion et audit* (pp. 1393–1402). Economica.

Chai, H., Tang, Q., Jiang, Y., & Lin, Z. (2010). The role of International Financial Reporting Standards in accounting quality: Evidence from the European Union. *Journal of International Financial Management & Accounting*, *21*(3), 220–278. DOI: 10.1111/j.1467-646X.2010.01041.x

Christensen, H. B., Lee, E., & Walker, M. (2008). Incentives or standards: What determines accounting quality changes around IFRS adoption? *Working paper*. [PDF file]

Colasse, B. (2004). Harmonisation comptable internationale: De la résistible ascension de l'IASC/IASB. *Gérer et Comprendre*, (75), 30–41.

Colasse, B. (2011). La crise de la normalisation comptable internationale, une crise intellectuelle. *Comptabilité Contrôle Audit*, *17*(1), 157–174. DOI: 10.3917/cca.171.0155

de Brébisson, H., et alphonse, P. (2018). Diversité des politiques d'adoption des IFRS: L'harmonisation financière est-elle possible? *Comptabilité Contrôle Audit*, *24*(2), 7–36. DOI: 10.3917/cca.242.0007

Degos, J.-G., Levant, Y., & Touron, P. (2019). The history of accounting standards in French-speaking African countries since independence: The uneasy path toward IFRS. *Accounting, Auditing & Accountability Journal*, *32*(1), 75–100. DOI: 10.1108/AAAJ-03-2016-2459

Dibi, A., & Amifi, H. (2024). Evolution du système comptable marocain à la lumière de la diffusion des normes comptables internationales. In *Systèmes comptables nationaux et normes IFRS: adoption ou adaptation?* ISBN 978-9969-9723-0-6

DiMaggio, P., & Powell, W. (1983). The iron cage revisited: Institutional isomorphism and collective rationality in organizational field. *American Sociological Review*, *48*(2), 147–160. DOI: 10.2307/2095101

El Quortobi, A. (2013). *Quel modèle de convergence pour le Maroc? 2ème assises de la profession comptable, mai 2013*. Skhirat.

Elhamma, A. (2023). Impact of mandatory IFRS adoption on economic growth: The moderating role of COVID-19 crisis in developing countries. *Journal of Accounting and Management Information Systems*, *22*(3), 554–568. DOI: 10.24818/jamis.2023.03007

Elhamma, A. (2024). Determinants of national IFRS adoption: Evidence from the Middle East and North Africa region. *International Journal of Accounting. Auditing and Performance Evaluation*, *20*(1/2), 69–90. DOI: 10.1504/IJAAPE.2024.135535

Elhamma, A. (2025). Perceived benefits of IFRS adoption in Morocco and French-speaking Sub-Saharan African countries. In F. Albuquerque & P. G. Dos Santos (Eds.), *Contemporary innovations in reporting and analysis* (pp. 183–210). IGI Global. https://doi.org/DOI: 10.4018/979-8-3693-5923-5.ch007

Feudjo, J. R. (2010). Harmonisation des normes africaines (OHADA) et internationales (IAS-IFRS): Une urgence ou une exigence? *La Revue des Sciences de Gestion*, (5), 149–158. DOI: 10.3917/rsg.245.0149

Hniche, O. (2009). Normes IAS-IFRS et analyse financière. *Revue Marocaine de Recherche en Management et Marketing*, (1), janvier.

Hoarau, C. (1995). L'harmonisation comptable internationale: Vers la reconnaissance mutuelle normative? *Comptabilité Contrôle Audit*, *1*(2), 75–88. DOI: 10.3917/cca.012.0075

Hopper, T., Lassou, P., & Soobaroyen, T. (2017). Globalisation, accounting and developing countries. *Critical Perspectives on Accounting*, *43*, 125–148. DOI: 10.1016/j.cpa.2016.06.003

Iatridis, G. (2010). International Financial Reporting Standards and the quality of financial statement information. *International Review of Financial Analysis*, *19*(3), 193–204. DOI: 10.1016/j.irfa.2010.02.004

Judge, W., Li, S., & Pinsker, R. (2010). National adoption of international accounting standards: An institutional perspective. *Corporate Governance*, *18*(3), 161–174. DOI: 10.1111/j.1467-8683.2010.00798.x

Khouatra, D. (2005). Le système comptable malgache entre modèle anglo-saxon et modèle continental. *Congrès de l'AFC*, Lille, 11–13 mai.

Khouatra, D. (2014). Évolution et diversité des systèmes comptables francophones. *Congrès de l'AFC*, Lille, mai.

Khouatra, D., & Merhoum, M. E. H. (2017). Élaboration et mise en œuvre d'un système comptable hybride par intégration de normes comptables internationales IAS-IFRS: Cas du système comptable financier algérien. *AFC Afrique – 2ème JEACC.*

Lenormand, G., & Touchais, L. (2009). Les IFRS améliorent-elles la qualité de l'information financière? Approche par la value relevance. *Comptabilité Contrôle Audit*, *15*(2), 145–164. DOI: 10.3917/cca.152.0145

Moussa, M. A. (2020). Les déterminants de la résistance à la production et à la publication des informations comptables et financières dans les entreprises au Tchad. *Revue de Consolidation Comptable et de Management de la Performance*, (5).

Oluwagbemiga, O. E. (2021). The influence of IFRS adoption on the quality of financial reporting in Nigerian listed companies. In *Advances in Pacific Basin Business, Economics and Finance*. Emerald Publishing. DOI: 10.1108/S2514-465020210000009005

Osinubi, I. S. (2020). The three pillars of institutional theory and IFRS implementation in Nigeria. *Journal of Accounting in Emerging Economies*, *10*(4), 575–599. DOI: 10.1108/JAEE-07-2019-0139

Ouarab, A., & Kaci, S. (2024). La comptabilité en normes IFRS: les chiffres et la valeur boursière de l'entreprise. In *Les systèmes comptables nationaux et les normes IFRS: adoption ou adaptation?* ISBN 978-9969-9723-0-6.

Plihon, D. (2007). Les nouvelles normes comptables internationales: Une réforme aux implications considérables. *Economics and Politics*, *36*(36), 74–80. DOI: 10.3917/leco.036.0074

Raffournier, B. (2007). Les oppositions françaises à l'adoption des IFRS: Examen critique et tentative d'explication. *Comptabilité Contrôle Audit*, *13*(3), 21–41. DOI: 10.3917/cca.133.0021

Ramanna, K., & Sletten, E. (2014). Network effects in countries' adoption of IFRS. *The Accounting Review*, *89*(4), 1517–1543. DOI: 10.2308/accr-50717

Wamba, R. T., Kouotou, A. C. M., Wanda, A. T., & Wanda, R. (2023). Le basculement du SYSCOHADA vers les normes IAS-IFRS, enjeux et perspectives dans les entités de l'Afrique subsaharienne: Un mariage ou un divorce? *Recherches en Sciences de Gestion*, *154*(1), 127–150. DOI: 10.3917/resg.154.0127

Watts, R. L., & Zimmerman, J. L. (1978). Towards a positive theory of the determination of accounting standards. *The Accounting Review*, *53*(1), 112–134.

Waweru, N. M., Peng, S., & Hopper, T. (2023). Two decades of African accounting research 2000–2019: Synthesis, reflection, gaps, and future directions. *Journal of International Accounting Research*, *22*(1), 99–136. DOI: 10.2308/JIAR-2021-078

Zori, S. G., & Kan, K. S. (2017). A qualitative comparative approach to the adoption of International Financial Reporting Standards (IFRS) in Africa. In Konan Anderson, A. (Ed.), *A qualitative comparative approach to the adoption of International Financial Reporting Standards (IFRS) in Africa*. DOI: 10.2139/ssrn.2992501

KEY TERMS AND DEFINITIONS:

Accounting harmonization: institutional process, aiming at convergence of national accounting standards and practices

IFRS: International Financial Reporting Standards, these standards established by the IFRS foundation aim to improve the intelligibility, relevance, reliability, comparability and transparency of financial information.

French-speaking Africa: an area composed of African countries which, for colonial reasons, speak French in whole or in part.

«Full IFRS»: a policy of outright adoption of IFRS

Adaptation: policy to incorporate IFRS into local standards

Convergence: policy of changing local standards to move closer to IFRS

1 The Organization for the Harmonization of Business Law in Africa (OHADA), created in 1993, brings together the West African Economic and Monetary Union (UEMOA), made up of 8 countries, the Economic Community of West African States (ECOWAS), which includes French-speaking countries (the UEMOA countries and Guinea Conakry), English-speaking countries (Nigeria, Ghana and Sierra Leone) and Portuguese-speaking countries (Guinea Bissau and Cape Verde), English-speaking countries (Nigeria, Ghana and Sierra Leone) and Portuguese-speaking countries (Guinea Bissau and Cape Verde), and the Economic and Monetary Community of Central Africa (CEMAC), which comprises 6 Central African countries.

[2] www.iasb.org

Chapter 12
Understanding the Impact of IFRS for SMEs in Morocco:
A Qualitative Study Based on Semi-Structured Interviews

Btissam Benga
https://orcid.org/0009-0007-9966-7292
ENCG, Ibn Tofail University, Kenitra, Morocco

ABSTRACT

This article examines the impact of IFRS adoption for SMEs in Morocco, in order to understand how these standards influence SMEs' accounting practices and financial reporting. The study is based on a qualitative approach, using semi-structured interviews with accounting professionals to gather in-depth information. The results highlight various effects: the adoption of IFRS for SMEs contributes to the modernization of accounting systems and improves the quality and comparability of financial information. However, a number of challenges were also identified, including high compliance costs, complex implementation and limited relevance to the specific needs of Moroccan SMEs. The study highlights the need for adaptations to better fit local business realities, while preserving the benefits of international harmonization.

DOI: 10.4018/979-8-3373-1902-5.ch012

1. INTRODUCTION

The harmonization of accounting practices on an international scale has been a major challenge in the globalization of economies for several decades. It was with this in mind that the International Financial Reporting Standards (IFRS) were conceived, to promote the transparency, comparability and quality of financial information between different countries (Hail et al., 2010; Barth et al., 2009). Although these standards were initially designed for large companies listed on financial markets, their application or adaptation to small and medium-sized enterprises (SMEs) is now raising several questions (Nobes, 2017).

In several jurisdictions, legislators and standard-setting bodies have encouraged (Chai et al., 2010), or even imposed, the use of IFRS or their simplified versions on SMEs (Kaya et al., 2015). However, due to their limited resources, their often more flexible organizational structure, and their limited exposure to international financial markets, SMEs do not necessarily have the technical, human or financial resources to implement these complex standards (Frost, 2017). This raises the central question of the relevance and appropriateness of IFRS for this specific entrepreneurial fabric, which in many countries represents the overwhelming majority of economic entities (Elhamma, 2025b).

The issue we wish to explore in this study is: what are the concrete effects of IFRS adoption on SMEs, in terms of both internal management and the production of financial information? In other words, to what extent do IFRS contribute to improving the quality of accounting information produced by SMEs, and what costs—technical, organizational and financial—do these companies face? This question is part of a wider debate on the universality of accounting standards, and the need to adapt regulatory frameworks to the specific characteristics of different types of company (Albu et al., 2013).

In this context, our research has several objectives. Firstly, we aim to understand how SMEs perceive the adoption of IFRS: is it seen as a regulatory constraint, a tool for improving financial management, or a lever for legitimizing their position vis-à-vis external partners? We will then identify the main challenges encountered in the implementation process: training of teams, cost of compliance, complexity of reporting obligations, etc.

To meet these objectives, we have chosen a qualitative approach, based on semi-structured interviews with SME managers and financial managers. The aim of this methodology is to gather rich and nuanced testimonies, providing access to the reality experienced by players in the field. The preliminary results of our survey reveal a wide range of experiences: while some SMEs acknowledge an improvement in the readability of their financial statements and a better structuring of their accounting information system, others express a feeling of inadequacy between the requirements of IFRS and their operational reality. A number of managers also point to the lack of institutional support and the administrative overload involved in applying these standards. In general, it appears that the effects of IFRS on SMEs are ambivalent, oscillating between benefits in terms of governance and constraints in terms of resources.

The originality of our study lies in the choice to give a voice directly to the actors concerned, by adopting an in-depth qualitative perspective. Whereas the majority of existing research adopts a quantitative or normative approach focused on large companies, our contribution aims to enrich the literature with an analysis rooted in the actual practices of SMEs. This approach enables us to gain a better understanding of the specific issues they face, and to open the way to a critical reflection on how to adapt normative frameworks to the needs of more modest economic structures.

The article is organized as follows. First, we review the literature on the evolution of IFRS and their application to SMEs, highlighting the tensions between standardization and contextualization. We will then present our methodology and survey. The third part will be devoted to an analysis of the empirical results obtained from the interviews. Finally, we will discuss the implications of our findings for practitioners, public policymakers and standardization bodies alike, before concluding with suggestions for future research.

2. LITERATURE REVIEW

In this section, we propose a literature review structured into four sub-sections to provide a better understanding of the issues involved in adopting IFRS, particularly in the context of SMEs.

2.1. IFRS: An Evolving Framework for Global Financial Communication

Over the past two decades, International Financial Reporting Standards (IFRS) have become the globally recognized framework for financial communication in the financial markets. By promoting harmonization, IFRS increases comparability, reliability, and transparency across corporate disclosures (Elhamma, 202a; Ebaid, 2023; Hail et al., 2010).

In emerging markets, the transition to IFRS has shown both promise and complexity. Ebaid (2023) demonstrates that while IFRS enhances the comparability of financial reports, it can reduce readability, especially for non-specialist stakeholders. The Moroccan context illustrates another dimension: (Oubahou et al., 2024) reveal that the adoption of IFRS by companies listed on the Casablanca Stock Exchange has led to more relevant and faster reporting but has also necessitated a major restructuring of internal accounting systems and staff training.

On the African continent, research into IFRS has intensified in recent years. A recent bibliometric examination of Effah (2024) highlights a significant increase in publications on the adoption and compliance with International Financial Reporting Standards (IFRS) in Africa since 2018. This development reflects an expanded intrigued in issues such as administrative compliance, authorization and organization differing qualities.

Past ponders, counting those by Boolaky et al., (2020), as well as Waweru et al., (2023), highlight the significance of relevant regulation components in effective IFRS usage. These ponders demonstrate that variables such as weight from universal bodies, the nearness of worldwide review firms and the quality proficient bookkeeping organizations have a solid impact on the selection of measures.

In spite of the far reaching selection of IFRS, there are major boundaries to their usage in creating nations. These incorporate an inadequately administrative foundation and a ineffectively created monetary culture, which ruin the reliable and successful application of guidelines. These confinements emphasize the require for nearby adjustment methodologies and focused on capacity building activities to guarantee viable usage of IFRSs (Van Wyk et al., 2009; Kamal et al., 2024).

2.2. IFRS for SMEs

2.2.1. Characteristics of IFRS for SMEs: Differences with Full IFRS

The IFRS for SMEs, issued in 2009 by the International Accounting Standards Board (IASB), was designed to supply a simlified accounting framework particularly tailored to entities without public accountability. Not at all like full IFRS, they exclude several complex accounting treatments such as detailed fair value measurements or segment reporting (Nobes, 2017; Barth et al., 2009).

This system proposes a secluded structure, went with by disentangled acknowledgment and valuation rules, in this way making the generation of monetary explanations more available to small entities (Hail et al., 2010; IFRS Foundation, 2022). It could be a compromise between straightforwardness and reasonableness, constraining the costs of compliance.

2.2.2. Global Adoption and Implementation Challenges

The adoption of IFRS by SMEs varies worldwide. In Europe and Latin America, many countries have adopted them in full or in part, while others have retained their national standards (Barker et al., 2016). Frost (2017) notes that institutional factors such as the strength of professional accounting bodies, legal systems and training provision influence adoption decisions.

In Turkey, Kilic et al., (2014) emphasize the importance of field-level engagement with stakeholders during implementation. Similarly, in Romania and Egypt (Boolaky et al., 2020), stakeholder resistance, training gaps, and lack of clarity from regulators have slowed the process (Albu et al., 2013; Kamal et al., 2024).

In India, Kumar et al., (2020) highlight that education and training gaps are among the biggest barriers. Nigeria faces similar issues, with SMEs often lacking the internal expertise to transition (Madawaki, 2014).

Several factors influence adoption success (Table 1):

Table 1. Factors Influencing IFRS Adoption by SMEs

Authors	Factor	Description
Albu et al., (2012), Kaya et al., (2015)	Institutional Capacity	Strong accounting education systems and effective regulatory enforcement support smoother adoption.
UNCTAD (2015), Kamal et al., (2024)	Cost Considerations	Initial implementation and ongoing compliance costs can be significant.
Hail et al. (2010)	Internationalization	SMEs involved in cross-border activities are more likely to adopt IFRS due to investor and creditor expectations.
Mhedhbi et al., (2022)	Cultural Dimensions	National cultural traits also influence openness to IFRS principles.

Source: Author construction

2.3 Positive Effects of Adopting IFRS for SMEs

One of the main benefits of adopting IFRS for SMEs is the improvement in the quality of financial information. Perera et al., (2015) argue that these standards increase the relevance and reliability of financial reporting in developing economies. The simplified framework reduces ambiguity and enhances the consistency of financial statements, especially when compared to diverse local GAAPs.

In emerging contexts such as Morocco or some French-speaking African countries (Zori et al..2017), Elhamma (2025) notes that the adoption of IFRS has improved the comparability of financial information, increased transparency, and better meet the expectations of international investors. This process is accompanied by a modernization movement, particularly visible through the introduction of digital accounting technologies such as ERPs, as illustrated by the work of Kaya et al., (2015) and Ghosh et al., (2020).

With the worldwide acknowledgment of the IFRS system, financial specialist certainty is tending to extend. Albu et al. (2013) and Nobes (2017) point out that this standard makes a difference to reduce data asymmetries, in this way encouraging benefactor relations and decision-making.

Elhamma (2023b) also contends that the adoption of IFRS within the MENA region advances more prominent monetary teach and more proficient asset allotment. According to the IFRS Foundation (2022), more than 80 nations allow or require their application for SMEs, reflecting its growing role in promoting financial transparency and integrity.

2.4 Challenges and Negative Impacts for SMEs

Despite its advantages, IFRS for SMEs presents several challenges (Delvaille et al.,2016), particularly in developing countries. The most cited constraint is the cost of implementation. SMEs often lack the financial and human resources to undertake system redesign, staff training and compliance assessments (UNCTAD, 2015; Kamal et al., 2024).

Elhamma (2023d) highlights that in Morocco and across the MENA region, the adoption of IFRS involves considerable administrative burdens, especially for small enterprises with limited resilience. These costs can significantly affect long-term performance, reducing the ability to innovate and expand. Although revised, IFRS for SMEs incorporate complex perspectives such as monetary disobedient or certain valuation strategies that require mastery seldom accessible in SMEs (IFRS Foundation, 2024; Ice, 2017; Zhang et al., 2021). Elhamma (2023e) cautions against applying these guidelines as well unbendingly, which could conflict with local structures or administrative systems.

The necessity to comply with national financial frameworks while adopting IFRS is another source of difficulty.This dual requirement often leads companies to maintain two parallel accounting frameworks, in this way expanding costs and regulatory complexity (Bonsón et al., 2023; Degos et al., 2019).

In addition, the lack of harmonization between IFRS and tax, legal or economic requirements creates inconsistencies that make financial reporting more difficult to establish. This phenomenon is particularly evident in African and Arab countries, where the weakness of institutions and the resistance of professionals are major obstacles to the full integration of the reference framework (Elhamma, 2024).

Finally, Elhamma (2025) emphasizes the importance of institutional resilience. His analysis shows that the lack of preparation of accounting professionals, combined with a lack of accompanying measures, has contributed to the increase in SME bankruptcies in some regions. It therefore calls for a gradual and contextualized adoption of IFRS, supported by active public policies and skills development programs.

3. METHODOLOGY

The following section outlines the main steps in the methodology adopted for this study. It is structured into two sub-sections: the first describes the data collection method, based on semi-structured interviews with professionals involved in the adoption of IFRS by Moroccan SMEs. The second details the qualitative data analysis process, based on thematic coding using NVivo software, to identify the perceptions, obstacles and effects associated with this adoption.

3.1 Data Collection Method

This study adopted a subjective approach with the aim of reaching a better understanding of the discriminations,e experiences, and representations of stakeholders involved in the choice of IFRS standards in Moroccan SMEs. This approach is especially pertinent when it comes to analyzing complex phenomena, as however small recorded locally, and getting to the subjective measurement of proficient hones (Ehamma, 2024b). The information collection strategy is based on semi-structured interviews with four complementary profiles: a chief financial officer, a finance manager, an administrative and financial manager and a SME manager who has worked on harmonization ventures within the private segment. These interviews were conducted between March and April 2025, either face-to-face or remotely, depending on the participants' accessibility. The average duration of the interviews was between 45 minutes and one hour.

Table 2. Profile of Interview Participants

Interviewee Code	Profession	Company activity	Interview Duration
Int.01	Chief Financial Officer	Handling – Services to airports and airlines	1 hour
Int.02	Finance Manager	Airport services	1 hour
Int.03	Administrative and financial manager	Industry	50 minutes
Int.04	SME manager	Agriculture	45 minutes

Source: Author construction

The choice of this strategy is based on a few contemplations. On the one hand, the semi-directive arrange offers the adaptability required to adjust addressing to the particular foundation and involvement of each interviewee, whereas guaranteeing generally consistency through the utilize of an organized meet direct. This direct, displayed in Reference section A, is organized around three fundamental topics:

the perception of IFRS within the SME setting, the deterrents and impediments encountered during usage, and the watched or expected impacts on bookkeeping and budgetary management. In expansion, this approach makes it conceivable to assemble wealthy, contextualized information established in Moroccan reality, by giving a voice to experts within the field.

3.2 Data Analysis Method

Once the interviews were complected, each recording was interpreted in its entirety, to ensure the rigor and accuracy to the respondents' statements. The subjective information was at that point analyzed using NVivo software, a recognized processing tool for organizing, coding and deciphering printed information within the social sciences. The study design was based on thematic coding, based on the lattice created upstream from the measurements of the meet direct. Three fundamental categories structure this expository system: the understanding of IFRS standards by the stakeholders interviewed, the difficulties encountered by SMEs in adopting IFRS standards, and the concrete or anticipated impacts on financial and accounting management.

This coding empowered us to recognize rambling repeats and inconsistencies, as well as critical subtleties based on the participants' profile and involvement. The utilize of NVivo encouraged the identification of emerging patterns and the visualization of the recurrence and transmission of topics, while ensuring the traceability of interpretations.

4. RESULTS AND DISCUSSION

This section presents the main findings of the qualitative analysis of the interviews, structured around three research questions. Based on thematic coding assisted by NVivo software, the study highlights a diversity of perceptions regarding the adoption of IFRS by Moroccan SMEs. The analysis reveals recurring themes linked to motivations, obstacles and perceived benefits, as well as contextual factors influencing this adoption. These results make it possible to identify both structural obstacles and the conditions necessary for the adoption of IFRS to bring real added value

Table 2. Summary of Key Findings on IFRS Adoption in SMEs

Research Question	Themes	Key Codes Nvivo/ Concepts
RQ1 – General Perceptions on IFRS Adoption for SMEs	Motivation and strategic goals	Access to foreign investments, Adoption for stock listing or sale, Optional adoption by holdings
	Perceived suitability	IFRS adapted to SMEs, Adaptation depends on sector, IFRS not practical for SMEs, IFRS unsuitable
	Conceptual perceptions	Economic vision of IFRS, Need for training and additional effort
	Expected accounting improvements	Improved international comparability, Modernization of accounting
RQ2 – Perceived Obstacles to IFRS Adoption	Capacity and training issues	Lack of IFRS knowledge, Need for training, Lack of IFRS tools and skills
	Financial and technical barriers	High adoption cost, IFRS too complex, Rare adoption in Morocco
	Institutional and regulatory support	Absence of institutional support, Lack of incentives from authorities
	Complexity as a non-barrier	Complexity not seen as a major issue by some participants
RQ3 – Expected Benefits of IFRS Implementation	Transparency and comparability	Improved financial transparency, Enhanced comparability across firms
	Financial and strategic advantages	Easier access to financing, Access to international markets, Enhanced competitiveness
	Relevance depending on firm type	Benefits only for certain SMEs, Useful mainly for well-known firms, IFRS beneficial for sale preparation
	Applicability to all SMEs	IFRS seen as useful for all SMEs by some participants
Other Observations	Adaptation and gradual implementation	Adapt IFRS to local context, Progressive adoption recommended, Digital and tax alignment necessary
	Role of institutions	Authorities should provide support and communication, Encourage through subsidies
	Readiness and timing	SMEs not yet ready, Long-term readiness, Adoption tied to tax modernization

Source: Table summarizing key themes and codes identified through NVivo software assisted qualitative analysis conducted by the author.

The interviews' analysis reveals divergent views regarding SMEs' adoption of IFRS. Some participants emphasized the advantages of such adoption, notably improved international comparability, modernized accounting practices and a more economic view of financial reporting, less focused on historical costs. These elements are seen as potential levers for companies considering opening their capital to foreign investors, an initial public offering (IPO) or a partial sale.

However, these advantages are perceived as being limited to certain SMEs, depending on their size, reputation or sector of activity. Due to their complexity, training requirements, and the necessary adjustments to accounting systems, some respondents believe that IFRS is impractical or unsuitable for the operating context of small businesses.

The adoption of IFRS is therefore considered feasible, but far from generalizable, and more suited to companies with sufficient resources or engaged in internationalization or restructuring strategies. However, these benefits do not apply uniformly to all SMEs. Several speakers pointed out that they are primarily aimed at SMEs that are more structured, have a certain reputation or are integrated into international value chains. There is a major obstacle to the adoption of IFRS by SMEs, and these were repeatedly identified by participants. The first is the high cost of the transition, which includes setting up appropriate tools, paying qualified professionals and providing ongoing training for teams. When it comes to small structures with limited resources, this factor is especially restrictive. A second major obstacle is the lack of in-house skills and specialized training.

Participants emphasized that IFRS standards require accounting and financial expertise that is often lacking in SMEs. This deficit is compounded by the lack of institutional support, as well as the absence of regulatory or tax incentives to encourage the transition to these standards. Finally, while some consider the complexity of IFRS to be harmless, others see it as an additional obstacle, notably because of the diversity of accounting treatments and the interpretation effort required.

Despite these challenges, the adoption of IFRS by SMEs offers numerous potential advantages. Respondents notably highlight improved comparability between companies, easier access to financing, and improved transparency of financial information. The gradual implementation of IFRS, backed by support measures and partial adaptation to the local context, is considered as an essential condition for maximizing these benefits. IFRS are seen as a strategic lever for strengthening the financial credibility of companies and attracting investors.

The results of this research reveal a diversity of perceptions among the professionals surveyed regarding the adoption of IFRS by SMEs. Overall, three main lines of interpretation emerge: the heterogeneity of perceptions according to company profile, the prevalence of structural obstacles, and the identification of a conditional strategic potential.

It is abundantly clear that not all SMEs agree that IFRS are appropriate. The respondents made a significant distinction between smaller, local businesses with limited operations and larger, more structured SMEs that frequently expand, have international goals, or are integrated into larger groups. For the latter, IFRS adoption can provide a competitive advantage, by facilitating access to capital, enhancing financial comparability and improving transparency. On the other hand, the standards are thought to be too complicated, pricey, and unsuitable for smaller structures' immediate requirements.

Several structural obstacles to SMEs' widespread adoption of IFRS are outlined in the analysis. Among these, the cost of implementation is a consistent factor: it includes the cost of training, buying the appropriate IT tools, and paying for qualified personnal. The lack of internal skills and institutional support accentuates these difficulties. Furthermore, the voluntary or non-mandatory nature of IFRS in many contexts makes their adoption unattractive in the absence of clear regulatory or tax incentives. It is interesting to note that the complexity of the standards, often mentioned in the literature, is not systematically perceived as a major obstacle by all respondents. Some believe that, with the adequate support, SMEs can gradually overcome this obstacle.

Participants acknowledge several advantages of adopting IFRS in spite of the challenges that have been identified. These include enhanced financial credibility, greater transparency of accounting information, and easier access to international markets or structured financing. However, these advantages are considered to be conditional on the existence of a supportive framework, an effort to popularize the standards and, above all, a clear political will.

The majority of respondents agreed that the adoption of IFRS by SMEs should be gradual, adapted to the local context and actively supported by the authorities.

In the light of the results and discussion points, a few recommendations can be formulated for public decision-makers, accounting authorities and SME development stakeholders:

Table 3. Measures to Ease IFRS Implementation for SMEs

Proposed Measure	Description
Gradual Adoption Strategy	Implement a phased approach to IFRS adoption, tailored to the size, sector, and international exposure of SMEs. This strategy helps limit initial costs and aligns the transition pace with companies' actual capabilities.
Strengthening Training and Technical Skills	Develop continuing education programs focused on IFRS for SMEs, integrated into university curricula and offered to professionals, especially in medium-sized firms. Practical guides can help simplify and popularize the standards.
Incentive and Support Mechanisms	Government and professional bodies should provide incentives such as training subsidies, temporary tax relief, or subsidized technical support. These actions would lower the perceived risks and foster a favorable environment for change.

continued on following page

Table 3. Continued

Proposed Measure	Description
Adapting Standards to Local Context	Contextualize IFRS by identifying key areas for local SMEs and proposing simplified versions or hybrid standards. These adaptations should remain aligned with core IFRS principles while facilitating a smoother transition for national adoption.
Communicating Positive Feedback	Promote successful IFRS adoption stories among SMEs to encourage wider implementation. Real-life testimonials can legitimize the standards and reduce initial resistance or apprehension among other companies.

Source: Table developed by the author based on analysis of Nvivo results.

5. CONCLUSION

The objective of this study was to analyze the impacts of IFRS adoption on SMEs in Morocco, centering on stakeholders' recognitions of the benefits, challenges and suggestions of this transition. To analyze these issues, a qualitative approach was used, based on semi-structured interviews with experts.

The results revealed a growing recognition of the benefits of IFRS adoption, particularly in terms of financial transparency, comparability of financial transactions, and increased attractiveness for investors.

This general recognition reflects a clear interest in IFRS, but moreover a require for backup and continuous adjustment, given the financial setting and constrained capacities of little structures. The main interest of this study lies in its experimental approach to a subject that has remained understudied in the Moroccan context.

By mobilizing a subjective qualitative based on the declarations of stakeholders specifically concerned, this study provides a better understanding of the local process of collecting and distributing IFRS standards. It also highlights the importance of an appropriate institutional framework and regulatory support for the successful adoption of international standards in the Moroccan entrepreneurial community.

The results identified several major challenges, including the high cost of implementation, the technical complexity of the standards and the lack of specialized training adapted to the context of Moroccan SMEs. The limited number of interviews and the geographical concentration of participants may also restrict the scope of the conclusions. Furthermore, the study does not consider companies that have not yet begun to think about IFRS, which could introduce a selection bias.

To complement the results obtained, future research could focus on a larger-scale quantitative approach, enabling hypotheses to be tested on a representative sample. It would also be relevant to study the impact of partial IFRS adoption on the economic performance of SMEs, or to evaluate the effects of training and support programs in the standards implementation process. Finally, comparisons with other developing countries that have experienced similar transitions could enrich our understanding of the conditions required for effective adoption of IFRS by small companies.

REFERENCES

Albu, C. N., Albu, N., Bunea, S., Calu, D. A., & Gîrbina, M. M. (2013). A framework for the analysis of the adoption of IFRS for SMEs. *Accounting in Europe, 10*(2), 193–215. DOI: 10.1080/17449480.2013.817393

Albu, C. N., Albu, N., Pali-Pista, S. F., Gîrbina, M. M., & Selimoğlu, S. K. (2013). Implementation of IFRS for SMEs in emerging economies: Stakeholder perceptions in Romania and Turkey. *Accounting and Management Information Systems, 12*(1), 73–101.

Albu, N., & Albu, C. (2012). International Financial Reporting Standards in an emerging economy: Lessons from Romania. *Australian Accounting Review, 22*(4), 341–352. DOI: 10.1111/j.1835-2561.2012.00196.x

Barker, R., & Shaikh, A. (2016). The adoption of IFRS for SMEs: A global perspective. *Accounting and Business Research, 46*(3), 35–56. DOI: 10.1080/00014788.2016.1147755

Barth, M. E., & Landsman, W. R. (2009). Transparency and the International Financial Reporting Standards (IFRS) for SMEs. *The Accounting Review, 84*(3), 15–42.

Bonsón, E., García-Borbolla, A., & Bednárová, M. (2023). IFRS for SMEs: Relevance, application and local challenges in European countries. *Journal of International Accounting Research, 22*(1), 1–21. DOI: 10.2308/JIAR-2022-020

Boolaky, P. K., Tawiah, V., & Soobaroyen, T. (2020). Why do African countries adopt IFRS? An institutional perspective. ***International***. *Journal of Accountancy, 55*(01).

Chai, H., Tang, Q., Jiang, Y., & Lin, Z. (2010). The role of International Financial Reporting Standards in accounting quality: Evidence from the European Union. *International Journal of Financial Management and Accounting, 21*(3), 220–278.

Degos, J.-G., Levant, Y., & Touron, P. (2019). The history of accounting standards in French-speaking African countries since independence: The difficult path towards IFRS. *Accounting, Auditing & Accountability Journal, 32*(1), 75–100. DOI: 10.1108/AAAJ-03-2016-2459

Delvaille, P., Le Manh, A., & Maillet, C. (2016). Challenges and limits of applying IFRS standards to SMEs. In Burlaud, A., & Thauvron, A. (Eds.), *Accounting in action* (pp. 183–194). L'Harmattan.

Ebaid, I. E.-S. (2023). IFRS adoption and the readability of corporate annual reports: Evidence from an emerging market. *Future Business Journal*, *9*(1), 13. Advance online publication. DOI: 10.1186/s43093-023-00244-x

Effah, N. A. A. (2024). A bibliometric review of IFRS adoption and compliance research in Africa. *Journal of Business and Socio-economic Development*, *4*(3), 193–209. DOI: 10.1108/JBSED-01-2023-0001

Elhamma, A. (2023a). Impact of mandatory IFRS adoption on foreign direct investment: The moderating role of conflict of interest regulation. ***Journal of Financial Reporting and Accounting***. https://doi.org/DOI: 10.1108/JFRA-04-2022-0145

Elhamma, A. (2023b). Impact of mandatory IFRS adoption on economic growth: The moderating role of the COVID-19 crisis. *Journal of Accounting and Management Information Systems*, *22*(3), 554–568. DOI: 10.24818/jamis.2023.03007

Elhamma, A. (2023c). Fifty years of IAS/IFRS standards: Adoption, consequences, and situation in Morocco. In R. M'Rabet & M. A. Issami (Eds.), ***50 years of management*** (pp. 121–136). Éditions EDISCA.

Elhamma, A. (2024a). Determinants of national IFRS adoption: Evidence from the MENA region. ***International Journal of Accounting***. *Auditing and Performance Evaluation*, *20*(1-2), 69–90. DOI: 10.1504/IJAAPE.2024.135535

Elhamma, A. (2024b). Participant observation as a qualitative research method in management sciences: Interests, conditions, and limitations. In Bentalha, B., & Alla, L. (Eds.), *Applying qualitative research methods to management science* (pp. 75–91). IGI Global., DOI: 10.4018/979-8-3693-5543-5.ch004

Elhamma, A. (2025a). Perceived benefits of IFRS adoption in Morocco and French-speaking Africa. In F. Albuquerque & P. G. Dos Santos (Eds.), ***Contemporary innovations in reporting*** (pp. 183–210). IGI Global. https://doi.org/DOI: 10.4018/979-8-3693-5923-5.ch007

Elhamma, A. (2025b). Lack of resilience and failure of SMEs in Morocco: Current situation. In Dias Rouco, J. C., & Nunes Figueiredo, P. C. (Eds.), *Improving resilience in business continuity management* (pp. 245–266). IGI Global., DOI: 10.4018/979-8-3693-8809-9.ch008

Frost, C. A. (2017). Barriers to the adoption of IFRS for SMEs in developing countries. *The International Journal of Accounting*, *52*(4), 322–340. DOI: 10.1016/j.intacc.2017.10.005

Ghosh, D., & Behera, A. (2020). Digital transformation in accounting: A study of cloud-based solutions in SMEs. *Journal of Accounting Technology*, *15*(2), 102–120.

Hail, L., Leuz, C., & Wysocki, P. (2010). Global accounting convergence and the potential adoption of IFRS for SMEs. *The Accounting Review*, *85*(6), 2043–2081. DOI: 10.2308/accr.2010.85.6.2043

IASB (2009). International Financial Reporting Standard for Small and Medium-sized Entities (IFRS for SMEs).

-IASB (2016). Guide to the IFRS for SMEs.

IFRS Foundation. (2022). IFRS for SMEs factsheet. Retrieved April 20, 2025, from https://www.ifrs.org

IFRS Foundation. (2024). SME Standard 2024 update. Retrieved April 19, 2025, from https://www.ifrs.org

Kamal, M., & Elbeltagi, I. (2024). Challenges in IFRS implementation among Egyptian SMEs: A capability perspective. *International Journal of Accounting and Finance*, *14*(2), 150–169.

Kaya, D., & Koch, M. (2015). Countries' adoption of the IFRS for SMEs: Early empirical evidence. *Accounting and Business Research*, *45*(1), 93–120. DOI: 10.1080/00014788.2014.969188

Kilic, M., & Uyar, A. (2014). Adoption process of IFRS for SMEs in Turkey: Insights from field research. *Accounting and Management Information Systems*, *13*(3), 492–519.

Kumar, S., & Singh, M. (2020). Bridging the education gap: Implementing IFRS for SMEs in India. *International Journal of Accounting Education*, *18*(3), 239–253.

Madawaki, A. (2014). Adoption of IFRS for SMEs in Nigeria: Perception of professional accountants. *International Journal of Business and Management*, *9*(1), 89–99. DOI: 10.5539/ijbm.v9n1p89

Mhedhbi, K., & Essid, M. (2022). National Cultural Dimensions and Adoption of IFRS for SMEs. *The International Journal of Accounting*. Advance online publication. DOI: 10.1142/S1094406022500044

Nobes, C. (2017). The development and adoption of IFRS for SMEs: An overview. *Journal of Financial Reporting and Accounting*, *15*(2), 127–139. DOI: 10.1108/JFRA-01-2016-0002

Oubahou, Y., & El Ouafa, K. (2024). The effect of adopting IFRS on the relevance of information: The case of Moroccan companies. *Investment Management and Financial Innovations*, *21*(2), 361–373. DOI: 10.21511/imfi.21(2).2024.32

Perera, H., & Chand, P. (2015). Issues in the adoption of IFRS in less developed countries. *Qualitative Research in Accounting & Management, 12*(3), 233–250. DOI: 10.1108/QRAM-02-2013-0012

UNCTAD. (2015). *Accounting and financial reporting guidelines for SMEs*. United Nations. Retrieved April 15, 2025, from https://unctad.org

Van Wyk, H. A., & Rossouw, J. (2009). IFRS implementation: The role of institutional factors in South Africa. *Meditari Accountancy Research, 17*(2), 117–137. DOI: 10.1108/10222529200900011

Waweru, N. M., Peng, S., & Hopper, T. (2023). Two decades of African accounting research 2000–2019: Synthesis, reflections, gaps, and future directions. *Journal of International Accounting Research, 22*(1), 99–136. DOI: 10.2308/JIAR-2021-078

Zhang, X., Li, H., & Zhao, S. (2021). The role of data analytics in SMEs' financial decision-making. *Journal of Financial Analytics, 19*(1), 57–68.

Zori, S. G., & Seny Kan, K. (2017). *A qualitative comparative approach to the adoption of International Financial Reporting Standards (IFRS) in Africa. SSRN.* https://doi.org/DOI: 10.2139/ssrn.2992501

KEY TERMS AND DEFINITIONS

IFRS:: These are international accounting rules designed to harmonize the presentation of financial statements worldwide. They enable greater transparency and comparability between companies in different countries.

SMEs:: These are small and medium-sized enterprises that play an essential role in the local economy. They generally have a smaller workforce, sales or balance sheet total than larger companies.

Modernization:: This is the process of adapting or improving working methods, often using new technologies. In the accounting context, this means adopting more efficient and up-to-date tools or standards.

Financial reporting:: This refers to the way in which a company communicates its financial results to stakeholders. This includes documents such as the balance sheet, income statement and notes.

Compliance challenges:: These are the difficulties companies face in complying with current laws, standards or regulations. These can include high costs, lack of training or complex procedures.

APPENDIX A. SEMI-DIRECTIVE INTERVIEW GUIDE

Participant Profile

Current Position:

Field of Practice:

Have you ever heard of IFRS for SMEs? (Yes / No)

If yes: How familiar are you with these standards? (General Notions / Good Knowledge / Current Practice)

Part 1 – General Perceptions

What are your general thoughts on the idea of adopting international accounting standards (such as IFRS) for SMEs?

Why do you think some countries or companies choose to adopt IFRS for SMEs?

Do you think these standards are suited to the realities of small and medium-sized enterprises?

Part 2 – Perceived Obstacles

In your opinion, what obstacles or difficulties do SMEs encounter when adopting these standards?

Do you think these obstacles are related to:

A lack of skills or training?

High costs?

The complexity of the standards?

A lack of external support?

Do you know of any companies that have encountered problems in this regard? Can you give an example?

Part 3 – Perceived Benefits

What potential benefits do you see in using IFRS for SMEs?

Do you think this could:

Improve the transparency of financial reporting?

Facilitate access to financing or partnerships?

Enable better comparability with other companies?

Do you see the benefits as affecting all SMEs or only some?

Part 4 – Opinion on Implementation

Do you think SMEs are ready to adopt this type of standard?

What role should authorities (state, accounting bodies, professional associations) play in supporting this process?

In your opinion, should these standards be further adapted to the local context?

Thank you very much for your responses. Would you like to add anything or share a final opinion on this topic?

Compilation of References

Abdul-Khaliq, S., Soufan, T., & Shihab, R. A. (2014). The relationship between unemployment and economic growth rate in Arab countries. *Journal of Economics and Sustainable Development, 5*(9), 56–59.

Abhayawansa, S. (2022). Swimming against the tide: Back to single materiality for sustainability reporting. *Sustainability Accounting. Management and Policy Journal, 13*(6), 1361–1385. DOI: 10.1108/SAMPJ-07-2022-0378

Acar, M. (2023). Who affects whom? Impact of the national culture of international audit firms and their affiliates on the financial reporting quality of audit clients. *Borsa Istanbul Review, 23*(1), 113–135. DOI: 10.1016/j.bir.2022.09.011

Ademola, A. O., Ben-Caleb, E., Madugba, J. U., Adegboyegun, A. E., & Eluyela, D. F. (2020). International public sector accounting standards (IPSAS) adoption and implementation in Nigerian public sector. *International Journal of Financial Research, 11*(1), 434–444.

Adhikari, P., & Mellemvik, F. (2010). The adoption of IPSASs in South Asia: A comparative study of seven countries. *Research in Accounting in Emerging Economies, 10*, 171–201. DOI: 10.1108/S1479-3563(2010)0000010012

African Business. (2022, April 5). *Unlocking SME potential through the power of emerging technology*. African Business. https://african.business/2022/04/technology-information/unlocking-sme-potential-through-the-power-of-emerging-technology

Agyei-Mensah, B. K. (2013). Adoption of international financial reporting standards (IFRS) in Ghana and the quality of financial statement disclosures. Macrothink Institute, *International Journal of Accounting and Financial Reporting*, ISSN, 2162-3082. https://doi.org/DOI: 10.5296/ijafr.v3i2.4489

Ahmadi, A., & Bouri, A. (2018). The accounting value relevance of earnings and book value: Tunisian banks and financial institutions. *International Journal of Law and Management, 60*(2), 342–354. DOI: 10.1108/IJLMA-11-2016-0131

Ahmed, A. S., Neel, M., & Wang, D. (2013). Does mandatory adoption of IFRS improve accounting quality? Preliminary evidence. *Contemporary Accounting Research, 30*(4), 1344–1372. DOI: 10.1111/j.1911-3846.2012.01193.x

Ahsina, K., Alaoui,O., Z., & Ellatife, E. (2013). L'adoption des normes comptables internationales IAS/IFRS par les sociétés cotées au Maroc: Un essai d'observation et de modélisation. *Revue Marocaine de Contrôle de Gestion*, N°5

Ahsina, K. (2012). Implementing IAS-IFRS in the Moroccan context: An explanatory model. *International Journal of Accounting and Financial Reporting*, *2*(2), 114–124. DOI: 10.5296/ijafr.v2i2.2524

Ahsina, K., Taouab, O., & Cherqaoui, M. B. (2014). L'impact de l'adoption des IFRS sur les sociétés cotées à la Bourse de Casablanca: Une étude exploratoire. *La Revue Gestion et Organisation*, *6*(2), 45–57. DOI: 10.1016/j.rgo.2014.09.003

Ahsina, K., Taouab, O., & Daghri, T. (2014). An empirical investigation of adopting IFRS accounting standards: Evidence from Morocco. *Research Journal of Finance and Accounting*, *5*(10), 120–131.

Ajibade, A. T., Okutu, N., Akande, F., Kwarbai, J. D., Olayinka, I. M., & Olotu, A. (2022). IFRS adoption, corporate governance and faithful representation of financial reporting quality in Nigeria's development banks. *Cogent Business & Management*, *9*(1), 2139213. DOI: 10.1080/23311975.2022.2139213

Akisik, O. (2013). Accounting regulation, financial development, and economic growth. *Emerging Markets Finance & Trade*, *49*(1), 33–67. DOI: 10.2753/REE1540-496X490103

Akisik, O. (2014). *Financial reporting and foreign direct investments in Latin America. Accounting in Latin America*. Emerald Group Publishing.

Akisik, O. (2014). Financial reporting and foreign direct investments in Latin America. In *Accounting in Latin America* (pp. 41–47). Emerald Group Publishing., DOI: 10.1108/S1479-356320140000014000

Akisik, O. (2020). The impact of financial development, IFRS, and rule of law on foreign investments: A cross-country analysis. *International Review of Economics & Finance*, *69*, 815–838. DOI: 10.1016/j.iref.2020.06.015

Akisik, O., Gal, G., & Mangaliso, M. P. (2020). IFRS, FDI, economic growth, and human development: The experience of Anglophone and Francophone African countries. *Emerging Markets Review*, *45*, 100725. DOI: 10.1016/j.ememar.2020.100725

Alabed, Q., Said, F. F., Karim, Z. A., Zaidi, M. A. S., & Mansour, M. (2022). Determinants of unemployment in the MENA region: New evidence using dynamic heterogeneous panel analysis. In A. E. Hassanien, R. Y. Rizk, V. Snášel, & R. F. Abdel-Kader (Eds.), *The 8th International Conference on Advanced Machine Learning and Technologies and Applications (AMLTA 2022).* https://doi.org/DOI: 10.1007/978-3-031-03918-8_34

Albu, N., & Albu, C. N. (2014). Strategies for and implications of the IFRS for SMEs implementation in emerging economies. *Comptabilités et innovations*, Grenoble, France.

Albu, C. N., Albu, N., & Alexander, D. (2014). When global accounting standards meet the local context-Insights from an emerging economy. *Critical Perspectives on Accounting*, *25*(6), 489–510. DOI: 10.1016/j.cpa.2013.03.005

Albu, C. N., Albu, N., Bunea, S., Calu, D. A., & Gîrbina, M. M. (2013). A framework for the analysis of the adoption of IFRS for SMEs. *Accounting in Europe*, *10*(2), 193–215. DOI: 10.1080/17449480.2013.817393

Albu, C. N., Albu, N., Pali-Pista, S. F., Gîrbina, M. M., & Selimoğlu, S. K. (2013). Implementation of IFRS for SMEs in emerging economies: Stakeholder perceptions in Romania and Turkey. *Accounting and Management Information Systems*, *12*(1), 73–101.

Albu, N., & Albu, C. (2012). International Financial Reporting Standards in an emerging economy: Lessons from Romania. *Australian Accounting Review*, *22*(4), 341–352. DOI: 10.1111/j.1835-2561.2012.00196.x

Al-Enzy, N. S. K., Monem, R., & Nahar, S. (2023). IFRS experience and earnings quality in the GCC region. *International Journal of Managerial Finance*, *19*(3), 670–690. DOI: 10.1108/IJMF-09-2021-0410

Alexander, D., Britton, A., & Jorissen, A. (2007). *International financial reporting and analysis* (3rd ed.). Thomson.

Alford, A., Jones, J., Leftwich, R., & Zmijewski, M. (1993). The relative informativeness of accounting disclosures in different countries. *Journal of Accounting Research, 31*, 183-223.Ben Salem, R., Damak-Ayadi, S., & Saïhi, M. (2017). Determinants of full IFRS adoption. *International Journal of Managerial and Financial Accounting*, *9*(2), 105–123.

Alhdiy, F. M., Johari, F., Daud, S. N. M., & Rahman, A. A. (2015). Short and long term relationship between economic growth and unemployment in Egypt: An empirical analysis. *Mediterranean Journal of Social Sciences, 6*(4), S3, 454–462. https://doi.org/DOI: 10.5901/mjss.2015.v6n4s3p454

Al-htaybat, K. A. (2018). IFRS adoption in emerging markets: The case of Jordan. *Australian Accounting Review*, *28*(1), 28–47. Advance online publication. DOI: 10.1111/auar.12186

Ali, A., & Hwang, L.-S. (2000). Country-specific factors related to financial reporting and the value relevance of accounting data. *Journal of Accounting Research*, *38*(1), 1–21. DOI: 10.2307/2672920

Almaqtari, F., Hashed, A., & Shamim, M. (2021). Impact of corporate governance mechanism on IFRS adoption: A comparative study of Saudi Arabia, Oman, and the United Arab Emirates. *Heliyon*, *7*(2), e05848. DOI: 10.1016/j.heliyon.2020.e05848 PMID: 33490662

Alnaas, A., & Rashid, A. (2019). Firm characteristics and compliance with IAS/IFRS: Evidence from North African companies. *Journal of Financial Reporting and Accounting*, *17*(3), 383–410. DOI: 10.1108/JFRA-06-2018-0052

Alnodel, A. A. (2018). The impact of IFRS adoption on the value relevance of accounting information: Evidence from the insurance sector. *International Journal of Business and Management*, *13*(4), 138–148. DOI: 10.5539/ijbm.v13n4p138

Alomair, A., Farley, A., & Yang, H. H. (2022). The impact of IFRS adoption on the value relevance of accounting information in Saudi Arabia. *Accounting and Finance*, *62*(2), 2839–2878. DOI: 10.1111/acfi.12902

Alon, A., & Dwyer, P. (2014). Early adoption of IFRS as a strategic response to transnational and local influences. *The International Journal of Accounting*, *49*(3), 348–370. DOI: 10.1016/j.intacc.2014.07.003

Alruwaili, W. S., Ahmed, A. D., & Joshi, M. (2023). IFRS adoption, firms' investment efficiency and financial reporting quality: A new empirical assessment of moderating effects from Saudi listed firms. *International Journal of Accounting & Information Management*, *31*(2), 376–411. DOI: 10.1108/IJAIM 10 2022 0226

Alsharif, A. H., Salleh, N. O. R. Z. M. D., & Baharun, R. O. H. A. I. Z. A. T. (2020). Bibliometric analysis. *Journal of Theoretical and Applied Information Technology*, 98(15), 2948-2962, E-ISSN: 1817-3195.

Alshujairi, M. H. (2014). Government accounting system reform and the adoption of IPSAS in Iraq. *Research Journal of Finance and Accounting, 5*(24), 1–20. https://www.iiste.org/Journals/index.php/RJFA/article/download/18490/19035

Alzeban, A. (2018). The association between internal audit department characteristics and IFRS compliance. *Asian Review of Accounting*, *26*(3), 336–358. DOI: 10.1108/ARA-03-2017-0054

Amaefule, L., Onyekpere, U., & Kalu, E. (2018). International Financial Reporting Standards and manufacturing firms' financial performance in Nigeria: A study of selected quoted firms. *International Journal of Accounting and Taxation*, *6*(1), 102–114. DOI: 10.15640/ijat.v6n1a9

Amidu, M., Yorke, S. M., & Harvey, S. (2016). The Effects of Financial Reporting Standards on Tax Avoidance and Earnings Quality: A Case of an Emerging Economy. *Journal of Accounting & Finance* (2158-3625), 16(2).

Andreu, A., Castilla, A., Gálvez, M., & García, I. (2024). Sustainability. The coming regulatory tsunami (III). *EY Rethinking Sustainability.* https://www.ey.com/es_es/insights/rethinking-sustainability/sostenibilidad-tsunami-regulatorio-iii

Armstrong, S. C., Barth, M. E., Jagolinzer, A. D., & Riedl, E. J. (2010). Market reaction to the adoption of IFRS in Europe. *The Accounting Review*, *85*(1), 31–61. DOI: 10.2308/accr.2010.85.1.31

Ashbaugh, H., & Pincus, M. (2000). Domestic accounting standards, international accounting standards, and the predictability of earnings. *Journal of Accounting Research, 39*(3), 417–434. DOI: 10.1111/1475-679X.00020

Asongu, S., Akpan, U. S., & Isihak, S. R. (2018). Determinants of foreign direct investment in fast-growing economies: Evidence from the BRICS and MINT countries. *Financial Innovation*, *4*(26), 26. Advance online publication. DOI: 10.1186/s40854-018-0114-0

Atu, O. E. O. K., Atu, O. G., & Okoye, A. F. (2013). International Public Sector Accounting Standards (IPSAS): Challenges and Way Forward in Nigeria. *Quarterly Journal of Associational of National Accountants of Nigeria*, *21*(1), 26–32.

Avelé, D. (2013). *La théorie positive de la comptabilité: Aspects théoriques et critiques* (Master's thesis). Université de Moncton, Canada.

Ayachi, G. (2018). La convergence de la comptabilité de l'État avec les normes IPSAS: Le cas du Maroc [MPRA Paper No. 90039]. University Library of Munich. https://mpra.ub.uni-muenchen.de/90039/

Baghar, N. (2017). *La normalisation comptable au Maroc: Actualités, enjeux et perspectives* (Master's thesis). École Nationale de Commerce et de Gestion, Université Hassan 1er, Settat.

Bajra, U., & Čadež, S. (2018). Audit committees and financial reporting quality: The 8th EU Company Law Directive perspective. *Economic Systems*, *42*(1), 151–163. DOI: 10.1016/j.ecosys.2017.03.002

Bakr, S. A., & Napier, C. J. (2022). Adopting the international financial reporting standard for small and medium-sized entities in Saudi Arabia. *Journal of Economic and Administrative Sciences*, *38*(1), 18–40. DOI: 10.1108/JEAS-08-2018-0094

Ball, R. (2006). International Financial Reporting Standards (IFRS): pros and cons for investors. *Accounting and Business Research, 36*(sup1), 5–27. https://doi.org/DOI: 10.1080/00014788.2006.9730040

Ball, I. (2015). Debate: Would IPSAS help Greece? *Public Money & Management*, *35*(6), 397–398. DOI: 10.1080/09540962.2015.1076954

Bampoky, B. (2019). Les difficultés de normalisation comptable dans l'espace OHADA. *ACCRA*, (2), 25–59. DOI: 10.3917/accra.005.0025

Barghathi, Y. (2019). Financial reporting quality and earnings management in Libyan banks: Stakeholders' perceptions. *African Journal of Accounting. Auditing and Finance*, *6*(3), 177–200. DOI: 10.1504/AJAAF.2019.10020488

Barker, R., & Shaikh, A. (2016). The adoption of IFRS for SMEs: A global perspective. *Accounting and Business Research*, *46*(3), 35–56. DOI: 10.1080/00014788.2016.1147755

Baron, R. M., & Kenny, D. A. (1986). The moderator–mediator variable distinction in social psychological research: Conceptual, strategic, and statistical considerations. *Journal of Personality and Social Psychology*, *51*(6), 1173–1182. DOI: 10.1037/0022-3514.51.6.1173 PMID: 3806354

Barth, M. E., Landsman, W. R., Lang, M., & Williams, C. (2007). Accounting quality: International accounting standards and US GAAP. Manuscript, Stanford University. https://citeseerx.ist.psu.edu/document?repid=rep1&type=pdf&doi=092af2d3624226dba00e8cd39e5fa302d635e0ae

Barth, M. E., Li, K., & McClure, C. G. (2017). Evolution in value relevance of accounting information. *Stanford University Graduate School of Business Research Paper No. 17-24*, 78. https://doi.org/DOI: 10.2139/ssrn.2933197

Barth, M. E., & Landsman, W. R. (2009). Transparency and the International Financial Reporting Standards (IFRS) for SMEs. *The Accounting Review, 84*(3), 15–42.

Bartov, E., Goldberg, S. R., & Kim, M. (2005). Comparative value relevance among German, US, and international accounting standards: A German stock market perspective. *Journal of Accounting, Auditing & Finance, 20*(2), 95–119. DOI: 10.1177/0148558X0502000201

Bassemir, M., & Novotny-Farkas, Z. (2018). IFRS adoption, reporting incentives and financial reporting quality in private firms. *Journal of Business Finance & Accounting, 45*(7-8), 759–796. DOI: 10.1111/jbfa.12315

Bayrak, R., & Tatli, H. (2018). The determinants of youth unemployment: A panel data analysis of OECD countries. *The European Journal of Comparative Economics, 15*(2), 231–248. DOI: 10.25428/1824-2979/201802-231-248

Bayraktar, N. (2013). Foreign direct investment and investment climate. *Procedia Economics and Finance, 5*, 83–92. DOI: 10.1016/S2212-5671(13)00013-0

Belkaoui, A. R. (1995). *The cultural shaping of accounting*. Quorum Books. DOI: 10.5040/9798216187097

Bellanca, S., & Vandernoot, J. (2013). Analysis of Belgian public accounting and its compliance with International Public Sector Accounting Standards (IPSAS) 1, 6, and 22. *International Journal of Business and Management, 8*(9), 122–133. DOI: 10.5539/ijbm.v8n9p122

Bellanca, S., & Vandernoot, J. (2013). Belgian public accounting: Evolution and compliance with IPSAS. *International Advances in Economic Research, 19*(1), 79–81. DOI: 10.1007/s11294-012-9386-8

Ben Slama, F., & Klibi, M. F. (2017). Accounting development in a changing environment: The case of Tunisia. *International Journal of Law and Management. Scopus., 59*(5), 756–775. Advance online publication. DOI: 10.1108/IJLMA-03-2016-0034

Beneish, M. D., Miller, B. P., & Yohn, T. L. (2015). Macroeconomic evidence on the impact of mandatory IFRS adoption on equity and debt markets. *Journal of Accounting and Public Policy, 34*(1), 1–27. DOI: 10.1016/j.jaccpubpol.2014.10.002

Bengtsson, M. (2022). *National Adoptions of IFRS: Accounting Perspectives*. IntechOpen., DOI: 10.5772/intechopen.103679

Bengtsson, M. M. (2021). Determinants of de jure adoption of international financial reporting standards: A review. *Pacific Accounting Review, 34*(1), 156–173. DOI: 10.1108/PAR-10-2020-0193

Benhayoun, I., El Amrani, M., Barhdadi, A., & Azzaoui, W. (2025). Adoption of ISSB standards in emerging markets – insights from Moroccan companies' organizational readiness. *Journal of Financial Reporting and Accounting*. DOI: 10.1108/JFRA-07-2024-0468

Benitez, J., Henseler, J., Castillo, A., & Schuberth, F. (2020). How to perform and report an impactful analysis using partial least squares: Guidelines for confirmatory and explanatory IS research. *Information & Management*, *57*(2), 103168. Advance online publication. DOI: 10.1016/j.im.2019.05.003

Benito, B., Brusca, I., & Montesinos, V. (2007). L'harmonisation des systèmes gouvernementaux d'information financière: Le rôle des IPSAS. *Revue Internationale des Sciences Administratives*, *73*(2), 323–350. DOI: 10.3917/risa.732.0323

Benito, B., Brusca, I., & Montesinos, V. (2007). The harmonization of government financial information systems: The role of the IPSASs. *International Review of Administrative Sciences*, *73*(2), 293–317. DOI: 10.1177/0020852307078424

Bentley-Goode, K. A., Simnett, R., Thompson, A., & Trotman, A. J. (2024). Choice of assurance provider and impact on quality of sustainability reporting: Evidence from sustainability reporting restatements. *Accounting and Finance*. https://www.scopus.com/inward/record.uri?eid=2-s2.0-85209989086&doi=10.1111%2facfi.13367&partnerID=40&md5=fe10fc893e605511235a86093e3a6733

Bergmann, A. (2012). The influence of the nature of government accounting and reporting in decision-making: Evidence from Switzerland. *Public Money & Management*, *32*(1), 15–20. DOI: 10.1080/09540962.2012.643050

Bernheim, Y., Escaffre de Mazars, L., & Guerard. (1999). Point de vue. Évaluation à la juste valeur. Un nouveau modèle comptable ? *Comptabilité - Contrôle – Audit*, *5*(2), 25–45.

Bessieux-Ollier, C., & Walliser, É. (2014). Sur la contingence du référentiel comptable: L'exemple des entreprises françaises cotées sur Alternext. *Revue Française de Comptabilité*, (100), 25–40. DOI: 10.3917/resg.100.0073

Biddle, G. C., & Hilary, G. (2006). Accounting quality and firm-level capital investment. *The Accounting Review*, *81*(5), 963–982. https://www.jstor.org/stable/4093094. DOI: 10.2308/accr.2006.81.5.963

Bilodeau, J., Chérief, I., Labelle, R., et al. (2005). Les caractéristiques des contrats de dettes et les clauses restrictives comptables: Quels liens ? *Comptabilité – Contrôle – Audit, 11(2),* 109–133.

Blessing, J. (2024). ESG frameworks and regulatory convergence: A global review. *Corporate Governance Journal*, *28*(1), 11–35.

Bonetti, P., Magnan, M. L., & Parbonetti, A. (2016). The influence of country-and firm-level governance on financial reporting quality: Revisiting the evidence. *Journal of Business Finance & Accounting*, *43*(9-10), 1059–1094. DOI: 10.1111/jbfa.12220

Bonito, A., & Pais, C. (2018). The macroeconomic determinants of the adoption of IFRS for SMEs. *Revista de Contabilidad*, *21*(2), 116–127. DOI: 10.1016/j.rcsar.2018.03.001

Bonsón, E., García-Borbolla, A., & Bednárová, M. (2023). IFRS for SMEs: Relevance, application and local challenges in European countries. *Journal of International Accounting Research*, *22*(1), 1–21. DOI: 10.2308/JIAR-2022-020

Boolaky, P. K., Omoteso, K., Ibrahim, M. U., & Adelopo, I. (2018). The development of accounting practices and the adoption of IFRS in selected MENA countries. *Journal of Accounting in Emerging Economies*, *8*(3), 327–351. DOI: 10.1108/JAEE-07-2015-0052

Boolaky, P. K., Tawiah, V., & Soobaroyen, T. (2020). Why do African countries adopt IFRS? An institutional perspective. ***International***. *Journal of Accountancy*, *55*(01).

Boolaky, P. K., Tawiah, V., & Soobaroyen, T. (2020). Why Do African Countries Adopt IFRS? An Institutional Perspective. *The International Journal of Accounting*, *55*(1), 2050005. Advance online publication. DOI: 10.1142/S1094406020500055

Botzem, S., Quack, S., & Zori, S. (2017). International Accounting Standards in Africa: Selective Recursivity for the 'Happy Few'? *Global Policy*, *8*(4), 553–562. DOI: 10.1111/1758-5899.12514

Boubakary, B., & Zerbib, R. (2019). Influence des modes managériales sur la culture d'entreprise: Une approche exploratoire dans le contexte camerounais. *La Revue des Sciences de Gestion*, (297–298), 33–44. DOI: 10.3917/rsg.297.0033

Braun, V., & Clarke, V. (2006). Using thematic analysis in psychology. *Qualitative Research in Psychology*, *3*(2), 77–101. DOI: 10.1191/1478088706qp063oa

British Petroleum. (2021). *Statistical review of world energy* (70th ed.). https://www.bp.com/content/dam/bp/business-sites/en/global/corporate/pdfs/energy-economics/statistical-review/bp-stats-review-2021-full-report.pdf

Brusca, I., & Condor, V. (2002). Towards the harmonisation of local accounting systems in the international context. *Financial Accountability & Management*, *18*(2), 129–162. DOI: 10.1111/1468-0408.00148

Brusca, I., & Martínez, J.-C. (2016). L'adoption des IPSAS: Un défi pour la modernisation et l'harmonisation de la comptabilité du secteur public. *Revue Internationale des Sciences Administratives, 82*(4), 761–781. DOI: 10.3917/risa.824.0761

Burlaud, A., & Colasse, B. (2010). Normalisation comptable internationale: Le retour du politique? *Comptabilité Contrôle Audit, 16*(3), 153–176. DOI: 10.3917/cca.163.0153

Bushman, R. M., & Piotroski, J. D. (2006). Financial reporting incentives for conservative accounting: The influence of legal and political institutions. *Journal of Accounting and Economics, 42*(1–2), 107–148. DOI: 10.1016/j.jacceco.2005.10.005

Callao, S., Jarne, J. I., & Laínez, J. A. (2007). Adoption of IFRS in Spain: Effect on the comparability and relevance of financial reporting. *Journal of International Accounting, Auditing & Taxation, 16*(2), 148–178. DOI: 10.1016/j.intaccaudtax.2007.06.002

Cameran, M., & Campa, D. (2020). Voluntary IFRS adoption by unlisted European firms: Impact on earnings quality and cost of debt. *The International Journal of Accounting, 55*(03), 2050013. DOI: 10.1142/S1094406020500134

Cameran, M., & Perotti, P. (2014). Audit fees and IAS/IFRS adoption: Evidence from the banking industry. *International Journal of Auditing, 18*(2), 155–169. DOI: 10.1111/ijau.12019

Camfferman, K., & Zeff, S. A. (2017). The Challenge of Setting Standards for a Worldwide Constituency: Research Implications from the IASB's Early History. *European Accounting Review, 27*(2), 289–312. DOI: 10.1080/09638180.2017.1296780

Can, G. (2021). Does Sharia compliance affect financial reporting quality? An evidence from Muslim majority countries. *International Journal of Islamic and Middle Eastern Finance and Management, 14*(1), 16–33. DOI: 10.1108/IMEFM-04-2019-0149

Caputo, F., & Pizzi, S. (2024). Bridging the gap between financial and sustainability reporting. What are the implications for sustainable development? In *The Routledge Handbook of Accounting for the Sustainable Development Goals.* Taylor and Francis; Scopus. DOI: 10.4324/9781003404118-20

Carvajal, M., & Cahan, S. (2024). International trade, mandatory IFRS adoption and financial reporting quality. *Pacific Accounting Review, 36*(2), 185–210. DOI: 10.1108/PAR-01-2023-0014

Carvalho, J. B. da C., Camões, P. J., Jorge, S. M., & Fernandes, M. J. (2007). Conformity and diversity of accounting and financial reporting practices in Portuguese local government. *Canadian Journal of Administrative Sciences / Revue Canadienne des Sciences de l'Administration*. Advance online publication. https://doi.org/DOI: 10.1002/cjas.1

Casta, J. F. (2009). Théorie positive de la comptabilité. In Colasse, B. (Ed.), *Encyclopédie de comptabilité, contrôle de gestion et audit* (pp. 1393–1402). Economica.

Castilla, A., Andreu, A., & García, I. (2021). Sustainability. The Coming Regulatory Tsunami. *EY Rethinking Sustainability*. https://www.ey.com/es_es/insights/rethinking-sustainability/sostenibilidad-tsunami-regulatorio

CDP. (2022). Disclosing through CDP. The business benefits. https://cdn.cdp.net/cdp-production/comfy/cms/files/files/000/006/049/original/CDP_Benefits_of_Disclosure_brochure_2022.pdf

CDP. CDSB, GRI, IIRC, SASB (2020). Statement of Intent to Work Together Towards Comprehensive Corporate Reporting. 11 September 2020. https://www.globalreporting.org/media/bixjk1ud/statement-of-intent-to-work-together-towards-comprehensive-corporate-reporting.pdf

Center for strategic and international studies. (2021). Supporting Small and Medium Enterprises in Sub-Saharan Africa through Blended Finance. Daniel F. Runde, Conor M. Savoy, and Janina Staguhn.

Chai, H., Tang, Q., Jiang, Y., & Lin, Z. (2010). The role of International Financial Reporting Standards in accounting quality: Evidence from the European Union. *International Journal of Financial Management and Accounting*, *21*(3), 220–278.

Chai, H., Tang, Q., Jiang, Y., & Lin, Z. (2010). The role of international financial reporting standards in accounting quality: Evidence from the European Union. *Journal of International Financial Management & Accounting*, *21*(3), 220–278. DOI: 10.1111/j.1467-646X.2010.01041.x

Chakroun, S., & Ben Amar, A. (2025). The IFRS adoption, corporate tax avoidance and the moderating effect of family ownership. *International Journal of Law and Management*, *67*(1), 16–36. DOI: 10.1108/IJLMA-06-2023-0135

Chalmers, J., Picard, N., Eastman, H., & Wilkinson, G. (2021). PwC`s Global investor survey 2021: The economic realities of ESG. PWC https://www.pwc.com/gx/en/corporate-reporting/assets/pwc-global-investor-survey-2021.pdf

Chalmers, J., Picard, N., Eastman, H., & Wilkinson, G. (2022). PwC`s Global investor survey 2022: The ESG execution gap. PWC https://www.pwc.com/gx/en/global-investor-survey/PwC-Global-Investor-Survey-2022.pdf

Chamisa, E. E. (2000). The relevance and observance of the IASC standards in developing countries and the particular case of Zimbabwe. *The International Journal of Accounting*, *35*(2), 267–286. DOI: 10.1016/S0020-7063(00)00049-2

Chan, J. L. (2010). *Government adoption of accounting standards, especially IPSAS.* http://www.jameslchan.com/papers/ChanPhDSem6.pdf

Chan, J. L. (2004). Une révolution mondiale dans la comptabilité publique? Une analyse des IPSAS et quelques recommandations. *Revue Française de Comptabilité*, (janvier), 27–31.

Chen, Y., & Rezaee, Z. (2012). The role of corporate governance in convergence with IFRS: Evidence from China. *International Journal of Accounting & Information Management.*

Chen, C., Young, D., & Zhuang, Z. (2013). Externalities of mandatory IFRS adoption: Evidence from cross-border spillover effects of financial information on investment efficiency. *The Accounting Review*, *88*(3), 881–914. DOI: 10.2308/accr-50384

Chen, J. J., & Zhang, H. (2010). The impact of regulatory enforcement and audit upon IFRS compliance–Evidence from China. *European Accounting Review*, *19*(4), 665–692. Advance online publication. DOI: 10.1080/09638180903384684

Chin, W. W. (1998). The partial least squares approach to structural equation modeling. *Modern Methods for Business Research*, 295–336.

Chourou, B. (2005). *Promoting human security: Ethical, normative and educational frameworks in the Arab states.* UNESCO.

Choy, L. Y. (2023). Climate disclosures and sustainability regulation in Southeast Asia. *Asian Journal of Accounting Research*, *8*(3), 210–227.

Christensen, H. B., Lee, E., & Walker, M. (2008). Incentives or standards: What determines accounting quality changes around IFRS adoption? *Working paper.* [PDF file]

Christensen, H. B., Lee, E., Walker, M., & Zeng, C. (2015). Incentives or standards: What determines accounting quality changes around IFRS adoption? *European Accounting Review*, *24*(1), 31–61. DOI: 10.1080/09638180.2015.1009144

Christiaens, J., Reyniers, B., & Rollé, C. (2010). Impact of IPSAS on reforming governmental financial information systems: A comparative study. *International Review of Administrative Sciences, 76*(3), 537–554. DOI: 10.1177/0020852310372449

Christiaens, J., Reyniers, B., & Rollé, C. (2010). Les conséquences des IPSAS sur la réforme des systèmes d'information financière publique: Étude comparative. *Revue Internationale des Sciences Administratives, 76*(3), 563–581. DOI: 10.3917/risa.763.0563

Christiaens, J., Vanhee, C., Manes-Rossi, F., Aversano, N., & Van Cauwenberge, P. (2014). The effect of IPSAS on reforming governmental financial reporting: An international comparison. *International Review of Administrative Sciences, 81*(1), 158–177. DOI: 10.1177/0020852314546580

Christiaens, J., Vanhee, C., Manes-Rossi, F., Aversano, N., & Van Cauwenberge, P. (2015). Les conséquences des IPSAS sur la réforme des rapports financiers du gouvernement: Comparaison internationale. *Revue Internationale des Sciences Administratives, 81*(1), 171–191. DOI: 10.3917/risa.911.0171

Chtourou, W. (2006). Le développement international des PME. *Gestion, 31*(1), 88–97. DOI: 10.3917/riges.311.0088

Chua, J. H., Steier, L. P., & Chrisman, J. J. (2006). How family firms solve intra-family agency problems using interlocking directorates: An extension. *Entrepreneurship Theory and Practice, 30*(6), 777–783. DOI: 10.1111/j.1540-6520.2006.00150.x

Ciocan, C. C., & Georgescu, I. (2019). Quality of financial reporting in Romania: Measuring qualitative characteristics pre and post IFRS adoption. *European Union Financial Regulation and Administrative Area EUFIRE, 2019*, 405–428.

Colasse, B. (2000). *Encyclopédie de comptabilité, contrôle de gestion et audit* (Vol. 1). Economica.

Colasse, B. (2004). Harmonisation comptable internationale: De la résistible ascension de l'IASC/IASB. *Gérer et Comprendre*, (75), 30–41.

Colasse, B. (2011). La crise de la normalisation comptable internationale, une crise intellectuelle. *Comptabilité Contrôle Audit, 17*(1), 157–174. DOI: 10.3917/cca.171.0155

Colibert, J., & Des Robert, J.-F. (2008). *Les normes IPSAS et le secteur public: Normes comptables applicables aux États et municipalités, établissements publics, organisations internationales*. Dunod. (Collection Management Public).

Commission Delegated Regulation (EU) 2023/2772 of 31 July 2023 supplementing Directive 2013/34/EU of the European Parliament and of the Council as regards sustainability reporting standards. 31 July 2023. https://eur-lex.europa.eu/legal-content/EN/TXT/HTML/?uri=OJ:L_202302772

Contractor, F. J., Nuruzzaman, N., Dangol, R., & Raghunath, S. (2021). How FDI inflows to emerging markets are influenced by country regulatory factors: An exploratory study. *Journal of International Management, 27*(1), 100834. DOI: 10.1016/j.intman.2021.100834

Cormier, D., Demaria, S., & Lapointe-Antunes, P. (2007). Le référentiel IFRS: Nous dirigeons-nous vers une comptabilité au-delà du réel ? *Comptabilité – Contrôle – Audit*, Numéro thématique, décembre, 43–56.

Cormier, D., Magnan, M., & Zéghal, D. (2000). Le contenu informationnel et la capacité prédictive des mesures de performance financière: Une comparaison France, États-Unis et Suisse. *Comptabilité – Contrôle – Audit, 6*(1), 77–105.

Cuijpers, R., & Buijink, W. (2005). Voluntary adoption of non-local GAAP in the European Union: A study of determinants and consequences. *European Accounting Review, 14*(3), 487–524. DOI: 10.1080/0963818042000337132

Daskalopoulos, E., Evgenidis, A., Tsagkanos, A., & Siriopoulos, C. (2016). Assessing variations in foreign direct investments under international financial reporting standards (IFRS) adoption, macro-socioeconomic developments and credit ratings. *Investment Management and Financial Innovations. Scopus., 13*(3), 328–340. Advance online publication. DOI: 10.21511/imfi.13(3-2).2016.05

Daske, H. (2006). Economic benefits of adopting IFRS or US-GAAP – Have the expected cost of equity capital really decreased? *Journal of Business Finance & Accounting, 33*(3–4), 329–373. DOI: 10.1111/j.1468-5957.2006.00611.x

Daske, H., Hail, L., Leuz, C., & Verdi, R. (2013). Adopting a label: Heterogeneity in the economic consequences around IAS/IFRS adoptions. *Journal of Accounting Research, 51*(3), 495–547. DOI: 10.1111/1475-679X.12005

de Arriba-Sellier, N. (2023). The International Regulation and Coordination of Sustainable Finance. In: Dam-de Jong, D., Amtenbrink, F. (eds) Netherlands Yearbook of International Law 2021. Netherlands Yearbook of International Law, vol 52. T.M.C. Asser Press, The Hague. https://doi.org/DOI: 10.1007/978-94-6265-587-4_8

de Brébisson, H., et alphonse, P. (2018). Diversité des politiques d'adoption des IFRS: L'harmonisation financière est-elle possible? *Comptabilité Contrôle Audit, 24*(2), 7–36. DOI: 10.3917/cca.242.0007

De George, E. T., Li, X., & Shivakumar, L. (2016). A Review of the IFRS Adoption Literature. *Review of Accounting Studies, 21*(3), 898–1004. DOI: 10.1007/s11142-016-9363-1

de Villiers, C., La Torre, M., & Molinari, M. (2022). The Global Reporting Initiative's (GRI) past, present and future: Critical reflections and a research agenda on sustainability reporting (standard-setting). *Pacific Accounting Review, 34*(5), 728–747. DOI: 10.1108/PAR-02-2022-0034

Deaconu, A., Buiga, A., & Strouhal, J. (2012). SMEs financial reporting: Attitudes towards IFRS for SMEs. *Studia Universitatis Babe -Bolyai, Oeconomica, 57*(1).

Defond, M. L. (2019). Why accounting matters: Evidence from accounting's ""big bang."' *Journal of International Accounting Research, 18*(3), 87–96. Advance online publication. DOI: 10.2308/jiar-52568

DeFond, M., Gao, X., Li, O. Z., & Xia, L. (2019). IFRS adoption in China and foreign institutional investments. *China Journal of Accounting Research, 12*(1), 1–32. DOI: 10.1016/j.cjar.2018.07.006

Degenne, A., & Forsé, M. (1994). *Social networks: A structural analysis in sociology* (U series, Sociology). Paris: Armand Colin.

Degos, J.-G., Levant, Y., & Touron, P. (2019). The history of accounting standards in French-speaking African countries since independence: The uneasy path toward IFRS. *Accounting, Auditing & Accountability Journal, 32*(1), 75–100. DOI: 10.1108/AAAJ-03-2016-2459

del Olmo, J., & López, F. (2024). Sustainability reporting standards, international harmonisation or global entanglement. *La Ley* https://dialnet.unirioja.es/servlet/articulo?codigo=9250447

Delvaille, P., Le Manh, A., & Maillet, C. (2016). Challenges and limits of applying IFRS standards to SMEs. In Burlaud, A., & Thauvron, A. (Eds.), *Accounting in action* (pp. 183–194). L'Harmattan.

Demaria, S. (2008). *Le choix d'options comptables lors de la première application des normes IAS/IFRS: Observation et compréhension des choix effectués par les groupes français* (Thèse de doctorat). Groupe de Recherche en Droit, Economie et Gestion. Université Nice Sophia Antipolis.

Depoers, F., Jeanjean, T., & Jérôme, T. (2016). Voluntary Disclosure of Greenhouse Gas Emissions: Contrasting the Carbon Disclosure Project and Corporate Reports. *Journal of Business Ethics, 134*(3), 445–461. DOI: 10.1007/s10551-014-2432-0

Devi, R., Firoz, M., & Saravanan, R. (2025). Unveiling redundancy in environmental, social, and governance reporting framework in India: An exploratory study. *Sustainability Accounting. Management and Policy Journal, 16*(2), 551–582. DOI: 10.1108/SAMPJ-10-2023-0786

Dibi, A., & Amifi, H. (2024). Evolution du système comptable marocain à la lumière de la diffusion des normes comptables internationales. In *Systèmes comptables nationaux et normes IFRS: adoption ou adaptation?* ISBN 978-9969-9723-0-6

DiMaggio, P. J., & Powell, W. W. (1983). The iron cage revisited: Institutional isomorphism and collective rationality in organizational fields. *American Sociological Review, 48*(2), 147–160. DOI: 10.2307/2095101

Ding, T., Jona, J., Potter, B., & Soderstrom, N. (2025). Are climate scenario analysis disclosures valued by investors? *Journal of Accounting and Public Policy, 51*, 107313. DOI: 10.1016/j.jaccpubpol.2025.107313

Directive (EU) 2022/2464 of the European Parliament and of the Council of 14 December 2022 amending Regulation (EU) No 537/2014, Directive 2004/109/EC, Directive 2006/43/EC and Directive 2013/34/EU, as regards corporate sustainability reporting. 14 December 2022. OJEU n. 322. https://eur-lex.europa.eu/legal-content/EN/TXT/PDF/?uri=CELEX:32022L2464

Directive 2014/95/EU of the European Parliament and of the Council of 22 October 2014 amending Directive 2013/34/EU as regards disclosure of non-financial and diversity information by certain large undertakings and groups. 22 October 2014. OJEU n. 330. https://eur-lex.europa.eu/legal-content/EN/TXT/PDF/?uri=CELEX:32014L0095

Do Hoon, K., Leem, W. B., & Yuk, J. H. (2019). The effect of IFRS adoption on the value relevance of accounting information: Evidence from South Korea. *Investment Management and Financial Innovations, 16*(2), 78–88. DOI: 10.21511/imfi.16(2).2019.07

Doan, D.-T., Nguyen, L.-N. T., & Phan, H. T. (2020). Factors affecting the application of IFRS through the perceptions of business managers and auditors in Vietnam. *Problems and Perspectives in Management. Problems and Perspectives in Management, 18*(1), 371–384. Advance online publication. DOI: 10.21511/ppm.18(1).2020.32

Donthu, N., Kumar, S., Mukherjee, D., Pandey, N., & Lim, W. M. (2021). How to conduct a bibliometric analysis: An overview and guidelines. *Journal of Business Research, 133*, 285–296. DOI: 10.1016/j.jbusres.2021.04.070

Doukakis, L. C. (2014). The effect of mandatory IFRS adoption on real and accrual-based earnings management activities. *Journal of Accounting and Public Policy, 33*(6), 551–572. DOI: 10.1016/j.jaccpubpol.2014.08.006

Doupnik, T. S., & Riccio, E. L. (2006). The influence of conservatism and secrecy on the interpretation of verbal probability expressions in the Anglo and Latin cultural areas. *The International Journal of Accounting*, *41*(3), 237–261. DOI: 10.1016/j.intacc.2006.07.005

Dumontier, P., & Raffournier, B. (1998). Why firms comply voluntarily with IAS: An empirical analysis with Swiss data. *Journal of International Financial Management & Accounting*, *9*(3), 216–245. DOI: 10.1111/1467-646X.00038

Dye, R. A. (1985). Disclosure of nonproprietary information. *Journal of Accounting Research*, *23*(1), 123–145. DOI: 10.2307/2490910

Ebaid, I. E.-S. (2023). IFRS adoption and the readability of corporate annual reports: Evidence from an emerging market. *Future Business Journal*, *9*(1), 13. Advance online publication. DOI: 10.1186/s43093-023-00244-x

Ebaid, I. E.-S. (2024). Does the implementation of IFRS improve transparency regarding the company's financial conditions?: Evidence from an emerging market. *PSU Research Review*, *8*(2), 498–513. DOI: 10.1108/PRR-11-2021-0063

Ed-Dafali, S., Adardour, Z., Derj, A., Bami, A., & Hussainey, K. (2025). A PRISMA-Based Systematic Review on Economic, Social, and Governance Practices: Insights and Research Agenda. *Business Strategy and the Environment*, *34*(2), 1896–1916. DOI: 10.1002/bse.4069

Effah, N. A. A. (2024). A bibliometric review of IFRS adoption and compliance research in Africa. *Journal of Business and Socio-economic Development*, *4*(3), 193–209. DOI: 10.1108/JBSED-01-2023-0001

EFRAG. (2021). Current Non-Financial Reporting Formats and Practices 2021. European Reporting Lab. https://www.efrag.org/sites/default/files/2024-07/EFRAG_PTF-NFRS_A6_FINAL%5B1%5D.pdf

EFRAG. (n.d.). EFRAG Sustainability Reporting Technical Group (EFRAG SR TEG). https://www.efrag.org/en/about-us/governance/efrag-sustainability-reporting-technical-expert-group-efrag-sr-teg

Eisenhardt, K. M. (1989). Building Theories from Case Study Research. *The Academy of Management Review, 14*(4), 532–550. JSTOR. DOI: 10.2307/258557

El Abbadi, A. (2011–2012). *L'adoption des normes IFRS par les groupes marocains: Les opportunités et contraintes et leurs apports à la bonne gouvernance: Cas pratique Banque Centrale Populaire* (Mémoire de master). Université My Ismail, Meknès.

El Guindy, M. N., & Trabelsi, N. S. (2020). IFRS adoption/reporting and auditor fees: The conditional effect of audit firm size and tenure. *International Journal of Accounting & Information Management, 28*(4), 639–666. DOI: 10.1108/IJAIM-09-2019-0107

El Hachimi, C., & Benthami, A. (2024). La modernisation des systèmes comptables de l'État marocain à la lumière des normes IPSAS. *European Scientific Journal, 20*(7), 155–170. DOI: 10.19044/esj.2024.v20n7p155

El Hamza, M. (2018). *La convergence du référentiel comptable marocain aux normes IFRS (analyse empirique)* (Thèse de doctorat en sciences de gestion). Groupe ISCAE.

El Quortobi, A. (2013). *Quel modèle de convergence pour le Maroc? 2ème assises de la profession comptable, mai 2013*. Skhirat.

Elemes, A., & Filip, A. (2022). Financial reporting quality and private firms' access to trade credit capital. *The International Journal of Accounting, 57*(02), 2250010. DOI: 10.1142/S109440602250010X

El-Gazzar, S. M., Finn, P. M., & Jacob, R. (1999). An empirical investigation of multinational firms' compliance with International Accounting Standards. *The International Journal of Accounting, 34*(2), 239–248. DOI: 10.1016/S0020-7063(99)00005-9

Elhamma, A. (2023). Cinquante ans des normes comptables internationales IAS/IFRS: Adoption, conséquences et où en est-on au Maroc? In R. M'Rabet & M. A. Issami (Eds.), *50 ans de management: Regards croisés d'un demi-siècle du management* (pp. 121–136).

Elhamma, A. (2023). Cinquante ans des normes comptables internationales IAS/IFRS: Adoption, conséquences et où en est-on au Maroc? In R. M'Rabet & M. A. Issami (Eds.), *50 ans de management: Regards croisés d'un demi-siècle du management* (pp. 121–136). EDISCA.

Elhamma, A. (2023). Cinquante ans des normes comptables internationales IAS/IFRS: Adoption, conséquences et où en est-on au Maroc? In R. M'Rabet & M. A. Issami (Eds.), *50 ans de management: Regards croisés d'un demi-siècle du management* (pp. 121–136). Éditions EDISCA.

Elhamma, A. (2023a). *Cinquante ans des normes comptables internationales IAS/IFRS: Adoption, conséquences et où en est-on au Maroc?* (pp. 121–136).

Elhamma, A. (2023b). *Cinquante ans des normes comptables internationales IAS/ IFRS: Adoption, conséquences et où en est-on au Maroc?* In R. M'Rabet & M. A. Issami (Eds.), *50 ans de management: Regards croisés d'un demi-siècle du management* (pp. 121–136). Éditions EDISCA.

Elhamma, A. (2023c). Fifty years of IAS/IFRS standards: Adoption, consequences, and situation in Morocco. In R. M'Rabet & M. A. Issami (Eds.), ***50 years of management*** (pp. 121–136). Éditions EDISCA.

Elhamma, A. (2025b). Perceived benefits of IFRS adoption in Morocco and French-speaking Sub-Saharan African countries. In F. Albuquerque & P. G. Dos Santos (Eds.), *Contemporary innovations in reporting and analysis* (pp. 183–210). IGI Global. https://doi.org/DOI: 10.4018/979-8-3693-5923-5.ch007

Elhamma, A., & Boutafrout, F. Z. (2025). Examining Creative Accounting as an Explanatory Factor of Taxpayer Behavior: Evidence From Morocco. In B. Alj, L. Alla, & B. Bentalha (Edts), *Modeling and Profiling Taxpayer Behavior and Compliance*, (pp. 165-184), IGI Global Scientific Pubishing. https://doi.org/DOI: 10.4018/979-8-3373-0422-9.ch007

Elhamma, A. (2012). *Comprendre les normes comptables internationales IAS/IFRS au Maroc (1re* (Edition, E. D. G. L., Ed.).

Elhamma, A. (2015). The relationship between budgetary evaluation, firm size and performance. *Journal of Management Development*, *34*(8), 973–986. DOI: 10.1108/ JMD-06-2014-0053

Elhamma, A. (2023a). Impact of mandatory IFRS adoption on economic growth: The moderating role of COVID-19 crisis in developing countries. *Journal of Accounting and Management Information Systems*, *22*(3), 554–568. DOI: 10.24818/ jamis.2023.03007

Elhamma, A. (2023c). The relationship between organisational decentralisation, balanced scorecard and its perceived benefits in Moroccan SMEs. International Journal of Accounting. *Auditing and Performance Evaluation*, *19*(2), 185–202. DOI: 10.1504/IJAAPE.2023.132384

Elhamma, A. (2024a). Determinants of national IFRS adoption: Evidence from the Middle East and North Africa region. *International Journal of Accounting. Auditing and Performance Evaluation*, *20*(1–2), 69–90. DOI: 10.1504/IJAAPE.2024.135535

Elhamma, A. (2024b). Participant observation as a qualitative research method in management sciences: Interests, conditions, and limitations. In Bentalha, B., & Alla, L. (Eds.), *Applying qualitative research methods to management science* (pp. 75–91). IGI Global., DOI: 10.4018/979-8-3693-5543-5.ch004

Elhamma, A. (2025). Perceived Benefits of IFRS Adoption in Morocco and French Speaking Sub-Saharan African Countries. In *Contemporary Innovations in Reporting and Analysis* (pp. 183–210). IGI Global Scientific Publishing.

Elhamma, A. (2025a). Impact of mandatory IFRS adoption on foreign direct investment: The moderating role of conflict of interest regulation. *Journal of Financial Reporting and Accounting*, *23*(3), 936–958. DOI: 10.1108/JFRA-04-2022-0145

Elhamma, A. (2025b). Lack of resilience and failure of SMEs in Morocco: Current situation. In Dias Rouco, J. C., & Nunes Figueiredo, P. C. (Eds.), *Improving resilience in business continuity management* (pp. 245–266). IGI Global., DOI: 10.4018/979-8-3693-8809-9.ch008

Elhamma, A. (2025c). A half-century of international accounting standards (IAS/IFRS): Assessing the mandatory adoption, impact, and Morocco's position in the convergence process. In Vardari, L., & Qabrati, I. (Eds.), *Aligning financial reporting standards with global trade needs* (pp. 185–204). IGI Global., DOI: 10.4018/979-8-3373-0887-6.ch007

Elhamma, A. (2025d). Digitalization of management control: Case of Moroccan companies. In Khalil, A., Bousselmi, H. E. W., & Ben Slimene, I. (Eds.), *Digital technologies for sustainability and quality control* (pp. 33–52). IGI Global., DOI: 10.4018/979-8-3693-4373-9.ch002

Elhamma, A., & El-Moumane, R. (2025). The role of strategic planning in resilience and crisis management: A case study of a public organization in Morocco. In Dias Rouco, J. C., & Nunes Figueiredo, P. C. (Eds.), *Enhancing resilience in business continuity management* (pp. 433–460). IGI Global., DOI: 10.4018/979-8-3693-8809-9.ch015

Elhamma, A., & Moalla, M. (2015). Impact of uncertainty and decentralization on activity-based costing use. *International Journal of Accounting and Economics Studies*, *3*(2), 148–155. DOI: 10.14419/ijaes.v3i2.4817

El-Helaly, M., Ntim, C., & Al-Gazzar, M. (2020). Diffusion theory, national corruption and IFRS adoption around the world. *Journal of International Accounting, Auditing and Taxation, 38*, 100305. Harvard Business School, available at: *SSRN*: https://ssrn.com/abstract=1590245. https://doi.org/DOI: 10.2139/ssrn.1590245

Ernst & Young. (2016). Accounting System of Enterprises and IFRS Standards for SMEs – Comparative Study, EY Tunisia Financial Reporting Group, 2016 Edition.

Expert-Comptable, T. P. E. (n.d.). *Ressources pour les petites entreprises*. Retrieved October 10, 2019, from https://www.expert-comptable-tpe.fr/

Falikou Traore, H. (2010). *Enjeux des normes IAS/IFRS pour les comptes consolidés: Cas Omnium Nord-Africain* (Mémoire de fin d'études). Université My Ismail, Meknès.

Fernández-Feijóo, B., Romero, S., & Ruiz, S. (2014). Commitment to corporate social responsibility measured through global reporting initiative reporting: Factors affecting the behaviour of companies. *Journal of Cleaner Production*, *81*, 244–254. DOI: 10.1016/j.jclepro.2014.06.034

Feudjo, J. R. (2010). Harmonisation des normes africaines (OHADA) et internationales (IAS-IFRS): Une urgence ou une exigence? *La Revue des Sciences de Gestion*, (5), 149–158. DOI: 10.3917/rsg.245.0149

Filion, L. J. (1991). Vision and relations: Elements for an entrepreneurial metamodel. *International Small Business Journal*, *9*(2), 26–42. DOI: 10.1177/026624269100900202

Florou, A., Morricone, S., & Pope, P. F. (2020). Proactive financial reporting enforcement: Audit fees and financial reporting quality effects. *The Accounting Review*, *95*(2), 167–197. DOI: 10.2308/accr-52497

Focus, I. F. R. S. (n.d.). *Site d'information sur les normes comptables internationales*. Retrieved February 22, 2020, from https://www.focusifrs.com/

Fornell, C., & Bookstein, F. L. (1982). Two structural equation models: LISREL and PLS applied to consumer exit-voice theory. *JMR, Journal of Marketing Research*, *19*(4), 440–452. DOI: 10.1177/002224378201900406

Foundation, F. R. S. (n.d.). *IFRS—International Financial Reporting Standards*. Retrieved August 1, 2019, from https://www.ifrs.org/

Francis, J., LaFond, R., Olsson, P. M., & Schipper, K. (2004). Costs of equity and earnings attributes. *The Accounting Review*, *79*(4), 967–1010. https://www.jstor.org/stable/4093083. DOI: 10.2308/accr.2004.79.4.967

Frost, C. A. (2017). Barriers to the adoption of IFRS for SMEs in developing countries. *The International Journal of Accounting*, *52*(4), 322–340. DOI: 10.1016/j.intacc.2017.10.005

Garanina, T. A., & Kormiltseva, P. S. (2013). The effect of International Financial Reporting Standards (IFRS) adoption on the value relevance of financial reporting: A case of Russia. *Research in Accounting in Emerging Economies*, *13*, 27–60. DOI: 10.1108/S1479-3563(2013)0000013007

Gardi, B., Aga, M., & Abdullah, N. N. (2023). Corporate governance and financial reporting quality: The Mediation Role of IFRS. *Sustainability (Basel)*, *15*(13), 9869. DOI: 10.3390/su15139869

Garza Sánchez, H. H., Cortez Alejandro, K. A., Méndez Sáenz, A. B., & Rodríguez García, M. D. P. (2017). Efecto en la calidad de la información ante cambios en la normatividad contable: Caso aplicada al sector real mexicano. *Contaduría y Administración*, *62*(3), 761–774. DOI: 10.1016/j.cya.2015.11.012

Gassen, J., & Sellhorn, T. (2006). Applying IFRS in Germany: Determinants and consequences. *German Economic Review*, *7*(2), 143–164.

Gaviria, D. A. G., Martínez, E. M. C., Polo, O. C. C., & Arcila, J. O. S. (2023). Accounting mechanism to measure the environmental impact of industries in the ABURRÁ VALLEY and its application of the general disclosure requirements related to financial information on sustainability (IFRS S1) and climate-related disclosures (IFRS S2). *Revista de Gestao Social e Ambiental*, *17*(5), e03639. Advance online publication. DOI: 10.24857/rgsa.v17n5-013

Gebhardt, M., Schneider, A., Siedler, F., Ottenstein, P., & Zülch, H. (2024). Climate reporting in the fast lane? The impact of corporate governance on the disclosure of climate-related risks and opportunities. *Business Strategy and the Environment*, *33*(7), 7253–7272. DOI: 10.1002/bse.3852

Ghosh, D., & Behera, A. (2020). Digital transformation in accounting: A study of cloud-based solutions in SMEs. *Journal of Accounting Technology*, *15*(2), 102–120.

Gietzmann, M. B., & Isidro, H. (2013). Institutional investors' reaction to SEC concerns about IFRS and US GAAP reporting. *Journal of Business Finance & Accounting*, *40*(7-8), 796–841. DOI: 10.1111/jbfa.12027

Golmohammadi Shuraki, M., Pourheidari, O., & Azizkhani, M. (2021). Accounting comparability, financial reporting quality and audit opinions: Evidence from Iran. *Asian Review of Accounting*, *29*(1), 42–60. DOI: 10.1108/ARA-06-2020-0087

Golubeva, O. (2020). Maximising international returns: Impact of IFRS on foreign direct investments. *Journal of Contemporary Accounting & Economics*, *16*(2), 100200. DOI: 10.1016/j.jcae.2020.100200

Gomes, L. R., & Costa, J. C. (2025). Financial reporting quality dynamics in India: The role of IFRS convergence and corporate governance. *Corporate Governance (Bradford)*, *25*(3), 441–454. DOI: 10.1108/CG-10-2023-0439

Goodwin, J., Ahmed, K., & Heaney, R. (2009). The effects of IFRS adoption and the influence of agency costs on earnings management: Evidence from Australia. *Journal of Contemporary Accounting & Economics*, *5*(2), 1–17. DOI: 10.1016/j.jcae.2009.08.001

Gordon, L. A., Loeb, M. P., & Zhu, W. (2012). The impact of IFRS adoption on foreign direct investment. *Journal of Accounting and Public Policy*, *31*(4), 374–398. DOI: 10.1016/j.jaccpubpol.2012.06.001

Gray, S. J. (1988). Towards a theory of cultural influence on the development of accounting systems internationally. *Abacus*, *24*(1), 1–15. DOI: 10.1111/j.1467-6281.1988.tb00200.x

GRI. (2024). About GRI. https://www.globalreporting.org/about-gri/

Griffiths, S. (2017). A review and assessment of energy policy in the Middle East and North Africa region. *Energy Policy*, *102*, 249–269. DOI: 10.1016/j.enpol.2016.12.023

Groebner, D. F., Shannon, P. W., Fry, P. C., & Smith, K. D. (2011). *Business Statistics: A Decision-Making Approach*. Prentice Hall/Pearson.

Grossi, G., & Soverchia, M. (2011). European Commission adoption of IPSAS to reform financial reporting. *Abacus*, *47*(4), 525–552. DOI: 10.1111/j.1467-6281.2011.00353.x

Guthrie, J. (1998). Application of accrual accounting in the Australian public sector – Rhetoric or reality. *Financial Accountability & Management*, *18*(2), 117–140. DOI: 10.1111/1468-0408.00047

Guthrie, J., Olson, O., & Humphrey, C. (1999). Debating developments in new public financial management: The limits of global theorizing and some new ways forward. *Financial Accountability & Management*, *15*(3–4), 209–228. DOI: 10.1111/1468-0408.00082

Habib, A., Bhuiyan, M. B. U., & Hasan, M. M. (2019). IFRS adoption, financial reporting quality and cost of capital: A life cycle perspective. *Pacific Accounting Review*, *31*(3), 497–522. DOI: 10.1108/PAR-08-2016-0073

Hail, L., Leuz, C., & Wysocki, P. (2010). Global accounting convergence and the potential adoption of IFRS for SMEs. *The Accounting Review*, *85*(6), 2043–2081. DOI: 10.2308/accr.2010.85.6.2043

Hail, L., Leuz, C., & Wysocki, P. D. (2010). Global accounting convergence and the potential adoption of IFRS by the U.S. (Part I): Conceptual underpinnings and economic analysis. *Accounting Horizons*, *24*(3), 355–394. DOI: 10.2308/acch.2010.24.3.355

Hand, J., & Skantz, T. (1998). The economic determinants of accounting choices: The unique case of equity carve-outs under SAB 51. *Journal of Accounting and Economics*, *24*(2), 175–203. DOI: 10.1016/S0165-4101(98)00005-6

Haoudi, K. (2015). Passage aux normes IFRS au Maroc: Fondements théoriques, intérêts et enjeux. *International Journal of Innovation and Applied Studies*, *10*(4), 1299–1311.

Hartman, L. P., Rubin, R. S., & Dhanda, K. K. (2007). The Communication of Corporate Social Responsibility: United States and European Union Multinational Corporations. *Journal of Business Ethics*, *74*(4), 373–389. DOI: 10.1007/s10551-007-9513-2

Hassan, E. A., Rankin, M., & Lu, W. (2014). The development of accounting regulation in iraq and the IFRS adoption decision: An institutional perspective. *The International Journal of Accounting*, *49*(3), 371–390. DOI: 10.1016/j.intacc.2014.07.001

Hassan, M. (2019). Analysis of effects of IFRS adoption on the comparability of financial reporting: Evidence from Saudi listed companies. *Journal of Emerging Issues in Economics. Finance and Banking*, *8*(1), 2698–2714.

Hassan, M. K. (2008). The development of accounting regulations in Egypt: Legitimating the International Accounting Standards. *Managerial Auditing Journal*, *23*(5), 467–484. DOI: 10.1108/02686900810875299

Hayat, A. (2018). FDI and economic growth: The role of natural resources? *Journal of Economic Studies (Glasgow, Scotland)*, *45*(2), 283–295. DOI: 10.1108/JES-05-2015-0082

Hedfi, M. R., & Sethom, K. (2010). *Norme IFRS pour PME: Présentation et étude d'opportunité pour la Tunisie*.

Hewa, S., Mala, R., Chen, J., & Dumay, J. (2025). Climate related disclosures and investor behaviour: An Australian study. *Advances in Accounting*, *68*, 100809. https://www.scopus.com/inward/record.uri?eid=2-s2.0-85218249704&doi=10.1016%2fj.adiac.2025.100809&partnerID=40&md5=70355b38f822282169b52235d05ca203. DOI: 10.1016/j.adiac.2025.100809

Himanshu, S., Singh, J. P., & Kumar, A. (2020). Prioritizing and establishing cause and effect relationships among financial reporting quality metrics. *Vision (Basel), 24*(3), 330–344. DOI: 10.1177/0972262920925600

Hjazeen, H., Seraj, M., & Ozdeser, H. (2021). The nexus between economic growth and unemployment in Jordan. *Future Business Journal, 7*(1), 42. DOI: 10.1186/s43093-021-00088-3

Hniche, O. (2009). Normes IAS-IFRS et analyse financière. *Revue Marocaine de Recherche en Management et Marketing*, (1), janvier.

Hoarau, C. (1995). L'harmonisation comptable internationale: Vers la reconnaissance mutuelle normative? *Comptabilité Contrôle Audit, 1*(2), 75–88. DOI: 10.3917/cca.012.0075

Hoarau, C., & Teller, R. (2007). IFRS: Les normes comptables du nouvel ordre économique global? *Comptabilité-Contrôle-Audit, 13*(3), 3–20. DOI: 10.3917/cca.133.0003

Hodgdon, C., Tondkar, R. H., Adhikari, A., & Harless, D. W. (2009). Compliance with International Financial Reporting Standards and auditor choice: New evidence on the importance of the statutory audit. *The International Journal of Accounting, 44*(1), 33–55. DOI: 10.1016/j.intacc.2008.12.003

Hofstede, G. (1980). *Culture's consequences: International differences in work-related values*. Sage Publications.

Hood, C. (1995). The "New Public Management" in the 1980s: Variations on a theme. *Accounting, Organizations and Society, 20*(2-3), 93–1009. DOI: 10.1016/0361-3682(93)E0001-W

Hope, O.-K., Jin, J., & Kang, T. (2006). Empirical evidence on jurisdictions that adopt IFRS. *Journal of International Accounting Research, 5*(2), 1–20. DOI: 10.2308/jiar.2006.5.2.1

Hopper, T., Lassou, P., & Soobaroyen, T. (2017). Globalisation, accounting and developing countries. *Critical Perspectives on Accounting, 43*, 125–148. DOI: 10.1016/j.cpa.2016.06.003

Hosseini, M. R., Martek, I., Zavadskas, E. K., Aibinu, A. A., Arashpour, M., & Chileshe, N. (2018). Critical evaluation of off-site construction research: A Scientometric analysis. *Automation in Construction, 87*, 235–247. DOI: 10.1016/j.autcon.2017.12.002

Houcine, A., Zitouni, M., & Srairi, S. (2022). The impact of corporate governance and IFRS on the relationship between financial reporting quality and investment efficiency in a continental accounting system. *EuroMed Journal of Business*, *17*(2), 246–269. DOI: 10.1108/EMJB-06-2020-0063

Houqe, M. N., van Zijl, T., Dunstan, K., & Karim, A. W. (2012). The effect of IFRS adoption and investor protection on earnings quality around the world. *The International Journal of Accounting*, *47*(3), 333–355. DOI: 10.1016/j.intacc.2012.07.003

Hsu, Y. L., & Yang, Y. C. (2022). Corporate governance and financial reporting quality during the COVID-19 pandemic. *Finance Research Letters*, *47*, 102778. DOI: 10.1016/j.frl.2022.102778 PMID: 35250396

Hulland, J. (1999). Utilisation des moindres carrés partiels (PLS) dans la recherche en gestion stratégique: Une revue de quatre études récentes. *Journal de gestion stratégique, 20*, 195–204.

Humphrey, C., Loft, A., & Woods, M. (2009). The global audit profession and the international financial architecture: Understanding regulatory relationships at a time of financial crisis. *Accounting, Organizations and Society*, *34*(6-7), 810–825. DOI: 10.1016/j.aos.2009.06.003

Iamsiraroj, S., & Ulubaşoğlu, M. A. (2015). Foreign direct investment and economic growth: A real relationship or wishful thinking? *Economic Modelling*, *51*, 200–213. DOI: 10.1016/j.econmod.2015.08.009

IASB (2009). International Financial Reporting Standard for Small and Medium-sized Entities (IFRS for SMEs).

-IASB (2016). Guide to the IFRS for SMEs.

Iatridis, G. (2010). International financial reporting standards and the quality of financial statement information. *International Review of Financial Analysis*, *19*(3), 193–204. DOI: 10.1016/j.irfa.2010.02.004

IBM. (n.d.). TCFD. https://www.ibm.com/es-es/topics/tcfd

ICAC. (2023). Sustainability Information. https://www.icac.gob.es/sostenibilidad/informacionsostenibilidad

Idrissi Chouahdi, A. (2019). *Les conditions d'applications des normes IPSAS au Maroc en comparaison avec la Belgique* [Doctoral thesis, Université de Liège]. ORBi. https://orbi.uliege.be/handle/2268/235459

IFAC & AICPA & CIMA. (2023). State of play: Sustainability Disclosure & Assurance 2019-2020. IFAC https://ifacweb.blob.core.windows.net/publicfiles/2023-12/IFAC_State%20of%20Play_Sustainability%20Disclosure%20%26%20Assurance%202019-2021_ES_Secure.pdf

IFRS Foundation (Ed.). (2020). *Due process handbook* (August 2020). IFRS Foundation Publications Department.

IFRS Foundation. (2018), Conceptual framework for financial reporting, Retrieved from https://www.ifrs.org/content/dam/ifrs/publications/pdf-standards/english/2021/issued/part-a/conceptual-framework-for-financial-reporting.pdf Isidro, H., Nanda, D., & Wysocki, P. D. (2020). On the relation between financial reporting quality and country attributes: Research challenges and opportunities. The Accounting Review, 95(3), 279-314. https://doi.org/DOI: 10.2308/accr-52607

IFRS Foundation. (2018). *Use of IFRS standards around the world.* https://www.ifrs.org/content/dam/ifrs/around-the-world/adoption/use-of-ifrs-around-the-world-overview-sept-2018.pdf

IFRS Foundation. (2018). *Use of IFRS standards around the world: Overview.* https://www.ifrs.org/content/dam/ifrs/around-the-world/adoption/use-of-ifrs-around-the-world-overview-sept-2018.pdf

IFRS Foundation. (2022). IFRS for SMEs factsheet. Retrieved April 20, 2025, from https://www.ifrs.org

IFRS Foundation. (2023). *IFRS S1 and S2: Sustainability disclosure standards.* IFRS Foundation Publications. https://www.ifrs.org

IFRS Foundation. (2024). SME Standard 2024 update. Retrieved April 19, 2025, from https://www.ifrs.org

IFRS. (2018). IFRS Foundation updates jurisdiction profiles to reflect decision by 17 African countries to adopt IFRS Standards from 2019. https://www.ifrs.org/news-and-events/news/2018/01/ifrs-foundation-updates-jurisdiction-profiles-to-reflect-decision-by-17-african-countries /

IFRS. (2020). Consultation Paper on Sustainability Reporting. *IFRS Foundation.* https://www.ifrs.org/content/dam/ifrs/project/sustainability-reporting/consultation-paper-on-sustainability-reporting.pdf

IFRS. (2023). Effects Analysis: IFRS Sustainability Disclosure Standards. *IFRS Foundation.* https://www.ifrs.org/content/dam/ifrs/project/general-sustainability-related-disclosures/effects-analysis.pdf

IFRS. (2023). Feedback Statement. IFRS Sustainability Reporting Standards. *IFRS Foundation.* https://www.ifrs.org/content/dam/ifrs/project/general-sustainability-related-disclosures/feedback-statement.pdf

IFRS. (2023). IFRS S1: General Requirements for Disclosure of Sustainability-related Financial Information. *IFRS Foundation.* https://www.ifrs.org/content/dam/ifrs/publications/pdf-standards-issb/english/2023/issued/part-a/issb-2023-a-ifrs-s1-general-requirements-for-disclosure-of-sustainability-related-financial-information.pdf

IFRS. (2023). IFRS S2: Climate-related Disclosures. *IFRS Foundation.* https://www.ifrs.org/content/dam/ifrs/publications/pdf-standards-issb/english/2023/issued/part-a/issb-2023-a-ifrs-s2-climate-related-disclosures.pdf

IFRS. (2023). Project Summary: IFRS Sustainability Disclosure Standards. *IFRS Foundation.* https://www.ifrs.org/content/dam/ifrs/project/general-sustainability-related-disclosures/project-summary.pdf

IFRS. (2024). New report sets out global progress towards both mandated and voluntary corporate climate-related disclosures. https://www.ifrs.org/news-and-events/news/2024/11/new-report-global-progress-corporate-climate-related-disclosures/?utm_source=chatgpt.com

IFRS. (2024). Progress towards adoption of ISSB Standards as jurisdictions consult. https://www.ifrs.org/news-and-events/news/2024/04/progress-towards-adoption-of-issb-standards-as-jurisdictions-consult/

IFRS. (n.d.). International Integrated Reporting. https://integratedreporting.ifrs.org/

IFRS. (n.d.). International Sustainability Standards Board. https://www.ifrs.org/groups/international-sustainability-standards-board/

IFRS. (n.d.). ISSB: Frequently Asked Questions. https://www.ifrs.org/groups/international-sustainability-standards-board/issb-frequently-asked-questions/

Ilie, E., & Miose, N.-M. (2012). IPSAS and the application of these standards in Romania. *Procedia: Social and Behavioral Sciences*, *62*, 35–39. DOI: 10.1016/j.sbspro.2012.09.008

International Accounting Standards Board. (2009). Basis of des conclusions. Available at: https://www.ifrs.org/use-around-the-world/use-of-ifrs-standards-by-jurisdiction (Accessed in 2022).

International Accounting Standards Board. (2022). International financial reporting standards for SMEs jurisdiction. Available at: https://www.ifrs.org/use-around-the-world/use-of-ifrs-standards-by-jurisdiction (Accessed in 2022).

International Federation of Accountants (IFAC). (2018). *Handbook of the International Code of Ethics for Professional Accountants.* https://www.ifac.org

International Labour Organization (ILO). (2021). *World employment and social outlook trends 2021.* International Labour Office.

International Labour Organization. (2024). *Employment trends for youth in the Middle East and North Africa.* https://doi.org/DOI: 10.54394/GFEA7064

International Monetary Fund. (2003). *Morocco: Report on the observance of standards and codes (ROSC)—Data module.* https://www.imf.org/en/Publications/CR/Issues/2016/12/30/Morocco-Report-on-the-Observance-of-Standards-and-Codes-ROSC-Data-Module-16468

International Monetary Fund. (2004). *Jordan: Report on the observance of standards and codes—Data module—Update.* https://www.imf.org/external/pubs/ft/scr/2004/cr0432.pdf

IR. (2013). The International IR Framework. Integrated Reporting. https://integratedreporting.ifrs.org/wp-content/uploads/2015/03/13-12-08-THE-INTERNATIONAL-IR-FRAMEWORK-SPANISH-1.pdf

Irvine, H. (2008). The global institutionalization of financial reporting: The case of the United Arab Emirates. *Accounting Forum, 32*(2), 125–142. DOI: 10.1016/j.accfor.2007.12.003

Jaafar, A., & El-Shawa, M. (2009). Ownership concentration, board characteristics and performance: Evidence from Jordan. In Tsamenyi, M., & Uddin, S. (Eds.), *Accounting in Emerging Economies* (Vol. 9, pp. 73–95). Emerald Group Publishing Limited., DOI: 10.1108/S1479-3563(2009)0000009005

Jayeoba, O. O., Ajibade, A. T., Olayinka, I. M., Ogundajo, G. O., & Kwarbai, J. D. (2016). Accounting standards and foreign direct investment inflows in selected African countries (1980–2015). *International Journal of Advanced Academic Research/Social and Management Sciences, 2*(10), 17–25.

Jeanjean, T. (1999). *La théorie positive de la comptabilité: Une revue de critiques. Cahier 99–12.* CEREG, Université Paris Dauphine.

Jeanjean, T., & Stolowy, H. (2008). Do accounting standards matter? An exploratory analysis of earnings management before and after IFRS adoption. *Journal of Accounting and Public Policy, 27*(6), 480–494. DOI: 10.1016/j.jaccpubpol.2008.09.008

Jensen, G. R. (2018). International Public Sector Accounting Standards (IPSAS). In Farazmand, A. (Ed.), *Global Encyclopedia of Public Administration, Public Policy, and Governance*. Springer., DOI: 10.1007/978-3-319-20928-9_2280

Jensen, M. C., & Meckling, W. H. (1976). Theory of the firm: Managerial behavior, agency costs and ownership structure. *Journal of Financial Economics, 3*(4), 305–360. DOI: 10.1016/0304-405X(76)90026-X

Johri, A. (2024). Examining the Impact of International Financial Reporting Standards Adoption on Financial Reporting Quality of Multinational Companies. *International Journal of Financial Studies, 12*(4), 96. DOI: 10.3390/ijfs12040096

Jorge, S., Brusca, I., & Nogueira, S. P. (2019). Translating IPSAS into national standards: An illustrative comparison between Spain and Portugal. *Journal of Comparative Policy Analysis, 21*(5), 445–462. Advance online publication. DOI: 10.1080/13876988.2019.1579976

Judge, W., Li, S., & Pinsker, R. (2010). National adoption of international accounting standards: An institutional perspective. Corporate Gouvernance. *International Review (Steubenville, Ohio), 18*(3), 161–174.

Judge, W., Li, S., & Pinsker, R. (2010). National adoption of international accounting standards: An institutional perspective. *Corporate Governance, 18*(3), 161–174. DOI: 10.1111/j.1467-8683.2010.00798.x

Kabir, I., & Hartini, J. (2013). Corporate governance and disclosure on segment reporting: Evidence from Nigeria. In *Global Business and Finance Research Conference, 5*(2), 98-113.

Kamal, M., & Elbeltagi, I. (2024). Challenges in IFRS implementation among Egyptian SMEs: A capability perspective. *International Journal of Accounting and Finance, 14*(2), 150–169.

Kao, T. H. W. H. S. (2014). The effect of IFRS, information asymmetry and corporate governance on the quality of accounting information. *Asian Economic and Financial Review, 4*(2), 226.

Kateb, I. (2024). The bridge to quality financial reporting: Audit committees' mediating role in IFRS implementation for emerging markets. *Journal of Corporate Accounting & Finance, 35*(1), 250–268. DOI: 10.1002/jcaf.22664

Katz, M. L., & Shapiro, C. (1985). Network externalities, competition, and compatibility. *The American Economic Review*, *75*, 424–440.

Kaufmann, D., Kraay, A., & Mastruzzi, M. (2007). *Worldwide Governance Indicators 2006*. World Bank.

Kaya, M., & Koch, D. (2015). Countries' adoption of the International Financial Reporting Standard for Small and Medium-sized Entities (IFRS for SMEs) – Early empirical evidence. *Accounting and Business Research, 45*(1), 93–120. DOI: 10.1080/00014788.2014.969188

Khattabi, L., & Elmallouki, L. (2023). Le passage aux normes IPSAS au Maroc: Vers un nouveau mode de gestion des finances publiques. *International Journal of Accounting, Finance, Auditing, Management and Economics, 4*(3–1), 466–480. https://doi.org/DOI: 10.5281/zenodo.8064041

Khlif, H., Kamran, A., & Manzurul, A. (2020). Accounting regulations and IFRS adoption in francophone North African countries: The experience of Algeria, Morocco, and Tunisia. *The International Journal of Accounting*, *55*(1), 2050004. Advance online publication. DOI: 10.1142/S1094406020500043

Kholeif, A. (2010). A new institutional analysis of ifrss adoption in egypt: A case study of loosely coupled rules and routines. In *Research in Accounting in Emerging Economies* (Vol. 10). https://doi.org/DOI: 10.1108/S1479-3563

Khouatra, D. (2005). Le système comptable malgache entre modèle anglo-saxon et modèle continental. *Congrès de l'AFC*, Lille, 11–13 mai.

Khouatra, D. (2014). Évolution et diversité des systèmes comptables francophones. *Congrès de l'AFC*, Lille, mai.

Khouatra, D., & Merhoum, M. E. H. (2017). Élaboration et mise en œuvre d'un système comptable hybride par intégration de normes comptables internationales IAS-IFRS: Cas du système comptable financier algérien. *AFC Afrique – 2ème JEACC*.

Kilic, M., & Uyar, A. (2014). Adoption process of IFRS for SMEs in Turkey: Insights from field research. *Accounting and Management Information Systems, 13*(3), 492–519.

Kiliç, M., Uyar, A., & Ataman, B. (2016). Preparedness of the entities for the IFRS for SMEs: An emerging country case. *Journal of Accounting in Emerging Economies*, *6*(2), 156–1. DOI: 10.1108/JAEE-01-2014-0003

Kim, J. B., Liu, X., & Zheng, L. (2012). The impact of mandatory IFRS adoption on audit fees: Theory and evidence. *The Accounting Review*, *87*(6), 2061–2094. DOI: 10.2308/accr-50223

Klish, A. A., Shubita, M. F. S., & Wu, J. (2022). IFRS adoption and financial reporting quality in the MENA region. *Journal of Applied Accounting Research*, *23*(3), 570–603. DOI: 10.1108/JAAR-08-2020-0155

Koleśnik, K. (2013). The role of culture in accounting in the light of Hofstede's, Gray's and Schwartz's cultural dimensions theories: A literature review. *Journal of Modern Accounting and Auditing*, *9*(10), 1365–1375.

Kosmidou, K., Kousenidis, D., Ladas, A., & Negkakis, C. (2020). Regulation of capital flows: Effects on liquidity and the role of financial reporting quality. *Journal of Economic Behavior & Organization*, *175*, 86–97. DOI: 10.1016/j.jebo.2020.04.005

Kossentini, A., & Ben Othman, H. (2014). A study of the institutional and economic determinants of IFRS adoption in emerging economies. *Business Illinois*. Available at: https://business.illinois.edu

Kothari, C. R. (2001). *Research methodology: Methods and techniques* (2nd rev. ed.). New Age International Publishers.

KPMG. (2022). Big shifts, small steps. Survey of Sustainability Reporting 2022. *KPMG*. https://assets.kpmg.com/content/dam/kpmg/xx/pdf/2022/10/ssr-small-steps-big-shifts.pdf

Kumari, R., & Naresh, G. (2023). Adoption of International Financial Reporting Standards and its effect on quality of financial reporting-a bibliometric study. *International Journal of Managerial and Financial Accounting*, *15*(3), 255–281. DOI: 10.1504/IJMFA.2023.131760

Kumar, S., & Singh, M. (2020). Bridging the education gap: Implementing IFRS for SMEs in India. *International Journal of Accounting Education*, *18*(3), 239–253.

Laouane, A. (2023). Informations financières issues du référentiel international et performance financière: Analyse de l'impact des IFRS sur la valeur des indicateurs comptables et boursiers. *Alternatives Managériales Economiques*, *5*(3), 200–218. https://doi.org/DOI: 10.48374/IMIST.PRSM/ame-v5i3.41917

Laouane, A., & El Hijazi, M. (2024). Le passage aux IFRS par les entreprises marocaines: Contexte d'avènement, voies de recherche et principales divergences par rapport au CGNC. *Revue de Gestion et d'Économie*, *1*(1), 91–108. DOI: 10.34874/PRSM.jbe.48062

Lee, S. J., Kang, S. J., & Lee, S. (2024). Economic, social and institutional determinants of FDI inflows: A comparative analysis of developed and developing economies. *Transnational Corporations Review, 16*(3), 200074. DOI: 10.1016/j.tncr.2024.200074

Lenormand, G., Bessieux-Ollier, C., & Piot, C. (2012). Les IAS/IFRS: Bilan et perspectives. *Revue Française de Gestion, 38*(222), 55–66. DOI: 10.3166/rfg.222.55-66

Lenormand, G., & Touchais, L. (2009). Les IFRS améliorent-elles la qualité de l'information financière? Approche par la value relevance. *Comptabilité Contrôle Audit, 15*(2), 145–164. DOI: 10.3917/cca.152.0145

Levitt, A. (1998). The importance of high quality accounting standards. *Accounting Horizons, 12*(2), 79–82. https://www.proquest.com/openview/113ef6fb20852f7024ae491923c7e84c/1?cbl=3330&pq-origsite=gscholar

Lin, S., Riccardi, W., & Wang, C. (2012). Does accounting quality change following a switch from US GAAP to IFRS? Evidence from Germany. *Journal of Accounting and Public Policy, 31*(6), 641–657. DOI: 10.1016/j.jaccpubpol.2012.10.006

Liu, H., & Lee, H. (2024). The Role of Ownership Structure in the Relationship Between Environmental, Social, and Governance Practices and Financial Reporting Quality: Evidence from China. *Sustainability (Basel), 16*(23), 10687. Advance online publication. DOI: 10.3390/su162310687

Liu, J., & Liu, C. (2007). Value relevance of accounting information in different stock market segments: The case of Chinese A-, B-, and H-shares. *Journal of International Accounting Research, 6*(2), 55–81. DOI: 10.2308/jiar.2007.6.2.55

Lohmöller, J. B. (1989). *Latent variable path modeling with partial least squares.* Springer., DOI: 10.1007/978-3-642-52512-4

Lopez, D. M., Schuldt, M. A., & Vega, J. G. (2022). Do industry specialist auditors enhance accounting quality in the EU? Evidence from the pre-IFRS and mandatory post-IFRS periods. *Asian Review of Accounting, 30*(4), 398–431. DOI: 10.1108/ARA-04-2022-0077

Lüder, K. (2000). National accounting, governmental accounting and cross-country comparisons of government financial condition. *Financial Accountability & Management, 16*(2), 117–128. DOI: 10.1111/1468-0408.00100

Lüder, K., & Jones, R. (2003). *Reforming governmental accounting and budgeting in Europe*. Fachverlag Moderne Wirtschaft.

Lungu, C. I., Caraiani, C., & Dascălu, C. (2017). The impact of IFRS adoption on foreign direct investments: Insights for emerging countries. *Accounting in Europe, 14*(3), 331–357. DOI: 10.1080/17449480.2017.1374546

Madawaki, A. (2014). Adoption of IFRS for SMEs in Nigeria: Perception of professional accountants. *International Journal of Business and Management, 9*(1), 89–99. DOI: 10.5539/ijbm.v9n1p89

Mahmoodi, M., & Mahmoodi, E. (2016). Foreign direct investment, exports and economic growth: Evidence from two panels of developing countries. *Ekonomska Istrazivanja, 29*(1), 938–949. DOI: 10.1080/1331677X.2016.1164922

Mahmood, K., Barghathi, Y., & Lasyoud, A. A. (2021). Exploring the potentials of clawbacks to check earnings management practices and enhance financial reporting quality: Perceptions from the UAE. *Qualitative Research in Financial Markets, 13*(3), 359–382. DOI: 10.1108/QRFM-05-2020-0081

Ma, L., Ma, T., & Friedman, H. L. (2021). Financial reporting quality and noise in stock returns: Evidence from Chinese AB Twin shares. *Journal of Financial Reporting, 6*(1), 137–162. DOI: 10.2308/JFR-2019-0019

Mameche, Y., & Masood, A. (2021). Macroeconomic evidence on the impact of mandatory IFRS adoption on FDI in the Gulf Cooperation Council (GCC) countries. *Journal of Accounting in Emerging Economies, 11*(4), 610–631. DOI: 10.1108/JAEE-04-2020-0084

Manawadu, I., Che Azmi, A., & Mohamed, A. (2019). Moderating effect of IFRS adoption on FDI and conditional accounting conservatism in South Asia. *Journal of Accounting in Emerging Economies, 9*(1), 51–74. DOI: 10.1108/JAEE-03-2017-0035

Marchal, S., Boukari, M., & Cayssials, J. L. (2007). L'impact des normes IAS/IFRS sur les données comptables des groupes français. *Bulletin de la Banque de France, 163*, 43–54.

Marien, B., & Beaud, J.-P. (2003). *Guide pratique pour l'utilisation de la statistique en recherche: Le cas des petits échantillons*. Réseau sociolinguistique et dynamique des langues, Agence Universitaire de la Francophonie.

Marquez-Ramos, L. (2008). The effect of IFRS adoption on trade and foreign direct investments. *International Trade and Finance Association Conference Papers,* 19.

Marquez-Ramos, L. (2008). The effect of IFRS adoption on trade and foreign direct investments. *International Trade and Finance Association Conference Papers, bepress*(19).

Masoud, N. (2017). The effects of mandatory IFRS adoption on financial analysts' forecast: Evidence from Jordan. *Cogent Business & Management*, *4*(1), 1–18. DOI: 10.1080/23311975.2017.1290331

Mbir, D. E. G., Agyemang, O. S., Tackie, G., & Abeka, M. J. (2020). IFRS compliance, corporate governance and financial reporting quality of GSE-listed non-financial firms. *Cogent Business & Management*, *7*(1), 1759856. DOI: 10.1080/23311975.2020.1759856

Medisoa (2023). Key sustainability reporting standards. https://medisoa.com/principales-estandares-para-el-reporte-de-sostenibilidad/

Mensah, E. (2021). The effect of IFRS adoption on financial reporting quality: Evidence from listed manufacturing firms in Ghana. *Economic research-. Ekonomska Istrazivanja*, *34*(1), 2890–2905. DOI: 10.1080/1331677X.2020.1860109

Meyer, J. W., & Rowan, B. (1977). Institutionalized Organizations: Formal Structure as Myth and Ceremony. *American Journal of Sociology*, *83*(2), 340–363. DOI: 10.1086/226550

Mhaka, C. (2014). IPSAS, a guaranteed way of quality government financial reporting? A comparative analysis of the existing cash accounting and IPSAS-based accounting reporting. *International Journal of Finance & Economics*, *3*(3), 134–141.

Mhedhbi, Z., & Essid, A. (2022). National cultural dimensions and adoption of the International Financial Reporting Standard (IFRS) for Small and Medium-sized Entities (SMEs). *The International Journal of Accounting*, *57*(1), 2250004. DOI: 10.1142/S1094406022500044

Misini, S., & Badivuku-Pantina, M. (2017). The effect of economic growth in relation to unemployment. *Journal of Economics and Economic Education Research*, *18*(2), 1–9.

Mita, A., Utama, S., Fitriany, F., & Wulandari, E. R. (2018). The adoption of IFRS, comparability of financial statements and foreign investors' ownership. *Asian Review of Accounting*, *26*(3), 391–410. DOI: 10.1108/ARA-04-2017-0064

Mohseni, M., & Jouzaryan, F. (2016). Examining the effects of inflation and unemployment on economic growth in Iran (1996–2012). *Procedia Economics and Finance*, *36*, 381–389. DOI: 10.1016/S2212-5671(16)30050-8

Moore, M. H. (1995). *Creating public value: Strategic management in government*. Harvard University Press.

Morshed, A. (2024). Assessing the Economic Impact of IFRS Adoption on Financial Transparency and Growth in the Arab Gulf Countries. *Economies. Scopus., 12*(8), 209. Advance online publication. DOI: 10.3390/economies12080209

Moukil, A. (2011). *L'impact des normes IFRS sur les banques: Cas du passage aux normes IFRS dans la BMCE Bank* (Master's thesis). Université My Ismail, Meknès.

Mou, R., & Ma, T. (2023). A Study on the Quality and Determinants of Climate Information Disclosure of A-Share-Listed Banks. *Sustainability (Basel), 15*(10), 8072. Advance online publication. DOI: 10.3390/su15108072

Moussa, M. A. (2020). Les déterminants de la résistance à la production et à la publication des informations comptables et financières dans les entreprises au Tchad. *Revue de Consolidation Comptable et de Management de la Performance*, (5).

Murphy, K. J. (1999). Executive compensation. Handbook of labor economics, 3, 2485-2563.

Musah, A., Adjei, E., & Ahmed, I. A. (2020). The effect of IFRS adoption on foreign direct investment in Africa. *Journal of Applied Accounting and Taxation, 5*(2), 117–126. DOI: 10.30871/jaat.v5i2.1481

Nahmias, M. (2004). *L'essentiel des normes IAS/IFRS*. Éditions d'Organisation.

Nam, H.-J., & Ryu, D. (2023). FDI and human development: The role of governance, ODA, and national competitiveness. *Journal of International Financial Markets, Institutions and Money, 85*, 101769. DOI: 10.1016/j.intfin.2023.101769

Nejad, M. Y., Ahmad, A., Salleh, M. F. M., & Rahim, R. A. (2018). International financial reporting standards foreign direct investment in ASEAN countries. *Gadjah Mada International Journal of Business, 20*(3), 303–329.

Nguyen, H. T. T., Nguyen, H. T. T., & Nguyen, C. V. (2023). Analysis of factors affecting the adoption of IFRS in an emerging economy. *Heliyon, 9*(6), e17331. DOI: 10.1016/j.heliyon.2023.e17331 PMID: 37389083

Nielsen, C. (2023). ESG Reporting and Metrics: From Double Materiality to Key Performance Indicators. *Sustainability (Basel), 15*(24), 16844. Advance online publication. DOI: 10.3390/su152416844

Nnadi, M., & Soobaroyen, T. (2015). International financial reporting standards and foreign direct investment: The case of Africa. *Advances in Accounting, 31*(2), 228–238. DOI: 10.1016/j.adiac.2015.09.007

Nobes, C. (1983). A judgmental international classification of financial reporting practices. *Journal of Business Finance & Accounting, 10*(1), 1–19. DOI: 10.1111/j.1468-5957.1983.tb00409.x

Nobes, C. (2017). The development and adoption of IFRS for SMEs: An overview. *Journal of Financial Reporting and Accounting, 15*(2), 127–139. DOI: 10.1108/JFRA-01-2016-0002

Nobes, C. W., & Zeff, S. A. (2016). Have Canada, Japan and Switzerland Adopted IFRS? *Australian Accounting Review, 26*(3), 284–290. DOI: 10.1111/auar.12131

Nobes, C., & Parker, R. (2006). *Comparative international accounting* (9th ed.). Prentice Hall.

Nunnally, J. C. (1978). *Psychometric theory* (2nd ed.). McGraw-Hill.

Nurunnabi, M. (2021). Implementation of international financial reporting standards (IFRS) in developing countries. In *International financial reporting standards implementation: A global experience (Contributions to International Accounting)* (pp. 11–76). Emerald Publishing. https://doi.org/DOI: 10.1108/978-1-80117-440-420211002

Obert, R. (2009). Des IFRS pour les PME. Revue Française de Comptabilité, 424.

Oduware U. (2012), IFRS Adoption in Nigeria and Optimizing the Gains of Global Investment Climate Akintola Williams Deloitte, 1-15.

Ofoegbu, G. N. (2014). New public management and accrual accounting basis for transparency and accountability in the Nigerian public sector. *IOSR Journal of Business and Management, 16*(7), 104–113. DOI: 10.9790/487X-1673104113

Okoh, L., & Ohwoyibo, O. (2010). Public Accountability: Vehicle for Socio- Economic Development of Nigeria. *International Journal of Investment and Finance, 3*(1&2), 145–149.

Okpala, K. E. (2012). Adoption of IFRS and financial statements effects: The perceived implications on FDI and Nigeria economy. *Australian Journal of Business and Management Research, 2*(5), 76–83. DOI: 10.52283/NSWRCA.AJBMR.20120205A10

Okun, A. (1962). Potential GNP: Its measurement and significance. In *The 1962 proceedings of business and economic statistics section*. American Statistical Association.

Oliveira, M. C., Ceglia, D., & Filho, F. A. (2016). Analysis of corporate governance disclosure: A study through BRICS countries. *Corporate Governance (Bradford), 16*(5), 923–940. DOI: 10.1108/CG-12-2015-0159

Oluwagbemiga, O. E. (2021). The influence of IFRS adoption on the quality of financial reporting in Nigerian listed companies. In Lee, C.-F., & Yu, M.-T. (Eds.), *Advances in Pacific Basin Business, Economics and Finance* (Vol. 9, pp. 137–160). Emerald Publishing Limited., DOI: 10.1108/S2514-465020210000009005

Önce, S., & Çavuş, G. (2019). Evaluation of the Effects of Corporate Governance on Financial Reporting Quality. *Journal of Modern Accounting and Auditing, 15*(8), 385–395.

Oppong, C., & Aga, M. (2019). Economic growth in the European Union: Does IFRS mandatory adoption matter? *International Journal of Emerging Markets, 14*(5), 792–808. DOI: 10.1108/IJOEM-01-2018-0010

Osinubi, I. S. (2020). The three pillars of institutional theory and IFRS implementation in Nigeria. *Journal of Accounting in Emerging Economies, 10*(4), 575–599. DOI: 10.1108/JAEE-07-2019-0139

Ouarab, A., & Kaci, S. (2024). La comptabilité en normes IFRS: les chiffres et la valeur boursière de l'entreprise. In *Les systèmes comptables nationaux et les normes IFRS: adoption ou adaptation?* ISBN 978-9969-9723-0-6.

Oubahou, Y., & El Ouafa, K. (2024). The effect of adopting IFRS on the relevance of information: The case of Moroccan companies. *Investment Management and Financial Innovations, 21*(2), 361–373. DOI: 10.21511/imfi.21(2).2024.32

Oubahou, Y., El Ouafa, K., & Bengrich, M. (2025). The impact of IFRS adoption on the relevance of financial reporting in emerging markets: The case of Moroccan listed companies. *EuroMed Journal of Business*. Advance online publication. DOI: 10.1108/EMJB-05-2024-0128

Outa, E., Ozili, P. K., & Eisenberg, P. (2017). IFRS convergence and revisions: Value relevance of accounting information quality from East Africa. *Journal of Accounting in Emerging Economies, 7*(3), 352–368. DOI: 10.1108/JAEE-11-2014-0062

Outellou, S., Taouab, O., & Abdelbaki, N. (2023). Les Déterminants de l'Adoption des IFRS par les Entreprises: Cas du Maroc. *European Scientific Journal, 19*(13), 13. Advance online publication. DOI: 10.19044/esj.2023.v19n13p158

Ouvrard, S. (2010). *IFRS for SMEs*. 17th IAE–Chartered Accountants Conference, Toulouse.

Owusu, G. M. Y., Suppiah, S. D. K., Saat, N. A. M., & Law, S. H. (2022). IFRS adoption and economic growth in developing economies. *International Journal of Economics and Accounting, 11*(1), 73–98. DOI: 10.1504/IJEA.2022.119613

Owusu, G. M., Saat, N. A. M., Suppiah, S. D. K., & Siong, H. L. (2017). IFRS adoption, institutional quality, and foreign direct investment inflows: A dynamic panel analysis. *Asian Journal of Business and Accounting, 10*(2), 43–75.

Owusu, G., Yaw, M., Saat, N. A. M., Suppiah, S. D., & Hook, L. S. (2017). Do accounting standards matter for foreign direct investment in developing countries? *International Journal of Economics & Management, 11*(S3), 891–915.

Özcan, A. (2016). Assessing the effects of IFRS adoption on economic growth: A cross-country study. *ACU International Journal of Social Sciences, 2*(2), 65–80. DOI: 10.22466/acusbd.v2i2.5000202321

Pacter, P. (2005). What exactly is convergence? *International Journal of Accounting. Auditing and Performance Evaluation, 2*(1/2), 67–83. DOI: 10.1504/IJAAPE.2005.006893

Palea, V. (2013). IAS/IFRS and financial reporting quality: Lessons from the European experience. *China Journal of Accounting Research, 6*(4), 247–263. DOI: 10.1016/j.cjar.2013.08.003

Păşcan, I.-D. (2015). Measuring the effects of IFRS adoption on accounting quality: A review. *Procedia Economics and Finance, 32*, 580–587. DOI: 10.1016/S2212-5671(15)01435-5

Paul, J., Lim, W. M., O'Cass, A., Hao, A. W., & Bresciani, S. (2021). Scientific procedures and rationales for systematic literature reviews (SPAR-4-SLR). *International Journal of Consumer Studies, 45*(4), O1–O16. DOI: 10.1111/ijcs.12695

Perera, H., & Chand, P. (2015). Issues in the adoption of IFRS in less developed countries. *Qualitative Research in Accounting & Management, 12*(3), 233–250. DOI: 10.1108/QRAM-02-2013-0012

Phuong, N. C., & Nguyen, T. D. (2012). International harmonization and national particularities of accounting: Recent accounting development in Vietnam. *Journal of Accounting and Organizational Change, 8*(3), 431–451. DOI: 10.1108/18325911211258371

Pina, V., & Torres, L. (2003). Reshaping public sector accounting: An international comparative view. *Canadian Journal of Administrative Sciences, 20*(4), 334–350. DOI: 10.1111/j.1936-4490.2003.tb00709.x

Plihon, D. (2007). Les nouvelles normes comptables internationales: Une réforme aux implications considérables. *Economics and Politics, 36*(36), 74–80. DOI: 10.3917/leco.036.0074

Pohlan, L. (2019). Unemployment and social exclusion. *Journal of Economic Behavior & Organization, 164*, 273–299. DOI: 10.1016/j.jebo.2019.06.006

Pollitt, C., & Bouckaert, G. (2011). *Public management reform: A comparative analysis—New Public Management, governance, and the Neo-Weberian State* (3rd ed.). Oxford University Press.

Pratama, A., Dewi, N., Sofia, P., Muhammad, K., & Megawati, L. R. (2024). Sustainability Reporting Ecosystem and IFRS S1 and S2: How Accounting Research Can Assist its Implementation. *Journal of Ecohumanism*, *3*(4), 3101–3168. DOI: 10.62754/joe.v3i4.3830

Pratama, A., Jaenudin, E., & Anas, S. (2022). Environmental, Social, Governance-Sustainability Disclosure Using International Financial Reporting Sustainability Standards S1 in Southeast Asian Companies: A Preliminary Assessment. *International Journal of Energy Economics and Policy*, *12*(6), 456–472. DOI: 10.32479/ijeep.13581

Pricope, C. F. (2017). The implications of IFRS adoption on foreign direct investment in poor countries. *Audit Financiar, 15*(146).

Psaros, J., & Trotman, K. (2004). The impact of the type of accounting standards on preparers judgments. *Abacus International Journal of Accounting. Finance and Business Studies*, *40*(1), 76–93.

PWC. (2024). SEC adopts climate-related disclosure rules. https://viewpoint.pwc.com/dt/us/en/pwc/in_briefs/2024/2024-in-brief/ib202402.html

Raffournier, B. (2009). IFRS et gouvernance d'entreprise: un cercle vertueux ? ». DerSchweizerTreuhänder = L'expert-comptable suisse, 11, 802-809.

Raffournier, B. (1995). The determinants of voluntary financial disclosure by Swiss listed companies. *European Accounting Review*, *4*(2), 261–280. DOI: 10.1080/09638189500000016

Raffournier, B. (2007). Les oppositions françaises à l'adoption des IFRS: Examen critique et tentative d'explication. *Comptabilité Contrôle Audit*, *13*(3), 21–41. DOI: 10.3917/cca.133.0021

Ramangalahy, C. (2001). Capacité d'absorption de l'information, compétitivité et performance des PME exportatrices: Une étude empirique (Absorptive capacity of information, competitiveness, and exporting SMEs' performance: Empirical study). Doctoral dissertation, University of Montréal, Montréal.

Ramanna, K., & Sletten, E. (2014). Network effects in countries' adoption of IFRS. *The Accounting Review*, *89*(4), 1517–1543. DOI: 10.2308/accr-50717

Raman, R., Subramaniam, N., Nair, V. K., Shivdas, A., Achuthan, K., & Nedungadi, P. (2022). Women entrepreneurship and sustainable development: Bibliometric analysis and emerging research trends. *Sustainability (Basel)*, *14*(15), 9160. DOI: 10.3390/su14159160

Ramond, O., Paugam, L., Casta, J. F., & Batsch, L. (2012). *Évaluation financière et normes comptables*. Economica.

Rani, R., Vasishta, P., Singla, A., & Tanwar, N. (2025). Mapping ESG and CSR literature: A bibliometric study of research trends and emerging themes. *International Journal of Law and Management*. DOI: 10.1108/IJLMA-09-2024-0301

Rashmi, K., & Kataria, A. (2021). Work–life Balance: A Systematic Literature Review and Bibliometric Analysis. *The International Journal of Sociology and Social Policy*, *42*(11/12), 1028–1065. DOI: 10.1108/IJSSP-06-2021-0145

Rechka, F., & Kabbaj, S. (2019). Les normes IPSAS et le passage d'une comptabilité de caisse à une comptabilité d'exercice au Maroc. *Revue du contrôle, de la comptabilité et de l'audit, 3*(4), 649–678.

Rehman, N. U. (2016). FDI and economic growth: Empirical evidence from Pakistan. *Journal of Economic and Administrative Sciences*, *32*(1), 63–76. DOI: 10.1108/JEAS-12-2014-0035

Riccardi, W. N. (2019). Do audit firm tenure and size moderate changes in financial reporting quality due to mandatory IFRS adoption? *Auditing*, *38*(4), 201–224. DOI: 10.2308/ajpt-52406

Ritsumeikan, L. (2011). An institutional perspective on international financial reportingstandards adoption in developing countries. *Academy of Accounting and Financial Studies Journal*, *15*(2), 61–71.

Robey, D. (1986). Evaluating the organizational impact of computer-based information systems. *Accounting Management and Information Technologies*, *1*(1), 3–15. DOI: 10.1016/0959-8022(86)90005-6

Robinson, T. R., & Henry, E. (2009). International financial statement analysis. CFA Institute Investment Series. Retrieved from https://books.mec.biz/tmp/books/G2L68QLOCEX7RSFY1UU1.pdf

Rodrigues, L. L., Schmidt, P., & dos Santos, J. L. (2012). The origins of modern accounting in Brazil: Influences leading to the adoption of IFRS. *Research in Accounting Regulation*, *24*(1), 15–24. DOI: 10.1016/j.racreg.2011.12.003

Rogers, E. M. (1962). *Diffusion of Innovations*. Free Press.

Roje, G., Vasiček, V., & Hladika, M. (2012). The perspectives of IPSASs introduction in Croatian public sector. *International Journal of Public Sector Performance Management*, *2*(1), 25–43. DOI: 10.1504/IJPSPM.2012.048742

Roy, J. K., & Vasa, L. (2025). Financial technology and environmental, social and governance in sustainable finance: A bibliometric and thematic content analysis. *Discover Sustainability*, *6*(1), 148. Advance online publication. DOI: 10.1007/s43621-025-00934-2

Sadiku, M., Ibraimi, A., & Sadikucal, L. (2015). Econometric estimation of the relationship between unemployment rate and economic growth of FYR of Macedonia. *Procedia Economics and Finance*, *19*, 69–81. DOI: 10.1016/S2212-5671(15)00009-X

SAFA (South Asian Federation of Accountants). (2006). *A study on accrual-based accounting for governments and public sector entities in SAARC countries*. South Asian Federation of Accountants.

Saji, T. G. (2022). Asymmetric financial reporting quality and firm size: Conditional evidence from an emerging market. *Journal of Applied Accounting Research*, *23*(5), 977–1004. DOI: 10.1108/JAAR-10-2021-0264

Samaha, K., & Khlif, H. (2016). Adoption of and compliance with IFRS in developing countries: A synthesis of theories and directions for future research. *Journal of Accounting in Emerging Economies*, *6*(1), 33–49. DOI: 10.1108/JAEE-02-2013-0011

Scheel, P. (2024). The potential of dual materiality in CSRD. *Magnus Commodities*. https://magnuscmd.com/es/el-potencial-de-la-doble-materialidad-en-la-csrd/

Schipper, K. (1991). Commentary on earnings management. *Accounting Horizons*, *5*(4), 91–102.

Securities and Exchange Commission. The Enhacement and Standardization of Climate-Related Disclosures for Investors. March 6, 2024. https://www.sec.gov/files/rules/final/2024/33-11275.pdf

Sellami, Y. M., & Gafsi, Y. (2018). What drives developing and transitional countries to adopt the IFRS for SMEs? An institutional perspective. *Journal of Corporate Accounting & Finance*, *29*(2), 34–56. DOI: 10.1002/jcaf.22331

Shao, M., & Xue, M. (2024). Firms' voluntary climate action disclosures and stock market reaction: A BERT-based analysis of earnings conference calls in China. *Journal of Climate Finance, 8,* 100047. DOI: 10.1016/j.jclimf.2024.100047

Sharairi, M. H. (2018). Factors that influenced the adoption of IFRS by Islamic banks in the UAE. *Accounting Research Journal, 33*(1), 75–91. DOI: 10.1108/ARJ-11-2017-0185

Shima, K. M., & Yang, D. C. (2012). Factors affecting the adoption of IFRS. *International Journal of Business, 17*(3), 276–298.

Sidley (2025). SEC Ends Defense of Climate-Related Disclosure Rules. https://www.sidley.com/en/insights/newsupdates/2025/04/sec-ends-defense-of-climate-related-disclosure-rules

Siggelkow, N. (2007). Persuasion with case studies. *Academy of Management Journal, 50*(1), 20–24. DOI: 10.5465/amj.2007.24160882

Silva, A., Jorge, S., Rodrigues, L. L., & Proença, C. (2025). The role of internal and external enforcers in enhancing financial reporting quality. *Journal of Accounting & Organizational Change*.DOI: 10.1108/JAOC-01-2024-0027

Simionescu, M., & Naros, M. S. (2019). The role of foreign direct investment in human capital formation for a competitive labour market. *Management Research and Practice, 11*(1), 5–14.

Simnett, R., Tan, Y., You, J., & Zhou, S. (2025). Australian Listed Entities' Preparedness for Mandatory Reporting and Assurance of Climate-related Disclosures. *Abacus*. https://www.scopus.com/inward/record.uri?eid=2-s2.0-85219160823&doi=10.1111%2fabac.12363&partnerID=40&md5=e4e09238299c6eadf40fe895aea27427

Soderstrom, N. S., & Sun, K. J. (2007). IFRS adoption and accounting quality: A review. *European Accounting Review, 16*(4), 675–702. DOI: 10.1080/09638180701706732

Stolowy, H., Lebas, M. J., & Langois, G. (2006). *Comptabilité et analyse financière: Une perspective globale* (1re éd.). Belgique: De Boeck & Larcier.

Street, D. L., & Gordon, E. A. (2023). An interview with IASB Chair Dr. Andreas Barckow. *Journal of International Financial Management and Accounting. 34*(2), 358–377. Advance online publication. DOI: 10.1111/jifm.12171

Suta, A., Molnár, P., Limbach, Z., & Tóth, Á. (2025). Dictionary-based assessment of European Sustainability Reporting Standard (ESRS) disclosure topics. *Discover Sustainability, 6*(1), 146. Advance online publication. DOI: 10.1007/s43621-025-00930-6

Tag, M. N., & Degirmen, S. (2022). Economic freedom and foreign direct investment: Are they related? *Economic Analysis and Policy, 73*, 737–752. DOI: 10.1016/j.eap.2021.12.020

Tahat, Y., Omran, M. A., & AbuGhazaleh, N. M. (2018). Factors affecting the development of accounting practices in Jordan: An institutional perspective. *Asian Review of Accounting*, *26*(4), 464–486. DOI: 10.1108/ARA-01-2017-0010

Tawiah, V., & Borgi, H. (2022). Impact of XBRL adoption on financial reporting quality: A global evidence. *Accounting Research Journal*, *35*(6), 815–833. DOI: 10.1108/ARJ-01-2022-0002

TCFD. (2022) Task Force on Climate-related Financial Disclosures. 2022 Status Report. *TCFD.* https://assets.bbhub.io/company/sites/60/2022/10/2022-TCFD-Status-Report.pdf

Toudas, K., Poutos, E., & Balios, D. (2013). Concept, regulations and institutional issues of IPSAS: A critical review. *European Journal of Business and Social Sciences*, *2*(1), 43–54.

Trabelsi, A. (2017). *Application des normes IPSAS en Tunisie*. Al Manhal.

Trabelsi, R. (2013). Vers un dispositif d'appréciation de la pertinence des IFRS dans un contexte pré-implémentation. *International Journal of Innovation and Applied Studies*, *3*(3), 626–650.

Turki, H., Wali, S., & Boujelbène, Y. (2017). Adoption obligatoire des IFRS et asymétrie d'information dans le contexte français: effet modérateur de l'endettement. *La revue Gestion et Organisation, Volume 9*, Issue 1, Pages 63-78. https://doi.org/ DOI: 10.1016/j.rgo.2017.01.001

Turki, H., Wali, S., Ali, Z., & Mohammed, M. (2020). IFRS and financial performance: Study in the French context. *International Journal of Financial Research*, *11*(2), 424–434. DOI: 10.5430/ijfr.v11n2p424

UNCTAD. (2015). *Accounting and financial reporting guidelines for SMEs*. United Nations. Retrieved April 15, 2025, from https://unctad.org

van der Lugt, C., van de Wijs, P., & Petrovics, D. (2020). Carrots & Sticks. Sustainability reporting policy: Global trends in disclosure as the ESG agenda goes mainstream. *Global Reporting Initiative (GRI) and the University of Stellenbosch Business School (USB).* https://www.carrotsandsticks.net/media/zirbzabv/carrots-and-sticks-2020-june2020.pdf

Van Wyk, H. A., & Rossouw, J. (2009). IFRS implementation: The role of institutional factors in South Africa. *Meditari Accountancy Research*, *17*(2), 117–137. DOI: 10.1108/10222529200900011

Veriest, A. (2011). *IFRS for SMEs: Evolution and challenges.*

Vilardell, I. (2013). *The Spanish accounting plan for SMEs and the IFRS for SMEs.* DRM/CREFIGE, University of Paris-Dauphine.

Vishnani, S., Gupta, S., & Gupta, H. (2021). Convergence of Indian accounting standards to IFRS: Impact on quality of financial reporting of Indian industries. *International Journal of Managerial and Financial Accounting*, *13*(1), 1–24. DOI: 10.1504/IJMFA.2021.116205

Vishnu Nampoothiri, M., Entrop, O., & Annamalai, T. R. (2024). Effect of mandatory sustainability performance disclosures on firm value: Evidence from listed European firms. *Corporate Social Responsibility and Environmental Management*, *31*(6), 5220–5235. DOI: 10.1002/csr.2860

Walsh, J. P., & Yu, J. (2010). Determinants of foreign direct investment: A sectoral and institutional approach. *IMF Working Paper*, *10*(187), 1. Advance online publication. DOI: 10.5089/9781455202218.001

Wamba, R. T., Kouotou, A. C. M., Wanda, A. T., & Wanda, R. (2023). Le basculement du SYSCOHADA vers les normes IAS-IFRS, enjeux et perspectives dans les entités de l'Afrique subsaharienne: Un mariage ou un divorce? *Recherches en Sciences de Gestion*, *154*(1), 127–150. DOI: 10.3917/resg.154.0127

Watts, R. L., & Zimmerman, J. L. (1978). Towards a positive theory of the determination of accounting standards. *The Accounting Review*, *53*(1), 112–134.

Watts, R. L., & Zimmerman, J. L. (1986). *Positive accounting theory.* Prentice Hall.

Watts, R. L., & Zimmerman, J. L. (1990). Positive accounting theory: A ten-year perspective. *The Accounting Review*, *65*(1), 131–156.

Waweru, N. M., Peng, S., & Hopper, T. (2023). Two decades of African accounting research 2000–2019: Synthesis, reflection, gaps, and future directions. *Journal of International Accounting Research*, *22*(1), 99–136. DOI: 10.2308/JIAR-2021-078

WEF. (2020). Explore from metrics. https://www.weforum.org/stakeholdercapitalism/our-metrics/

World Bank. (2016). *Governance index.* Retrieved June 23, 2016, from http://info.worldbank.org/governance/wgi/index.asp

World Bank. (2021). *World development indicators.* https://databank.worldbank.org/source/world-development-indicators

World Trade Organization. (1996). *Trade and foreign direct investment*,57. https://www.wto.org/english/news_e/pres96_e/pr057_e.htm

Xesibe, Z., & Nyasha, S. (2020). Unemployment and economic growth in South Africa: A re-examination. *International Journal of Sustainable Economy, 12*(2), 101–116. DOI: 10.1504/IJSE.2020.110261

Yin, R. K. (2009). *Case Study Research: Design and Methods.* SAGE Publications. https://books.google.co.ma/books?id=k0WrN3rBz_sC

Yousefinejad, M., Ahmad, A., Salleh, F. M., & Rahim, R. A. (2018). Causal relationship between international financial reporting standard (IFRS) and foreign direct investment (FDI): A panel data analysis of ASEAN countries. *Asian Journal of Accounting and Governance, 10*, 61–72. DOI: 10.17576/AJAG-2018-10-06

Yurisandi, T., & Puspitasari, E. (2015). Financial reporting quality-before and after IFRS adoption using NiCE qualitative characteristics measurement. *Procedia: Social and Behavioral Sciences, 211*, 644–652. DOI: 10.1016/j.sbspro.2015.11.091

Zahid, R. M. A., & Simga-Mugan, C. (2019). An analysis of IFRS and SME-IFRS adoption determinants: A worldwide study. *Emerging Markets Finance & Trade, 55*(2), 391–408. DOI: 10.1080/1540496X.2018.1500890

Zaidi, S., & Huerta, E. (2014). IFRS adoption and enforcement as antecedents of economic growth. *International Journal of Accounting and Financial Reporting, 4*(1), 1. Advance online publication. DOI: 10.5296/ijafr.v4i1.5410

Zaid, M. A. A., & Issa, A. (2023). A roadmap for triggering the convergence of global ESG disclosure standards: Lessons from the IFRS foundation and stakeholder engagement. *Corporate Governance (Bradford), 23*(7), 1648–1669. DOI: 10.1108/CG-09-2022-0399

Zeghal, D., & Mhedhbi, K. (2006). An analysis of the factors affecting the adoption of international accounting standards by developing countries. *The International Journal of Accounting, 41*(4), 373–386. DOI: 10.1016/j.intacc.2006.09.009

Zehri, F., & Chouabi, J. (2013). Adoption determinants of the international accounting standards IAS/IFRS by developing countries. *Journal of Economics, Finance and Administrative Science, 18*(35), 56–62. DOI: 10.1016/S2077-1886(13)70030-1

Zhang, G. (2013). Accounting standards, cost of capital, resource allocation, and welfare in a large economy. *The Accounting Review, 88*(4), 1459–1488. DOI: 10.2308/accr-50375

Zhang, X., Li, H., & Zhao, S. (2021). The role of data analytics in SMEs' financial decision-making. *Journal of Financial Analytics, 19*(1), 57–68.

Zhao, X., Lynch, J.Jr, & Chen, Q. (2010). Reconsidering Baron and Kenny: Myths and truths about mediation analysis. *The Journal of Consumer Research, 37*(2), 197–206. DOI: 10.1086/651257

Zori, S. G., & Kan, K. S. (2017). A qualitative comparative approach to the adoption of International Financial Reporting Standards (IFRS) in Africa. In Konan Anderson, A. (Ed.), *A qualitative comparative approach to the adoption of International Financial Reporting Standards (IFRS) in Africa*. DOI: 10.2139/ssrn.2992501

Zouak, H. (2012). *Les normes IFRS dans la mission d'audit: Cas de REDAL.* (Mémoire de master en Finance, Audit et Contrôle de gestion). Université Moulay Ismail, Meknès.

About the Contributors

Azzouz Elhamma is a Full Professor of Accounting and Finance at the National School of Business and Management (ENCG), Ibn Tofail University in Kenitra, Morocco. He earned his Ph.D. in Management Sciences in 2011, followed by his Habilitation to Supervise PhD Research (HDR) in the same field in 2017. Professor Elhamma teaches a variety of undergraduate and graduate courses, including Advanced Financial Accounting and International Financial Reporting Standards (IFRS). His research interests focus on IFRS, Sustainability, and Management Control. He has published numerous scientific articles on the adoption and impact of IFRS, particularly in emerging economies, in internationally recognized journals such as the "Journal of Financial Reporting and Accounting", the "International Journal of Accounting, Auditing and Performance Evaluation", the "Journal of Management Development".

***

Buket Atalay Aycan has been working as a lecturer in the Department of Accounting and Tax at the University of Ufuk since 2024. She graduated from Baskent University, Department of Economics. After getting her master's degree in finance from Ankara University in 2008, she started to work as an assistant commerce specialist at Ziraat Bank in 2010 and worked at the bank for about 3 years. She worked as a foundation specialist assistant for about two years from 2013 to 2015. While she was working as a research assistant (5 years) in the Department of Management at Baskent University, she received her PhD (2018) in Accounting and Finance from Baskent University and became a lecturer at the same department. She became a Certified Public Accountant in 2019 before working as a finance specialist and an Enterprise Risk Management Supervisor at private sector. She worked as an assistant professor in the Department of Business Management at Ostim Teknik University in 2022. She attended several conferences on accounting and finance.

She has several publications such as articles and book chapters on accounting and finance. She has taught Principles of Accounting, Cost Accounting, Managerial Accounting, Auditing, Financial Statement Analysis, Corporate Finance, Financial Markets, E-Trade courses. Her interest academic field covers Corporate Finance, Financial Accounting, International Financial Reporting, Sustainability Reporting, Financial Statement Analysis and Data Analysis.

Abdessamad Dibi PHD and HDR professor at Hassan 2 University in Casablanca, Morocco, founding member of the PRISME multidisciplinary research laboratory in social engineering and business management. Former teacher-trainer for national education executives in the preparatory cycle for the agrégation in economics and management. Former member of the national jury for the agrégation in economics and management. Former teacher of economics and business preparatory classes. The author of several national and international publications, his operational and academic research focuses on the challenges of organisational and managerial innovation and the ways in which individuals and organisations can act in a context of uncertainty and complexity. Main publications over the last three years: Dibi, A. (2025). The creation of organizational value by controlling hidden costs: Lessons from a qualimetric intervention research study. Management & Avenir, 145(1), 89-108. Dibi, A., Mharzi, H., Hebaz, A., & Laroussy, A. (2025). Le management du potentiel humain: expérimentation d'un outil de pilotage dans le contexte d'un établissement éducatif marocain. @ GRH, I4-XXV. Dibi, A., El Moussaoui, T., El Moussaoui, A. E., & Loqman, C. (2024). Qualimatric intervention research: interest for management sciences researchers. In Applying qualitative research methods to management science (pp. 92-127). IGI Global. Dibi, A., & Amifi, H. (2023). Le contrôle de gestion des coûts-performance cachés, une pratique managériale innovante pour des organisations plus résilientes. DE LA GESTION DES CRISES A LA RESILIENCE: Quelles pratiques dans les organisations aujourdhui?. Dibi, A., & Benlakouiri, A. (2022). The valorization of human potential through socio-economic management: Case of a Moroccan public administrative organization. Recherches en Sciences de Gestion, 150(3), 219-249. Dibi, A. (2022). Managing the overall performance of educational establishments: Some ways to do better with little. ACCRA, 15(3), 61-91. Dibi, A. (2022). Diagnostic organisationnel d'un établissement éducatif: identification des dysfonctionnements, évaluation des coûts cachés et prescription d'actions correctives. Revue Alternatives managériales et économiques AME, 4(3), 81-101.

Ayoub Jroundi is a PhD researcher at the National School of Business and Management of Kenitra, Ibn Tofail University, Morocco. He holds a Research Master's degree in Finance from Hassan II University of Casablanca. His academic interests lie broadly in the fields of business, management, and organizational sciences. He is affiliated with the Research Laboratory in Organizational Management Sciences and is actively involved in academic research and higher education. His current research is focused on management control, extra-financial performance, sustainability reporting, IFRS, ESG disclosure and emerging reporting frameworks.

Rubén Lado-Sestayo is Professor of Finance at the University of Santiago de Compostela. He has a degree in Economics and Business Administration, a master's in Economics: Industrial Organization and Financial Markets, and a PhD in Economics (Honours) from the University of Santiago de Compostela. His research is focused primarily on the study of spatial issues, with interests in profitability, risks, entry barriers, survival and failure determinants.

Adil Laouane is a faculty member and researcher at the Faculty of Law, Economics, and Social Sciences (FSJES) of Ain Sebâa, part of Hassan II University of Casablanca. He holds a PhD in Management Sciences and specializes in issues related to international accounting, with a particular focus on the adoption and impact of IFRS (International Financial Reporting Standards) in the context of emerging economies, especially Morocco. Areas of Expertise and Research Interests Professor Laouane's research lies at the intersection of accounting standardization, corporate financial performance, and financial reporting transparency. His scholarly approach integrates both quantitative and qualitative empirical methods to assess the economic and informational effects of international accounting standards.

Andrea Martínez-Salgueiro serves as Assistant Professor at University of Vigo (Spain). She is accredited as Associate Professor by ANECA, has one recognized research period, and currently coordinates the Master's Degree in International Trade. She holds a PhD in Finance from Autonomous University of Barcelona (UAB). She earned a Bachelor's degree in Business Administration from University of Vigo (2015) and a Master's in Economics and Business Administration (UAB, 2019). Her research focuses on corporate risk management (climate-related financial risk and weather derivatives, and the impact of sustainability on business risk). She has published several articles in top-tier journals, contributed to academic books, and presented at numerous international conferences.

Hamide Özyürek is a faculty member in the Department of Business Administration at Ostim Technical University. She holds a Bachelor's degree in Business Administration from Anadolu University, a Master's degree from Ufuk University, and a Ph.D. from Kırıkkale University. Her doctoral dissertation is titled *"Time-Driven Activity-Based Costing Method: Its Application in the Manufacturing Sector."* Dr. Özyürek became a Certified Public Accountant (CPA) in 2004 and gained professional experience as an accounting manager in various private companies. Since beginning her academic career in 2007, she has focused on cost accounting, managerial accounting, financial performance analysis, sustainability, blockchain technologies, and crypto assets. She was awarded the title of Associate Professor in 2018. She has published over 50 academic works, including articles in WoS- and Scopus-indexed journals, as well as books and book chapters. She has presented her research at numerous international conferences in countries such as Hong Kong, Italy, Switzerland, Spain, and France. In 2013, she participated in a professional development project in Germany titled "Developing Professional Skills on EU Tax Practices and Tax Audits." As part of the Erasmus Teaching Mobility Program, she has delivered accounting and finance courses at several European institutions, including the Technical University of Košice in Slovakia, Vilnius University in Lithuania, and Warsaw Management University in Poland. Her academic contributions, international collaborations, and dedication to teaching and research continue to shape her career in accounting, finance, and emerging technologies in business.

Sandra Tenorio-Salgueiro holds a Bachelor's degree in Business Administration and Management from the University of Vigo, complemented by several master's degrees in Auditing, Financial Management, and Teacher Training. With significant professional experience in financial auditing and corporate finance, she is currently undertaking a Ph.D. in Economics and Business at the University of Santiago de Compostela. Additionally, she is a faculty member in the Department of Financial Economics and Accounting at the University of Vigo, where she contributes to both teaching and research.

Milagros Vivel-Búa is a professor of financial economics and accounting at the University of Santiago de Compostela. Her main line of research is risk-return management and sustainability in European companies. She has published in various journals, books and other types of publications. She has also won several awards for her research work.

Index

A

B

C

D

E

F

I

J

L

M

N

P